An Illustrated Survey of the

WEST'S MODERN FIGHTERS

Doug Richardson

Technical details of today's most advanced fighting aircraft

THE MILITARY PRESS
New York

A SALAMANDER BOOK

This 1984 edition is published by
The Military Press,
distributed by Crown Publishers, Inc.,
One Park Avenue,
New York, NY 10016,
United States of America.

All correspondence concerning the content of this
volume should be addressed to Salamander
Books Ltd., 27 Old Gloucester Street, London
WC1N 3AF, United Kingdom.

This book is not to be sold outside the United
States of America and Canada.

ISBN 0-517-441144

h g f e d c b a

CREDITS

Editor: Ray Bonds
Designer: Mark Holt
Color artwork: Stephen Seymour,
Terry Hadler, Kai Choi
Cutaway drawings and line plan views:
Mike Badrocke
Diagrams: TIGA
Filmset by SX Composing Ltd.,
and Tradespools Ltd.
Color reproduction by Tempus Litho Ltd.
Printed in Belgium by Henri Proost et Cie

The publishers wish to thank wholeheartedly the
many organisations and individuals in the
aerospace industry and the armed forces of
various nations who have all been of considerable
help in the preparation of this book. In particular,
thanks are due to Mike Spick, aviation author, for
his assistance.

CONTENTS

INTRODUCTION

The mid-1980s are a crucial time for the defence of the Western World. During the late 1970s and early 1980s, the NATO allies sunk a large portion of their defence budgets into new aircraft programmes such as the F-14, F-15, F-16, F-18, Mirage 2000 and Tornado, with the goal of maintaining the qualitative edge which they have traditionally enjoyed over the more simply-equipped but numerically far superior air arms of the Warsaw Pact.

Now the Soviet bloc is itself modernising its own air strength—a return move in the delicate balance of military power which has maintained the fragile peace of Central Europe for the duration of the lives of the writer, most of his readers, and their equivalents in Eastern Europe. The balance is being re-adjusted, and if it's to be maintained, the warplanes described in these pages must be able to cope with aircraft such as the new MiG-29 Fulcrum, MiG-31 Foxhound, Su-25 Frogfoot and Su-27 Flanker, designs drawn up some five or more years behind their Western counterparts. The designers of these new Soviet fighters knew from Western publications and trade shows just what performance and capabilities their new creations had to match. In contrast, the teams which created many of the aircraft described here had to predict the likely pattern of the threat which their new designs would one day face.

When this delicate process of predicting technological change is carried out correctly, and is backed up by a speedy production commitment, the result is timely designs such as the Hurricane, Me 109, Zero, Mustang and Sabre, MiG-15 and -21, Mirage III, Harrier and Phantom. Failure could result in modern-day equivalents of the Gloster Gladiator, Curtiss P-40 Warhawk, Gloster Meteor, Republic F-84 Thunderjet, or Supermarine Swift—aircraft less fit (or even completely unfit) for combat operations in the era in which they served.

The 25 aircraft described in these pages are the types on which the balance of power must depend for the rest of the 1980s and into the 1990s. Not all can claim to be total successes, but the ratio of good to merely adequate is higher than would have been the case a decade ago. New aircraft are more thoroughly evaluated before entry to service than was sometimes the case in the past, while the high cost of fuel and manpower has hurried the less successful older types into retirement.

This book is intended as a review of the Western powers' most important modern fixed-wing tactical aircraft, and therefore the inclusion of such potent attack aircraft as the A-10, F-111 and aging but still important Buccaneer under the main title of "West's Modern Fighters" is justified. The book should serve not only as a reference guide to the individual aircraft, but also to aquaint the reader with the technology which they embody. Instead of attempting to describe in full detail the development, structure, power-

plant, avionics and weaponry of each of the 25 aircraft—impossible within the space available—I have presented summaries, expanding upon such topics in cases where it seemed relevant. Some chapters will refer the reader to another for fuller details of an engine, missile or item of avionics.

Fifteen of the types described have already seen combat, sometimes against Soviet types but often against each other. The Mirage, Kfir and A-4 have fought against Mirages in the Middle East, and against Sea Harrier in the South Atlantic; Eagles downed Phantoms above the waters of the Arabian Gulf a few days before these words were written; F-4, F-5, F-14, Mirage F1 and Super Etendard seemed likely to be unleashed against one another in a long-predicted new and still more violent phase of the long-running war between Iran and Iraq. In addition to documenting Western air power, "The West's Modern Fighters" seems likely to be a guide to the warplanes in tomorrow's headlines, unless in the new few years there is a dramatic reduction in the number of wars between developing nations.

Chapter by chapter, the book hopefully develops into a loosely-structured encyclopedia of modern aerospace technology, giving the reader a glimpse of the technology which lies beneath the aluminium or carbon-fibre skins of the individual aircraft. An additional chapter discusses new projects such as the X-29, Advanced Technology Fighter, Stealth Fighter, Lavi and Gripen which are currently taking shape on Western drawing boards, while another describes how new technology is creating the "smart" precision-guided weapons which many Western fighters carry or are due to carry—highly-accurate versions of existing missiles and all-new designs intended to make optimum use of this new technology.

Both the publishers and I thank the air forces and aircraft manufacturers of the West for their wholehearted assistance in supplying the many colour photographs which appear in these pages, plus original reference material—in some cases for aircraft no longer in production. (One individual even loaned us the last file copy of a brochure we needed.)

Doug Richardson

London
August, 1984

COMPARATIVE SPECIFICATIONS

This table is based on figures released by the manufacturers of the individual aircraft, and must be treated with some reserve. Figures for weight and size are all directly comparable, but performance data is not; tactical radius is dependent on the mission profile being flown, and on the warload being carried, for example. Figures for maximum speed apply at altitude, unless stated. Each manufacturer tends to make differing assumptions, and in some cases does not make clear the conditions which have been assumed. The minimum runway length is dictated by take-off run, which is itself dependent on take-off weight. (The spectacular performance of some types at air-show demonstrations is in some cases the result of flying with modest fuel loads and external "ordnance" consisting of empty casings!) Once an aircraft has dropped its ordnance and burned most of its fuel, it may land well within the distance needed for take-off. This is not always the case with the latest generation of fighters, whose high thrust-to-weight ratio often results in short take-off runs.

Symbols indicate the following:
* hi-lo-hi;
† lo-lo-lo;
n/a not available.

TYPE	LENGTH	SPAN	WEIGHT		SPEED (at alt)	TIME TO HEIGHT	CEILING	MIN RUNWAY	COMBAT RADIUS	WARLOAD
			empty	max t/o						
British Aerospace **Buccaneer**	63ft5in (19.32m)	44ft0in (13.41m)	30,000lb (13,610kg)	62,000lb (28,123kg)	Mach 0.9 (sea level)	n/a	40,000ft? (12,192m?)	3,800ft (1,160m)	2,000nm (3,700km)	12,000lb (5,400kg)
British Aerospace **Harrier GR.3**	46ft10in (14.27m)	25ft3in (7.7m)	12,300lb (5,580kg)	25,000lb (11,350kg)	640kt+ (1,186km/h+)	2min23sec to 40,000ft (12,200m)	50,000ft (15,240m)	VSTOL	150nm,STOL (278km, STOL)	8,000lb (3,600kg)
British Aerospace **Sea Harrier**	47ft7in (14.5m)	25ft3in (7.7m)	12,500lb (5,670kg)	26,015lb (11,880kg)	640kt+ (1,186km/h+)	n/a	50,000ft (15,240m)	VSTOL	250nm (460km)	8,000lb (3,600kg)
Dassault-Breguet **Mirage IIIE**	49ft3in (15.0m)	27ft0in (8.2m)	15,540lb (7,050kg)	30,200lb (13,700kg)	Mach 2.2	6min 50sec to 49,000ft (15,000m)	56,000ft (17,000m)	2,300ft (700m)	650nm (1,200km)	8,800lb (4,000kg)
Dassault Breguet **Mirage 5**	51ft0in (15.55m)	27ft0in (8.2m)	14,550lb (6,600kg)	30,200lb (13,700kg)	Mach 2.2	6min50sec to 49,000ft (15,000m)	56,000ft (17,000m)	2,300ft (700m)	700nm* (1,300km)	8,800lb (4,000kg)
Dassault Breguet **Mirage 50**	51ft0in (15.55m)	27ft0in (8.2m)	15,765lb (7,150kg)	30,200lb (13,700kg)	Mach 2.2	5min 24sec to 40,000ft (12,200m)	59,000ft (18,000m)	3,000ft (915m)	340nm† (630km)	8,800lb (4,000kg)
Dassault-Breguet **Mirage F1.C**	49ft2in (15.0m)	27ft7in (8.4m)	16,315lb (7,400kg)	33,510lb (15,200kg)	Mach 2.2	41,930ft/min (12,780m/min)	65,600ft (20,000m)	2,100ft (640m)	399nm† (740km)	8,800lb (4,000kg)
Dassault-Breguet **Mirage 2000**	47ft1in (14.35m)	29ft6in (9.0m)	16,315lb (7,400kg)	36,375lb (16,500kg)	Mach 2.3	59,050ft/min (18,000m/min)	65,600ft (20,000m)	n/a	399nm+ (740km+)	13,200lb+ (6,000kg+)
Dassault-Breguet **Super Etendard**	47ft0in (14.32m)	31ft6in (9.60m)	14,200lb (6,450kg)	25,350lb (11,500kg)	Mach 1.0	19,700ft/min (6,000m/min)	45,000ft (13,700m)	2,300ft (700m)	390nm* (720km)	5,000lb (2,270kg)
Fairchild **A-10A Thunderbolt**	53ft4in (16.26m)	57ft6in (17.53m)	24,959lb (11,310kg)	50,000lb (22,700kg)	381kt (S/L) (706km/h)	6,000ft/min (1,830m/min)	n/a	1,450ft (440m)	500nm+ (930km+)	16,000lb (7,300kg)
General Dynamics **F-16A Fighting Falcon**	49ft6in (15.09m)	32ft10in (10.01m)	15,586lb (7,060kg)	35,400lb (16,060kg)	Mach 2+	n/a	59,000ft+ (18,000m+)	2,500ft (760m)	500nm+ (930km+)	20,450lb (9,275kg)

TYPE	LENGTH	SPAN	WEIGHT		SPEED (at alt)	TIME TO HEIGHT	CEILING	MIN RUNWAY	COMBAT RADIUS	WARLOAD
			empty	max t/o						
General Dynamics **F-111E**	73ft6in (22.4m)	32/63ft0in (9.74/19.2m)	46,172lb (20,943kg)	91,300lb (41,400kg)	Mach 2.5	n/a	50,000ft+ (15,240m+)	3,000ft (915m)	1,500nm* (2,780km)	28,000lb (12,700kg)
Grumman **A-6E Intruder**	54ft9in (16.69m)	53ft0in (16.15m)	26,456lb (12,000kg)	58,600lb (26,580kg)	561kt(S/L) (1,040km/h)	7,570ft/min (2,300m/min)	42,500ft (12,950m)	3,890ft (1,185m)	765nm* (1,415km)	18,000lb (8,165kg)
Grumman **F-14 Tomcat**	62ft8in (19.1m)	38ft2in/64ft1in (11.67/19.54m)	39,762lb (18,036kg)	74,348lb (33,720kg)	Mach 2.4	30,000+m/min (9,150+m/min)	50,000ft+ (15,000m+)	2,700ft (825m)	n/a	14,500lb (6,580kg)
IAI **Kfir C-7**	53ft8in (16.36m)	26ft11in (8.22m)	16,060lb (7,300kg)	35,715lb (16,200kg)	Mach 2+	5min 10sec to 50,000ft(15,250m)	58,000ft (17,700m)	4,750ft (1,450m)	640nm* (1,185km)	13,400lb (6,085kg)
McDonnell Douglas **A-4M Skyhawk**	40ft3¼in (12.27m)	27ft6in (8.38m)	11,016lb (4,997kg)	25,500lb (11,566kg)	583kt (1,080km/h)	5,500ft/min (1,676m/min)	52,000ft (15,850m)	3,950ft (1,204m)	n/a	9,195lb (4,170kg)
McDonnell Douglas **AV-8B**	46ft4in (14.12m)	30ft4in (9.25m)	13,000lb (5,900kg)	29,750lb (13,495kg)	550kt (1,020km/h)	13,068ft/min (3,960m/min)	44,950ft (13,700m+)	VSTOL	599nm (1,110km)	9,200lb (4,175kg)
McDonnell Douglas **F-4E Phantom**	63ft0in (19.20m)	38ft5in (11.7m)	29,535lb (13,397kg)	58,000lb (26,309kg)	Mach 2.2	1min 18sec to 30,000ft (9,144m)	56,120ft (17,105m)	n/a	700nm (1,297km)	16,000lb (7,257kg)
McDonnell Douglas **F-15C Eagle**	63ft9in (19.43m)	42ft10in (13.05m)	27,315lb (12,390kg)	67,990lb (30,840kg)	Mach 2.4+	1min to 12,000ft (3,657m)	64,960ft (19,800m)	2,755ft (840m)	n/a	17,989lb (8,160kg)
McDonnell Douglas **F/A-18A Hornet**	56ft0in (17.07m)	40ft5in (12.31m)	23,060lb (10,460kg)	49,200lb (22,320kg)	Mach 1.8	n/a	50,000ft (15,240m)	2,788ft (850m)	400nm+ (740km)	17,000lb (7,710kg)
Northrop **F-5E Tiger II**	48ft2in (14.68m)	26ft8in (8.13m)	9,722lb (4,410kg)	24,724lb (11,215kg)	Mach 1.64	34,500ft/min (10,515m/min)	51,800ft (15,790m)	2,500ft (762m)	138nm (256km)	7,000lb (3,175kg)
Northrop **F-20 Tigershark**	46ft7in (14.2m)	26ft7in (8.1m)	12,125lb? (5,500kg?)	27,462lb (12,475kg)	Mach 2.0	55,774ft/min (17,000m/min)	56,300ft (17,160m)	3,543ft (1,080m)	350nm† (650km)	8,300lb (3,765kg+)
Panavia **Tornado ADV**	59ft3in (18.06m)	28ft2in/45ft7in (8.6/13.9m)	c.31,000lb (c.14,000kg)	60,120lb (27,270kg+)	Mach 2.2	2 min to 30,000ft (9,150m)	49,212ft+ (15,000m+)	2,493ft (760m)	400nm+ (740km+)	19,840lb (9,000kg+)
Panavia **Tornado IDS**	54ft9in (16.70m)	28ft2in/45ft7in (8.6/13.9m)	31,065lb (14,090kg)	c.60,000lb c.(27,200kg)	Mach 2.2	2 min to 30,000ft (9,150m)	49,212ft+ (15,000m+)	n/a	755nm* (1,400km)	19,840lb (9,000kg+)
Saab-Scania **JA 37 Viggen**	53ft10in (16.40m)	34ft9in (10.60m)	c.15,400lb (c.7,000kg)	37,750lb+ (17,000kg+)	Mach 2+	1min 40sec to 32,800ft (10,000m)	n/a	1,640ft (500m)	270nm+ (500km+)	15,432lb (7,000kg)
SEPECAT **Jaguar Intl**	50ft11in (15.52m)	28ft6in (8.69m)	16,975lb (7,700kg)	34,016lb (15,430kg)	728kt (1,350km/h)	1min 30sec to 45,930ft (14,000m)?	n/a	2,887ft (880m)	289nm† (535km)	10,493lb (4,760kg)
Vought **A-7E Corsair II**	46ft2in (14.10m)	38ft9in (11.80m)	19,400lb (8,800kg)	42,000lb (19,050kg)	600nm (1,100km/h)	n/a	42,000ft (13,000m)	4,000ft (1,220m)	450nm* (835km)	15,000lb (6,800kg)

BUCCANEER

DEVELOPMENT

When USAF F-15 crews first set eyes on the portly lines of the RAF Buccaneer on the flight line at Nellis AFB, Nevada, during a mid 1970s "Red Flag" air-combat exercise, they could not believe their luck. Were the "Limies" really going to take on the brand-new F-15 Eagle in a plump, underpowered, subsonic bomber fitted with antediluvian avionics? Those Eagle crews just couldn't wait for the "turkey shoot" to begin. But the first few days of action soon showed that the Buccaneer was a tricky adversary indeed: the RAF aircraft were getting to their targets, but unobserved by the F-15s. Eventually, a disorientated Buccaneer crew were forced to risk a brief "pop-up" manoeuvre to re-locate themselves, and a waiting Eagle obtained a radar lock-on and pounced. As the exercise continued, the Eagles did manage to "kill" more Buccaneers, but this veteran design had shown its capabilities in no uncertain terms.

Originally developed for the Royal Navy, ignored and despised by the Royal Air Force until circumstances forced its adoption, the Buccaneer is a hard-hitting bomber strong enough to fly at treetop height for long periods of time. Given more vigorous backing and support it could have been an even bigger success, with further-improved and uprated versions entering service in the mid-to-late 1960s.

In June 1952 the Royal Navy issued a specification for a two-seat bomber able to fly at Mach 0.85 at a height of only 200ft (60m). The company finally selected to build the aircraft was Blackburn, an organisation with a reputation for building some of the ugliest, modestly-performing but solidly-built aircraft ever accepted into British military service.

The timing of the project was crucial.

Left: Buccaneer S.2As of 208 Sqn pass the Needles during a maritime training mission. As the more modern Tornado enters service, Buccaneers are being re-assigned to the anti-ship role.

The technique of blowing a layer of high-pressure air across the upper surface of a flap in order to prevent separation of the airflow at large flap angles had been pioneered in the USA only a few years earlier and had been much studied by Blackburn. It allowed the designers to obtain the required lift from a smaller wing than would otherwise have been the case. Turbofan engines were available for installation in the definitive S.2 model (the early Gyron Junior turbojet-powered version was woefully underpowered). The attractions of digital technology could not be resisted by the rival Grumman team who designed the slightly later A-6 Intruder, but the British decision to stick with analogue electronics was a wise one. Had the Buccaneer become bogged down in the avionics problems which plagued early-model Intruders, the project would prob-

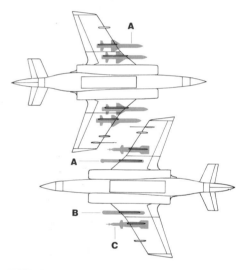

Typical weapons:
Top: Despite its age, the Buccaneer will be a formidable maritime strike weapon when retrofitted with the new BAe Dynamics Sea Eagle anti-ship missile (**A**), a long-range turbojet powered weapon

Above: For over-land operations, the aircraft can carry a Westinghouse Pave Strike target-designator pod (**A**), an ALQ-101 jamming pod (**B**), and Texas Instruments Paveway II LGBs (**C**). Sky Shadow may be fitted.

Left: Buccaneer S.2B (XV359) of 12 Sqn RAF. When this drawing was prepared, the aircraft was stationed at RAF Akrotiri in Cyprus. Aircraft from this location flew sorties in support of British troops stationed in the Lebanon as part of the short-lived international peacekeeping force. Designed for use aboard the Royal Navy's carriers of the 1960s, Buccaneer had folding wings, and this uppersurface view shows to good effect the massive wing hinges. Like every part of the Buccaneer structure, these had to be built tough enough to survive the rigours of prolonged low-level flight at high speed. Normal low-level cruise speed is up to 540kt (1,000km/h), but the twin Spey turbofans can give Mach 0.9+.

Below left: The external warload consists of a single AIM-9G Sidewinder, Westinghouse ALQ-101-1C jammer, plus two 430gal (1,955lit) slipper tanks. The internal weapons bay carries up to 4,000lb (1,800kg) of ''iron'' bombs or other free-falling ordnance. The Sidewinder is not for show—the Buccaneer can bite back! RAF crews flying Red Flag training exercises in the USA have successfully engaged in mock air-to-air combat, scoring many ''kills''.

Below: The bulge beneath the Buccaneer fuselage is not flab but fuel. As a retrofit, the aircraft's unique rotary weapons-bay door was bulged in order to create an extra fuel tank. Fuel is also carried in eight fuselage tanks plus integral tanks in the wings. The fuselage tanks are fitted with an explosion-suppression system, and an elaborate arrangement of transfer and cross-feed pipes ensures that less than a quarter of the total would be lost if one tank were damaged as a result of combat.

ably have been added to the long list of British aircraft cancellations. The original S.1 version was powered by a pair of Gyron Junior turbojets, and flew for the first time in April 1958. Originally designated NA.39, the Buccaneer S.1 entered service in the early 1960s. The RN already had its sights set on a longer-ranged S.2 aircraft, flying the first example in May 1963. By 1965, deliveries to the RN were under way. The days of the S.1 were numbered, although some were used briefly as trainers by the RAF in 1968 until the S.2B became available.

Spey-powered Buccaneer S.2s were to serve aboard Royal Navy carriers until HMS *Ark Royal*, the last catapult-equipped vessel, was paid off in the late 1970s. The surviving 64 aircraft were passed over to the Royal Air Force to supplement the 26 examples ordered by that Service in 1968, when the proposed Anglo-French

Variable Geometry (AFVG) strike aircraft followed the F-111K and TRS.2 into cancellation.

Attempts to sell a land-based version of the aircraft to the West German Luftwaffe were ineptly handled, but an order for 16 was finally placed by South Africa in 1963. These were duly built and handed over to the South African Air Force, but the Labour Government which came to power in 1964 refused to supply a further batch or even to replace one aircraft which crashed while on its delivery flight.

Around 60 Buccaneers remain in service, numbers having been thinned as a result of structural problems. These aircraft are being switched back to the maritime role as Tornado IDS strength builds up, and some may be reworked with new avionics. The prospect of some aircraft being modified as tankers or as EW aircraft has also been considered.

STRUCTURE

Fatigue was clearly going to be a problem in an aircraft designed to cruise in at low altitude where air turbulence is greatest. A Canberra used during Operation Swifter low-level flight trials in Libya was fit only for scrapping afterwards, but the Buccaneer was required to take this sort of punishment as a matter of routine. The Blackburn designers made no real attempt to "rewrite the book" on how fatigue-free structures should be created—they simply followed the existing rules rigorously, improvising where necessary.

High-grade metals, large forgings, extensive use of milling, and avoidance of structural shapes or features which might result in a local concentration of stress were all features of the design, and this attention to detail paid off in a generally trouble-free structure. Fatigue problems

British Aerospace Buccaneer S Mk.2B
1. Radome.
2. Multi-mode search and fire control radar module.
3. Weapon control computer.
4. Cockpit pressurisation valves.
5. Windscreen rain dispersal air duct.
6. Windscreen wiper.
7. Rudder pedals.
8. Pilot's instrument panel.
9. Head-up display.
10. Pilot's ejection seat.
11. Canopy breaker head fairing.
12. Observer's windscreen.
13. Radar hand controller.
14. Observer's ejection seat.
15. Sliding cockpit canopy cover.
16. Fuel system accumulator.
17. Canopy actuator.
18. Starboard wing boundary layer air ducting.
19. Wing fold hinge joint.
20. Wide band homing aerial.
21. Leading edge blowing air duct.
22. Vortex generators.
23. Starboard navigation light.
24. No.1 UHF aerial.
25. Anti-collision light.
26. Starboard blown flap.

27. Formation light.
28. Blown, drooping aileron.
29. Starboard wing folded position.
30. No.2 UHF aerial.
31. Fuselage integral fuel tanks.
32. Internal weapons load, 4 × 1,000lb bombs.
33. Cable ducting.
34. Rotating weapons bay.
35. Weapons bay door actuating jack.
36. Avionics equipment racks.
37. HF notch aerial.
38. Electrical system panel.
39. Tailplane trim and variable gearing mechanism.
40. Rear equipment bay cooling air intake.
41. Tailplane hydraulic actuator.
42. Forward radar warning antenna.
43. Tailplane pivot bearing.
44. Tailplane blowing air ducting.
45. Blown leading edge duct.
46. All-moving tailplane.
47. Tailplane flap.

48. Tailplane flap hydraulic actuator.
49. TACAN aerial.
50. Tail navigation light.
51. Aft formation light.
52. Rear radar warning antenna.
53. Rudder.
54. Rudder hydraulic actuator.
55. Split tailcone airbrake.
56. Airbrake hinge link and drag strut.
57. Catapult hold back.
58. Airbrake hydraulic jack.
59. Arrester hook.
60. Yaw damper.
61. Fuel vent.
62. Arrester hook hydraulic jack and damper.

63. Tail bumper hydraulic jack.
64. Tail bumper.
65. Rear equipment bay air conditioning system.
66. Jet pipe.
67. Ventral doppler aerial.
68. Port formation light.
69. Port blown, drooping aileron.
70. Aileron blowing air duct.
71. Port navigation light.
72. Aileron hydraulic actuator.

73. Aileron control linkage.
74. Leading edge blowing air duct.
75. Chaff and flare dispenser.
76. Wide band homing aerial.
77. Port blown flap.
78. Pitot head.
79. Flap hydraulic jack.
80. Outboard wing stores pylon.
81. Wing fold hydraulic jack and linkage.

82. Missile launch rail adaptor.
83. Martel air-to-surface missile.
84. Inward-retracting main undercarriage.
85. Main undercarriage leg pivot bearing.
86. Hydraulic retraction jack.
87. Retractable catapult strop hook.

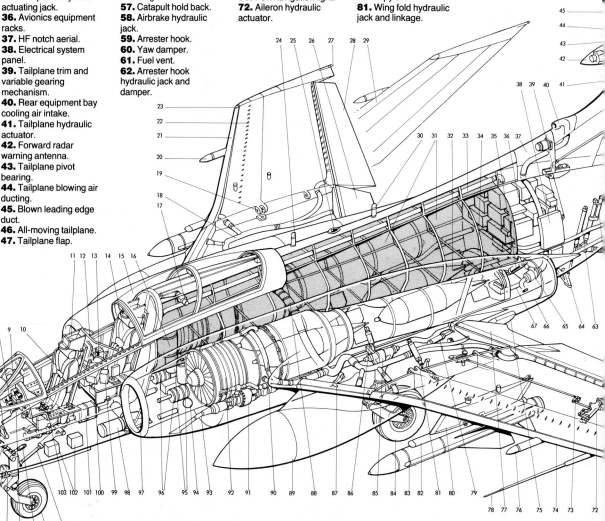

were not experienced until 1980, some 15 years after the first S.2s were handed over to the Royal Navy.

The wings and horizontal stabiliser are blown by air tapped from the HP compressor of the engine. Air is ducted along these surfaces in Nimonic (high-temperature alloy) pipes, then released through slits of almost microscopic width. These are located along the leading edge of the wing and just ahead of the ailerons and flaps, and on the underside of the tailplane leading edge.

Installation of the larger and more powerful Spey turbofan and its larger-diameter inlet ducts and jetpipes in the S.2 version required a fair degree of airframe surgery, but this was accomplished with a minimum of fuss. Other changes introduced at the same time added air blowing to the inner wing and extended the wingspan by means of glass-fibre tips.

South African aircraft are generally similar to the UK standard, complete with tail hooks, but the wing-folding mechanism is unpowered.

Inspection of the Buccaneer fleet was ordered in 1980 following the loss of a wing (and subsequent crash) by an aircraft jinking at low altitude to avoid interception during a Red Flag exercise. Careful checks showed that almost half the fleet had serious fatigue problems. These were due to the higher level of stress associated with overland operations—all fatigue testing had assumed maritime operations! Inspection and minor repairs restored many aircraft to operational status, but a repair scheme had to be devised for some of the more badly-fatigued examples. Others were deemed beyond economic repair and had to be scrapped, with one squadron disbanding so that its aircraft might be used to "top up" the others.

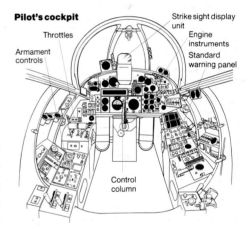

POWERPLANT

The Rolls-Royce Spey 101 turbofan used in all current Buccaneers offers more thrust, better SFC and less thrust-loss when air is diverted from the final stages of the compressor for use in the flap and tailplane-blowing system. Broadly similar to the engine used in the UK's Phantoms (see F-4 entry), the 101 has no afterburner and is rated at 11,250lb (5,100kg).

To give the South African S.50 additional thrust, a retractable twin-barrelled BS.605 rocket engine is installed in the lower fuselage, aft of the weapons bay. This burns kerosene fuel plus hydrogen peroxide oxidiser, and develops 8,000lb (3,630kg) of thrust for 30 seconds.

AVIONICS

The 1950s-vintage avionics of the Buccaneer greatly reduce the effectiveness of the aircraft. Designed for the naval strike role, they may have been adequate back in the 1960s for locating and attacking large surface vessels, but are not really suited to the conditions of modern combat, particularly overland attack. Compared with the digital equipment carried by the Grumman A-6, the Buccaneer avionics are crude.

The need for an update was recognised in the eary 1980s by the issue of Air Staff Target 1012, a proposed avionics updating scheme for 32 aircraft which will be used for maritime operations into the late 1980s. It is not clear whether this work will in fact be carried out, given the modest number of aircraft involved and other pressures on the defence budget. The original Blue Parrot forward-looking radar has already been given a minor rework to improve performance in the overland role, but would now be modified for improved maritime performance and a new HUD would be added. The original Doppler/twin-gyro platform navigation system would be replaced by an INS similar in performance to that in the Jaguar, while a new data link would provide secure communications with NATO

Above: The extended nose probe marks this Buccaneer as a trials aircraft. The external load consists of an ALQ-101 and slipper tank on the starboard wing, plus a Pave Spike target designator and Paveway LGB on the port side. The bomb door is of the original "dry" pattern without an integral fuel tank, and was an ingenious means of creating a low-drag alternative to conventional doors, rotating 180deg to expose the weapons.

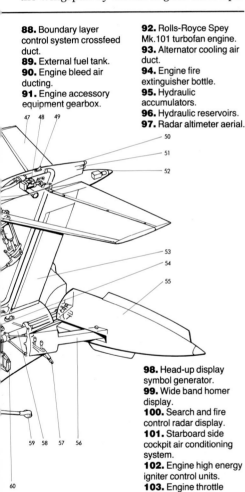

88. Boundary layer control system crossfeed duct.
89. External fuel tank.
90. Engine bleed air ducting.
91. Engine accessory equipment gearbox.
92. Rolls-Royce Spey Mk.101 turbofan engine.
93. Alternator cooling air duct.
94. Engine fire extinguisher bottle.
95. Hydraulic accumulators.
96. Hydraulic reservoirs.
97. Radar altimeter aerial.

98. Head-up display symbol generator.
99. Wide band homer display.
100. Search and fire control radar display.
101. Starboard side cockpit air conditioning system.
102. Engine high energy igniter control units.
103. Engine throttle levers.
104. Nose undercarriage hydraulic lock strut.
105. Aft retracting nosewheel.
106. Nosewheel steering jack.
107. Control column.
108. Artificial feel system pressure head.
109. Landing/taxiing lamp.
110. Nose undercarriage hydraulic retraction jack.
111. Lower UHF aerial.
112. Weapon system recorder.
113. Radar scanner.
114. In-flight refuelling probe.

Pilot's cockpit

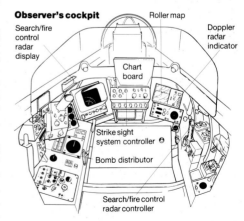

Above: Mounted on the instrument panel of the front cockpit is the strike sight – a primitive HUD – which gives the pilot the visual signals he requires in order to fly the aircraft to the target and perform the planned delivery manoeuvre.

Observer's cockpit

Above: To the left of the observer's centrally located chartboard and strike sight system controller is the radar display; a roller map and Doppler radar are on the other side. The joystick on the right-hand side controls the radar.

surface vessels and AEW aircraft. The cockpits of the current aircraft have been described as "large and comfortable steam-driven slums", so some effort would be expended on bringing these to an updated standard which would ease aircrew workload.

At present the aircraft carries Westinghouse ALQ-101-10 ECM pods. These would be further improved, and supplemented by the new Marconi Space and Defence Systems Sky Shadow. Two Tracor ALE-40 dispensers for chaff and flares would be internally mounted within the rear fuselage. The ESM and ECM systems would also require modernisation. Current RWR is the Marconi Space and Defence Systems ARI 18228. This uses the same RF sub-systems as the AR 18223

fitted to Harrier and Jaguar but, instead of a simple lamp display able to show data on only a single threat, features a CRT able to show bearing, transmission type and other data for multiple threats. Operating frequency is probably E to J band. Forward- and rearward-facing antennas for the system are located in the bullet fairing at the junction of the fin and tailplane.

ARMAMENT

Normal payload for strike missions can include 4,000lb (1,800kg) of ordnance in the weapons bay, plus up to 12,000lb (5,500kg) on underwing hardpoints. This can consist of "iron bombs", pods for unguided rockets, napalm tanks, or nuclear weapons (probably the 600lb/270kg

variable-yield weapon reported to have the designation "Green Parrot"). The aircraft can also carry a "buddy pack" beneath the wing for in-flight refuelling.

Anti-radar and TV-guided versions of the Anglo-French Martel air-to-surface missile may be carried beneath the wing. The anti-radar version was originally withdrawn from use when the last carrier-based Buccaneer unit came ashore in 1979 with the paying-off of the carrier *Ark Royal*, but these missiles have now been returned to service. Martel is due to be replaced by the longer-ranged Sea Eagle (see Sea Harrier entry). Sea Eagle-related modifications to the aircraft will begin early in 1985, with the new missile becoming operational by the autumn.

The only other powered missiles nor-

mally carried are the AIM-9G and -9L versions of Sidewinder, carried for self-defence since the autumn of 1983. Pave-way laser-guided bombs are used in conjunction with the Pave Spike laser designator. In the maritime role, the weapon would probably not be used against ship targets, but more probably for attacks on land sites such as port installations.

PERFORMANCE

The massively strong structure of Buccaneer allows pilots to fly at the lowest altitudes with impunity. Normal low-level cruise height is around 100ft (30m), but experienced crews can take the aircraft lower. At these heights the aircraft is very difficult to detect and intercept. Maximum

Below: The large internal weapons bay allows Buccaneer to carry ordnance without the normal drag penalty associated with external hardpoints. The latter are available for shorter-range missions.
Possible weapons:
1. Guided missiles (such as the Martel, AS.30 and Sea Eagle).
2. Rocket flares.
3. Reconnaissance flares.
4. 1,000lb (454kg) "iron" bombs on triple ejector racks (a total of 12 may be carried on the underwing hardpoints), BL.755 cluster munitions or

Paveway LGBs.
5. 500lb (227kg) "iron" bombs (up to 24 on the underwing hardpoints).
6. 18-round launchers for 68mm unguided rockets.
7. 36-round launchers for 2in unguided rockets.
8. 250gal (1,136lit) slipper tank.
9. 430gal (1,955lit) slipper tank.
10. 440gal (2,000lit) auxiliary fuel tank in weapons bay (often used when externally mounted weapons must be carried).
11. Nuclear weapons or 1,000lb "iron" bombs in weapons bay.
12. Ventral recce pack.

speed at sea level has been reported as beyond Mac 0.9. The aircraft's service ceiling of at least 40,000ft (12,200m) is of academic interest except on long range ferry missions.

Naval targets are often located by Nimrod maritime-patrol aircraft, which are able to use their Searchwater radar to plot both target and attacker and to pass positional data to the Buccaneer. This allows the initial approach to the target to be made with the radar switched off, to avoid warning enemy ESM operators.

Occasionally, Buccaneer can display a performance which is surprising for an aircraft of its class. At the 1976 Greenham Common Air Show in the UK, a USAF F-14 thrilled the crowd by carrying out a vertical climb over the airfield from near ground level, using full afterburner and "standing on its tail". The next aircraft on show was an RAF Buccaneer, which astonished the spectators by performing its own version of the same trick. After running in at high speed "on the deck", it pulled up into a graceful climb, trading speed for height until it matched the height reached by the US fighter.

The feat might not have been so impressive as the F-14's rocket-like ascent, and was really intended as a joke against the USN. It certainly impressed the crowd, and must have given at least one of the onlooking East European military attachés reason to reach for a camera. A similar manoeuvre carried out in wartime could develop into a full toss-bombing attack, with a nuclear weapon being released during the climb.

It is often forgotten that the aircraft was—and still is—an effective Euro-strategic bomber. Basic tactical range in a hi-lo-hi attack is 2,000nm (3,700km).

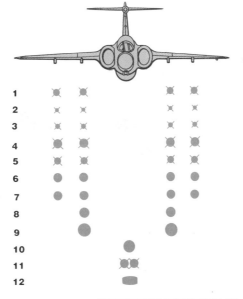

Below: The designers of Buccaneer relied on the fact that vulnerability to SAMs falls sharply with decreasing cruise height, while Mach 0.9 will give most of the anti-SAM protection conferred by high speed. Designers of modern fast-reacting SAM systems might argue with these figures!

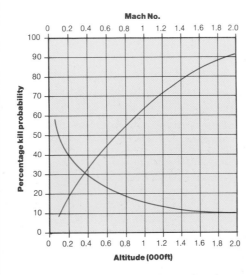

Left: The folding wings and tailcone were essential features in an aircraft originally designed for naval use. Note the streaks of dirt extending backwards across the starboard wing of this Buccaneer. Each is located immediately behind each of the vortex generators, and could be due to the wing-blowing system.

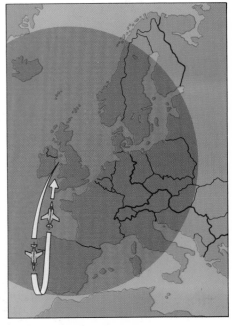

Above: In May 1966 a Buccaneer S.2 of 801 Sqn was launched from the carrier *Victorious* in the Irish Sea, flew to Gibraltar, carried out a simulated nuclear attack, then returned to the carrier – a round trip of 2,000nm (3,700km). Projected into East Europe, this tactical radius displays the aircraft's capability.

HARRIER GR.3 AND AV-8A

DEVELOPMENT

Despite the growing range of anti-runway weapons which may be carried by modern strike aircraft, most of the world's air forces continue to place their faith in aircraft which require a conventional runway. Only the Royal Air Force and US Marine Corps are firm exponents of V/STOL (Vertical/Short Takeoff and Landing) operation. Until some future war sees a modern air force pinned to the ground by the destruction of its runways in a massive pre-emptive strike, the current "anti-V/STOL" myopia will continue; it must be hoped that the runways chosen for any future demonstration of "runway-busting" will not be those of NATO.

The first two prototypes were built using company money, but were given Government funding just before roll-out. Under a further contract awarded in November 1960, four more prototype P.1127s were built. All six were little more than technology-demonstration aircraft intended to provide initial VTOL operating experience, but the nine swept-wing P.1127 Kestrels built under a joint UK/USA/West German programme had uprated Pegasus 5 engines and were able to carry a modest warload. These aircraft equipped a short-lived trinational squadron tasked with exploring the military usefulness of VTOL aircraft.

Experience with Kestrel had shown the RAF that the aircraft could match the tactical radius and endurance of the Hunter, so studies were continued in parallel with the supersonic P.1154 V/STOL programme. By the time that a Socialist Government came to power in 1964, with the avowed intention of cancelling most—if not all—of the then-current British military aircraft programmes, the RAF had prepared an Air Staff Requirement for a subsonic V/STOL aircraft able to replace the Hunter. A development batch of six

Above: Dispersed basing for an RAF Harrier GR.3. Hidden beneath camouflage netting, the aircraft rests on a temporary metal taxiway which spreads its weight over the ground.

Pegasus 6-powered aircraft was ordered in February 1965. The first example started flying trials with a brief VTOL hover on August 31, 1966. Tests went well, and 60 production aircraft were ordered early in 1967, the first of these being were handed over to the RAF in January 1969.

The initial RAF model was the Harrier GR.1, which was followed by the improved GR.1A (with the Pegasus 102 engine) and GR.3 (with the Pegasus 103 and additional avionics). The first production GR.1 flew on December 28, 1967, and a total of 114 were delivered. The T Mk 2, 2A and 4 were two-seat trainers with full combat capability.

Existing GR.1s were rebuilt to the definitive GR.3 standard, while further examples were built from scratch. Production of this version has almost been completed, with the construction of a final batch to replace combat losses in the Falklands war.

In FY69 the US Congress approved

funds for an initial batch of 12 Harriers for test and evaluation by the USMC, but made it clear that no further purchases would be authorised unless the aircraft were produced in the United States. Hawker Siddeley and McDonnell Douglas signed a licence agreement under which the US company could build the aircraft for any US orders. Rolls-Royce granted Pratt & Whitney a similar licence for productio_ of the Pegasus engine. However, because of cost it was decided to build the planned USMC fleet of 102 AV-8A single-seaters and 8 TAV-8A trainers in the UK. Generally similar to the GR.3, these aircraft lack the nose-mounted laser ranger and marked-target seeker fitted to the RAF aircraft.

More than 60 examples are still in service with the USMC and will remain operational until the AV-8B is deployed. To maintain front-line strength in the meantime, the surviving AV-8As are being rebuilt to the improved AV-8C standard under a Conversion in Lieu of Procurement (CILOP) programme which will improve aircraft survivability, reliability and maintainability, and have lift-improvement devices, and improved avionics.

The only other export order for the basic Harrier was placed in the eary 1970s by Spain. A total of 13 Mk 55 Harriers, including two two-seat trainers, was ordered for service aboard the Spanish

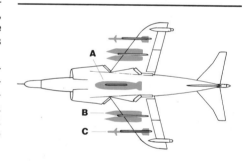

Typical weapons: The relatively short tactical radius of Harrier makes the type better suited to close-support than to longer-ranging strike missions. In the configuration shown here, the aircraft carries a centreline tank (**A**) to extend the range, pods for unguided rockets (**B**), plus AIM-9 missiles for self-defence. Combat experience in the Falklands and earlier Red Flag training exercises showed that the aircraft could take on faster opponents such as Mach 2 fighters. Alternatives to the rocket pods include the BL755 cluster munition and the Paveway laser-guided bomb.

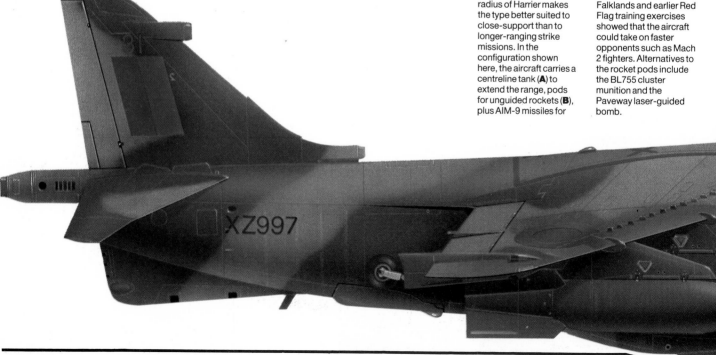

Below left: Harrier's plump fuselage lines are dictated by the size of the Pegasus vectored-thrust turbofan engine, while the shape of the triple-spar swept wing is evidence of its Hawker parentage. This company never flew a true supersonic fighter but Harrier can manage Mach 1.3 in a shallow dive. The planned supersonic P.1154 was never built.

Below left: When ground-based laser designators finally became available in Falklands front-line positions, carrier-based Harriers used Paveway LGBs to good effect. This view also shows the four nozzles of the Pegasus. In a world which has seen experimental VTOLs come and go, this "four-poster" arrangement is the only scheme to have proved a success.

Below left: The distinct "hump" aft of the cockpit is the point at which the wing structure passes over the engine. If the latter needs to be changed, the entire wing must be removed, easy in a conventional hangar, but a major operation in the field. The shape of the vertical fin is another Hawker "trademark".

British Aerospace Harrier GR Mk.3

1. Pitot head.
2. Laser Ranger and Marked Target Seeker (LRMTS).
3. Windscreen washer reservoir.
4. IFF aerial.
5. Yaw vane.
6. Windscreen wiper.
7. Pilot's head-up display (HUD).
8. Martin-Baker Type 9D zero-zero ejection seat.
9. Boundary layer air exhaust ducts.
10. Cockpit air conditioning system.
11. Engine oil tank.
12. Twin alternators.
13. Engine accessory gearbox.
14. Auxiliary power unit
15. Starboard wing pylons.
16. Starboard wing integral fuel tank.
17. Aileron hydraulic actuator.
18. Starboard navigation light.
19. Roll control reaction air valve.
20. Outrigger wheel fairing.
21. Starboard aileron.
22. Hydraulic reservoir.
23. Plan flap.
24. Anti-collision light.
25. Water-methanol tank.
26. Water-methanol filler cap.
27. Flap.jack.
28. Rear fuselage fuel tank.
29. Emergency ram air turbine.
30. Turbine release control.
31. Equipment bay air conditioning system.
32. HF aerial tuner.
33. HF notch aerial.

34. Starboard all-moving tailplane.
35. Rudder control linkage.
36. Total temperature probe.
37. Forward radar warning receiver.
38. VHF aerial.
39. Rudder.
40. Rudder trim tab.
41. Yaw control reaction air valves.
42. Rear radar warning receiver.
43. Pitch control reaction air valve.
44. Port all-moving tailplane.
45. Tail bumper.
46. Tailplane hydraulic actuator.
47. UHF aerial.
48. Control system linkages.
49. Twin batteries.
50. Chaff and flare dispensers.
51. Avionics equipment racks.
52. Airbrake hydraulic jack.
53. Liquid oxygen converter.

54. Hydraulic system nitrogen pressurising bottle.
55. Airbrake.
56. Fuel jettison.
57. Aileron hydraulic actuator.
58. Port aileron.
59. Aileron/roll reaction valve mechanical linkage.
60. Hydraulic retraction jack.
61. Outrigger wheel leg fairings.
62. Port outrigger wheel.
63. Roll control reaction air valve.
64. Port navigation light.
65. Bleed air ducting.
66. Rocket pack.
67. Outboard wing pylon.
68. Aileron control linkage.
69. Port wing integral fuel tank.
70. 1,000lb HE bomb.
71. Rear (hot stream) swivelling exhaust nozzle.
72. Main wheels.
73. Inboard wing pylon.

74. Pressure refuelling connection.
75. Ammunition tank.
76. Main undercarriage hydraulic jack.
77. Fuselage flank fuel tank.
78. 30mm Aden cannon.

79. Forward (fan air) swivelling exhaust nozzle.
80. Engine monitoring and recording equipment.
81. Ventral gun pod, port and starboard.

82. Hydraulic system ground connectors.
83. Forward fuselage fuel tank.
84. Rolls-Royce Pegasus Mk.103 vectoring thrust turbofan engine.

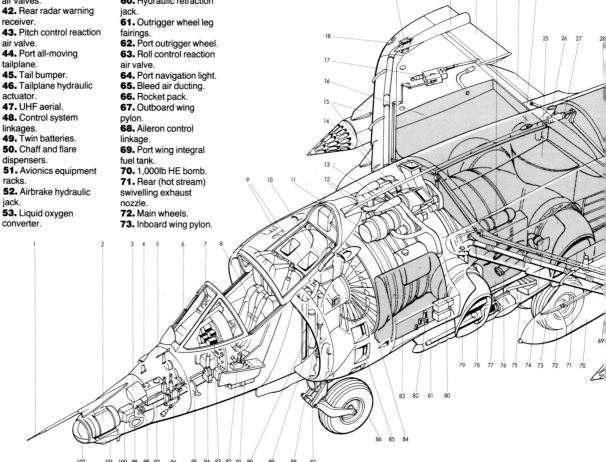

Navy's sole aircraft carrier, the *Dedalo*. To avoid political embarassment to Britain's Socialist Government, which was unwilling to be seen supporting a right-wing regime, the aircraft were ordered by the US Navy, which passed them on to Spain, where they remain in service as AV-8S and TAV-8S Matadors. They will serve on the new carrier *Principe de Asturias*.

Fourteen RAF Harrier GR.3 fighters were deployed to the South Atlantic to supplement the Sea Harrier. Pilots quickly converted to carrier operations, while their aircraft were modified within a week to use AIM-9L Sidewinder missiles. Once committed to action, these aircraft clocked up 125 ground-attack and tactical reconnaissance sorties. Lack of defence-suppression weapons capable of attacking Argentinian radars meant that the Harrier force had to cope with alerted defences—mostly light anti-aircraft weapons. "Most aircraft engaged in offensive support survived damage, which usually resulted from intense Argentinian anti-aircraft gunfire," said the British Government's official report. Three aircraft were lost in action, all believed to have been the victims of anti-aircraft gunfire.

STRUCTURE

In creating the Harrier, the design team at Kingston had to redesign much of the structure of the original P.1127 and Kestrel. The airframe is designed to have a 3,000-hour service life, and is stressed to cope with loads of up to 7g. Most of the structure is made from aluminium alloy, but titanium is used in the engine bay and other high-stress areas.

The wing is small, ideal for high-speed flight at low level where its low gust response will minimise the buffeting experienced by the airframe and pilot. It is of three-spar construction, with an anhedral of 12deg and an integral fuel tank. The leading edge has a dog-tooth at around one-third span, while the trailing edge is fitted with ailerons and plain flaps.

Since the horizontal stabiliser shares the 12deg anhedral of the wing, its drooped surfaces are in close proximity to the hot efflux from the rear nozzles. Severe vibration problems were experienced on the Kestrel, but the redesigned surface used on Harrier provides the needed strength for only a minimal increase in weight. The vertical fin is supplemented by a small

ventral surface, and incorporates a manually-operated rudder made from aluminium honeycomb.

The fuselage houses the cockpit, nose and aft-mounted avionics bays, the Pegasus engine and five integral fuel tanks. The inlets used on the original P.1127 prototypes were tested with inflatable rubber lips. These provided the large-radius lips suited to hovering flight, but could be deflated to give a sharper profile for high-speed flight. In practice, the stress of high-speed flight proved too much for the rubber material and the scheme had to be abandoned. The lip profile adopted for the production aircraft resembles that of the wing. Eight blow-in doors on each inlet provide the additional airflow needed during take-off and landing.

Visibility from the cockpit is poor, particularly towards the rear. The forward view is restricted by the HUD and items of equipment located at the bottom of the windscreen, while the general shape of the canopy and the large air intakes for the Pegasus engine impair rearward vision.

Conventional control surfaces are of no use in the hover or at very low airspeeds, so the Harrier has a second control system

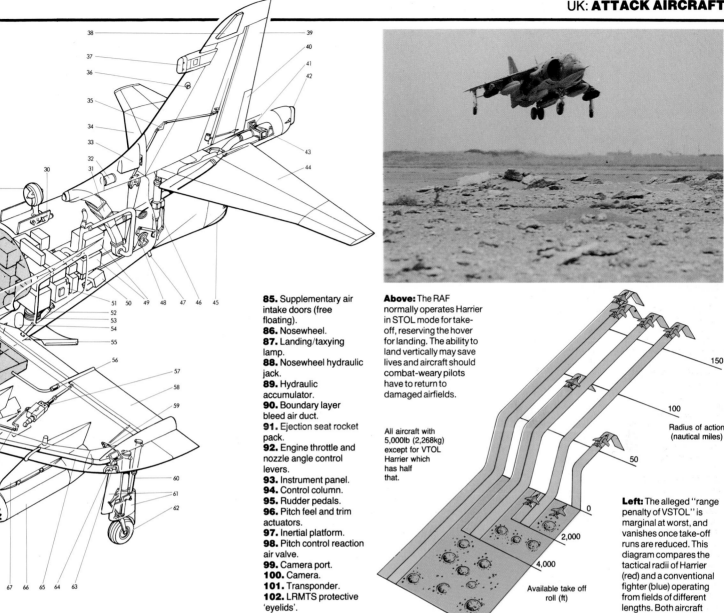

85. Supplementary air intake doors (free floating).
86. Nosewheel.
87. Landing/taxiing lamp.
88. Nosewheel hydraulic jack.
89. Hydraulic accumulator.
90. Boundary layer bleed air duct.
91. Ejection seat rocket pack.
92. Engine throttle and nozzle angle control levers.
93. Instrument panel.
94. Control column.
95. Rudder pedals.
96. Pitch feel and trim actuators.
97. Inertial platform.
98. Pitch control reaction air valve.
99. Camera port.
100. Camera.
101. Transponder.
102. LRMTS protective 'eyelids'.

Above: The RAF normally operates Harrier in STOL mode for take-off, reserving the hover for landing. The ability to land vertically may save lives and aircraft should combat-weary pilots have to return to damaged airfields.

All aircraft with 5,000lb (2,268kg) except for VTOL Harrier which has half that.

150
100
Radius of action (nautical miles)
50
2,000
4,000
Available take off roll (ft)
5,000

Left: The alleged "range penalty of VSTOL" is marginal at worst, and vanishes once take-off runs are reduced. This diagram compares the tactical radii of Harrier (red) and a conventional fighter (blue) operating from fields of different lengths. Both aircraft carry 5,000lb (2,300kg).

comprising wingtip, nose and tail-mounted reaction jets. These are fed with air tapped from the engine's HP section and distributed around the airframe by Nimonic pipes able to cope with the 350deg C temperature of the airflow leaving the engine.

PROPULSION

The Rolls-Royce Pegasus is the Western world's only twin-shaft, vectored-thrust turbofan. Its medium bypass ratio allows the design to match the thrust of the front and rear nozzles (fed by cold fan air and hot core efflux respectively), and gives the high thrust levels needed for V/STOL, plus modest specific fuel consumption. In its present form the engine is rated at 21,500lb (9,750kg). The two shafts of the engine rotate in opposite directions. A three-stage axial flow fan and an eight-stage HP compressor are each driven by a two-stage turbine. A portion of the airflow from the fan is fed to the two forward-mounted nozzles, while the hot efflux from the core feeds the two aft nozzles.

The front nozzles are made from steel, the aft nozzles from Nimonic high-tem-perature alloy. Early engines used glass-fibre forward nozzles until the failure of one nozzle resulted in asymmetric thrust and the loss of the second prototype. All four nozzles may be rotated from fully aft to 10deg forward of vertical by means of a drive system incorporating duplicated motors and transmission elements based on shafts and chains.

The current Pegasus 11 Mk 103 features a redesigned fan giving an increased air mass flow, pressure ratio and bypass ratio, while the turbine inlet temperature has been raised. This version is also cleared for the use of vectoring in forward flight (VIFF) to enhance aircraft combat manoeuvrability.

Short-term development work is concentrated on the needs of the AV-8B, but Rolls-Royce has studied the Pegasus 18, a 26,000 to 28,000lb (11,800 to 12,700kg) engine with a new fan, HP compressor and turbine.

AVIONICS

Much of the avionics which went into the RAF's Harrier GR.1 were systems under development for the cancelled P.1154 supersonic V/STOL fighter. This included the Ferranti FE 541 nav-attack system, a Specto (now part of Smiths Industries) HUD, and a projected-map display. The later GR.3 standard introduced additional items of avionics, several of which affected the external appearance of the aircraft. A modified and extended nose houses a Ferranti Type 106 laser ranger and marked-target seeker, while the glass-fibre fairing in the fin of the Harrier (and Jaguar) houses the forward- and rearward-facing antennas of the Marconi Space and Defence ARI 18223 radar warning receiver.

The broadly similar AV-8A lacks the nose-mounted electro-optics of the Harrier GR.3, so has a nose profile similar to that of the GR.1. Some items of avionics such as the radio and IFF systems were changed to US-standard equipment.

Both the RAF and USMC aircraft are being updated with more modern avionics. RAF GR.3s are to be fitted with the Zeus internally-mounted jamming system. This combines a Marconi-developed radar warning receiver (RWR) with Northrop jamming transmitters.

The control unit and display are located in the cockpit, while the antennas are positioned in the best locations to ensure good coverage. On the Harrier this will almost certainly be in the traditional fin fairing currently favoured by the RAF for the RWR antennas. Transmitter antennas for the jamming transmitter may be located in the nose and tail. All the remaining units are mounted in the aircraft's main avionics bay aft of the wing.

As part of the Conversion in Lieu of Procurement (CILOP) programme which updates USMC AV-8As to the AV-8C standard, the aircraft is being fitted with new items of avionics including the ALR-45 radar warning receiver, ALE-39 flare/chaff dispenser, ARC-159 radio, and KY-28 crypto set.

ARMAMENT

The Harrier and the AV-8A have seven external hardpoints—two beneath each wing and three beneath the fuselage. Ordnance which may be carried includes conventional bombs, "smart" bombs, and pods for unguided rockets. Paveway laser-guided bombs were used in the final stages of the Falklands war. Ferranti laser target marker and ranger units located on Two Sisters were used to designate targets on Tumbledown on the final day of combat. Four Paveway laser-guided bombs (LGBs) were toss-bombed from a stand-off range of 3 to 4nm (6 to 7km) by Harrier GR.3s. Two attacks were mounted—one in the morning and the other in the afternoon. On both occasions a single Harrier carrying two LGBs flew in from the south-west, releasing the ordnance at an angle of 30deg during a 3g pull-up. As the aircraft turned away to safety, the LGBs flew over Mount Harriet, reaching a maximum height of around 1,500ft (500m) before dropping into the target area.

During both attacks, errors in target-designation procedure resulted in the illuminating laser being turned on too soon, causing one of the two bombs to miss the target, but the other scored a direct hit.

An anti-armour weapon for future service on Harriers (and other aircraft) follows the failure of the Hunting Engineering VJ291 guided cluster munition developed to meet the requirements of an RAF Air Staff Target. The original requirement was downgraded to eliminate off-boresight attack capability, and is being met by a new version of the Hunting Engineering BL755 cluster bomb. The revised weapon carries the same number of bomblets (147) as the current model, but these have been redesigned to increase lethality and reduce the range at which the weapon must be released. Each bomblet will be fitted with a tail-mounted retarding parachute intended to slow its forward flight and pitch it into a nose-down attitude. The modified bomblet will descend on the target in a more vertical attitude than at present, particularly if released at short range. This will ease the task of penetrating tank armour, ensuring that the bomblet's shaped-charge warhead is fired against the relatively thin upper surface armour of a tank rather than the sides or turret front and glacis plate.

The V-8A and Matador are equipped to carry AIM-9 Sidewinder missiles, while RAF GR.3s were hastily fitted with the missile during the Falklands war. The AV-8C will probably be able to carry AGM-65 Maverick missiles. Twin fairings beneath the belly each contain a 30mm ADEN cannon.

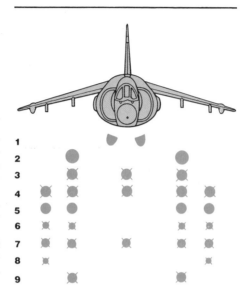

Possible weapons:
1. ADEN gun packs.
2. 100 or 330gal tanks.
3. 1,000lb (450kg) free-falling or retarded bombs.
4. Cluster munitions.
5. Launchers for unguided rockets.
6. Flares or light firebombs.
7. Carriers for practice bombs.
8. AIM-9 Sidewinders.
9. Laser-guided bombs or guided missiles.

Below: Most obvious features of the Harrier GR.3 cockpit are the HUD and the circular projected-map display for the FE 541 navigation/attack system. Maps stored in a cassette show a tactical area of up to some 800 to 900nm (1,500 to 1,700km) in diameter.

PERFORMANCE

The Harrier is capable of vertical take-off, but the technique is rarely used. Tests with the Kestrel showed that even a minimal take-off run could substantially increase range/payload. Vertical landing remains a useful facility, allowing pilots fatigued by multiple sorties to land at airfields whose runways have been partially or totally destroyed.

Like the Hunter it replaced in RAF service, the Harrier is a subsonic aircraft, although capable of supersonic speed in a shallow dive. Maximum speed at low level is more than 640kt (1,186km/h), while the aircraft can reach Mach 1.3 in a dive. From a standing start the GR.3 can carry out a vertical take-off and climb to 40,000ft (12,200m) in less than 150 seconds. Service ceiling is greater than 50,000ft (15,250m).

If the Harrier does have a weak point, it is probably range. Tactical radius on a hi-lo-hi strike mission on which external tanks are not carried is around 225nm (415km). A typical Jaguar tactical radius under similar conditions would be double this figure. Normal ferry range is 1,800nm (3,330km), but RAF aircraft may be fitted with a flight refuelling probe to extend their range. Maximum ferry range with a single in-flight refuelling is more than 3,000nm (5,550km).

The Harrier and AV-8B have an undeserved reputation for being accident prone, their safety record being questioned in the late 1970s. Neither the RAF nor USMC makes any secret that attrition has been heavy, but deny that this is any

Right: A fully loaded and fuelled Harrier taxies beneath trees to hide from enemy strike aircraft. This manoeuvre may be carried out at regular airfields (freeing the hardened aircraft shelters for conventional aircraft) or dispersed temporary airstrips.

reflection on the aircraft. The fact remains that, though the fast-and-low tactics favoured by the RAF and RN and combat-proven in the South Atlantic do reduce combat attrition, they leave the pilot with little margin for error in an emergency.

The RAF considers the Harrier's safety record to be good when compared with that of the Hunter, while the USMC has pointed out that the AV-8A has an accident rate well below that of the F-8 Crusader. Both types used for comparison are widely considered to be "pilot's aircraft", and no-one had seriously suggested that either was a danger to its crews.

One factor which led to the high US accident rate was overconfidence. Initial operating experience with hand-picked and highly-experienced pilots led the USMC to regard the aircraft as forgiving, and to assign newly-trained pilots to VTOL duty. The resulting accident rate forced a re-evaluation of the type's qualities. Talking to *Flight International* in the late 1970s, the USMC likened the AV-8A to the World War II Corsair. Like the piston-engined fighter, the AV-8A is safe, offers high performance, but has to be *flown*—it is unforgiving of any lack of attention by less-experienced aircrew. The ultimate vote in favour of the Harrier must surely be that both operators plan to deploy the follow-on AV-8B.

OPERATORS

UK (143 GR.3); Spain (11 AV-8S, 2 TAV-8S); US Marine Corps (102 AV-8A, 8 TAV-8A; approximately 60 still in service are being rebuilt as AV-8C).

Operations from unsupported sites

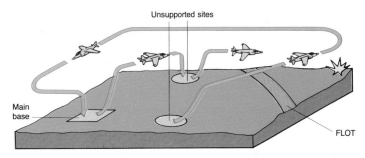

Left: Harrier can operate from unsupported sites, using the main base only for logistics and support. Once fuelled and armed, the aircraft fly to an unsupported forward location close to the forward line of troops (FLOT), land vertically then await calls for close-air support. Having delivered their ordnance, the aircraft return to the main base.

Operations from pre-stocked sites

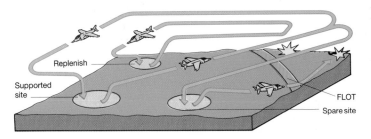

Left: In true dispersed-base operations, all flying is carried out from hard-to-target sites rather than from main airfields. Take-offs would be STOL, landings vertical. Some bases are prestocked with fuel and ordnance, but have only limited servicing facilities, while others are air bases in miniature, offering full servicing, briefing and communication facilities.

Rapid-reaction operations

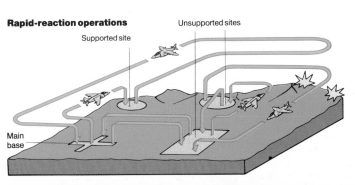

Left: Troops are normally supported either by aircraft flying pre-planned "set piece" strikes which may arrive too late, or by aircraft flying "cab rank" patrols so as to be available at short notice. By holding ready-for-action aircraft on the ground, rather than on fuel-wasting loiter patterns, Harrier units can be on call for long periods.

SEA HARRIER FRS.1

DEVELOPMENT

Without the Sea Harrier, the Falkland Islands would still be in Argentinian hands. Like all wars, the Falklands campaign of 1982 was finally won by the infantry, but without the air cover given to the UK task force by Royal Navy Sea Harrier fighters, the fleet could not come within range of the Argentinian A-4s and Mirages, and the landings would not have been possible.

Sea Harrier FRS Mk 1 is a multirole, shipborne V/STOL fighter able to perform attack, reconnaissance, and air superiority missions.

The first serious evidence that Harriers might one day fly from RN carriers came in March 1970, when GR.1 fighters of No. 1 Sqn of the RAF flew trials sorties from HMS *Ark Royal*. Dogged persistence by some Royal Navy planners who wanted to see a reversal of the 1966 decision by a Labour Government to end RN fixed-wing flying finally paid off late in August 1972 with the issue of a Naval Staff Target for a minimal-modification version of the Harrier GR.3 able to operate from "Invincible"-class light carriers. An order for 24 aircraft was repeatedly delayed, and was not placed until May 1975. First flight was in August 1978, with delivery of the first aircraft to the Royal Navy taking place in June 1979.

India's long-standing requirement for new aircraft to replace the totally obsolescent Sea Hawk fighters originally deployed aboard the carrier *Vikrant* was finally met by ordering eight Sea Harriers—six FRS Mk 51 single-seaters and two T Mk 4 trainers. Total value of the contract is estimated to be worth over $90 million. Deliveries began on January 27, 1983, and all aircraft are to become operational aboard the *Vikrant*. An option on a further

batch of eight aircraft has not yet been taken up.

Having lost five Sea Harriers during the Falklands war and two others in accidents, the Royal Navy placed a follow-on order for 14 further aircraft—seven to replace losses plus a further seven to increase the fleet size following the decision not to sell *Invincible* to the Royal Australian Navy. Production is running at around one aircraft per month, and is likely to end in the mid-1980s.

Soon after the Falklands war BAe was reported to be studying the feasibility of a specialised airborne early-warning version. This would have had extended wings equipped with conformal radar antennas. There have been no subsequent reports of this project, so it has probably been abandoned.

The need for some improvements to Sea Harrier was highlighted by the Falklands

Above: During the Falklands War, a force of 28 carrier-based Sea Harriers, backed up by the surface-to-air missile firepower of the British Task Force, broke the back of the Argentine Air Force. Wave after wave of Mirages, Daggers and A-4s clashed with the small force of defending Sea Harriers, which claimed 20 "kills" without losing any of their own number in air combat. This brilliant combat record is partly an accident of geography – had the Argentines not been operating at the limit of their range, some Sea Harriers might have been lost.

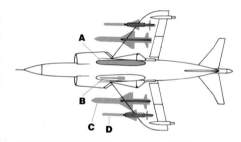

Typical weapons: Above: Combat effectiveness of the Sea Harrier will be improved by the availability of new weaponry in the mid-to-late 1980s. The BAeD Sea Eagle anti-ship missile (**C**) is about to enter service, while the same company's new ALARM anti-radar missile (**D**) could be retrofitted in the late 1980s. The aircraft can be fitted with 30mm ADEN cannon packs (**B**) but during the Falklands War one of these was replaced by a similarly-shaped pod Blue Eric jamming system (**A**). The latter could be replaced by a more advanced pod or even by the new Marconi/ Northrop Zeus.

ZA177

Below: Seen from above, the Sea Harrier is almost identical to the RAF's GR.3. Only the broader nose profile, the radome for the Blue Fox radar and the RN-style grey paint scheme immediately identify this aircraft as a Sea Harrier, although many other minor modifications were needed to suit the aircraft to long-term shipboard service. The Falklands War proved that land-based Harriers could be ship-based if needed.

Below: The Royal Navy can only afford a single shipboard fighter, so the Sea Harrier must be able to fly fighter, recce and strike missions. The loading shown here of two external tanks, two AIM-9L Sidewinders and a single BL755 cluster bomb could be used by an aircraft attempting reconnaissance of a hostile coastline but having orders to attack any target of opportunity.

Below left: The raised cockpit of the Sea Harrier is a distinct recognition feature, and a great improvement on the ''front office'' of the land-based GR.3. The FRS.1 might be mistaken at first sight for the AV-8B, but the latter has a slimmer nose and lacks the radome and nose-mounted pitot head of the RN aircraft.

campaign. The need for greater endurance and weapon-carrying capability was swiftly met by fitting aircraft embarked aboard the carrier *Illustrious* with larger drop tanks and four Sidewinders instead of two. In the longer term, the RN plans improvements to the Ferranti Blue Fox airborne radar and to the aircraft's radar-warning receiver.

As part of a mid-life improvement programme, RN Sea Harriers will be equipped with a new Ferranti pulse-doppler radar, plus up to four AIM-120 AMRAAM missiles and two AIM-9 Sidewinders, giving the aircraft a multi-shot look-down/shoot-down capability. Two drop tanks fitted to underwing pylons would increase the aircraft's endurance, improving range and loiter capability. New leading-edge root extensions (LERXs) could improve manoeuvrability, and an improved radar warning receiver may also be fitted.

STRUCTURE

The Sea Harrier has great commonality with the airframe, powerplant and mechanical systems of the Harrier GR.3 but has an entirely different nose and forward fuselage, a larger fin to allow for this, and magnesium alloy has been largely eliminated from the airframe as an anti-corrosion precaution.

Air turbulence caused by ship superstructure can be a problem in naval aviation, so the Sea Harrier has greater control authority while in the hover and transition—the reaction-control jets are more powerful than those on Harrier. The fin has been increased in height by around 4in (10cm), while the horizontal stabiliser has been strengthened and given an extra 2deg of travel.

The cockpit has been raised to incorporate revised displays and to give a better rear view, while the nose is increased in size to house the Blue Fox radar. The nose, complete with its radar set, may be hinged to port for storage within the carrier's hangar. Other minor modifications to the Sea Harrier added an emergency wheel-brake system, a different pattern of liquid-oxygen converter, and various lashing lugs on the nosegear.

POWERPLANT

The Sea Harrier is powered by the Pegasus 11 Mk 104. A marinised version of the Mk 103 used to power the RAF's GR.3 fleet, this offers the same 21,000lb (9,500kg) of thrust but incorporates LP and intermediate casings made from corrosion-resistant materials, and has a strengthened gearbox able to drive the more powerful 15kVA electrical generators of the naval aircraft.

AVIONICS

When the Royal Navy decided to adopt a navalised version of Harrier as its next shipboard fighter, part of the navalisation process involved the addition of a virtually all-new avionics suite to what was originally a low-level strike aircraft. This includes a Ferranti Blue Fox radar, a Smiths Industries head-up display of improved design, a self-aligning Ferranti FIN 1040 attitude and heading reference system and digital computer, a Decca 72 Doppler radar, radar altimeter, and improved radar warning system.

British Aerospace Sea Harrier FRS.1
1. Pitch reaction control air valve.
2. Pitch feel and trim actuators.
3. Inertial platform.
4. IFF aerial.
5. Yaw vane.
6. Rudder pedals.
7. Control column.
8. Windscreen wiper.
9. Instrument panel.
10. Pilot's head-up display (HUD).
11. Martin-Baker Mk.9D zero-zero ejection seat.
12. Boundary layer air exhaust ducts.
13. Cockpit air conditioning system.
14. Engine oil tank.
15. Alternator.
16. Engine accessory gearbox.
17. Auxiliary power unit (APU).
18. Starboard wing pylons.
19. Starboard wing integral fuel tank.
20. Aileron hydraulic actuator.

21. Starboard navigation light.
22. Roll control reaction air valve.
23. Outrigger wheel fairing.
24. Starboard aileron.
25. Hydraulic reservoir.
26. Plain flap.
27. Anti-collision light.
28. Water-methanol tank.
29. Water-methanol filler cap.
30. Flap hydraulic jack.
31. Rear fuselage fuel tank.
32. Emergency ram air turbine.
33. Turbine release control.
34. Equipment bay air conditioning system.
35. HF aerial tuner.
36. HF notch aerial.
37. Starboard all-moving tailplane.

38. Rudder control linkage.
39. Total temperature probe.
40. Forward radar warning receiver.
41. VHF aerial.
42. Rudder.
43. Rudder trim tab.
44. Yaw control reaction air valves.

45. Rear radar warning receiver.
46. Pitch control reaction air valve.
47. Port all-moving tailplane.
48. Tail bumper.
49. Radar altimeter aerials.
50. Tailplane hydraulic actuator.
51. UHF aerial.

52. Control system linkages.
53. Twin batteries.
54. Chaff and flare dispensers.
55. Avionics equipment racks.
56. Airbrake hydraulic jack.
57. Liquid oxygen converter.

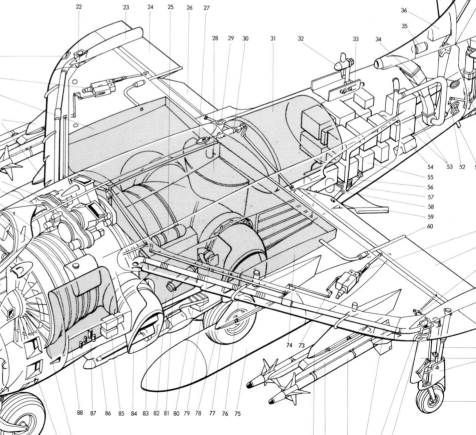

Above: A Sea Harrier is launched from the ski ramp of an RN carrier – probably *Invincible*. This manoeuvre is easier than it looks, and was swiftly mastered by GR.3 pilots in the Falklands War.

Right: The cockpit of Sea Harrier is generally similar to that of the GR.3. The CRT display for the Blue Fox radar has not yet been installed in this aircraft (see grey-painted blank plate).

77. Mainwheels.
78. Inboard wing pylon.
79. Pressure refuelling connection.
80. Ammunition tank.
81. Main undercarriage hydraulic jack.
82. Fuselage flank fuel tank.
83. 30mm Aden cannon.
84. Forward (fan air) swivelling exhaust nozzle.
85. Engine monitoring and recording equipment.
86. Ventral gun pod, port and starboard.

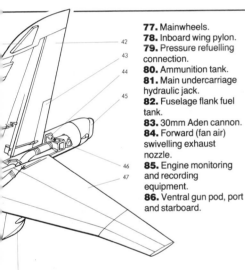

58. Hydraulic system nitrogen pressurising bottle.
59. Airbrake.
60. Fuel jettison.
61. Aileron hydraulic actuator.
62. Port aileron.
63. Aileron/roll reaction valve mechanical linkage.
64. Hydraulic retraction jack.
65. Outrigger leg fairings.
66. Port outrigger wheel.
67. Roll control reaction air valve.
68. Port navigation light.
69. Bleed air ducting.
70. Twin AIM-9L Sidewinder air-to-air missiles.
71. Missile launch rails.
72. Outboard wing pylon.
73. Aileron control linkage.
74. Port wing integral fuel tank.
75. 190gal jettisonable fuel tank.
76. Rear (hot stream) swivelling exhaust nozzle.

87. Hydraulic system ground connectors.
88. Forward fuselage fuel tank.
89. Rolls-Royce Pegasus Mk.104 vectoring thrust turbofan engine.
90. Supplementary air intake doors, free floating.
91. Nosewheel.
92. Landing/taxiing lamp.
93. Nosewheel hydraulic jack.
94. Hydraulic accumulator.
95. Boundary layer bleed air duct.
96. Pitot head.
97. Radar hand controller.
98. Ejection seat rocket pack.
99. Engine throttle and exhaust nozzle angle control levers.
100. Doppler radar.
101. Radar scanner.
102. Radome, folded to port.
103. Ferranti 'Blue-Fox' radar equipment.

Blue Fox was developed from the earlier Seaspray set devised for the Sea King helicopter. This is a frequency-agile I-band dual-role set, and can be used to guide the aircraft during interception missions or during attacks against surface targets. The four main operating modes are search (for target detection), attack (for use against air and surface targets), boresight (used for ranging on targets of opportunity), and transponder (for the identification of "friendlies").

Pulse-Doppler techniques are not used, since this technique—widely used in current-generation radars—is mainly intended to improve rejection of ground clutter. Blue Fox was designed for the simpler role of detecting large targets such as Backfire bombers or Il-38 May maritime-patrol aircraft over the sea.

The antenna is a stabilised planar array, and the basic set is built up from a series of LRUs in order to ease maintenance. It is air-cooled and weighs 186lb (84kg).

ARMAMENT

Being a modified version of the land-based fighter, the Sea Harrier can carry the same range of ordnance as RAF GR.3s. Since air-to-air combat was always seen as one of Sea Harrier's roles, Royal Navy aircraft were fitted with AIM-9 Sidewinder missiles and are scheduled to receive the AIM-120 AMRAAM. Indian Navy FRS.51 aircraft carry the Matra R.550 Magic. All versions carry two 30mm ADEN cannon in ventral packs.

One weapon not carried by the GR.3 but an important part of Sea Harrier's armament is the new BAe Dynamics Sea Eagle, an anti-ship missile based on the proven aerodynamic form of the earlier rocket-powered Anglo-French Martel. It is probably the most advanced anti-ship missile currently available, and likely to remain so for some time in view of the long delays

likely before supersonic weapons such as the Franco-German ANS fly in definitive form and are cleared for service.

Flight trials have demonstrated the round's ability to separate from the launch aircraft at various altitudes, light up the built-in turbojet engine, descend to low level, then fly under autopilot control to the point where the built-in MSDS radar seeker can take over for the final run in to the target. Seeker performance in the face

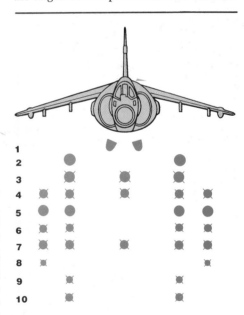

Possible weapons:
Current and proposed armament loads for the Sea Harrier include:
1. Gun packs for the 30mm ADEN cannon.
2. External tanks of 100, 190 or 330 gallons.
3. 1,000lb (450kg) free-falling or retarded bombs.
4. BL755 cluster bombs.
5. Matra 116/116

launchers for 2in (50mm) unguided rockets.
6. Bofors Lepus flares.
7. Carriers for practice bombs.
8. AIM-9L or R.550 Magic missiles.
9. Sea Eagle anti-ship missiles.
10. Harpoon anti-ship missiles (offered as armament for export aircraft).

of ECM has also been demonstrated, while warhead penetration and detonation tests have confirmed the likely destructive effect.

PERFORMANCE

The Royal Navy Air Staff Target for Sea Harrier asked for a fighter able to fly a 400nm (740km) tactical radius air-to-air mission, a strike mission of at least 250nm (460km) tactical radius, or a search mission covering at least 27,000 square miles (70,000sq km) at low level.

Test flights carried out in the early 1970s by company pilots showed that, as on land, a short take-off run greatly improves load-carrying capability. In the case of a shipboard fighter, the wind over the deck resulting from the carrier's own speed gives a further performance boost if STOL takeoffs are used. The most drama-

tic improvement comes with the use of a "ski-lift" take-off ramp. The aircraft can take off with a heavier load of fuel and weapons, or from a shorter take-off run, if the foward roll ends on a curved ramp which will give a degree of upward momentum. The aircraft can leave the ramp without the speed and wing lift needed for sustained flight. While in what amounts to a semi-ballistic flight, it can gain normal flying speed.

Tests with a land-based ramp started in August 1977, and angles of up to 20 deg were used, though it was established that the optimum was around 15deg. The basic procedure is simple. Aircraft begin their take-off roll with the nozzles pointing aft, and the pilot applies a downward nozzle angle as he reaches the top of the ramp.

A ramp was added to the carrier *Invincible* while the vessel was still under construction, and was incorporated in the

design of follow-on vessels. The 1950s-vintage *Hermes* was also retrofitted with a ramp.

The top speed of Sea Harrier is 640kt (1,190km/h) at sea level, but the aircraft can manage Mach 1.25 in a dive. Normal cruise speed is 350 to 450kt (650 to 835km/h) at low altitude, but the massive thrust of the Pegasus allows a swift acceleration to 600kt (1,110km/h). At height, the aircraft can comfortably cruise on internal fuel for up to an hour at Mach 0.8. Service ceiling is 51,200ft (15,600m). Reaction time is fast: from the moment of scramble the aircraft can arrive at a combat area 30nm (55km) from the carrier in less than 6 minutes.

Below: The "H" and "N" on the two aircraft nearest the camera indicate their being based on *Hermes* and *Invincible* respectively. The third is from 899 Sqn, a land-based unit stationed at Yeovilton, Somerset.

Ski ramp increases STOL capability

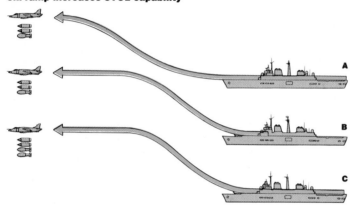

Left: The use of a ski ramp allows shipboard or land-based aircraft to carry a larger warload or rely on a shorter takeoff run. On a conventional flat-deck carrier, a Sea Harrier carrying a 10,000lb (4,500kg) load leaves the deck at 120kt (222km/h) after a 600ft (180m) run (**A**). Given a ski ramp, it can either make do with a 200ft (60m) roll and 70kt (130km/h) takeoff speed (**B**) or use the full deck length and resulting 120kt (222km/h) to carry 13,000lb (5,900kg) (**C**).

Anti-ship attack (hi-lo-hi)
Mission radius 280nm (520km)

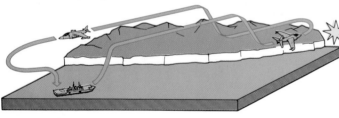

Left: Operating in hi-lo-hi mode in order to conserve fuel while still approaching the target at low level, Sea Harrier has a typical tactical radius of 280nm (520km). If the target is a warship and may be attacked with Sea Eagle missiles, the tactical radius is further increased.

Reconnaissance role
Mission radius 450nm (837km)

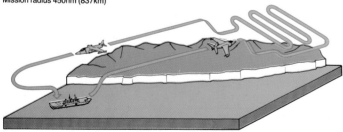

Left: The "R" in the FRS.1 designation of the Royal Navy's Sea Harriers indicates the type's reconnaissance role. Depending on the size of the area to be searched, tactical radius can be up to 450nm (840km). Missions of this type were flown during the Falklands War in order to monitor enemy warship movements.

High-altitude combat air patrol
Mission radius 100nm (185km)

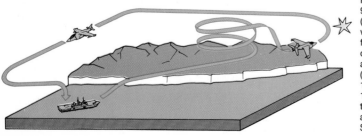

Left: When used for combat air patrol, a Sea Harrier can loiter for up to 90min at up to 100nm (185km) from its carrier, while still having enough fuel for 3min of air combat using its cannon and Sidewinder missiles (plus medium-range AIM-120A AMRAAMs from 1986 onwards). Like all the diagrams shown above, this assumes a STOVL mission.

During the Falklands war 28 Sea Harriers flew 1,100 combat air patrol missions plus 90 offensive support operations. Availability at the beginning of each day was 95 per cent, and 99 per cent of all planned missions were flown. On April 1, 1982, *Hermes* launched 12 Sea Harriers to carry out attacks on Port Stanley and Goose Green. An hour after their return, the same aircraft were once more airborne on air-defence patrols.

In action against the Argentinian Air Force, Sea Harriers scored 20 "kills" and three probables, despite being outnumbered six to one. The AIM-9L Sidewinder air-to-air missile dominated in air-to-air combat, accounting for 16 of the "kills" plus one probable. The other enemy aircraft were shot down by 30mm cannon fire from the Sea Harrier's twin ADEN.
Two Sea Harriers were lost in combat—one to small-arms fire and the other to a Roland surface-to-air missile. Four more were lost in accidents—one crashed after take-off, two went missing while on patrol and are believed to have collided in bad weather, while another rolled off the deck and into the sea.

OPERATORS

UK (34 FRS Mk 1 and 4 T Mk 4 trainers originally delivered; 14 more aircraft ordered); India (6 FRS Mk 51, two T Mk 4 trainers).

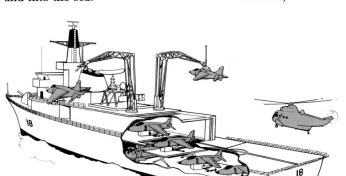

Left: Land-based trials of the proposed Skyhook method of operating Sea Harriers from small naval vessels have already been carried out. The aircraft hovers close to the stabilised crane arm, which is then automatically mated with a pick-up point on top of the aircraft. The arm can either refuel the Harrier via a probe/receptacle incorporated within the arm/aircraft coupling, or bring the Harrier down to the flight deck.

MIRAGE III

DEVELOPMENT

Ever since the Mirage IIICJs of the Israeli Air Force shattered the air arms of Egypt, Syria and Jordan in a series of surprise raids in the opening hours of the 1967 Six-Day War, Dassault has enjoyed an enviable reputation as a builder of jet fighters. Yet this very success tends to obscure the fact that the company's reputation is largely based on a single product—the delta-winged family of aircraft based on the Mirage III. The company has flown and placed in production other types, but none has come close to matching the success of the Mirage III.

Low cost and Mach 2 performance were the selling points of the Mirage III. While Britain and the USA built complex, heavy, expensive, and highly-specialised interceptors such as the Lightning and F-106 Delta Dart, France produced an affordable and workmanlike multi-role fighter—just what many customers needed and what only Dassault had the foresight to build.

The basic Mirage III design is a single-engined, delta wing, multi-mission type available in a family of variants suitable for interception, air-superiority, ground-attack, reconnaissance, and operational-training roles. By using a common airframe for a series of different aircraft, Dassault was able to keep the price of the aircraft to a minimum. Back in 1960, the original IIIC cost just over $1 million each. The IIIE is no longer in production, but at today's prices would cost at least six or seven times the 1960 figure.

Only 10 Mirage IIIA preproduction aircraft were built, the first production versions being the IIIC all-weather interceptor and ground-attack fighter, and IIIB two-

seat trainer. A total of 224 single-seat and 110 two-seaters were built. (The IIID was a two-seat trainer built in Australia.) First flight of a Mirage IIIC took place in October 1960, and production deliveries to the Armée de l'Air started in December of that year.

Export versions of the IIIC were sold to Israel (IIICJ) and South Africa (IIICZ). Production ended in 1964, the more powerful Mirage IIIC2 having been built only in prototype form, flying in 1965 with a prototype of the uprated Atar which later became the 9K-50.

Definitive export model was the IIIE, originally developed as a fighter/bomber for nuclear strike missions. By extending the fuselage length by about 12 inches (30cm), the internal fuel capacity was increased to 733gal (3,332 litres), while additional avionics coped with the new navigation and attack duties. Final production total for this version was 523. The basic range of aircraft was rounded out by

the Mirage IIIR reconnaissance version.

Main production facility is the Avions Marcel Dassault Breguet Aviation plant at Merignac in France, but aircraft have also been built under licence by the Government Aircraft Factory at Melbourne, Australia, and by the Swiss Federal Aircraft Factory at Emmen, Switzerland. Unlicenced production under the designations Nesher and Dagger was also carried out in Israel by Israel Aircraft Industries, who further developed the type into the J79-powered IAI Kfir.

The most controversial Mirage III variant was the IIIS adopted by the Swiss Air Force. Instead of buying an off-the-shelf Mirage, the Swiss opted to order a version customised to meet their own specialised requirements. The Mirage IIIS has revised armament, new avionics, and the fuselage is strengthened to allow rocket-assisted take-offs and arrested landings. To add further problems, the aircraft were to be built in Switzerland. The end result was a

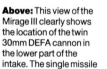

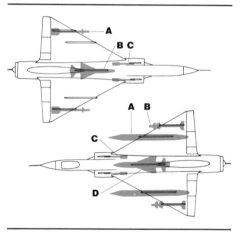

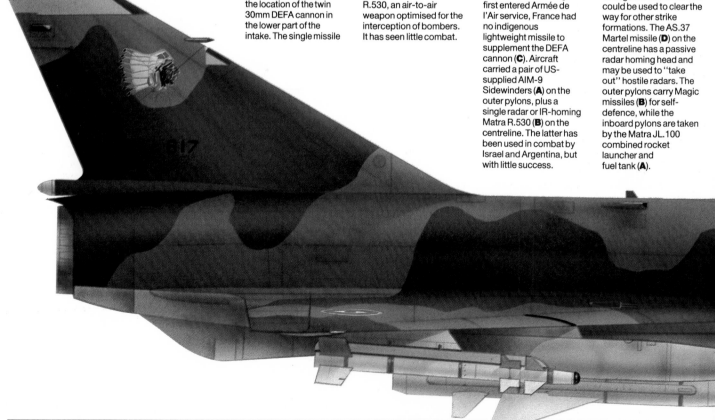

Above: This view of the Mirage III clearly shows the location of the twin 30mm DEFA cannon in the lower part of the intake. The single missile carried on the aircraft centreline is a Matra R.530, an air-to-air weapon optimised for the interception of bombers. It has seen little combat.

Typical weapons:
Top: When the Mirage III first entered Armée de l'Air service, France had no indigenous lightweight missile to supplement the DEFA cannon (**C**). Aircraft carried a pair of US-supplied AIM-9 Sidewinders (**A**) on the outer pylons, plus a single radar or IR-homing Matra R.530 (**B**) on the centreline. The latter has been used in combat by Israel and Argentina, but with little success.

Above: The Mirage IIIE configuration shown here could be used to clear the way for other strike formations. The AS.37 Martel missile (**D**) on the centreline has a passive radar homing head and may be used to "take out" hostile radars. The outer pylons carry Magic missiles (**B**) for self-defence, while the inboard pylons are taken by the Matra JL.100 combined rocket launcher and fuel tank (**A**).

Below left: The distinctive delta wing of the Mirage III has a leading edge swept back at just over 60deg, and a thickness to chord ratio of between 3.5 and 4.5 per cent. Dassault's first delta wing was that of the tiny MD 550 Mirage I, but a technical agreement with Fairey Aviation in the UK provided design data which was used in the Mirage II and III.

Above right: Features of the Mirage IIIE visible from below include the shallow radome for the Doppler navigation radar (just forward of the door for the nose section of the undercarriage); gun ports beneath the intakes; a distinct gap between the intake centrebody and the fuselage side; the doors for the inward-retracting main undercarriage; the red-painted airbrakes; and the elevons at the trailing edge of the wing.

Stores carried on this aircraft are R.550 Magic "dogfight" missiles on the outer pylons, external fuel tanks on the inboard pylons, and a single AS.37 Martel. This was built in TV guided (AJ.168) and passive-radar (AS.37) forms by Aérospatiale and Britain's Hawker Siddeley Dynamics. France and UK fielded the AS.37, but France had no requirement for the AJ.168.

Below left: Most Mirage IIIs are of the IIIE pattern shown here. The earlier IIIC has a shorter forward fuselage. Doors located in the centre of the roundel on the inlet wall open to admit extra air during take-off. The bullet-shaped fairing on the fin houses an antenna for the radar-warning receiver, while the fairing at the base of the fin holds the braking parachute.

disaster. Costs escalated, and the first Swiss-built aircraft did not fly until October 1965. The planned buy had to be cut back from 100 aircraft to only 58, and the final unit cost was twice that of an off-the-shelf Mirage IIIE.

Dassault has received orders for at least 1,430 Mirage deltas, some 1,100 of which remain in service. Not all are Mirage IIIs—the company does not differentiate between this aircraft and the later Mirage 5 and 50 when releasing production figures.

Although the latter version had probably supplanted the Mirage III on the line by the late 1970s, the older designation is unlikely to disappear. Dassault's new generation Mirage IIING flew for the first time on December 21, 1982. Powered by the Atar 9K50 engine used in the Mirage 50, the new variant introduces fly-by-wire systems and new ECM equipment.

STRUCTURE

The delta wing which gives the Mirage III its characteristic appearance (and which has almost become a Dassault "trademark") has a leading-edge sweep of 60deg, a slight anhedral of 1 deg, and a thickness:chord ratio of between 3.5 and 4.5 per cent. Some 15in (38cm) deep at its root, it is much easier to manufacture than a swept wing, which would have had to be around one-third of that thickness in order to obtain Mach 2 performance. Small airbrakes are mounted on the upper and lower surfaces, while the trailing edge is fitted with hydraulically-powered elevons. Two integral fuel tanks have a total internal capacity of 360 US gallons (1,370 litres).

The fuselage is "waisted" in accordance with the area rule in order to minimise drag. This is not obvious in side view, but can clearly be seen from above. The nose section incorporates a dielectric radome for the interception radar, while the aft end is topped by the single vertical fin.

The semi-circular air inlets are of a type which was to be used on subsequent members of the Mirage family. The conical centre-sections (known to Dassault engineers as "mice") move to vary the cross section according to aircraft speed. The space between the inlets houses either a 124gal (470 litre) fuel tank, or the second seat on training aircraft. The remainder of the fuel is housed in four flexible tanks arranged around the duct which carries the inlet air to the engine.

The canards on the new Mirage IIING are based on those flight-tested on the experimental Mirage 4000. Made on numerically-controlled machines, they were flight-tested for the first time on a Mirage 50 testbed. Trials started in May 1981.

By the autumn, Dassault designers had enough data to begin the design of the IIING. In addition to the canards, this also has a modified delta wing featuring a slight leading-edge extension at the wing root in order to improve handling at high angles of attack, a quadruplex digital fly-by-wire control system, and a modified hydraulic system featuring some components from the Mirage F1 and 2000.

Following installation of the new equipment in a full-scale mock-up (based on the

Dassault-Breguet Mirage IIIE
1. Pitot head.
2. Radome (removed).
3. Total pressure heads.
4. Rudder pedals.
5. Radar (head down) display.
6. Pilot's instrument display.
7. Head-up display.
8. Martin-Baker ejection seat.
9. Cockpit canopy cover.
10. Canopy jack.
11. Canopy emergency release.
12. Avionics system equipment.
13. Oxygen bottles.
14. Voltage regulator.
15. Fuel system inverted flight accumulator.
16. Air system filter.
17. Engine bleed air ducting.
18. Starboard wing integral fuel tanks.
19. Hydraulic reservoir.
20. Starboard navigation light.
21. SNECMA Atar 9C engine.
22. Bleed air pre-cooler.
23. Generator.
24. Engine oil tank.
25. Engine accessory equipment.
26. Starboard elevons.
27. HF aerial.
28. Fuselage ventral fuel tank.
29. Rudder artificial feel unit.
30. Rudder hydraulic actuator.
31. UHF aerial.
32. Radar warning aerial.
33. VHF aerial.
34. Tail navigation and anti-collision lights.
35. Radar warning aerial.
36. Rudder.
37. Parachute release link.
38. Brake parachute housing.
39. Afterburner nozzle jacks.
40. Variable area afterburner nozzle.
41. Afterburner duct.
42. Auxiliary fuel tank.
43. Elevon compensator hydraulic actuator.
44. Elevon compensator.
45. Inboard elevon.
46. Outboard elevon.
47. Port navigation light.
48. Outboard elevon hydraulic actuator.
49. Port wing main fuel tanks.
50. Inboard elevon hydraulic actuator.
51. Outboard stores pylon.
52. Missile launch rail.
53. AIM-9 Sidewinder air-to-air missile.
54. Elevon control rod.
55. External fuel tank.
56. Pylon mounting.
57. Inboard stores pylon.
58. Leading edge aerodynamic notch.
59. Main undercarriage pivot bearing.
60. Inward retracting mainwheel.
61. Hydraulic retraction jack.
62. Hydraulic accumulator.
63. Hydraulic lock strut.
64. Airbrakes.
65. Leading edge fuel tank.
66. Airbrake hydraulic jack.
67. Engine starter housing.
68. Fuselage fuel tanks.
69. AS.30 air-to-air missile.
70. Electrical system equipment.
71. DEFA 30mm cannon (2).
72. Intake suction relief door.
73. Ventral gun pack ammunition magazine.
74. Air conditioning system.
75. Intake variable half cone screw jack.
76. Intake half cone centre-body.
77. Battery.
78. Elevon artificial feel unit.
79. Nose undercarriage hydraulic jack.
80. Aft retracting nosewheel.
81. Landing/taxiing lamps.
82. Engine throttle lever.
83. Control column and linkages.
84. Doppler navigation radar.

airframe of a crashed Mirage 5), work was started to convert the canard-equipped testbed to the full IIING standard. This was completed by June 1982 and, following a long series of ground tests, the aircraft flew for the first time on December 21. Its first public appearance was at the 1983 Paris Air Show.

POWERPLANT

Without doubt the most important French jet-engine programme, the SNECMA (Societe Nationale d'Etude et de Construction de Moteurs d'Aviation) Atar owes its origins to wartime German BMW axial-flow designs. From these SNECMA developed the much-improved Atar 9, with a redesigned compressor and new pattern of two-stage turbine. The Mirage IIIA was powered by the 9B which developed 13,225lb (5,999kg) in full afterburner, but this was replaced in the Mirage IIIC by the slightly more powerful 9B3 version rated at 13,320lb (6,042kg). For all subsequent versions of the Mirage III, Dassault used

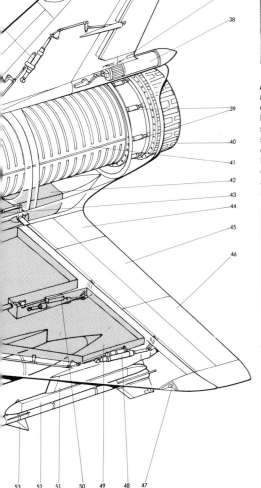

85. Doppler aerial fairing.
86. Incidence probe.
87. Thomson CSF Cyrano II radar pack.
88. Radar scanner.

the Atar 9C rated at 13,670lb (6,200kg). This features a revised compressor with steel blades in the most thermally-stressed stages, a self-contained starter, and an improved overspeed which automatically engages at Mach 1.4 to boost the thrust at high supersonic speeds by up to eight per cent.

In addition to production by SNECMA, the Atar has been built under licence by Commonwealth Aircraft Corporation, Australia (for the Mirage IIIO), Fabrique Nationale, Belgium (for the Mirage 5), and by Sulzer Brothers, Switzerland (for the Mirage IIIS).

The Rolls-Royce Avon 67 turbojet was flight-tested in the Mirage back in February 1961, in the hope that the RAAF might specify this engine for its planned Mirage buy. Australia was already an Avon user, non-afterburning versions of the British engine having been installed in locally-built F-86 Sabres, and the engine offered significant performance. But when the RAAF finally signed for its new fighters, the Atar was specified, and this power-

Above: The aerodynamic configuration of the Mirage III was so successful that Dassault scaled-up the design to create the larger Mirage IV bomber. Seen head-on, this twin-engined aircraft could be mistaken for the fighter.

Below: The dorsal radome and long forward fuselage on these patrolling Mirage III interceptors identifies them as the IIIE multi-role variant. These aircraft do not carry AIM-9s or Magics, so against manoeuvring targets would have to rely on cannon.

plant was to be used in one form or another for all delta-winged Mirage fighters until the late-1970s Mirage 2000.

It was inevitable that later and more powerful versions of the Atar would find their way into the Mirage III airframe. The Atar 9K-50 was developed for use in the Mirage F1 and 50 (see Mirage F1 entry for full details of this engine), but was also offered in the Mirage III.

The full story of uprated Mirage IIIs is buried deep in classified Dassault and French government archives. The first production version of the delta Mirage to offer the Atar 9K-50 was a small batch of Mirage IIIs delivered to what Dassault Breguet coyly describes as "a foreign operator already using Mirage III planes, and wishing a combat aircraft with a very high penetration speed".

The "foreign operator" in question was South Africa, which took delivery of these uprated Mirages between 1974 and 1975. Single-seat recce and two-seat trainer versions were designated IIIR2Z and IIID2Z respectively, and it would be surprising if the IIICZ fleet had not been reworked to accept the new engine. The Atar 9K-50 was also selected for the Mirage 50 (see Mirage 5/50 entry), but was to make a re-appearance in the Mirage III series with the Mirage IIING flown in 1982.

The SEPR 844 rocket motor is an optional unit, and replaces one of the internal fuel tanks. It burns red fuming nitric acid (RFNA) oxidiser contained in a tank within the rocket pack, plus aniline fuel carried in a special pack which replaced the DEFA cannon and their ammunition. These propellants are supplied to the engine by pumps driven by a shaft on the Atar, and the motor develops 3,300lb (1,500kg) of thrust.

AVIONICS

The IIIC entered service with a CSF Cyrano I air-interception radar, but the later IIIE introduced more complex avionics able to cope with multi-role missions. The Cyrano IIbis carried in the nose is a 200kW I/J-band radar offering air-to-air, air-to-ground, ranging, ground mapping, and terrain-warning modes, presenting data to the pilot on a radar display or CSF 97 sighting unit.

A low-profile ventral radome (just ahead of the cockpit) houses the antenna of a Marconi Doppler navigation radar—the aircraft was designed before the days of compact low-cost inertial navigation systems. The nav/attack computer used a series of plastic plug-in cards to enter the co-ordinates of up to 12 waypoints or targets. A TACAN system provides bearing and distance data.

ARMAMENT

When the Mirage IIIC entered service in late 1960, the aircraft was more impressive than its armament. The DEFA 30mm cannon were (and still are) powerful and reliable weapons, albeit slow-firing by modern standards, but in the absence of a French lightweight air-to-air missile the aircraft usually carried a pair of AIM-9 Sidewinders. Longer-range armament at first consisted of a single Matra R.511 carried on the centreline. This was a primitive weapon equipped with passive optical homing or a simple semi-active radar seeker which was virtually useless at heights below 10,000ft (3,048m).

The definitive Matra R.530 was a more sophisticated weapon, offering alternative radar or infra-red homing seekers. Designed to combat non-manoeuvring targets such as bombers, it was really suitable for

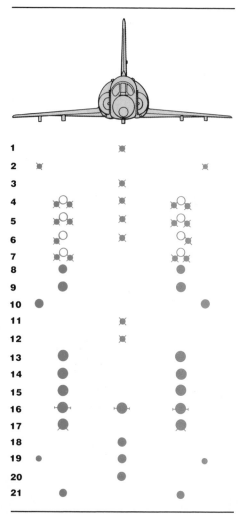

Possible weapons:
Left: Realising that the French Air Force could no longer afford to design customised aircraft for each mission, Dassault deliberately designed the Mirage III as a multirole airframe which could be adapted for interception, air-superiority, strike or reconnaissance missions. As a result, the Mirage III, 5 and 50 are cleared to carry a wide range of stores, plus a cannon, including:
1. Matra R.530 radar or infra-red homing missile.
2. AIM-9 or Matra R.550 Magic IR-homing missiles.
3. Aerospatiale AS.30 air-to-surface missile.
4-7. Various combinations of bombs, including free-falling and retarded bombs, napalm, cluster munitions such as the Matra Beluga, or anti-airfield weapons such as the Matra Durandal. The aircraft could probably carry the new Matra laser-guided bombs.
8, 9, 10. Launchers for unguided rockets, including the novel Matra JL.100 combined rocket launcher/external tank.
11. Practice bombs.
12-16. Various patterns of external tank.
17. Target systems.
18-21. Pod-mounted guns, jammers or reconnaissance equipment.

Above: Cockpit of the prototype Mirage IIING. Although based on the Mirage IIIE, the new aircraft incorporates much experience gained in the Mirage 2000 programme. The aircraft has a zero-zero ejection seat, fly-by-wire controls, a modern inertial navigation and attack system including a head-up display. The production aircraft could carry a laser rangefinder plus a radar – the Electronique Serge Dassault Aida range-only radar from the Mirage 5, the Thomson-CSF Cyrano IV from the Mirage F1 or the Thomson-CSF Agave used in the Super Etendard.

Right: The prototype Mirage IIING. The addition of canards has little effect on the external appearance of the aircraft, but creates a degree of static instability. When allied to the new quadruplex fly-by-wire control system (based on experience gained with the Mirage 2000) they give the IIING a dogfight performance approaching that of the newer Dassault fighter. The Mirage IIING has nine hardpoints for armament, four beneath the wing and five under the fuselage.

use against fighters. The more modern Matra R.550 Magic was developed as a Sidewinder replacement; it arms the Mirage IIIs of the French and Egyptian Air Forces, and could be carried by the IIING. Israeli Mirage IIICJs carry the Rafael Shafrir, as do the Mirage IIIs of some export customers.

For air-to-surface missions, the aircraft can carry one Aérospatiale AS.30 missile or two 1,000lb (454kg) bombs under the fuselage, plus two 1,000lb bombs beneath the wings. Alternative weapons which may be carried in place of iron bombs include rocket pods or the Beluga bomblet dispenser and Durandal anti-runway weapon.

PERFORMANCE

The spectacular performance of the Mirage III at air displays is backed up by an impressive specification. The aircraft can climb to 36,000ft (11,000m) in only three minutes, and reach 49,200ft (15,000m) in just under seven minutes. Service ceiling is 55,700ft (17,000m) at Mach 1.7, but use of the SEPR rocket motor raises this to 75,500ft (22,860m).

At low level, a clean aircraft can manage 750kt (1,390km/h), but the gust response of the 375sq ft (35sq m) of wing area will make for a bumpy ride. In a straight and level dash at 39,000ft (12,000m) the delta planform performs well, allowing the Mirage IIIE to attain Mach 2.2.

The aircraft's main weaknesses stem from the use of a delta wing. Highly efficient at supersonic speeds at low angles of attack, the delta is not really suited to the low speeds and high angles of attack associated with take-off and landing—or dogfighting. As a result, a fully-loaded Mirage III needs about a mile (1.6km) of runway for its take-off run, although it can land in less than half this length by using a braking parachute. In combat, the Mirage III pilot should in theory avoid tangling with agile opponents, although the Israelis have shown that this rule may be overlooked given good pilot training and the optimum tactical situation.

OPERATORS

Argentina (11), Australia (89), Brazil (17), France (319), Israel (40), Lebanon (11), Pakistan (33), South Africa (56), Spain (25), Switzerland (50), Venezuela (9).

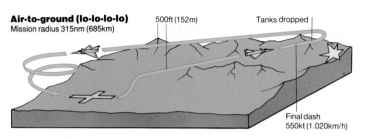

Air-to-ground (lo-lo-lo-lo)
Mission radius 315nm (685km)

500ft (152m)

Tanks dropped

Final dash 550kt (1.020km/h)

Left: In the demanding lo-lo-lo-lo strike role, a Mirage IIING fitted with two 450 US gal (1,700lit) tanks (dropped near target) can attack an airfield 315nm (685km) away using 16 BASP 100 anti-runway bombs. Final 50nm (90km) dash is at 550kt (1,020km/h).

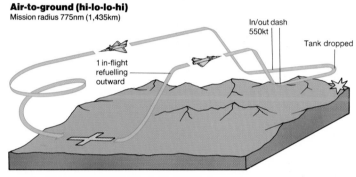

Air-to-ground (hi-lo-lo-hi)
Mission radius 775nm (1,435km)

In/out dash 550kt

Tank dropped

1 in-flight refuelling outward

Left: Given support from a tanker aircraft, the Mirage IIING is capable of impressive long-range hi-lo-lo-hi strike missions. An aircraft fitted with one 350 US gallon (1,300lit) drop tank can carry eight 550lb (250kg) bombs to a target 775nm (1,435km) away, flying the final 50nm (90km) at 550kt (1,020km/h). The Mirage refuels once on the outward leg, and jettisons tanks over target.

MIRAGE 5, 50

DEVELOPMENT

Three years after taking delivery of the first batch of Mirage IIICJs, the Israeli Air Force asked Dassault to design a new version of the aircraft customised to meet the requirements of the IDFAF. Given the good weather conditions and high visibility of the Middle Eastern skies, plus the high degree of training of Israeli pilots, the IDFAF was willing to swap avionics for fuel and weaponry.

Studies carried out showed that elimination of the complex avionics suite of the Mirage IIIC could shave around 1,000lb (450kg) off the weight of the Mirage, some $200,000 off the price, and cut down on the maintenance demands which the aircraft would make on the IDFAF's conscript ground crews. (Current figures claim only 13 maintenance manhours per flying hour for a basic Mirage 5 similar in build standard to the 5J.)

In September 1966, Israel placed a $60 million order for 50 examples of what was then known as the Mirage 5J. Dassault started cutting metal, and flew the first example on May 19, 1967. Within days of the flight, the Middle East was on the brink of an Arab/Israeli war. On June 3, President de Gaulle ordered an embargo on all supplies of military equipment to Israel. This policy, apparently intended to deter Israel from carrying out a pre-emptive strike against her neighbours, may well have been the final factor which persuaded the Israeli cabinet to unleash the IDFAF. On the morning of June 5, the Mirage IIICJ fleet spearheaded the Israeli air attacks which opened the Six-Day War.

In the months which followed, the first Mirage 5Js rolled off the line at the Dassault Breguet works at Merignac, and by the end of the year eight were ready for delivery. Victims of de Gaulle's embargo, they remained in France.

In April of the following year, Israel paid the final instalment of $20 million for the complete batch, and even took out an option on 50 of the even newer Mirage F1 swept-wing fighters. By this time almost half the Mirage 5s were ready. By November, 40 had been completed, and an embarrassed Dassault had billed the Israeli Government for $200,000 to cover maintenance work on the impounded aircraft. Declining to pay, the Israeli Government politely suggested that the bill be forwarded to the Elysee Palace.

Offered a refund of its $60 million payment in September 1969, Israel declined, and put into motion plans to "kidnap" the Mirage 5s and other hardware being built in France. Israeli pilots had been stationed in France to test-fly the embargoed warplanes, and to maintain a programme of familiarisation training on the type. As winter approached, the Israelis asked if this training programme could be transferred to airfields in Corsica, where the winter weather would be more favourable to flying. This move was duly

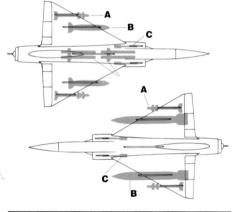

Above: Belgian Air Force Mirage 5BA fighter bomber at altitude during a training sortie. Although the basic Mirage delta configuration was developed as a high-altitude interceptor for the French Air Force, these Belgian strike aircraft will spend most of their time at low level.

Typical weapons:
Top: On an anti-airfield strike mission, the Matra R.550 Magic (**A**) and twin DEFA cannon (**C**) would be used for self-defence; Matra Durandal ordnance (**D**) would crater runways and taxiways, while the same company's Beluga cluster munition (**B**) would be lethal against anti-aircraft defences or vital airfield facilities such as the control tower.

Above: For many Third-World nations, the Mirage 5 and 50 are the main front-line interceptors. The configuration shown here has the 30mm cannon (**C**) and two Magics (**A**) as armament, plus two large external tanks to maximise the endurance and range (**B**). The latter would allow large areas of terrain to be patrolled and protected from a few bases.

Below left: The Mirage 5 is one of the lowest-cost Mach 2 fighters available from the West. Its simple delta wing is the best method of creating a fighter able to fly dashes of up to Mach 2 while still being easy to build, fly and maintain. Since the Mirage 5 lacks the complex avionics suite (including nose radar) of the Mirage IIIC, the nose is of long and slim proportions, while the weight saved by eliminating "black boxes" allows extra fuel to be carried in the fuselage tanks. The aircraft shown here is Mirage 5F 13-PJ of Esc 2/13 "Alpes" of the French Air Force. Originally built for the Israeli Air Force, it was never delivered.

Above: Being a low-cost fighter for less sophisticated applications, the Mirage 5 tends to carry only simple armament. The aircraft shown here is equipped with a pair of Matra R.550 Magic infrared homing missiles, two launchers for unguided rockets, plus two 400kg bombs carried on the centreline. This sort of armament would be ideal for close-support missions – the rockets and cannon could deal with personnel or soft-skinned vehicles, while the bombs could provide the heavier punch needed to cope with bunkers or other hard targets. On short-range missions, the Mirage 5 can carry up to 8,800lb (4,000kg) of stores on its five hard points. The Magic missiles have a range of 0.2-6.2 miles (0.32-10km).

Below: Aft of the cockpit, the Mirage 5 is externally identical to the Mirage IIIE, and uses the same SNECMA Atar 9C turbojet engine. Changes beneath the skin include the deletion of an avionics bay located just behind the cockpit of the Mirage IIIE. The 5/50 is similar to the 5, but has the more powerful Atar 9K engine.

Dassault-Breguet Mirage 5

1. Total pressure heads.
2. Rudder pedals.
3. Radar display.
4. Pilot's instrument display.
5. Attack sight.
6. Martin-Baker ejection seat.
7. Cockpit canopy cover.
8. Canopy jack.
9. Canopy emergency release.
10. Fuel filler cap.
11. Forward fuselage fuel tank.
12. Oxygen bottles.
13. Voltage regulator.
14. Fuel system inverted flight accumulator.
15. Air system filter.
16. Bleed air ducting.
17. Starboard wing fuel tanks.
18. Starboard navigation light.
19. TACAN aerial.
20. Hydraulic reservoir.
21. Bleed air pre-cooler.
22. Generator.
23. Engine oil tank.
24. Engine accessory equipment.
25. Starboard elevons.
26. SNECMA Atar 9C engine.
27. Fuselage ventral fuel tank.
28. Rudder artificial feel unit.
29. Rudder hydraulic actuator.
30. Artificial feel system pitot.
31. VHF aerial.
32. Tail navigation and anti-collision lights.
33. Rudder.
34. Brake parachute housing.
35. Parachute release link.
36. Afterburner nozzle jacks.
37. Variable area afterburner nozzle.
38. Afterburner duct.
39. Auxiliary fuel tank.
40. Elevon compensator hydraulic actuator.
41. Elevon compensator.
42. Inboard elevon.
43. Outboard elevon.
44. Port navigation light.
45. Outboard elevon hydraulic actuator.
46. 150Kg bomb.
47. Outboard stores pylon.
48. Inboard elevon hydraulic actuator.
49. Elevon control rod.
50. 250Kg bombs.
51. Port wing main fuel tanks.
52. Pylon mounting.
53. Leading edge aerodynamic notch.
54. Inboard stores pylon.
55. Main undercarriage pivot bearing.
56. Hydraulic accumulator.
57. Inward-retracting mainwheel.
58. Hydraulic retraction jack.
59. Hydraulic lock strut.
60. External fuel tank.
61. Air brakes.
62. Airbrake hydraulic jack.
63. Engine starter housing.
64. Leading edge fuel tank.
65. Fuselage fuel tanks.
66. Electrical system equipment.
67. 400Kg bombs.
68. DEFA 30mm cannon (2).
69. Intake suction relief door.
70. Ventral gun pack ammunition magazine.
71. Air conditioning system.
72. Intake variable half cone screw jack.
73. Intake half cone centre-body.
74. Battery.
75. Elevon artificial feel unit.
76. Nose undercarriage hydraulic jack.
77. Aft-retracting nosewheel.
78. Landing/taxiing lamps.
79. Engine throttle lever.
80. Control column and linkages.
81. Incidence probe.
82. VHF aerial.
83. Avionics system equipment.
84. Radar cooling air exhaust duct.
85. Aida II ground attack radar.
86. Radome.
87. Pitot head.

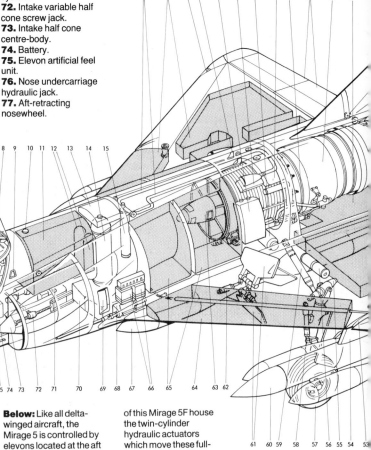

Below: Like all delta-winged aircraft, the Mirage 5 is controlled by elevons located at the aft edge of the wing. The four small fairings visible on the underside of the wing of this Mirage 5F house the twin-cylinder hydraulic actuators which move these full-span control surfaces. These devices incorporate artificial feel.

approved by the French Defence Ministry, so the Israelis next asked for the supply of external tanks, which would have greatly extended the range of the aircraft.

The move to Corsica was scheduled for December 25 but, 24 hours before it could take place, a suspicious French Government cancelled the move, ordering the aircraft to be partly dismantled and placed in storage. Part of the secret Israeli plan went ahead on December 25, when five gunboats built for the Israeli Navy "escaped" from France, arriving in Tel Aviv on December 31. The IDFAF was never to see its 50 Mirage 5Js, but accepted a refund of its money. The aircraft were reworked to a modified build standard in 1972/3 and taken into French Air Force service as the Mirage 5F. Some 30 still serve with two squadrons.

Like the Mirage III, the Mirage 5 has "spawned" a family of variants. The basic Mirage 5 is a single-seat ground attack fighter, and this is supplemented by the 5D two-seat trainer and 5R reconnaissance version. Despite the adverse publicity generated by the Israeli deal and subsequent embargo, the type has sold well.

In the late 1960s and early 1970s, the aircraft seemed perpetually at the centre of some controversy. Peruvian interest in February 1967 sparked off a political furore at the prospect of supersonic warplanes entering service with a Latin American air arm. The order for 14 Mirage 5s announced in April 1968 sparked off a chain of orders from the region.

The largest single order for the type—and probably the most controversial—was that placed by Libya in the winter of 1969/

70. An air arm short of trained pilots and ground crew was prepared to spend more than $400 million on a fleet of 110 Mirage 5s. In practice, only 60 were supplied. In the spring of 1973, the Israeli Air Force announced that at least one squadron had been supplied to Egypt, and the type was encountered in combat by Israeli aircraft during the 1973 Yom Kippur War.

The only sale to a NATO nation came in 1968, when Belgium finally adopted the type as a replacement for aging F-84F

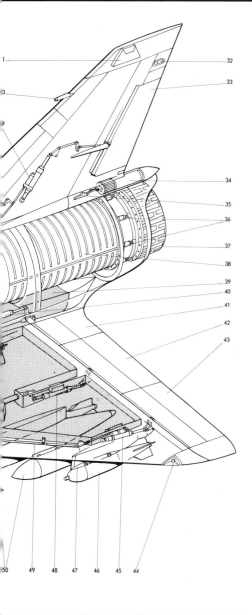

craft to maintain front-line strength. Financially, the latter deal was undoubtedly attractive, involving 100 per cent offset of the refurbishment work plus 80 per cent on the new aircraft, but the new Mirages would have had to be ordered for delivery in 1985—a timescale which could not be fitted into Belgian financial planning. The Mirages will be phased out in the late 1980s and replaced by a wing of F-16s.

MIRAGE 50

Following the installation of the improved Atar 9K-50 in Mirage IIIs for South Africa, the application of this engine to other export models was an obvious move. The result was the Mirage 50, which was launched at the 1975 Paris Air Show. First flight of a Mirage 50 prototype took place on 15 April 1979.

The original intention was just to "hot up" the Mirage 5, but the 50 is now offered in two versions based on the Mirage III and 5 respectively. The 5/50 is similar in fuselage design to the Mirage 5, having the slim nose section and extra fuel tank. A modified nose available as an option allows the Thomson-CSF Agave nose radar from the Super Etendard to be carried.

The Mirage 3/50 is essentially a hybrid aircraft, offering the engine and much of the avionics of the Mirage F1 in a Mirage III airframe. It retains the nose and avionics bay of the Mirage III, plus modified intakes able to handle the airflow of the new engine, but may be considered a

member of the Mirage III family rather than a true part of the Mirage 5 and 50 series.

Sole customer announced to date for the Mirage 50 has been Chile, which operates 16 aircraft – a mixture of Mirage 50C single-seaters and Mirage 50DC two-seat trainers. Launching of the more advanced Mirage IIING seems a tacit admission by Dassault-Breguet that the Mirage 50 must be considered a failure.

Production of the Mirage 5 is now tailing off as the number of new orders dwindles—recent customers have tended to favour the Mirage F1. Only six were ordered in 1982, a year which saw some 30 aircraft leave the line. Production is currently running at between one and two aircraft per month.

STRUCTURE

The Mirage 5 differs little from the basic Mirage III design, so readers should refer to the latter entry for full details. The main change in the Mirage 5 was the substitution of a long, slim nose section for the standard pattern, plus the provision of extra hardpoints for ordnance on some aircraft.

The basic aircraft has an additional internal fuel tank located just behind the cockpit in the space used by the avionics equipment bay in the Mirage III. This holds an extra 110 gallons (500 litres) of internal fuel, raising the internal fuel capacity by 15 per cent to a total of 843 gallons (3,830 litres). Fuel load can be traded off for extra avionics should the customer so desire.

Installation of the more powerful Atar 9K-50 engine in the Mirage 50 posed few structural problems. Diameter, length and attachment points are unchanged, although the slightly increased weight of the new engine gives slightly different centre

Below: Technicians prepare a Mirage 5 for flight. This head-on view shows the intakes – complete with movable conical centrebodies which alter position to match the intake to aircraft speed – as well as the distinct anhedral of the wing. The wide-track undercarriage makes taxying easy, reducing ground accidents. The huge drop tanks here add to the already increased fuel capacity of the Mirage 5 over the III.

Thunderstreaks, placing an order for 106 aircraft—a mixture of single-seat Mirage 5BA, two-seat 5BD and single-seat 5BR recce aircraft to be built under licence by SABCA (Societe Anonyme Belge de Constructions Aeronautiques) at Charleroi. The wisdom of adopting an aircraft with such simplified avionics for service in the often-foul weather of Western Europe seems questionable, but the Mirage had the dual advantage of bringing work to the local aerospace industry and of being affordable. Even at today's inflated prices, the likely unit cost of a Mirage 5 is around $10 million—half the cost of an F-16. Unless an air arm is prepared to buy from the Soviet Union or is on friendly terms with Israel Aircraft Industries, the Mirage 5 is probably the cheapest Mach 2 fighter available.

The Mirage 5B currently serves with Numbers 2 and 3 Wings of the Belgian Air Force, attrition having reduced the operational aircraft to around 60. In the early 1980s Dassault Breguet offered to refurbish and rework the remaining aircraft, stretching out their service life, and to supply between 12 and 40 new-build air-

Above: Despite having been developed to Israeli specifications, the Mirage 5 has proved popular with Arab air arms. This is one of the 5AD single-seaters supplied to the Abu Dhabi Air Force. The original fleet of 12 plus two 5DAD trainers was supplied in 1974, and was supplemented in 1976/77 by 14 5EADs, plus three 5RAD reconnaissance aircraft.

Below: Belgium ordered a batch of 106 Mirage 5BA (single seat), 5BR (recce) and 5BD (two-seat trainers) in 1968. Although lacking the avionics needed for use in Western European weather conditions, these were deployed as replacements for obsolete F-84s. Despite an attractive Dassault offer of more Mirage 5s, the Belgians chose a follow-on batch of F-16s.

of gravity conditions. The maximum airflow of 158lb/sec (72kg/sec) is only six per cent above that of the original engine, so only minor changes to the moving parts of the intake were necessary. The movable cones had been initially designed to handle this level of airflow.

POWERPLANT

For the Mirage 5, Dassault retained the proven SNECMA Atar 9C engine used in the Mirage IIIE, making this the most common powerplant of the Mirage delta series. It was built under licence by Fabrique Nationale, Belgium, for installation in that nation's licence-built aircraft.

The Atar 9K-50 used in the Mirage 50 is the powerplant originally developed for the Mirage F1, and offers an additional 1,625lb (737kg) of dry thrust, and an increase of 2,130lb (966kg) in full afterburner. The new engine is some 360lb (160kg) heavier than the Atar 9C, but offers improved specific fuel consumption and longer engine life. Being based on the earlier engine, it is compatible with the existing equipment-drive gearbox.

AVIONICS

The space formerly occupied by the main avionics bay having been usurped by a fuel tank, the Mirage 5 must carry its "black boxes" in the new slim-profile nose. Instead of an air-interception radar (as on the Mirage III), the nose of the Mirage 5 houses equipment such as a laser rangefinder and Aida II ranging radar.

The precise avionics fit has always been a matter for the customer to decide. In early Mirage 5s, the entire nose volume was required by the avionics units which made up the aircraft's limited fit. In recent years, the ever-increasing miniaturisation of electronics has allowed Dassault to pack systems of greater complexity into the same space. Installation of inertial-navigation systems, nav/attack computers and multi-purpose radars is now possible. The most complex avionics fit specified

Above: Mirage 5SDD in the markings of the Royal Saudi Arabian Air Force. These aircraft plus a batch of single-seaters were ordered by Saudi Arabia then transferred to Egypt's Air Defence Command. The two-seat trainer has an extended fuselage and a second seat located aft of the inlets which displaces some of the internal fuel (see page 36 for details of fuel tankage in single-seater).

Above: Mirage 5DV two-seater of Venezuela. Note the red-painted airbrake close to the wing root. The red line is a "No Step" warning intended to guard against ground crew walking along the wing and on the elevon. The raised rear cockpit gives the instructor an adequate forward view but displaces one of the internal fuel tanks.

Below: Mirage 5 with a heavy load of Matra general-purpose bombs whose design is a compromise between aerodynamic form, the desired explosive effect, and the mechanical strength which a bomb casing requires in order to penetrate the structure of a target without breaking up or exploding prematurely.

for a Mirage 5 is probably that carried by Egypt's Mirage 5.E2. The nav/attack system on these aircraft includes an inertial platform, HUD, and laser rangefinder, all linked by a Digibus alphanumeric multiplex link system.

Most Mirage 5 operators face relatively unsophisticated opposition, so few currently require a comprehensive ECM system. But Belgian Air Force Mirage 5R and 5BA fighters would have to cope with Soviet radar and electronic-warfare expertise in any Central Front war, so are equipped with the Rapport II (Rapid Alert Programmed Power Management of Radar Target) internally-mounted ECM system. This was developed for the Belgian Air Force following a study of Mirage 5 survivability carried out in the light of Israeli experience during the 1973 Yom Kippur War.

Requests for proposals for an internal ECM installation were circulated to US and European electronics companies early in 1974. Three companies were contracted to carry out feasibility studies, a team consisting of Loral and MBLE being chosen to develop prototype equipment. Flight tested in 1977, this entered production a year later as the Rapport II. It is compatible with the more modern Rapport III equipment now being installed on Belgian F-16s.

Avionics fit of the Mirage 5/50 is similar to that of the Mirage 5, but it is possible to fit the Thomson-CSF Agave radar if the customer so wishes. Air arms requiring an air-defence/air-superiority fighter would find the Mirage 3/50 a better choice, since the latter can carry the Cyrano IV radar from the Mirage F1. Details of these sets may be found in the entries for the Super Etendard and Mirage F1, respectively.

Left: Despite its attractive performance, the uprated Mirage 50 has not brought in the orders which Dassault expected. To date, only Chile operates the type.

Below: This French Air Force Mirage 5F carries one of the odder stores in the Armée de l'Air inventory – a combined underwing fuel tank and tandem bomb rack. Internal capacity of the tank section is 265 US gallons (1,000 litres). There are two 551 lb (250kg) bombs each side.

ARMAMENT

The Mirage 5 retains the two 30mm DEFA 552A cannon of the Mirage III, but can carry up to 8,800lb (4,000kg) of stores on five hardpoints. Some aircraft have two additional attachment points under the fuselage. Typical stores include 1,000lb (450kg) bombs, JL-100 rocket pods each with 18 68mm unguided rockets, napalm tanks, and AS.30 air-to-surface missiles.

PERFORMANCE

Not surprisingly in view of its Mirage III ancestry, the Mirage 5 is broadly similar in performance to the earlier aircraft. Combat radius with a 2,000lb (900kg) weapon load is 700nm (1,300km) in hi-lo-hi profile, and 350nm (650km) lo-lo-lo.

Installation of the Atar 9k in the Mirage 50 has a significant effect on performance. Climb rate is increased by 80 per cent at sea level, while the time to climb to a Mach 1.8 interception at 39,000ft (12,000m) is halved to only 2.5 minutes. Service ceiling at Mach 2 is increased by 6,500ft (2,000m) to 60,700ft (18,500m). Range is increased by 75nm (140km), while the take-off run is reduced by between 15 and 20 per cent compared with the Mirage III and 5.

Customers entering the Mach 2 market might be forgiven for preferring the swept-wing Mirage F1, but it seems strange that users of the existing deltas have not topped up their fleets with the Mirage 50. To date, only South Africa has done so, although its aircraft were delivered before the Mirage 50 designation was coined.

OPERATORS

Belgium (78), Chile (16 Mirage 50), Colombia (18), Egypt (66), France (38), Gabon (7), Libya (108), Pakistan (62), Peru (32), United Arab Emirates (24), Venezuela (6), Zaire (7).

Mirage 50 ground attack (lo-lo-lo)
Mission radius 235nm (435km)

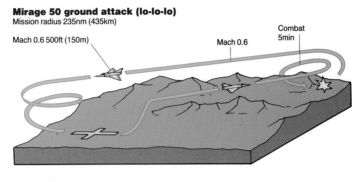

Left: Mirage 50 lo-lo-lo mission with eight 550lb (250kg) bombs, two 265 US gallon (1,000 litre) fuel-tank/bomb carriers and a single 350 US gallon (1,300 litre) tank. The aircraft can take off in full afterburner, fly 235nm (435km) at Mach 0.6 at an altitude of 500ft (150m), carry out five minutes of combat flying in the target area, then return at Mach 0.6/500ft.

Mirage 50 high-altitude interception
Mission radius 175nm (325km)

Left: High altitude 175nm (325km) interception mission for a Mirage 50 using internal fuel only and armed with two Magic missiles. Following take-off the fighter climbs in full afterburner to an intermediate cruise height, then up to 55,000ft (16,800m). The aircraft begins a final Mach 2 dash of almost 4 minutes to intercept the target. Return to base would be at Mach 0.9.

Mirage 50 long-range interception
Mission radius 710nm (1,315km)

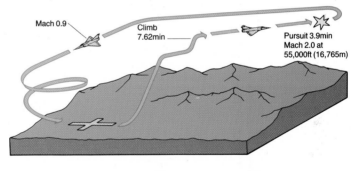

Left: For longer-range interception missions, the aircraft could be fitted with two 450 US gallon (1,700 litre) drop tanks. This would allow a long cruise at intermediate height, a climb in afterburner to engage a target flying at 710nm (1,310km) from the take-off point, then 1.5 minutes of Mach 1.8 combat using the cannon and two Magic missiles. Return is at Mach 0.9.

Mirage 50 combat air patrol
Patrol time 2 hours 20 minutes

Left: On a combat air patrol mission with two Magics plus two 450 US gallon (1,700 litre) drop tanks, the aircraft could take off in afterburner, climb to a patrol height of 36,000ft (11,000m) using maximum military power, then loiter for up to 2 hours and 20 minutes. A 2.8 minute pursuit in afterburner at speeds of up to Mach 1.8 would be followed by 1.5 minutes of air-to-air combat using guns and missiles, then a subsonic return flight to base.

DASSAULT-BREGUET
MIRAGE F1

DEVELOPMENT

Developed as a private-venture successor to the Mirage III and 5, the Mirage F1 is a multi-role aircraft designed to have the high rate of climb needed for interception missions, a heavy payload for ground attack, and good low-altitude handling to suit it to the likely arena of future air combat. Design work started in the mid-1960s, at a time when Dassault was test-flying the larger Mirage F2, a two-seat swept-wing design powered by a single Pratt & Whitney TF306 turbofan.

Although the F2 was being developed to meet a French Air Force requirement, Dassault could foresee a potential requirement for a small single-seat aircraft which could be powered by the existing Atar engine. Such foresight was rewarded in September 1967 when the French Government switched its support to the new small aircraft, ordering three prototypes. The first aircraft flew in March 1969, and first production deliveries from an initial batch of 105 F1.C fighters were made to the French Air Force in 1973.

Designed for primary use as all-weather interceptors, these aircraft have a limited ground-attack capability. Several variants were devised for other roles. A modified F1.C, the F.1C-200 interceptor, is intended to support overseas deployment of French troops and is fitted with a permanently-mounted flight refuelling probe mounted on the starboard side of the nose. These aircraft would be able to provide air cover for any operations by the French equivalent of the US Rapid Deployment Force.

The F1.A is clearly aimed at the same market as the Mirage 5. Intended as a clear-weather fighter and ground-attack aircraft, it has simplified avionics and extra internal fuel. It has been built under

licence by Atlas Aircraft in South Africa as well as by Dassault. First flight of a two-seat training version of the F1 did not take place until May 1976, with the debut of the Mirage F1.B. Twenty had been ordered by the French Air Force.

Development of the F1.E International was approved in March 1973, with the aircraft making its first flight in December 1974. Fitted with the more powerful SNECMA M53 turbofan and a more advanced avionics suite suitable for all-weather operations, this version was offered to Belgium, Denmark, the Netherlands and Norway as an alternative to the General Dynamics F-16, Northrop YF-17 and Saab-Scania Viggen. One wonders why Dassault bothered. The F1 is a good aircraft, and had the virtue of being of European design, but even its most enthusiastic supporter would not suggest that it was in the performance class of the US fighters. Following the selection of the

F-16 by the four NATO air arms, the F1.E was cancelled, although its designation was later to be revived for an Atar-powered version having similar avionics to the NATO aircraft.

The F1.CR reconnaissance version was developed to replace the French Air Force's Mirage IIIR and IIIRD aircraft, with the first example flying in November 1981. In addition to the normal Thomson-CSF Cyrano radar, this version also carries Omera 40 panoramic cameras, Omera 35 cameras, an Omera 360 flight recorder, IR equipment, and a SAGEM inertial navigation system. It is also fitted with an in-flight refuelling boom. More than 60 were ordered by the French Air Force, and the F1.CR entered service in the autumn of 1983.

With an estimated unit cost of $12.5 million, the F1 is relatively inexpensive by contemporary standards, so it is hardly surprising that the type has sold well. A

Above: With hindsight, the Mirage F1 appears to be an aberration on the part of the Dassault company, as it is the only Mirage not to be a tail-less delta. This example, from EC 1/5 Vendee, is armed with two Magics, two R.530s, and is notable for its refuelling probe.

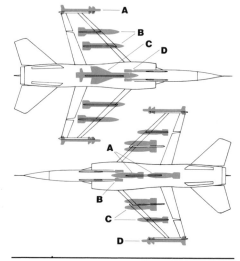

Typical weapons:
Top: A, Matra 550 Magic AAM; **B**, Beluga cluster bomb; **C**, AS.37 Martel; **D**, 30mm DEFA cannon with 135 rounds per gun. The Beluga CBU is a braked-bomb container with Thomson-Brandt submunitions, of which three different types exist: anti-armour, area saturation, and general purpose. AS.37 Martel is a radiation seeking missile which will home on a radar within a preset band.

Above: A, 500lb (250kg) bomb; **B**, 30mm DEFA cannon; **C**, 500lb (250kg) bomb; **D**, Matra 550 Magic AAM. This load can be described as general purpose and can be used against a wide variety of targets, unlike the load shown in the top illustration, which would probably be used in a battlefield scenario or against an airfield. The Martel anti-radiation missile can be carried on the centreline station only.

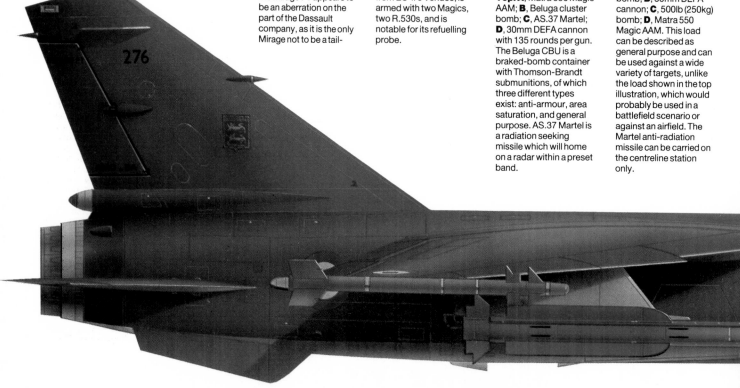

Below: At a time when most other nations were opting for twin-engined safety and reliability, the French have been remarkably consistent in sticking to the single engined concept. One result of this is that their fighters have generally been small, which makes them difficult to see at long ranges, and the F1 is no exception. The conventional layout in no way detracts from performance; the makers claim an 80 per cent improvement in combat agility over the Mirage III, while radius of action and patrol endurance have also shown remarkable increases compared to the earlier Dassault aircraft.

Above: This Mirage F1.C is the -200 variant, which is fitted with a fixed air refuelling probe to extend its ferry range. It is intended to be deployed rapidly over very long distances to give air cover to French forces overseas. The weapon load shown is for the attainment of air superiority over hostile territory. Two Matra 550 Magics are mounted on wingtip rails for close-range use, and Matra Super 530s occupy inboard wing pylons for medium range and BVR (beyond visual range) use. The twin 30mm DEFA cannon round out the armament, and a DB 3613 ECM pod is carried under the port wing to counter hostile radars. With the export market in mind, Magic has been made interchangeable with Sidewinder, and is roughly comparable with the US missile but more manoeuvrable. Like Sidewinder, it is IR-guided.

Below: The aircraft depicted is from ECTT 2/30 "Normandie-Niemen" which was founded by the Soviet Air Force in WWII as a squadron of French volunteer pilots. The flamboyant fin markings are being toned down on Armée de l'Air F1.Cs; the insignia is reduced in size; the yellow striping on the wings and yellow outer ring on the roundels have been deleted; and two-tone grey has replaced the earlier camouflage finish.

total of 678 aircraft for 11 nations may not seem a lot compared with the massive orders placed for the earlier Mirage III and 5, but these orders were won at a time when the market was largely saturated by the Mirage deltas and the Northop F-5, not to mention the MiG-21. Production is currently running at around five aircraft a month, and the 500th example was delivered in May 1982. Even without further orders, the line would stay open through 1985, but it seems safe to predict that small follow-on orders will keep low-rate production running for the next five years.

STRUCTURE

The wing of the Mirage F1 represented a break from the traditional delta planform used for the Mirage III and 5. Swept at a leading-edge angle of 47deg, it is of two-spar construction and incorporates many milled or chemically-milled components.

Port and starboard wings each have two differentially-operating double-slotted flaps, one aileron and two spoilers. Full-span leading-edge flaps may be drooped to increase lift—manually during landing but automatically when in combat.

Like the wing, the fuselage makes much use of milled and chemically milled components. Most of the structure is of aluminium alloy, but steel is used for the wing attachment points, and titanium for the engine firewall, landing gear trunnions and other critical areas. Airbrakes are located in the lower side of the air intake trunking. The vertical fin is supplemented by two smaller ventral fins, one on each side of the rear fuselage, while the horizontal stabiliser is of all-moving type.

Integral fuel tanks replace the bag tanks used on the Mirage III and 5, giving a total internal capacity of 790 Imp gal (3,600 litres), a 40 per cent increase.

As part of the offset deal associated with the Belgian Air Force's procurement of the Mirage 5, all Mirage F1 rear fuselages are built in Belgium.

POWERPLANT

Having decided to use the SNECMA Atar engine for the Mirage F1, Dassault was able to take advantage of the increased thrust available from the latest developments of this veteran powerplant. Derived from the Atar 9K engine of the Mirage IV

strategic bomber, and based on the earlier Atar 9C used in the Mirage III and 5, the 9K-50 has a slightly lower subsonic SFC, increased thrust and a longer life between overhauls.

The first and eighth compressor stages were modified to raise the pressure ratio from 6:1 to 6.5:1 and to increase the mass flow, while the turbine was redesigned with cast blades coated with a refractory material. Maximum dry thrust was increased to 11,055lb (5,015kg), rising to 15,870lb (7,200kg) with afterburner. The Atar 9K-50 was approved for service in 1969 and deliveries started in 1972.

The enhanced performance of the abortive Mirage F1.E International was almost entirely due to the installation of the SNECMA M53 turbofan in place of the Atar 9K-50 turbojet. The air intakes were increased in area to cope with the 190lb/sec (86kg/sec) mass flow of the new powerplant. (For details of the engine, see the Mirage 2000 entry.)

AVIONICS

The Thomson-CSF Cyrano IV radar carried by the Mirage F1.C offers about twice

Dassault-Breguet Mirage F1-C-200
1. Pitot head.
2. Radome, removed.
3. Flight refuelling probe.
4. Thomson-CSF Cyrano IV radar equipment.
5. Temperature probe.
6. Incidence probe.
7. Rudder pedals.
8. Pilot's instrument display.
9. Head-up display.
10. Martin-Baker Mk.4 ejection seat.
11. Cockpit canopy cover.
12. Canopy jack.
13. Canopy emergency release.
14. Intake half-cone central drive motor.
15. Air conditioning system.
16. Avionics equipment bay.
17. Power amplifier.
18. IFF aerial.
19. Inverted flight accumulator.
20. Centre fuselage fuel tank.
21. Forward fuselage fuel tanks.
22. Electrical system equipment.
23. Starboard drooped leading edge flap.
24. Starboard wing integral fuel tank.
25. Missile launch rail.
26. Matra 550 Magic air-to-air missile.
27. Starboard navigation light.
28. Starboard aileron.
29. Engine starter housing.
30. Starboard spoilers.
31. Asymmetric double-slotted flaps.
32. Engine bleed air pre-cooler.
33. SNECMA Atar 9K50 afterburning engine.

34. Engine oil tank.
35. Rear fuselage fuel tanks.
36. Flap hydraulic jack.
37. Spoiler actuator.
38. Hydraulic reservoir.
39. Flap operating push rods and linkages.
40. Starboard all-moving tailplane.
41. Afterburner duct.
42. Rudder trim actuator.
43. Rudder hydraulic actuator.
44. Radar warning aerial.
45. UHF aerial.
46. Compass remote transmitter.
47. VOR aerial.
48. VHF aerial.
49. Tail navigation and strobe lights.
50. Tail warning radar aerial.
51. Rudder.
52. Parachute release mechanism.
53. Brake parachute housing.
54. Afterburner nozzle control jacks.

55. Variable area afterburner nozzle.
56. Port aileron.
57. Port double slotted flaps.
58. Port all-moving tailplane.
59. Tailplane pivot bearing.
60. Tailplane hydraulic actuator.
61. Ventral fin.
62. Autopilot equipment.
63. Missile launch rail.
64. Port navigation light.
65. Flap guide rail.
66. Matra 550 Magic air-to-air missile.
67. Aileron hydraulic actuator.
68. Aileron trim actuator.
69. Structural provision for outboard stores pylon.

70. Aileron/spoiler interconnecting spring strut.
71. Port drooped leading edge flap.
72. Leading edge flap push rod and linkages.
73. Port wing integral fuel tank.
74. Main undercarriage hydraulic jack.

75. Main undercarriage leg pivot bearing.
76. Wing stores pylon.
77. Forward-retracting mainwheels.

78. Main undercarriage hydraulic lock strut.
79. Engine accessory equipment.

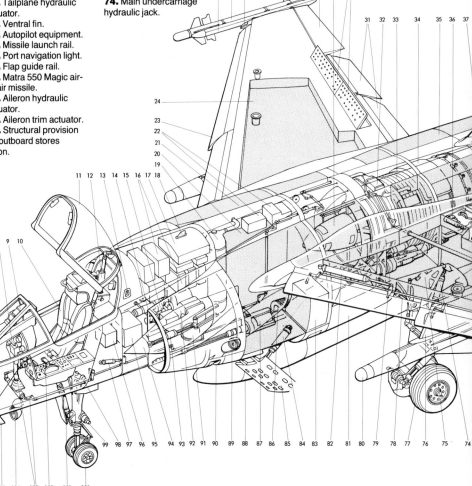

the range of the Cyrano II set which equipped the Mirage III. Weighing 348lb (158kg), this set has an inverted Cassegrain antenna and can pass data to a gunsight or head-up display. Standard operating modes allow searches for airborne targets at medium and high altitude, automatic tracking and subsequent interception, jammer tracking and air-to-ground mapping. Upgraded sets incorporate optional modes such as contour mapping, terrain avoidance and air-to-ground ranging. Advanced versions offered by the company include the Cyrano IVM with limited track-while-scan facilities, and the IVMR with additional air-to-ground modes such as terrain avoidance and blind let-down.

The tail surfaces of the Mirage F1 carry the forward and rearward facing "bullet" radomes of the Thomson-CSF Type BF radar-warning receiver. Two flush-mounted spiral antennas also provide signals to the equipment, covering the left and right-hand sectors. Audible warning is given to the pilot if a radar signal is detected, while cockpit-mounted display lamps show the general direction and nature of the threat. No frequency indica-

tion is given, but the system will distinguish between pulse or CW radar, and will indicate if the threat is a "track-while-scan" radar.

The more advanced Type BK probably offers more sophisticated signal processing. According to Thomson-CSF, it will respond only to tracking radars and will not generate false alarms due to signals from search radar, which unlike trackers do not represent a direct threat to the aircraft.

Several jamming pods are available from the same company. Developed to protect strike aircraft, the DB 3141 I/J-band pod is a noise jammer, while the more complex DB 3163 Remora probably uses noise and deception techniques. Remora is designed to counter pulse and CW airborne and ground threats, and can monitor and jam up to three of six pre-set ranges of frequency in I or J band. A power-management system is incorporated. Few details of the custom-designed Alligator pod have been announced but it is thought to be similar in concept to the DB 3163. An optional reconnaissance pod carries cameras, infrared linescan and side-looking radar.

ARMAMENT

The Mirage III interceptor relied on the US AIM-9 Sidewinder for short-range missile armament, but for the F1 Dassault was able to turn to Matra, which had started development of the R.550 Magic back in 1966–68. Begun as a private-venture alternative to the AIM-9, Magic received French Government funding in 1969. The end product was a short-range heat-seeking weapon suitable for use on interceptors and air-superiority fighters, and able to provide self-defence for ground-attack aircraft.

The first guided launch took place in January 1972, and production was under way by the summer of 1975. Deliveries of preproduction rounds to the French Air Force started in 1974, and the weapon entered operational service in the following year.

An effective "dogfight" weapon must be suitable for use under most likely conditions of combat; pilots cannot expect their target obligingly to fly the sort of medium altitude low-speed flight profile associated with many patterns of training target. Magic has no minimum launch

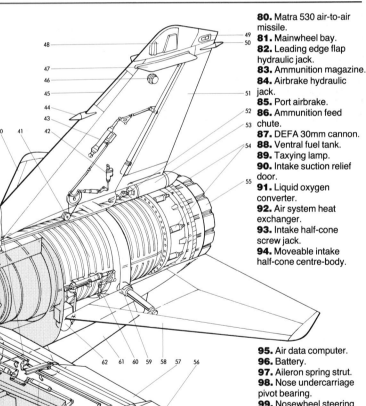

80. Matra 530 air-to-air missile.
81. Mainwheel bay.
82. Leading edge flap hydraulic jack.
83. Ammunition magazine.
84. Airbrake hydraulic jack.
85. Port airbrake.
86. Ammunition feed chute.
87. DEFA 30mm cannon.
88. Ventral fuel tank.
89. Taxying lamp.
90. Intake suction relief door.
91. Liquid oxygen converter.
92. Air system heat exchanger.
93. Intake half-cone screw jack.
94. Moveable intake half-cone centre-body.

95. Air data computer.
96. Battery.
97. Aileron spring strut.
98. Nose undercarriage pivot bearing.
99. Nosewheel steering jack.
100. Aft-retracting nosewheels.
101. Nose undercarriage hydraulic retraction jack.
102. Engine throttle lever.
103. Control column and linkages.
104. Retractable landing lamp.
105. TACAN aerial.
106. Total pressure head.
107. Cyrano IV radar flat plate antenna.
108. Radar antenna glass-fibre protective housing.

Above: An early Mirage F1.C launches a Matra R.550 Magic from its wingtip rail. Magic is a dogfight missile.

Below: Mirage F1.C in typical air defence configuration, with two R.550 Magics on the wingtip rails and two

Super 530 SARH missiles under the wings. Some fighter pilots feel that four on-board kills is insufficient.

Above: A Mirage F1 sets out on a tactical mission with a Thomson-CSF DB 3163 jamming pod and a recce pod on the underfuselage hard point. The latter store is probably a sideways-looking infra-red line scanning sensor able to create thermal images of targets from long range.

Below: A Mirage F1 prototype tries out a different role, with eight Durandal runway busting bombs. Dropped from low level, Durandal is braked by parachute, then tilted nose-down, when a rocket motor fires. It can pierce reinforced concrete up to 15½in (400mm) thick.

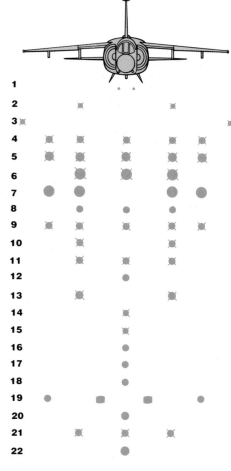

Possible weapons:
1. 30mm DEFA cannon.
2. Super 530 AAM.
3. Magic or Sidewinder.
4. 250 or 500lb bomb.
5. 800lb bomb.
6. 2,000lb bomb.
7. Rocket launcher.
8. 30mm gun pod.
9. Durandal.
10. BAP 100 or BAT 120.
11. Beluga cluster bomb.
12. Laser designator.
13. Laser-guided bomb.
14. AS.37 Martel.
15. Air/surface missile.
16. Recon pod.
17. ELINT pod.
18. SLAR pod.
19. Countermeasures pods (active/passive).
20. ECM jamming pod.
21. Training munitions.
22. Towed target.

speed, while its g limitations at launch are well beyond those of any aircraft on which it is likely to be mounted. The 196lb (89kg) round has a maximum speed of greater than Mach 2.0 and can pull up to 30g on its way to the target.

Basic configuration is similar to Sidewinder, with fixed cruciform fins at the rear of the missile and canard fins at the nose. Unlike the US missile, Magic has twin canards. The front pair are fixed, and designed to maintain an airflow over the rear movable pair at angles of attack of up to 20deg.

Target acquisition in combat is likely to be visual. The nitrogen-cooled seeker head carries out an autonomous search procedure and is capable of detecting targets from virtually any angle, and signalling the pilot once lock-on has been achieved.

Typical engagement ranges are 1.5nm (2.5km) at medium altitude and 5nm (10km) at high altitude. The 27.6lb (12.5kg) fragmentation warhead contains 13.2lb (6kg) of explosive, and is fitted with an electromagnetic proximity fuze. It is armed 1.8sec after launch, giving the missile a minimum engagement range of just under 1,000ft (0.3km).

To provide the Mirage F1 with a long-range punch, Matra developed the Super 530 long-range air-to-air missile. The design emphasises lift and manoeuvrability, with cruciform wings of long chord

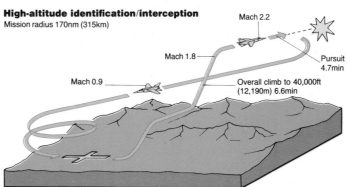

Ground attack (lo-lo-lo)
Mission radius 325nm (600km)

400kt (740km/h)

50nm (80km)
at 550kt
(1,020km/h)

Left: In the lo-lo-lo attack profile, loaded with six 500lb (250kg) bombs and two external fuel tanks, the Mirage F1 has a mission radius of 325nm (600km). When within 50nm (80km) of the target, speed is 500kt (920km/h). Transit is flown at 500ft (150m), and 400kt (735km/h). Dry power only is used.

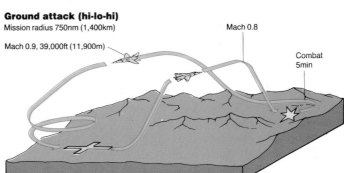

High-altitude identification/interception
Mission radius 170nm (315km)

Mach 2.2

Mach 1.8

Mach 0.9

Pursuit 4.7min

Overall climb to 40,000ft (12,190m) 6.6min

Left: The high level interception mission, flown clean with gun armament only, has a maximum mission radius of 170nm (315km). The profile calls for takeoff, followed by a stepped climb-out using full afterburner to 40,000ft (12,200m) in 6.6 minutes, reaching a speed of Mach 1.8, then accelerating to Mach 2.2 in 4.7 minutes. Gun interceptions at Mach 2.2 are unlikely.

Ground attack (hi-lo-hi)
Mission radius 750nm (1,400km)

Mach 0.9, 39,000ft (11,900m)

Mach 0.8

Combat 5min

Left: The hi-lo-hi attack profile with two 500lb (250kg) bombs and three fuel tanks, with 5 minutes combat, gives a mission radius of 750nm (1,400km). Full military power is used for the climb to optimum altitude on takeoff and egress only, the rest of the mission being flown at cruise settings, Mach 0.8 outbound, and Mach 0.9 on the return, to economise on fuel.

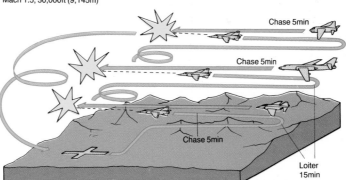

Triple interception
Mach 1.5, 30,000ft (9,145m)

Chase 5min

Chase 5min

Chase 5min

Loiter 15min

Left: The accompanying diagram shows a Mirage F1 configured with guns only, intercepting three targets inbound at Mach 1.5 and 30,000ft (9,150m). Each interception involves flying out to meet the intruder, turning in behind for a 5 minute full throttle pursuit, with a loiter time of 15 minutes on station between combats. All mission profiles shown here are based on information supplied by the manufacturers, Dassault-Breguet.

providing maximum lift and smoothing the airflow over the rear control fins. Super 530 is powered by a high-impulse solid-propellant rocket motor, which accelerates the 550lb (250kg) missile to an initial speed of Mach 4 to 5. Maximum range is 24nm (45km).

The target has no chance of out-manoeuvring the missile. At heights of up to 55,000 to 59,000ft (17,000 to 18,000m) the weapon can achieve lateral accelerations of up to 20g, falling to around 6g at 88,000ft (27,000m). If the victim is flying above the cruise height of the Mirage F1, the Super 530 may carry out a "snap-up" attack, gaining up to 30,000ft (9,000m) of altitude. The 66lb (30kg) warhead is of the fragmentation type and is fitted with an electromagnetic proximity fuze.

Design of the Super 530 started in 1968, but the first fully-guided air launch did not take place until 1975, when a round fired from a subsonic Vautour bomber flying at a height of 36,000ft (11,000m) intercepted a Mach 1.6 target drone flying at 59,000ft (18,000m). The first firing from a Mirage F1 followed in 1976, and entry into French Air Force service was in December 1979.

For ground-attack missions, the F1 can carry up to 8,800lb (4,000kg) of stores on external hardpoints. Weapons carried can include eight 1,000lb (450kg) bombs, four 36-round rocket launchers, or guided missiles such as the AS.30 or AS.37 Martel. The twin DEFA 553 30mm cannon each has 125 rounds of ammunition, and may be used against air or ground targets.

PERFORMANCE

The Mirage F1 is a much more impressive fighting machine than the Mirage III or 5. Maximum speed at high altitude is Mach 2.2, while the Mach 1.2 attainable at low altitude is useful when chasing high-speed terrain-following intruders. Maximum sea-level rate of climb is 41,930ft/

min (12,780m/min), giving a stabilised supersonic ceiling of 60,700ft (18,500m) and a service ceiling of 65,600ft (20,000m).

The swept wing allows an approach speed of only 141kt (260km/h), falling to 124kt (230km/h) at touchdown. Field length at maximum take-off weight is 20 per cent below the 5,300ft (1,600m) typical for a heavily loaded Mirage IIIE. Take-off and landing runs for a typical interception mission are 2,100ft (640m). The increased fuel load has a dramatic effect on range compared with the Mirage III and 5. Patrol endurance at high level is tripled, as is supersonic dash endurance, while low-level tactical radius is doubled.

Installation of the M53 turbofan in the

F1.E International gave the aircraft a rapid acceleration, but the rate of climb and top speed were largely unaffected, apart from a Mach 2.5 dash capability. Despite the attraction of the new engine, Dassault no longer offers it as an option for the F1, preferring to standardise production on the basic Atar-powered aircraft.

OPERATORS

The French Air Force took 252 F1s into service. It has been a highly successful export aircraft, with operators including Ecuador (18), Greece (40), Iraq (89), Jordan (36), Kuwait (20), Libya (38), Morocco (50), Qatar (14), South Africa (48), Spain (72).

DASSAULT-BREGUET
MIRAGE 2000

DEVELOPMENT

If the Mirage III and 5 were the "flagships" of the French aerospace industry during the late 1960s and early 1970s, the delta-winged Mirage 2000 is playing an equally dominant role in the 1980s. Like the earlier Mirage deltas it is fast but affordable, and on at least one occasion has captured an order which had been widely expected to go to a US fighter.

Early 1970s French plans for future fighters were bold to the point of being foolhardy. The Mach 2 "speed plateau" might be acceptable to the USAF, but l'Armée de l'Aire was made of more ambitious stuff, seriously proposing a Mach 3 top speed for its next interceptor. As realism crept slowly into official thinking, the magic figure dropped to Mach 2.7 and lower, but the swept-wing Super Mirage G-8A "Avion de Combat Futur" was never to leave the drawing board. Its cancellation in 1975 left the French Air Force without an aircraft able to replace the Mirage III (in the short term) and eventually the Mirage F1.C.

Never short of ideas for the future, though, Dassault-Breguet promptly announced not one new design but two—the single-engined Mirage 2000 and the private-venture Super Mirage 4000. Both combined the SNECMA M53 turbofan with a new version of the traditional delta layout used on earlier designs.

The main reason behind the use of the delta wing on the Mirage III and IV was

to ease fabrication problems, but in the case of the new Mirage 2000 and 4000, the Dassault design team had re-thought the delta concept. Studies had shown that a modern delta design taking advantage of artificial stability and the latest developments in aerodynamics could be an effective way of creating a new generation of fighters able to match the performance of the F-16 and F-15. The Mirage 2000 was the result of a French Air Force requirement for a lightweight, multi-role fighter able to replace the Mirage III fleet. Five prototypes were built and flown. The first flew on March 10, 1978, little more than two years after the project was launched. A second followed in the autumn, a third in April 1979, but the fourth was probably delayed by modifications resulting from

experience with the earlier aircraft. Representative of a production aircraft, it flew in May 1980, followed by a fifth—the first two-seat version—in October of the same year.

Each was assigned to a specific area of flight test, with the fleet clocking up more than 1,000 hours. Although initial procurement funding was allocated in 1979, a series of technical problems in areas such as propulsion and flight-control, plus severe slippage of the radar programme, delayed production deliveries. The first production aircraft was not to fly until November 20, 1982, while the third was the first to be delivered to the user.

The French Air Force is expected to buy up to 400, half configured as interceptors, the remainder as attack, reconnaissance or

Left: The prototypes of the Mirage 2000, (nearest camera) and the Super Mirage 4000, showing that the Mirage 4000 is much the larger of the two; what is not so readily apparent in this photo is that it has two engines. Other features are the better rearward visibility for the pilot, and the larger, though aerodynamically similar fin and rudder. The 2000 will serve l'Armée de l'Air; the 4000 has yet to find a buyer, despite Dassault assurances that it is superior to any other aircraft in its class.

Typical weapons:
Top: A, Matra R.550 Magic AAM; **B**, external fuel tank; **C**, ASMP nuclear air-to-surface missile; **D**, 30mm DEFA cannon. The ASMP is an air-launched cruise missile with a range of 190nm (350km).
Bottom: A, 30mm DEFA cannon; **B**, AS.30 AGM; **C**, Matra R.550 Magic. The AS.30 is a very accurate, supersonic air-to-surface missile, the original versions using optical tracking and command guidance, the latest models being laser-guided. Magics are heat-homing.

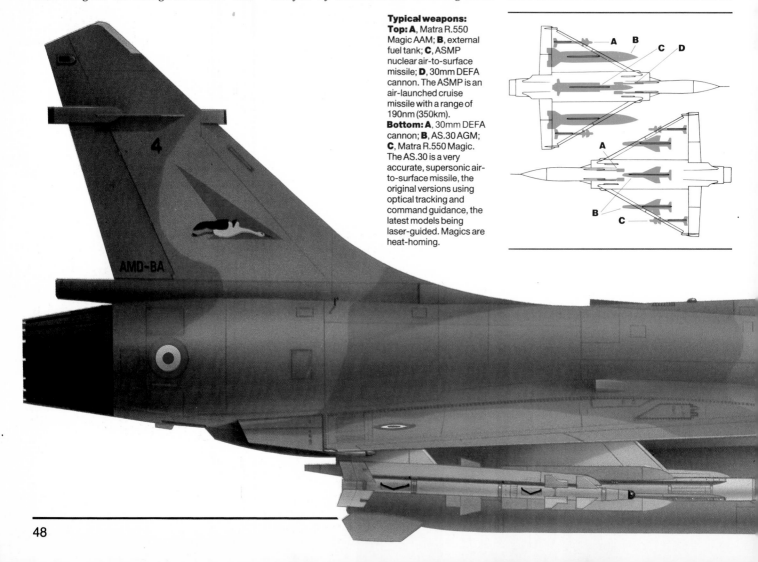

Below: The Mirage 2000 clearly shows its pedigree from the battle-tested Mirage III, but is far more capable. The tail-less delta configuration has been thought out-dated in the fighter world, but the use of relaxed static stability coupled with digital fly-by-wire, and the addition of vortex-inducing strakes on the inlets (one can hardly call them foreplanes) to improve high angle-of-attack qualities have all given the layout a new lease of life. High-altitude handling of the Mirage 2000 is excellent.

Above: The Mirage 2000 is here depicted in typical air defence configuration, with Matra Magic infra-red homing missiles on the outer pylons; and Matra Super 530D (D for doppler) semi-active radar-homing missiles mounted inboard. This missile has been built specifically to match the RDI radar carried by the Mirage 2000, and is believed to have good snap-down capability. The Super 530 is one of the fastest air-to-air missiles today, with a maximum speed of Mach 4.6 and a manoeuvre capability of 20g up to 56,000ft (17,000m) and 6g at 82,000ft (25,000m). The Mirage 2000 also has two 30mm DEFA 554 cannon with 125 rounds each, and shown on the centreline is an external fuel tank. The centreline and inner wing pylons are "wet", and are stressed to a maximum load of 3,968lb (1,800kg), while the outer wing points can carry up to 661lb (300kg). Four hardpoints on the wingroots each hold 862lb (400kg), maximum. Total external capacity is thus some 16,750lb (7,600kg).

Below left: One weakness of the Mirage 2000 highlighted by this side view is the limited rearward visibility from the cockpit. The SNECMA M53 engine cannot match the massive thrust of the latest US powerplants such as the F100 and F101, so Dassault could not afford the drag penalty associated with an F-16-style bubble canopy. The aircraft shown here is in the markings of Escadre de Chasse 1/2 "Cicognes", the first Armée de l'Air unit to be equipped with the type.

training aircraft. Likely unit cost is around $20 million. By 1988 more than 240 aircraft will have been ordered, and around half that number should be in service. Initial deliveries to the French Air Force will be of Mirage 2000C1 aircraft optimised for the ground attack role. Interceptor deliveries will not begin until 1986 when the RDI radar is available.

The first 2000B two-seat version flew for the first time in 1980. This is intended for the training role, but a two-seat cockpit is also fitted to the next version—the 2000N low-altitude strike variant. This flew for the first time on November 20, 1982, and will enter service with the Armée de l'Air in 1986.

As was the case with the Mirage III and F1, most 2000s to be built are likely to be for export; Dassault expects to export two aircraft for every one delivered to the

French Air Force. No really substantial orders have been received so far, but the market could hot up around 1985.

India first expressed serious interest in the Mirage 2000 in early 1981, discussing a possible purchase and licence production of up to 150 aircraft—a deal estimated to be worth some $3,500 million. The first 40 would have been delivered by Dassault, a further 45 provided as kits for local assembly, with the prospect of 60 or more further aircraft being licence-built by Hindustan Aeronautics. On April 1, 1982, a contract was signed for 36 single-seat and four two-seat Mirage 2000s, with delivery starting in 1984. Co-production plans were eventually shelved when India decided not to go ahead with the construction of the Mirage 2000 and SEPECAT Jaguar by HAL. Studies had apparently shown that the cost of building

the MiG-27 Flogger would be only 25 per cent of the likely cost of the Mirage 2000. HAL now plans to set up a production line for the Soviet aircraft.

In January 1982, Egypt signed a $1,000 million deal for 20 Mirage 2000s. The Egyptian Air Force has a requirement for up to 60, but follow-up orders will only be placed if favourable financing terms can be agreed.

Next nation to sign was Peru, which ordered 26 Mirage 2000 fighters in December 1982. Deliveries are due to begin in the summer of 1985. This came as a blow to the USA, which had seen Peru as a likely launch customer for the F-16/79 version of the Fighting Falcon. Peru is apparently having problems in financing the deal, so the future of the Mirage order remains in some doubt. Abu Dhabi followed in May 1983 with an order for 18 for

Dassault-Breguet Mirage 2000
1. Pitot head.
2. Radome (removed).
3. Flight refuelling probe.
4. Temperature probe.
5. Total pressure head.
6. Rudder pedals.
7. Pilot's instrument display.
8. Head-up display.
9. Martin-Baker ejection seat.
10. Cockpit canopy cover.
11. Canopy jack.
12. Canopy emergency release.
13. IFF aerial.
14. Avionics system equipment.
15. TACAN aerial.
16. Electrical system equipment.
17. Starboard leading edge slats.
18. Radar warning receiver.
19. Anti-collision light.
20. Fuel system equipment.
21. Bleed air pre-cooler.
22. Air turbine starter/auxiliary power unit.
23. Starboard wing integral fuel tank.
24. Alternators.
25. Accessory gearbox drive shaft.
26. SNECMA M53 engine.
27. Engine electronic control units.
28. Rear fuselage fuel tank.
29. Engine accessory equipment.
30. Rudder artificial feel unit.
31. Rudder hydraulic actuator.
32. Formation lighting strip.
33. Forward radar warning receiver.
34. VHF aerial.
35. Tail navigation lights.
36. Aft radar warning receiver.
37. Rudder.
38. ECM aerial.
39. ECM transmitter.
40. Afterburner nozzle jacks.
41. Variable area afterburner nozzle.
42. Afterburner duct.
43. Formation lighting strip.
44. Brake parachute housing.
45. Emergency arrester hook.
46. Inboard elevon.
47. Elevon hydraulic actuators.
48. Outboard elevon.
49. Port navigation light.
50. Radar warning receiver.
51. Outboard leading edge slat.
52. Outboard pylon mounting.
53. Outboard stores pylon.
54. Slat screw jacks.
55. Missile launch rail.
56. Matra Magic air-to-air missile.
57. Port wing main fuel tank.
58. Inboard pylon mounting.
59. Inboard stores pylon.
60. Slat drive motor and gearbox.
61. Main undercarriage pivot bearing.
62. Inward retracting mainwheel.
63. Missile launch rail.
64. Hydraulic retraction jack.
65. Airbrakes.
66. Airbrake hydraulic jack.
67. Slat drive shaft.
68. Matra Super 530 air-to-air missile.
69. Airframe mounted accessory gearbox.
70. Inboard leading edge slat.
71. Hydraulic accumulator.
72. Forward wing fuel tank.
73. Forward fuselage fuel tanks.
74. Ammunition magazine.
75. DEFA 30mm cannon.
76. External fuel tank.
77. Pressure refuelling connection.
78. Intake strake.
79. Intake suction relief door.
80. Air conditioning system.
81. Intake variable half cone screw jack.
82. Intake half cone centre-body.
83. Cockpit pressurisation valve.
84. Engine throttle lever.
85. Ejection seat rocket pack.
86. Nosewheel steering jacks.
87. Aft retracting nose undercarriage.
88. Hydraulic retraction jack.
89. VHF aerial.
90. Control column.

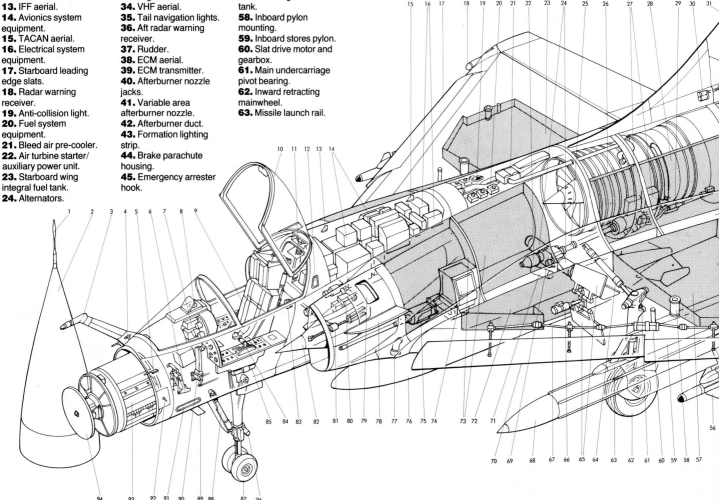

delivery in 1985, plus an option for 18 more.

At one point in the autumn of 1982, Dassault seemed on the brink of receiving a major order from China. Although reports of an impending deal were formally denied by the French Government, Peking was apparently seeking a co-production agreement. Cost proved an insurmountable stumbling block, and the following summer China announced that the scheme had been dropped.

Several other nations are known to have expressed serious interest in the Mirage 2000. Iraq was reported in the summer of 1982 to be contemplating the purchase of 70 for delivery in 1985 to 1986, while Argentina was apparently trying to raise funds early in 1984 for a purchase. Other potential customers are reported to include Libya and the United Arab Emirates.

The twin-engined Super Mirage 4000 has been less successful. Developed as a private venture to meet what Dassault predicted would be a significant market for an aircraft in the 40,000lb (18,000kg) weight class, it was displayed in mockup form in December 1977, but the sole prototype did not fly until March 9, 1979. In the following three years the aircraft was extensively flight-tested, clocking up several hundred flight hours. The bill for the development of what is virtually an aerodynamic prototype into a fully-equipped service aircraft could be well in excess of $1,000 million—a price tag likely to deter all but a handful of nations.

Dassault's optimism in building the aircraft now seems rash, since no order is in prospect. Persistent reports have mentioned a possible Saudi Arabian interest, but this has never been officially confirmed or denied. The possibility of an Iraqi purchase seems unlikely, although some interest has been reported. The project must be considered on "back burner", if not virtually moribund.

STRUCTURE

One problem faced by the Mirage 2000 design team was the fact that the M53 engine was not in the thrust class of the F100 turbofan used in the rival F-16. If the vital combat thrust:weight ratio of greater than unity was to be achieved, structural weight had to be kept to a minimum. Components made from composite materials had already been tested in the form of a carbon-fibre Mirage III rudder and a boron horizontal stabiliser on the Mirage F1, so Dassault had the experience and confidence to use these lightweight ma-

91. Formation lighting strip.
92. Incidence probe.
93. Thomson-CSF RDM radar unit.
94. Radar scanner.

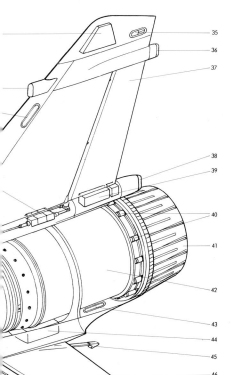

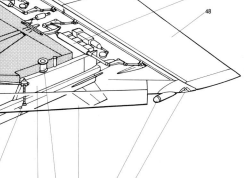

Right: The prototype two-seater Mirage 2000B. Intended for training and conversion, this variant differs from the single-seater in the raised dorsal spine in which are housed the avionics displaced by the second seat.

Composite materials save weight

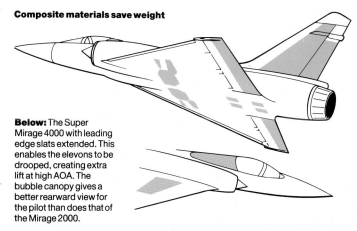

Below: The Super Mirage 4000 with leading edge slats extended. This enables the elevons to be drooped, creating extra lift at high AOA. The bubble canopy gives a better rearward view for the pilot than does that of the Mirage 2000.

Left: Weight-saving is a critical factor in all modern fighters. The use of advanced composites has become common. The Mirage 2000 utilises a proportion of carbon and boron fibre composites as illustrated here. The experience levels of French industry are not high and this is reflected by the (by modern standards) relatively small usage of these materials, compared with aircraft such as the Anglo-American Harrier II and the F-18 Hornet.

terials in the airframe of the Mirage 2000, particularly for skin panels.

The delta wing has a leading edge swept at 58deg, slightly less than the 60deg used on the Mirage III. It has a cambered profile, while the wing root is smoothly blended into the fuselage. Full-span automatic leading-edge flaps operate in conjunction with the two-section elevons fitted to the entire length of the trailing edge to provide variable camber when maximum lift is required—during combat and landing. When the aircraft is accelerating or cruising at low-altitude, the leading-edge flaps remain retracted, giving the wing the lowest-possible drag. These moving surfaces are under the control of the fly-by-wire system. Like the airbrakes (mounted one above and one below each wing), they are actuated by hydraulic power. The elevons have carbon-fibre skins. The airframe of the 2000N is strengthened for flight at speeds of up to 600kt (1,100km/h) at a height of only 200ft (60m) above the terrain.

The fuselage is area ruled, like that of the earlier Mirage III, and is largely of metal construction. An avionics compartment is located just aft of the cockpit, and is fitted with an access panel of carbon-fibre/metal honeycomb construction. Most of the skin of the vertical fin, and all the rudder skin are manufactured from composite materials.

In selecting an air-intake configuration, Dassault retained the semi-circular design with a movable half-cone centrebody used on the Mirage III, 5 and F1. A small fixed strake is located on the upper side of each, just aft of the lip.

In the two-seat models, the rear seat occupies some of the space used for fuel in the single-seaters, reducing the total internal load from 835 Imp gal (3,800 litres) to 813 Imp gal (3,700 litres), a figure still well in excess of the 733 Imp gal (3,330 litres) carried by the Mirage IIIE.

PROPULSION

The SNECMA M53 was originally intended as a powerplant for the Mirage F1.E offered to NATO in the mid-1970s, and for the Avion de Combat Futur. It is of unusual configuration—a single-shaft turbofan—probably a result of SNECMA's extensive experience with single-shaft designs gained during the Atar turbojet programme. It is of modular construction and is suitable for speeds of Mach 2.5 at high altitude.

Three versions have been tested, starting with the M53-2, developing 18,740lb (8,500kg) with afterburner. This was used for the prototype Mirage F1.E, 2000 and 4000 aircraft. The production M53-5 develops 19,840lb (9,000kg) and powers the Mirage 2000. It is likely to be replaced by the 21,340lb (9,680kg) M53-P2.

The three-stage fan has a bypass ratio of around 0.35:1, while the compressor has five stages. Both sections have titanium blades and are driven by a two-stage axial turbine. The low bypass ratio and moderate (8.5:1) pressure ratio of the M53 gives a higher subsonic SFC than might be desirable, but the engine is well suited to the supersonic interception mission. Specific fuel consumption of the M53-5 is 0.87lb/lb/hr, 0.92 in the case of the M53-P2. With the afterburner lit, both variants consume 2.07lb/lb/hr.

The -P2 has the same overall dimensions as the -5, and is interchangeable with the earlier unit. Internally it is somewhat different, with a revised LP compressor and turbine. It has been specified for all export Mirage 2000s, but was not fitted to French Air Force aircraft until the first 15 2000Ns.

AVIONICS

The Mirage 2000 incorporates a digital quadruplex fly-by-wire flight control sys-

tem, an essential feature in any relaxed-stability aircraft. No mechanical back-up control system is fitted. In the event of the system suffering a massive failure of all channels (virtually impossible under normal circumstances, but possible in the event of combat damage), an emergency fifth channel powered from an independent battery would provide the control facilities needed to allow the pilot to get the aircraft back to base.

A major problem in the Mirage 2000 programme has been a serious underestimation of the time required to develop the definitive pulse-doppler radar system. Two sets were developed for the Mirage 2000—the Thomson-CSF/Electronique Serge Dassault RDI (Radar Doppler a Impulsions) for the French Air Force and the Thomson-CSF RDM (Radar Doppler Multifunction) for export aircraft. RDI is an I-band track-while scan radar with a TWT transmitter and a high PRF. It uses a planar-array antenna, and has a maximum range of around 55nm (100km). Operating modes include air-to-air search; target tracking and missile guidance; air-to-ground ranging; ground and contour mapping.

The multi-role RDM is a medium-PRF set which uses a conventional Cassegrain antenna instead of a planar array. Similar in concept to the RDI, it offers additional operating modes for air-to-ground use, including terrain avoidance and air-to-ground attack. It was proposed as the radar for the Mirage 4000.

Delays with the RDI have resulted in the French Air Force having to accept its first production aircraft with the RDM export set, and with the standard Super 530 missile rather than the upgraded 530D devised to work with the pulse-Doppler radar.

The nuclear strike role demanded new avionics, so the 2000N will carry an Electronique Serge Dassault Antilope V terrain-following radar, two SAGEM inertial platforms, a Thomson-CSF colour CRT display and additional but classified ECM systems. Antilope V is a multi-mode pulse-Doppler set working in J-band and offering terrain-following, ground mapping and updating modes.

A new radar-warning receiver was developed for the Mirage 2000 by Thomson-CSF. Designated Serval, it is probably based on experience gained on the earlier BF and BK series RWRs. This may operate in conjunction with an internally-mounted dual-mode (noise/deception) ECM system reported to be under development by the same company. Thomson-CSF jamming pods such as the DB3141, DB 3163 and Alligator could also be carried (see Mirage F1 entry for details of all the above systems). Electronique Serge Dassault has developed a pod-mounted jammer covering H, I and J bands. Known as Barax, this may also be intended for use on the Mirage 2000.

ARMAMENT

To update Magic for use on the Mirage 2000, and to allow it to cope with the latest threats, Matra has developed the Magic 2. This uses a new pattern of infrared homing head, plus digital technology and signal processing. The seeker can be slaved to the aircraft fire-control system, and incorporates a multi-element detector cell of high sensitivity. According to Matra, this gives the missile "all-sector attack capability at ranges greater than those of other existing missiles". Magic 2 is fully interchangeable with the current version and its firing envelope is intended to match the performance of the Mirage 2000. It can manoeuvre at up to 50g.

Development started in 1978, and the first round was fired from a Mirage III in November 1981—a test which involved a head-on attack. Firings from the Mirage 2000 followed, and the weapon is due to enter service in 1985 with the French Air Force and Navy, and with export customers.

To provide the Mirage 2000 with long-range armament, Matra developed the Super 530D missile, taking advantage of recent improvements in digital technology. Carriage trials on the Mirage 2000 began in November 1979, followed by the first live firing in July 1981. Test firings against higher-flying targets started in April of the following year.

On the Mirage F1, the target is detected and illuminated by the Thomson-CSF Cyrano IV radar, but the Mirage 2000 carries the RDM I/J band pulse-Doppler set and a new Doppler semi-active radar homing head developed to work with the new radar will allow targets to be intercepted at low altitude, giving the missile

Possible weapons, Mirage 2000:
1. 30mm DEFA 554 cannon (125 rounds).
2. Matra Super 530 AAM.
3. Matra 550 Magic AAM.
4. Underwing fuel tank.
5. Centreline fuel tank.
6. 500lb (250kg) bomb.
7. 500lb (250kg) LGB.
8. 2,200lb (1,000kg) LGB or "iron" bomb.
9. 900lb (400kg) modular bomb.
10. BAP 100 penetration bomb.
11. BAT 120 tactical bomb.
12. Beluga cluster bomb.
13. 531 grenade launcher.
14. Grenadier.
15. F2 practice launcher.
16. F4 rocket launcher.
17. EO guidance pod.
18. Air/surface missile.
19. CC 421 gun pod.
20. Recce pod.
21. ECM jamming pod.

Possible weapons, Mirage 4000:
1. 30mm DEFA cannon.
2. Long-range AAMs.
3. Short-range AAMs.
4. Advanced AAMs.
5. Air/ground missiles.
6. Air/surface missiles.
7. Durandal anti-runway bombs.
8. BAP 100 penetration bombs.
9. 500lb (250kg) bombs.
10. 500lb (250kg) bomb, standard or retarded.
11. 2,200lb (1,000kg) laser guided or conventional bomb.
12. 68mm rocket launcher.
13. Beluga cluster bomb.
14. External fuel tanks.
15. FLIR pod.
16. Laser illuminator pod.
17. ECM jamming pod.
18. Reconnaissance pod.

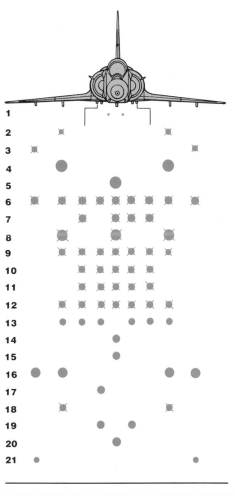

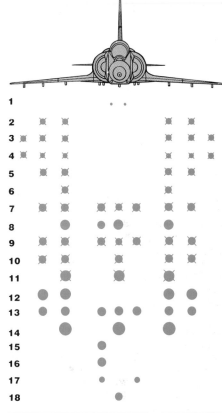

Below: A Mirage 2000 demonstrates its load-carrying capability, with eight 500lb (250kg) bombs, two external fuel tanks, and two Magic 550 heat-homing air-to-air missiles.

the "snap-down" capability needed in order to deal with low-level intruders. The new seeker also offers greater resistance to enemy electronic countermeasures.

Digital data processing within the round provides a faster reaction time. Super 530D can intercept aircraft flying at up to 80,000ft (24,380m) at speeds of up to Mach 3, so should have no difficulty in dealing with MiG-25 Foxbat reconnaissance aircraft. Thanks to an uprated pattern of motor and modified radome, the performance of the Super 530D will be generally superior to that of the standard version, including increased range. To cope with the increased capability of the seeker and guidance electronics, the aerodynamics of the round have been improved, while its new structure can withstand higher temperatures.

The first Super 530D missiles are scheduled to enter service in 1986. Early production French Air Force Mirage 2000s fitted with the export-standard RDI radar will initially carry standard Super 530 missiles, receiving the RDM radar and Super 530D in a later retrofit programme. Evaluation firings from a Mirage 2000 fitted with the pulse-Doppler RDM radar started in May 1983.

The Mirage 2000N will carry the most exotic missile currently being developed by the French aerospace industry—the Aérospatiale ASMP (Air-Sol Moyenne Portée) nuclear stand-off missile. Designed for strike missions against hardened targets, this is 17.6ft (5.38m) long, 3.1ft (96cm) in diameter and weighs around 2,200lb (1,000kg). The warhead is a 150kT thermonuclear weapon.

Before the Mirage 2000N takes off on its mission, the inertial navigation systems of the missile and launch aircraft will be loaded with details of the target and flight path, including any preplanned evasive manoeuvres to be flown during the final approach to the target. In cruising flight, ASMP is powered by a liquid-fuel ramjet, but a solid-propellant booster is used immediately after launch to bring the round up to the Mach 2 speed needed for ramjet operation. The booster is housed within the ramjet exhaust pipe. At burnout, it is ejected, the air intakes are opened, then kerosene fuel is injected into the combustion chamber. The ramjet lights, taking the round up to its cruising speed of above Mach 3. Maximum range is 54nm (100km).

In 1988, the ASMP will be deployed

tactically on the first of 85 Mirage 2000Ns, the first 15 of which were funded in the 1983 defence budget; a total of 100 rounds will be procured for use on the Mirage 2000N, the Mirage IVP nuclear bomber and the Super Etendard naval fighter. Air-launched powered flight testing of the missile started in 1983.

For conventional attack missions, the Mirage 2000 can carry up to 13,200lb (6,000kg) of ordnance, including 1,000lb (450kg) bombs, Durandal anti-runway weapons, Beluga cluster munitions, AS.30L laser-guided air-to-surface missiles or the new ARMAT anti-radar missile. The two 30mm DEFA 554 cannon each have 125 rounds of ammunition.

PERFORMANCE

In designing the Mirage 2000, the Dassault team has ingeniously provided the high-speed, brisk acceleration, and good manoeuvrability required for the air-superiority role in an aircraft which is small in size and of only modest power. Maximum level speed is Mach 2.2 at height, but a clean aircraft can probably manage dashes of Mach 2.3 or more. Loaded with eight 550lb (250kg) bombs and two Magics, the

Mirage 2000 turning advantage

Right: The turning ability of the original Mirage III was never very good, suffering as it did from the limitations of the tail-less delta planform. As the AOA increases to create the extra lift, needed in a hard turn, so does profile drag, resulting in a dramatic reduction of velocity. The Mirage 2000, with its slatted wing and vortex-inducing strakes, plus its higher thrust:weight ratio, turns far better than its Mirage III ancestor at subsonic speeds, and twice as well at Mach 1.5. The delta wing and advanced flight controls create an effective dogfighter.

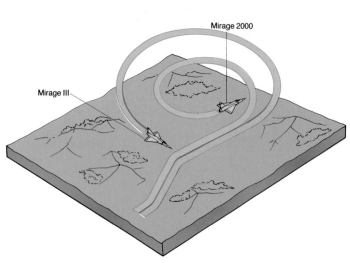

Mirage 2000

Mirage III

Mirage 2000 climb rate

Right: Examination of the bare statistics appears to show that the Mirage 2000 does not produce startling improvements over the 1950s-designed Mirage III, with a 5 per cent higher operational ceiling, and about the same increase in top speeds, both at high altitude and at sea level. However, the time to altitude is some 25 per cent better and the initial climb has increased by a factor of three; from 16,400ft/min (5,000m/min), to 49,000ft/min (14,934m/min). Its avionics, of course, put the Mirage 2000 in a totally different class. It could be in production until the 1990s.

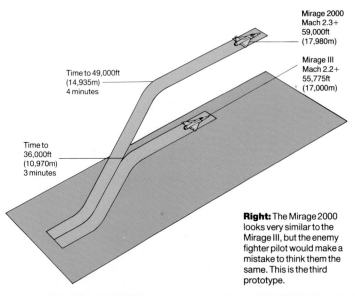

Mirage 2000
Mach 2.3+
59,000ft
(17,980m)

Mirage III
Mach 2.2+
55,775ft
(17,000m)

Time to 49,000ft
(14,935m)
4 minutes

Time to 36,000ft
(10,970m)
3 minutes

Right: The Mirage 2000 looks very similar to the Mirage III, but the enemy fighter pilot would make a mistake to think them the same. This is the third prototype.

Ground attack

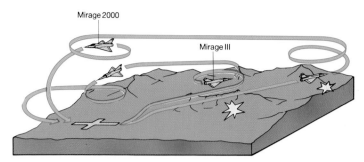

Combat air patrol

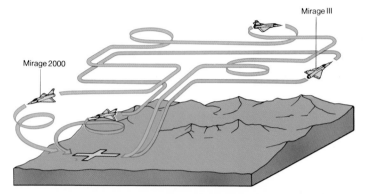

Left: In the ground attack role, the Mirage 2000 shows a marked improvement over the Mirage III, giving approx. 30 per cent greater radius of action when both aircraft are similarly configured, regardless of mission profile (hi-lo-hi, lo-lo-lo, etc). The tactical radius of the Mirage 2000 is quoted as being 435nm (700km), although with what type of load is not specified.

Left: For the combat air patrol mission, which would normally be flown configured with two Magics, two Super 530s and drop tanks, the Mirage 2000 is stated by Dassault to have three times the capability of the Mirage III. This could be interpreted in many ways. It could mean that the same time on patrol could be flown at three times the radius, or that time on patrol could be tripled at the same radius or, most likely, that the fuel allowance for full throttle combat is tripled.

aircraft can fly at over 600kt (1,110km/h) at low level without the use of afterburner. Approach is a comfortable 140kt (260km/h), but the aircraft handles comfortably down to 90kt (167km/h). Prototypes have flown at speeds from a mere 50kt (93km/h) to more than Mach 2.

Sea level rate of climb is 59,000ft/min (18,000m/min), 40 per cent better than that of the Mirage F1, and well into the F-16 class. Time from brake release to interception of an 80,000ft (24,400km/h) Mach 3 target is less than five minutes, while the service ceiling is 65,600ft (20,000m).

The quadruplex fly-by-wire flight-control system gives good handling characteristics at low and high speeds, and excellent manoeuvrability at subsonic and supersonic speeds. The airframe is stressed to accept +9g, and the aircraft can be rolled at up to 270deg/sec at subsonic or supersonic speed even when loaded with four air-to-air missiles.

OPERATORS

Potential purchasers of the Mirage 2000 are: France (400+ planned), Abu Dhabi (18), Egypt (20), India (40), Peru (26).

SUPER ETENDARD

DEVELOPMENT

Two aircraft emerged from the 1982 Falklands War with greatly-enhanced reputations—the BAe Sea Harrier and the Exocet-armed Super Etendard. Although the French fighter, at best marginally supersonic, is an uninspired design which breaks no new ground in aeronautical technology, it has two important operational features which catapulted it into the headlines in 1982—a long-range missile armament which allows it to strike heavily-defended naval targets with minimal risk of interception, plus the ability to operate from small aircraft carriers such as Argentina's *25 de Mayo*.

The fact that many of its missiles actually missed their targets in the Falklands War, and that the Argentinian Navy was not able to deploy the newly acquired aircraft aboard its single carrier, has tended to be overlooked in many subsequent analyses. Hastily rushed by its manufacturers to another customer (Iraq) and another war—this time in the Middle East—the type was once again displaying its indiscriminate missile fire as these words were being written.

The Super Etendard owes its origins to the early 1970s, when the French Aeronavale seemed unable to select a new aircraft to replace the Dassault Etendard IVMs deployed aboard the carriers *Foch* and *Clemenceau*. In theory, these were to be replaced by the SEPECAT Jaguar, and a single prototype of the planned Jaguar M shipboard strike fighter had flown for the first time in November 1969.

In 1970, the Aeronavale rejected the aircraft, indicating a preference for the Vought A-7. The motive for this decision was undoubtedly political rather than financial or technical. Troubles with Jaguar's Adour engine were well on the way to being cleared up, while the US aircraft would have been marginally more expensive than Jaguar. In addition to the A-7, studies were also carried out on a proposed A-4T version of the McDonnell Douglas Skyhawk, but the entire procurement exercise was fraught with political wrangling.

The Aeronavale had a long history of operating foreign aircraft. Its carriers were already equipped with Vought F-8 Crusaders, and the service had previously flown a licence-built version of the de Havilland Sea Venom. There was undoubtedly pressure to "buy French", and Dassault was able to offer a solution—a redesigned version of the existing Etendard.

The Super Etendard was to be a transonic aircraft with sufficient performance to meet the needs of the Aeronavale without exceeding the limits of the budget for aircraft re-equipment. The original proposal called for the existing airframe

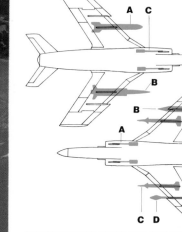

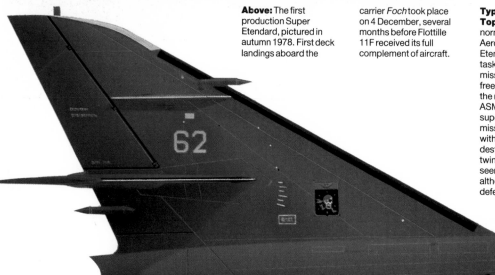

Above: The first production Super Etendard, pictured in autumn 1978. First deck landings aboard the carrier *Foch* took place on 4 December, several months before Flottille 11F received its full complement of aircraft.

Typical weapons:
Top: In addition to their normal shipboard role, Aeronavale Super Etendards will also be tasked with nuclear strike missions using the AN52 free-falling weapon (**A**) or the new Aerospatiale ASMP ramjet-powered supersonic stand-off missile (**B**). Compared with such formidable destructive power, the twin DEFA cannon (**C**) seem almost irrelevant, although useful for self-defence.

Above: Argentina's Super Etendards were not ready for carrier deployment at the time of the Falklands War, so were confined to long-range Exocet missions from land bases. The force has now worked up with weapons such as the internal cannon (**A**), Matra launcher for unguided rockets (**B**), and the indigenously developed Martin Pescador air-to-surface missile (**C**) and its guidance pod (**D**).

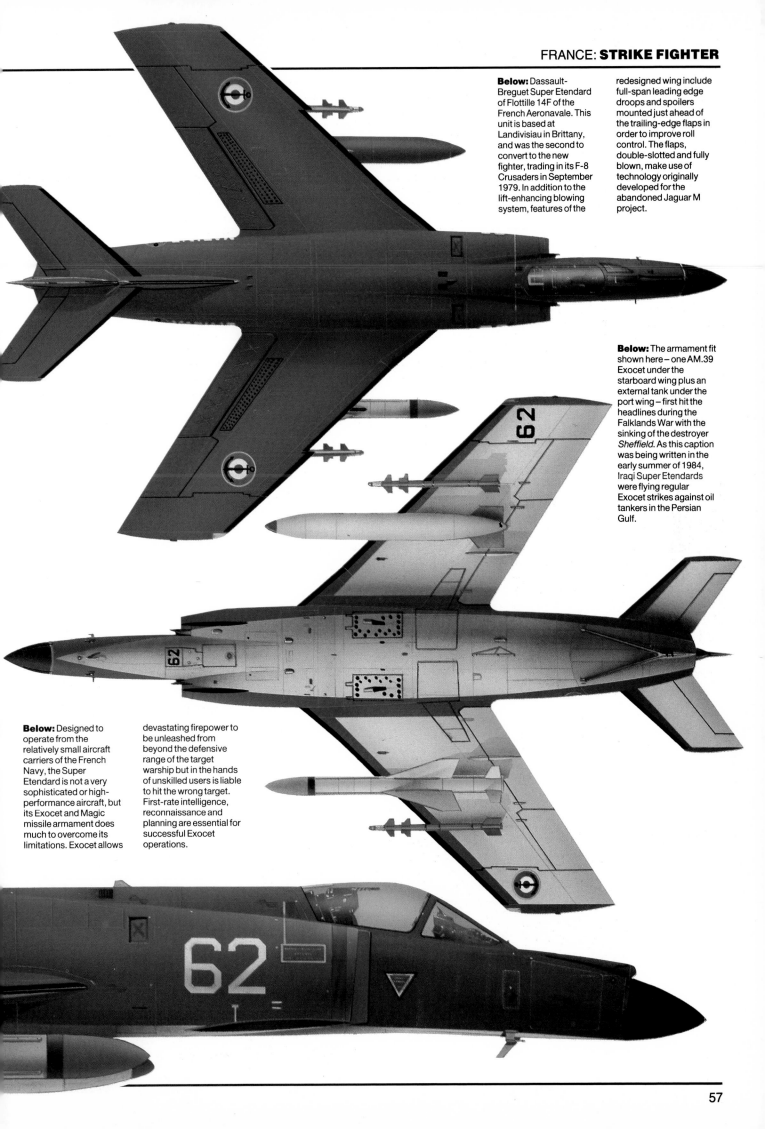

Below: Dassault-Breguet Super Etendard of Flottille 14F of the French Aeronavale. This unit is based at Landivisiau in Brittany, and was the second to convert to the new fighter, trading in its F-8 Crusaders in September 1979. In addition to the lift-enhancing blowing system, features of the redesigned wing include full-span leading edge droops and spoilers mounted just ahead of the trailing-edge flaps in order to improve roll control. The flaps, double-slotted and fully blown, make use of technology originally developed for the abandoned Jaguar M project.

Below: The armament fit shown here – one AM.39 Exocet under the starboard wing plus an external tank under the port wing – first hit the headlines during the Falklands War with the sinking of the destroyer *Sheffield*. As this caption was being written in the early summer of 1984, Iraqi Super Etendards were flying regular Exocet strikes against oil tankers in the Persian Gulf.

Below: Designed to operate from the relatively small aircraft carriers of the French Navy, the Super Etendard is not a very sophisticated or high-performance aircraft, but its Exocet and Magic missile armament does much to overcome its limitations. Exocet allows devastating firepower to be unleashed from beyond the defensive range of the target warship but in the hands of unskilled users is liable to hit the wrong target. First-rate intelligence, reconnaissance and planning are essential for successful Exocet operations.

**Dassault-Breguet
Super Etendard**
1. Agave radar unit.
2. Retractable in-flight refuelling probe.
3. Planar radar scanner.
4. Scanner tracking mechanism.
5. Refuelling probe housing.
6. Forward avionics equipment bay.
7. Refuelling probe retraction linkage.
8. Total pressure head.
9. Rudder pedals.
10. Instrument panel.
11. Head-up display.
12. Engine throttle lever.
13. Martin-Baker ejection seat.
14. Cockpit canopy cover.
15. Canopy jack.
16. Canopy emergency release.
17. Avionics equipment bay.
18. Fuel system accumulator.
19. Engine bleed air pre-cooler.
20. IFF aerial.
21. Leading edge dog-tooth.

22. Starboard wing integral fuel tank.
23. Wing fold hinge joint.
24. Starboard formation and strobe lights.
25. Starboard navigation light.
26. Fuselage fuel tanks.
27. Starboard wing tip folded position.
28. Aileron.
29. Double slotted Fowler-type flap.
30. Engine starter housing.
31. Bleed air ducting.
32. Engine oil tank.
33. SNECMA Atar 08K-50 non afterburning turbojet engine.
34. Tailplane trim actuator.
35. Elevator hydraulic actuator.
36. Rudder trim control unit.
37. Starboard trimming tailplane.
38. Rudder hydraulic actuator.
39. Forward radar warning antenna.

40. VHF aerial.
41. Command telemetery aerial.
42. Rudder.
43. Brake parachute housing (land based operations).
44. Tail navigation and anti-collision lights.
45. Rear radar warning antenna.
46. Elevator.
47. Port wing tip folded position.
48. Port trimming tailplane.
49. Port aileron.
50. Arrester hook.
51. Jet pipe.
52. Port double slotted Fowler-type flap.
53. Radar warning power amplifier.
54. Arrester hook pivot bearing.
55. Aft avionics equipment.
56. Engine fuel system.
57. Port navigation light.

58. Port formation and strobe lights.
59. Wing fold hinge joint.
60. Wing fold hydraulic jack.
61. Aileron hydraulic actuator.
62. Leading edge flap control rod.
63. Outboard stores pylon.
64. Port wing integral fuel tank.
65. Spoiler.
66. Spoiler hydraulic jack.
67. Flap hydraulic jack.

68. Matra rocket launcher.
69. Inboard stores pylon.
70. Inward-retracting mainwheel.
71. Main undercarriage pivot bearing.
72. Hydraulic reservoir.
73. Engine gearbox drive shaft.

74. Engine accessory equipment gearbox.
75. External fuel tank.
76. Main undercarriage hydraulic jack and lock strut.
77. Catapult strop link.
78. Airbrake hydraulic jack.

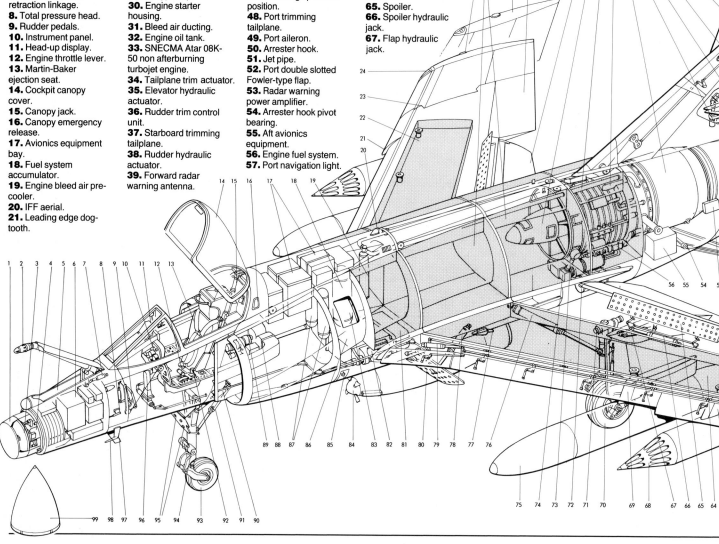

simply to be modified to accept modern avionics and other systems, retaining most of the structure unchanged. The first two prototypes were in fact rebuilt Etendard IVMs. But, by the time the Dassault team were finished, the end product was virtually an all-new aircraft having little in common with the existing model apart from the general configuration. If the Aeronavale realised the degree of redesign which was taking place, it chose not to complain. It thus obtained a better aircraft than a minimally-modified Etendard IVM would have been, but at a high price. Unit cost of the aircraft when the first export order was placed in 1979 was more than $10 million.

The first true Super Etendard flew on November 24, 1977, and production deliveries began the following summer. A total of 100 aircraft was planned, but shortage of funds forced the number to be cut to 71. This was no great hardship,

79. Leading edge flap hydraulic jack.
80. Airbrake.
81. Ammunition feed chute.
82. DEFA 30mm cannon.
83. Intake suction relief door.
84. Centreline auxiliary fuel tank/flight refuelling pack.
85. Ground intercom socket.
86. Gun pack ammunition magazine.

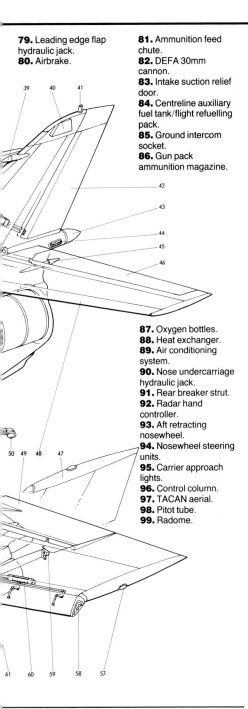

87. Oxygen bottles.
88. Heat exchanger.
89. Air conditioning system.
90. Nose undercarriage hydraulic jack.
91. Rear breaker strut.
92. Radar hand controller.
93. Aft retracting nosewheel.
94. Nosewheel steering units.
95. Carrier approach lights.
96. Control column.
97. TACAN aerial.
98. Pitot tube.
99. Radome.

Above This view of the first prototype shows the underside of the blown wing, the perforated airbrakes beneath the fuselage, and tail hook, and the large bullet fairing for the braking parachute which is used for operations at land bases.

Below: Elevators raised for take-off, a Super Etendard taxies to the catapult aboard a French carrier. The new type had not at this stage totally supplanted the Etendard IV, an example of which may be seen at the far right.

Left: The obvious resemblance between the Super Etendard and the earlier Etendard IV shown here is misleading: Super Etendard is essentially an all-new design.

since France maintains only one of its two carriers in fully-equipped condition. The other is used only as an ASW vessel, operating with a reduced crew.

An order for 14 Super Etendards was placed in 1979 by Argentina, which wanted to replace elderly A-4Q Skyhawks serving aboard the carrier *25 de Mayo*. Once these had been delivered, the line was closed, a total of 85 aircraft having been built.

The next customer was Iraq, which badly needed an anti-shipping capability for use against Iran. In an unprecedented deal, France agreed to lease five Aeronavale aircraft to the Iraqi Air Force. The actual transfer of aircraft and Exocet missiles took place under conditions of extreme secrecy in the autumn of 1983.

The Super Etendards were finally ready for action by the next spring, making their first attacks against targets near the Kharg Island oil terminal on March 28.

STRUCTURE

The wing has 45deg of sweepback and is fabricated with a two-spar torsion-box structure with integrally-stiffened machined panels. The outer panels fold to ease storage below deck. The ailerons are located inboard of the fold, and are supplemented by spoilers mounted on the upper surface of each wing just ahead of the flaps. Like all aerodynamic control surfaces on the aircraft, these are powered by duplicated hydraulic systems.

Super Etendard was clearly going to be heavier than the existing Etendard IVM on which it was based, so a series of aerodynamic improvements were needed in order to keep the carrier-approach speed within acceptable limits. Like the IVM, the wing of the new aircraft featured an outboard section of increased chord, creating a distinctive dog-tooth in the leading edge. The earlier pattern of leading-edge flap used in the IVM was replaced in the Super Etendard by new full-span drooping leading edges, while the trailing edge was fitted with redesigned double-slotted flaps capable of a greater deflection than those on the earlier aircraft.

The fuselage is of semi-monocoque design, waisted according to the area rule in order to reduce transonic drag. The only section known to incorporate armour is the cockpit area. Instead of the existing Atar 8, the new aircraft is powered by a non-afterburning version of the uprated Atar used in the Mirage F1. The air intakes and ducting had to be modified to handle the flow of air to new engine, while the aft fuselage (detachable to ease engine changes) required significant redesign. In place of the small Aida radar carried by the Etendard IVM, the new fighter would have much larger multi-role set, so the nose section had to be redesigned to provide storage space and a radome, while still retaining the retractable refuelling probe fitted to the earlier aircraft.

The general configuration of the tail and horizontal stabiliser is unchanged from the IVM, although the revised rear fuselage dictated some redesign of these components. The drag chute is carried in a bullet-shaped fairing at the junction between vertical and horizontal surfaces.

A carrier deck is no place for an unstable aircraft, so the main undercarriage retains the wide track which was a feature of the original design. Perforated airbrakes are located on the lower sides of the fuselage just below the wing, while an arrester hook is positioned further aft.

POWERPLANT

The SNECMA (Societe Nationale d'Etude et de Construction de Moteurs d'Aviation) Atar 8 engine installed in the Etendard IVM was a non-afterburning version of the Atar powerplant used in the Mirage III/5 series. The newer Mirage F1 used the more modern Atar 9K-50, a more powerful engine with a lower specific fuel consumption and longer overhaul life. The creation of a non-afterburning version to power the new Super Etendard was an obvious move.

The resulting Atar 8K-50 has a simple unaugmented jetpipe with a fixed nozzle.

Above: The first Super Etendard prototype started life as Etendard IV No. 68. Fitted with the new Atar 8K-50, it later received the blown wing originally tested on the third prototype and the nav/attack system and Agave radar from the second.

Below: Moments before launch on the catapult, the pilot of an Aeronavale Super Etendard awaits the signal to run up his engine. The catapult is ready, the deck-mounted blast deflector is in position, and the flight deck crew give a final visual check.

Right: Argentinian Navy Super Etendards fly in formation during a training mission in France prior to delivery of the aircraft. France played an ambiguous role during the Falklands War: at the time when her air force and naval air arm were flying Mirage and Super Etendard "aggressor" missions to hone the air combat skills of the British task force, French technicians were helping Argentina to install and commission Exocet, a move which would help the Argentinian Navy to sink vessels of the same task force.

It ran on the test bench for the first time in June 1972. The complete engine is 155in (393.6cm) long and 40.2in (102cm) in diameter. It weighs 2,541lb (1,155kg) and develops a thrust of 11,025lb (5,000kg), only 25lb (11kg) less than the dry thrust of the 9K-50 on which it is based.

Integral fuel tanks within the wings and fuselage of the Super Etendard hold a total of 845 US gallons (3,270 litres) of fuel. This can be supplemented by a single 290 gallon (1,100 lit) tank under each wing, plus a single 158 gallon (600 litre) tank beneath the fuselage. A "buddy" pack for in-flight refuelling is also available for installation on the fuselage centreline in place of the 600 litre tank.

AVIONICS

Most dramatic changes between the Super Etendard and its predecessor were in the field of avionics. The aircraft is fitted with a complex suite of systems which include a Thomson-CSF Agave multi-role radar, Thomson-CSF VE 120 HUD, plus a SAGEM-Kearfott Etna inertial navigation and attack system.

The radar weighs only 100lb (45kg) and is smaller than the Cyrano IV set carried by the Mirage F1, but of much the same capability. Basic operating modes include air-to-surface and air-to-air search, target tracking and ranging, target designation for the AS.39 Exocet missile, and navigation. Typical range against a fast patrol boat is 22 to 30nm (40 to 55km), or 10 to 15nm (18 to 28km) against a fighter target.

The antenna can scan plus or minus 70deg on either side of the centreline, carrying out one- or two-bar scan patterns at low or high altitudes respectively. Pulse width and repetition frequency are varied automatically to match the selected range. Data is passed to the pilot via the HUD or on a combined map/head-down display.

One novel scheme which seems to have been abandoned was an in-flight alignment system for the Etna INS. Before launch, the gyroscopes on the four-axis inertial platform must be run up, a process which takes eight minutes or more. When operating from carriers, the system must be provided with data on the carrier's current position. This is derived from the ship's own INS, and fed into the aircraft

via an electrical cable. In an attempt to speed up the process, an infra-red data link was proposed. Using this, aircraft could be catapulted from the flight deck before the alignment process was fully completed. As each climbed away, a rear-ward-facing infra-red sensor would have received final navigational data via a modulated infra-red beam from the carrier. Without such refinements, Etna is a more than adequate navigation aid, maintaining a record of current aircraft position with an error of no more than 1.2nm/hr (2.2km/hr). Like all INS systems, it can be updated in flight to minimise the remaining errors. This is done either by overflying a geographic point of known location, or by inserting navigational fixes obtained by the Agave radar.

ARMAMENT

Super Etendard has five hardpoints—two under each wing plus one on the fuselage centreline. These are stressed to carry a total of 8,100lb (3,675kg). Maximum weapon load if full internal fuel is carried is 4,630lb (2,100kg).

Above: A Super Etendard manoeuvres into position on the catapult aboard a French carrier (probably *Clemenceau*). In a few moments, the flight deck crew will fit the cable which connects the aircraft to the black and yellow striped pick-up point of the catapult.

Below: Elevators up and double-slotted flaps deflected, an Exocet-armed Super Etendard is flung down the deck by the power of the steam catapult. The nose-high attitude (common to all catapult take-offs by naval aircraft) maximises wing lift at the relatively low take-off speed.

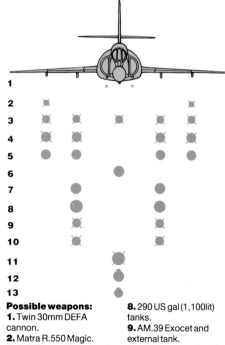

Possible weapons:
1. Twin 30mm DEFA cannon.
2. Matra R.550 Magic.
3, 4. 250kg or 400kg bombs.
5. 18-round launchers for 68mm unguided rockets.
6, 7. 160 US gal (600lit) tanks.
8. 290 US gal (1,100lit) tanks.
9. AM.39 Exocet and external tank.
10. AN52 nuclear bomb.
11. ASMP nuclear missile.
12. "Buddy" refuelling pack.
13. Recce pod.

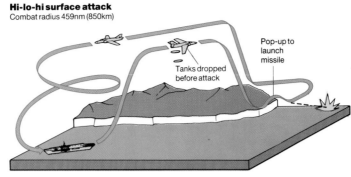

Hi-lo-hi surface attack
Combat radius 459nm (850km)

Pop-up to launch missile

Tanks dropped before attack

Left: Hi-lo-hi tactical mission from a carrier. After dropping external tanks during the high-altitude outbound cruise, Super Etendard can descend to sea level to attack a target 650nm (1,200km) distant using short-range or free-falling ordnance. On anti-ship missions, it can release AM.39s at the same point therefore further extending effective tactical range.

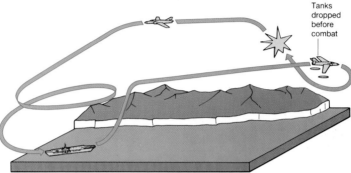

High-altitude interception
Combat radius 847nm (1,200km)

Tanks dropped before combat

Left: On an air-to-air interception mission, the aircraft would cruise out at high altitude with a payload of two Magics plus two external tanks. The latter would be dropped before entering combat up to 650nm (1,200km) from the take-off point. Despite the aircraft's marginally supersonic performance, the high lift from the large wing plus the off-boresight capability of the Magic missiles should make it an effective opponent.

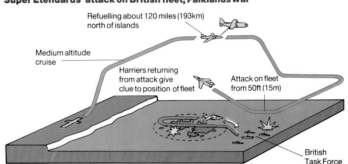

Super Etendards' attack on British fleet, Falklands War

Refuelling about 120 miles (193km) north of islands

Medium altitude cruise

Harriers returning from attack give clue to position of fleet

Attack on fleet from 50ft (15m)

British Task Force

Left: The Super Etendards which sank *Atlantic Conveyer* on 24 May 1982 refuelled from a KC-130 tanker. The radars at Port Stanley tracked the homeward flight of Sea Harriers, giving a clue to the location of the task force. Attacking from the north, the Super Etendards released their Exocets against "blips", mistaking the container ship for a carrier.

Typical ordnance loads include 550lb (250kg) and 880lb (400kg) bombs, launchers for unguided 68mm rockets, or the AS.39 version of Exocet. Performance of the basic aircraft may be limited by modern standards, but the use of Exocet allows it to remain out of range of the defences of the naval targets it is attempting to attack. Although used successfully in combat during the 1982 Falklands War, the Super Etendard was the only combat type in Argentinian service which did not suffer losses.

One problem resulting from long range "shoot and scoot" attacks is that target intelligence must be first class. The missile will be fired against a target seen only on radar, and thus hard to identify. Should the seeker break lock as a result of enemy countermeasures, an automatic target-re-aquisition routine will begin, but the round is likely to lock on to the largest radar target it can find—which may not be the correct one.

The Super Etendard/Exocet combination in combat has resulted in rounds striking the wrong target. An Argentinian attack against the British Task Force saw a hit scored on the container ship *Atlantic Conveyer* instead of the aircraft carrier assumed to have been the true target,

while the first Iraqi combat launch in 1984 resulted in a hit on the Greek oil tanker *Filikon* rather than a military target.

Aeronavale Super Etendards are also tasked with the nuclear strike role. The first such weapon to be carried was the 15kT AN52 free-falling tactical nuclear bomb, but work started in 1984 to modify the first batch of Super Etendards due to carry the air-breathing ASMP air-to-surface missile. Approximately 50 aircraft will be updated by 1988.

With the retirement of the Aeronavale's F-8s from shipboard service, Super Etendard must provide whatever fighter cover the French Navy may need when operating out of range of land-based aircraft. The twin DEFA 553 30mm cannon fire a heavy projectile well able to deal with aircraft structure, or that of ships or land targets for that matter, and may be supplemented in air combat by a pair of R.550 Magics.

PERFORMANCE

The large wing of the Super Etendard does much to ensure good handling characteristics. It has an area of 305sq ft (28.4sq m), so even at maximum take-off weight of 26,500lb (12,000kg), the wing loading is only 87lb/sq ft (424kg/sq m).

The flight decks of French aircraft carriers are only 781ft (238m) long, 15 per cent less than that of a US carrier, so low landing speed was an essential ingredient of the design. On final approach, the Super Etendard can be flown at only 125kt (230km/h).

Maximum level speed at 36,000ft (11,000m) is Mach 1, impressive performance for an aircraft without an afterburner. On trials, the aircraft is reported to have gone marginally supersonic, clocking up Mach 1.1. At low level, the aircraft can manage 650kt (1,204km/h).

Its performance in the air-to-air role is limited. Dassault has never released figures for climb performance, but the service ceiling is only 45,000ft (13,700m). This would allow the aircraft to dispose of snooping Tu-16s, Tu-95s or Il-38s. Launched on an interceptor mission complete with two Magics and two external tanks, Super Etendard has a tactical radius of 650nm (1,200km).

The AM.39 Exocet is a large and "draggy" store, but only one round is carried at a time. Its effect is offset by the carriage of external tanks under the opposite wing and on the fuselage centreline. In this configuration, Super Etendard has a hi-lo-hi range of 460nm (850km).

A-10A THUNDERBOLT II

DEVELOPMENT

At first sight, the Fairchild A-10 seems an unlikely combat aircraft for the 1980s. In size, this single-seat close-support aircraft rivals the World War II B-25 Mitchell bomber, while its top speed of 380kt (700km/h) could be comfortably exceeded by World War II piston-engined fighters such as the P-51 Mustang, Tempest and FW-109. Despite these apparently unambitious figures, the A-10 plays a major role in maintaining USAF ground-attack strength, and would be one of the major anti-armour weapons deployed against a present-day Westward thrust by the Warsaw Pact.

Although fielded as a specialised anti-tank/close support aircraft intended to operate in the European environment, the A-10 owes its origins to a late 1960s requirement for a low-cost aircraft to replace the Douglas A-1 Skyraider. As was the case in Korea during the early 1950s, the USAF found itself fighting an infantry war without a suitable close-support aircraft. High-technology aircraft such as the A-6 Intruder and F-111 were designed to penetrate the best defensive systems which Soviet technology could create, delivering heavy ordnance loads or even nuclear weapons onto fixed targets, but were hardly suitable for laying down heavy loads of iron bombs, cluster munitions, napalm and unguided rockets on near-invisible targets close to friendly troop positions. Toggling ordnance loads on to enemy bunkers and defensive positions was seen as a prosaic task best left to older fighters such as the F-100.

Experience showed that one of the best aircraft for close-support work was the A-1 Skyraider. A veteran of the 1950s, this aircraft was cheap to operate, carried four 20mm cannon in the wings, had enough hardpoints to carry a heavy ordnance load, and was tough enough to take combat damage and still get home. Unfortunately,

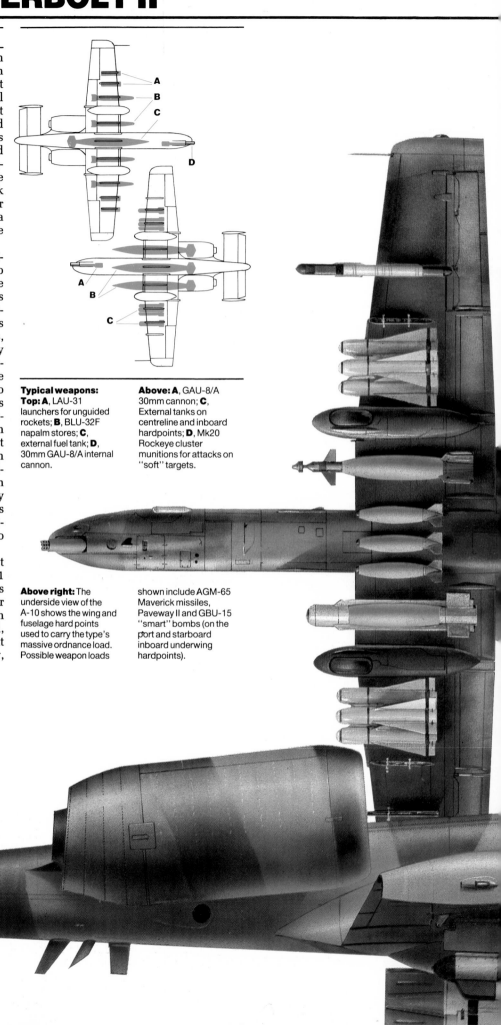

Typical weapons: Top: A, LAU-31 launchers for unguided rockets; **B**, BLU-32F napalm stores; **C**, external fuel tank; **D**, 30mm GAU-8/A internal cannon.

Above: A, GAU-8/A 30mm cannon; **C**, External tanks on centreline and inboard hardpoints; **D**, Mk20 Rockeye cluster munitions for attacks on "soft" targets.

Above right: The underside view of the A-10 shows the wing and fuselage hard points used to carry the type's massive ordnance load. Possible weapon loads shown include AGM-65 Maverick missiles, Paveway II and GBU-15 "smart" bombs (on the port and starboard inboard underwing hardpoints).

Left: The predominant element in the plan view of the A-10 is the straight line. Curves result in engineering and manufacturing complexity, and thus cost, so the austere lines of the A-10 reflect the decision to go for a relatively low-cost, battleworthy aircraft. Wherever possible, components were designed to be interchangeable between the right and left-hand sides in order to reduce spares holdings and to ease maintenance. The sheer size of the A-10 would make it a conspicuous target in crowded European skies. The Soviet Union has many obsolescent MiG-17 and early-model MiG-21s in reserve. These could form a potent anti-A-10 force. The A-10 would be relatively easy to acquire by eyeball if the USAF pilot allowed himself to be briefly silhouetted against the sky.

Below: A-10As of the 917th TFG from Carswell AFB, Texas. The green camouflage scheme would do a good job at low level, but if these aircraft ever go to war, someone should paint the add-on Pave Penny and ECM pods!

Below left: The raised canopy of the A-10A gives the pilot good all-round visibility, while the pod-mounted Pave Penny laser spot tracker (just below the cockpit) helps him find laser-marked targets. The slanted rear edge of the jetpipes is intended to minimise the thermal target presented to Soviet SA-7 SAMs.

there were just not enough of these veterans left, and combat attrition was slowly thinning out the remaining examples.

At one point, the Pentagon even considered returning the Skyraider to production, but cost studies suggested that the design could not economically be resurrected. Instead, USAF planners drew up a specification for an aircraft A-X. Studies were carried out in 1966 starting from a blank sheet of paper—no-one had any idea just how a dedicated close-support aircraft should be configured, but the USAF was determined to find out. Key areas of the new requirement were manoeuvrability, survivability, lethality, simplicity, long endurance, fast reaction time, and the ability to operate from unprepared airstrips.

In the late 1960s General Dynamics, Grumman, McDonnell Douglas and Northrop worked with the USAF to refine further the A-X concept, and in May 1970

Northrop and Fairchild were asked to develop and test-fly rival designs designated YA-9A and YA-10A respectively. The YA-10 flew for the first time on May 10, 1972, beating the YA-9A by 20 days, and two examples of both designs were in the hands of USAF evaluation pilots by October. Selection of the Fairchild design as the winner was announced on January 18, 1973, and the company was given a $159.2 million contract for the first 10 production aircraft.

Congress required some convincing that the A-X concept was valid, and insisted on a second fly-off, this time against the Vought A-7. This took place in April and May of 1974, with the A-10A being declared the winner on June 20.

Original planning assumed a total buy of 600, but this was soon increased. The target figure was to fluctuate between 707 and 825 during the life of the programme. Production was slowly built up to a peak

of 144 aircraft per year, and by the early 1980s most had been delivered. President Carter's FY82 budget request allocated no funding to the A-10, but the new Reagan Administration restored money for 20 aircraft a year to keep the line rolling, but abandoned the planned A-10B two-seat Combat-Ready Trainer version.

Funding for the first 14 trainers had originally been planned in the FY82 budget. Broadly similar in appearance and performance to the single-seater, the A-10B would have carried a revised cockpit with an enlarged canopy, a second ejection seat and systems for the second crewman. These changes would have added less than 1,500lb (680kg) to the aircraft weight.

Another abortive two-seat development was the planned Night/Adverse Weather version. A two-seat A-10 was originally devised in 1976 as a possible FAC-X forward air control aircraft for the USAF.

Fairchild A-10 Thunderbolt II
1. Cannon muzzles.
2. Forward radar warning antennae.
3. ILS aerial.
4. Air refuelling ramp door.
5. Air refuelling receptacle.
6. Pave Penny laser ranger and marked target seeker pod.
7. Rudder pedals.
8. Hinged windscreen panel, instrument access.
9. Head-up display.
10. Control column.
11. Pilot's instrument display.
12. Engine throttle levers.
13. McDonnell-Douglas ACES 2 ejection seat.
14. Canopy jettison strut.
15. Canopy actuator.
16. Leading edge stall strip.
17. Starboard wing stores pylons.
18. Cockpit canopy cover.
19. Pitot tube.
20. Starboard navigation and strobe lights.
21. Starboard aileron.
22. Split aileron/deceleron.
23. Deceleron operating jack.
24. Aileron hydraulic actuator.
25. Aileron tab.
26. Cockpit air valves.
27. IFF aerial.
28. Tab balance weight.
29. Anti-collision light.
30. UHF/TACAN aerial..
31. Starboard single slotted Fowler-type flaps.
32. Flap guide rail.
33. Flap hydraulic actuator.
34. Fuselage fuel cells.
35. Conditioned air delivery duct.
36. General Electric TF34-GE-100 turbofan engine.
37. Engine oil tank.
38. Engine accessory equipment gearbox.
39. Bleed air ducting.
40. Air conditioning system intake and exhaust duct.

41. Heat exchanger.
42. Fire extinguisher bottle.
43. Starboard tailfin.
44. X-band aerial.
45. Rudder mass balance.
46. Rudder.
47. Fan air exhaust duct.
48. Core engine exhaust duct.
49. Trim tab actuator.
50. Elevator tab.
51. Starboard elevator.
52. Elevator hydraulic actuators.
53. Rear radar warning receiver.

54. Tail navigation light.
55. Port elevator.
56. Port tailfin.
57. Rudder hydraulic actuator.
58. Formation light.
59. IFF aerial.
60. Elevator mechanical linkage.
61. UHF/TACAN aerial.
62. VHF/AM aerial.

63. Fuel jettison.
64. Air system ground connection.
65. Hydraulic reservoir.
66. VHF aerial.
67. Hydraulic system ground connections.
68. APU exhaust.

69. Auxiliary Power Unit (APU).
70. Air conditioning unit.
71. Port Fowler flaps.
72. Flap self-aligning torque shaft.
73. Trim tab control rod.
74. Aileron trim tab.

75. Split aileron/deceleron.
76. Strobe light.
77. Port navigation light.
78. Port aileron.
79. Cambered wing tip fairing.
80. Deceleron operating jack.
81. Aileron hydraulic actuator.
82. ECM pod.
83. Aileron mechanical linkage.

84. Flap hydraulic actuators.
85. Hydraulic retraction jack.
86. Main undercarriage pivot bearing.
87. Chaff/flare dispenser.
88. Forward-retracting mainwheel.
89. Leading edge stall strip.
90. Port wing stores pylons.
91. Maverick air-to-ground missiles.

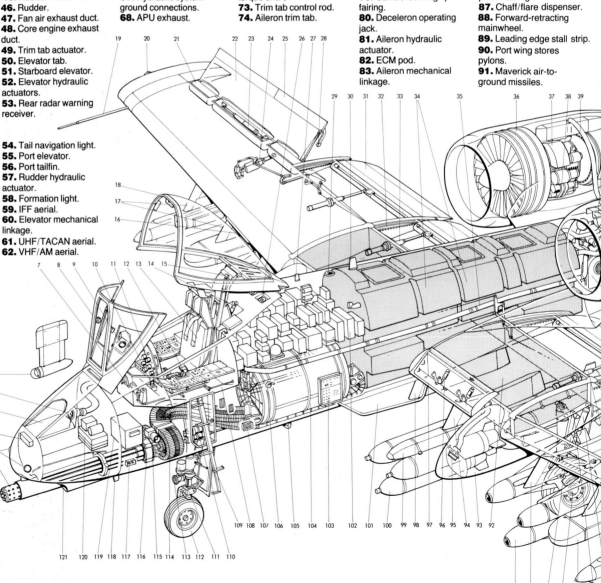

This project never came to fruition, but Fairchild decided to press ahead with a private-venture two-seater in the hopes of selling the result to the USAF as a specialised night/all-weather attack aircraft. The new variant would have a 94 per cent structural commonality and some 80 per cent equipment commonality with the basic A-10A, the company claimed, while new items of specialised nav/attack avionics would allow operation with cloud ceilings down to 300ft (90m) and in visibility of down to a mile (1.6km).

An experimental prototype using pod-mounted systems was flown for the first time on May 4, 1979. Following four months of company flight test, it was handed over to the USAF for 300 hours of flying at Eglin AFB, Florida. Despite successful night operations against moving targets such as armoured vehicles, the USAF declined to place an order, hoping to obtain much of the night/adverse

weather capability it would need from the LANTIRN pod system being developed for both this aircraft and the F-16.

Fairchild tried hard to obtain export orders, but the fact remains that few air forces outside the superpowers can afford to deploy a specialised single-mission aircraft costing some $10 million a copy at early 1980s prices. Potential customers included Chile, Egypt, Morocco, Pakistan, Peru, Thailand, and Venezuela. At one time Peru seemed likely to be the first export customer, evaluating the type in late 1981 as a possible Canberra replacement, only to turn it down the following year.

As the line began to run down, Fairchild proposed a number of other variants of the A-10 in the hope of obtaining further orders, but none attracted an order. The 713th and final A-10A was delivered to the USAF in April 1984, ending the 11-year production run.

STRUCTURE

The shape of the A-10 looks distinctly odd by modern standards, almost as if the team which designed the Heinkel 162 Volksjäger in 1944 had returned to their drawing boards to create a modern twin-engined version. Form has been dictated by function, however, and the aircraft's shape is the result of careful design.

Best-known feature of the fuselage is the armoured "bathtub" which protects the cockpit area. Manufactured from titanium, it is designed to withstand direct hits from cannon shells of 23mm calibre—the type fired by the Soviet ZSU-23-4 Shilka self-propelled anti-aircraft gun. The remainder of the fuselage is of more orthodox design, and built from aluminium alloy.

The wing is of straight form and three-spar construction, and has 7 degrees of dihedral on the outer panels. Control surfaces consist of two-section trailing-edge

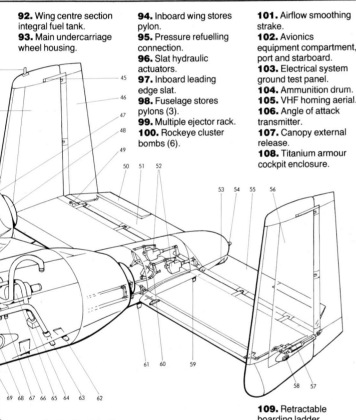

92. Wing centre section integral fuel tank.
93. Main undercarriage wheel housing.
94. Inboard wing stores pylon.
95. Pressure refuelling connection.
96. Slat hydraulic actuators.
97. Inboard leading edge slat.
98. Fuselage stores pylons (3).
99. Multiple ejector rack.
100. Rockeye cluster bombs (6).
101. Airflow smoothing strake.
102. Avionics equipment compartment, port and starboard.
103. Electrical system ground test panel.
104. Ammunition drum.
105. VHF homing aerial.
106. Angle of attack transmitter.
107. Canopy external release.
108. Titanium armour cockpit enclosure.

Above: The A-10 cannot be called a beautiful aircraft, but this photo captures its power and sheer size. A 1940s aircraft of this size would have had several gun turrets and a crew of five or six men.

Below: The sole prototype of the two-seat Night/Adverse Weather A-10. Despite a successful test programme, the USAF declined to order this version. In the author's opinion, this was a wrong decision. The A-10 NAW would have given the USAF what it often needs but rarely has – a close support aircraft able to hit the bad guys in any weather by day or by night. Have the lessons of Vietnam been forgotten?

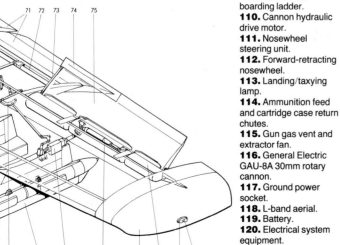

109. Retractable boarding ladder.
110. Cannon hydraulic drive motor.
111. Nosewheel steering unit.
112. Forward-retracting nosewheel.
113. Landing/taxiing lamp.
114. Ammunition feed and cartridge case return chutes.
115. Gun gas vent and extractor fan.
116. General Electric GAU-8A 30mm rotary cannon.
117. Ground power socket.
118. L-band aerial.
119. Battery.
120. Electrical system equipment.
121. Gun compartment venting intake.

flaps, a small leading edge slat on the inboard wing sections, and ailerons which split into upper and lower sections to serve as airbrakes. Large fairings buried in the wing house the main legs of the undercarriage. Even when the latter is retracted, the tyres protrude slightly, a feature designed to allow the aircraft to carry out "wheels-up" landings with minimal damage should the undercarriage fail to extend.

The novel rear-fuselage engine installation keeps the powerplants well apart, minimising the risk that combat damage to one will also affect the other. The engines are in a good position to avoid ingesting gun gas or runway dirt (a good feature for an aircraft intended for deployment at temporary airstrips). They are also in a good position to ingest turbulent air should the wing stall, a problem discovered in early trials, but soon fixed.

The twin tails offer further aids to survivability. If one is shot away or suffers rudder damage, the pilot can still maintain control with the other. In combat, the vertical and horizontal surfaces screen the hot aft section of the engines from the attention of simple man-portable heat-seeking missiles such as the SA-7.

Much attention was given at the design stage to survivability and maintainability. The fuel tanks—two tear-resistant, self-sealing tanks in the fuselage and two integral tanks in the wing centre section—are filled with reticulated foam to minimise the chance of fire following a hit, while all pipework external to the cells is fitted with a self-sealing cover. Total internal capacity is 10,700lb (4,850kg), and may be supplemented by up to three 600 gallon (2,270 litre) external tanks.

All control surfaces are hydraulically actuated, the control systems have built-in redundancy and being protected by armour. To minimise front-line spares holdings, right and left-hand flaps, control surfaces and their actuators, undercarriage legs, and engines are interchangeable between right and left-hand sides.

The only significant structural modifications which the aircraft has seen are the revised two-seat cockpit proposed for the abandoned trainer and night/all-weather attack versions. The sole prototype of the latter was the only aircraft to have an enlarged tail, whose vertical surfaces were increased in height by some 20in (50cm).

POWERPLANT

The General Electric TF34-GE-100 is a twin-spool, high bypass-ratio turbofan originally developed as the 9,275lb (4,207kg) thrust powerplant of the US Navy's S-3A Viking ASW aircraft. The slightly downrated TF34-100 selected for the A-10 is rated at 9,065lb (4,112kg), and has a specific fuel consumption of 0.371lb/lb/hr. This is slightly higher than the 0.363lb/lb/hr figure of the Navy's -400A engine, but is good news for a pilot who intended to fly long sorties, loitering near the FEBA to await requests for close-

support to be made by the troops on the ground.

The first TF34-GE-100 ran in July 1973, and completed its MQT trials in October of the following year, in good time to meet the February 1975 flight date of the first A-10 DT&E aircraft. Delivery of production engines started in June of the same year, and more than 1,700 examples of this variant have now been built.

The engine is 100in (254cm) long, 49in (124cm) in diameter, and weighs 1,439lb (653kg). A simple intake of annular form without inlet struts or guide vanes leads to a single-stage fan with 28 wide-chord titanium blades. This is followed by a 14-stage axial compressor whose first five stators are variable—a common feature on GE engines. The early stages are manufactured from titanium, the remainder from nickel alloy. An annular combustor fitted with 18 burners and borescope ports for engine inspection passes hot gas to a two-stage high-pressure and four-stage low-pressure turbine.

AVIONICS

By modern avionics standards, the A-10 started life not so much austere as near-naked. The most complex items fitted to the basic aircraft were the RWR and the equipment associated with the AGM-65 Maverick missile, but an inertial navigation system was soon added. Most of the remaining equipment was a versatile communications fit including VHF/AM, VHF/

FM, UHF/AM and UHF/ADF radios, plus IFF and crypto equipment for secure voice communications.

Inevitably, this simple fit has since been supplemented. Normally carried on a short pylon on the lower right-hand side of the fuselage (just forward of the cockpit), the 32lb (14.5kg) Westinghouse Pave Penny laser-designation pod detects targets marked by laser designators carried by ground troops or in other aircraft, passing data to the pilot's HUD and to the aircraft weapon-delivery system.

A complex suite of avionic systems was test-flown on the prototype Night/All-Weather version of the aircraft. This included a Westinghouse WX-50 terrain-following radar, Ferranti laser rangefinder, Texas Instruments AN/AAR-42 FLIR, and a Litton LN-39 inertial navigation set. The prototype installation was pod-mounted, but the definitive aircraft would have carried the new sensors internally.

In the long-term, the USAF hopes to retrofit the aircraft with the Martin Marietta LANTIRN (Low Altitude Navigation Targeting Infrared for Night), a pod-mounted thermal imaging sight intended to provide a night low-altitude attack capability. Currently under engineering development for use on the A-10 and F-16, it consists of two externally-mounted pods. The navigation pod weighs about 400lb (180kg) and contains a Ku-band terrain-following radar plus a wide field-of-view FLIR whose output is displayed in the form of imagery on the pilot's raster-scanned HUD. The 500lb (225kg) targeting pod houses an optical stabilisation system which is shared by wide and narrow field-of-view FLIR, a laser designator/range-finder, plus dual-mode automatic trackers. Plans for the installation of an automatic target-recogniser facility within the targeting pod have been postponed due to the degree of technological risk involved.

The USAF is pressing ahead with development of the system, despite the fact that LANTIRN has been heavily criticised by Congress. At one point, the cost of the programme almost led to cancellation, but the US Department of Defense finally accepted the USAF's claim that the project was essential to its future plans. Flight tests are currently under way, and Congress has asked that the system be tested in competition with the AAS-38 FLIR pod being developed for use on the F-18.

Shortage of defense funds prevented this competitive evaluation from being carried out, and at the time this text was prepared the USAF had been allocated only sufficient LANTIRN money to continue performance evaluation of the first development pods. Production or any preparations for production have been ruled out by Congress until alternatives to LANTIRN have been fully explored. At an estimated unit price of more than $5 million per aircraft, the system seems

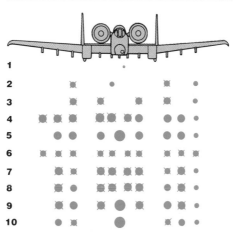

1
2
3
4
5
6
7
8
9
10

Possible weapons:
1. Internal GAU-8/A 30mm cannon.
2. AGM-65 Maverick air-to-surface missiles and pylon-mounted Pave Penny sensor.
3. GBU-10 laser-guided bombs (interdiction missions).
4. Mk 20 Rockeye cluster munitions (counter-insurgency missions or other strikes against soft targets).
5. LAU-3 rocket launchers plus a centreline fuel tank (FAC missions).
6. Mk82 GP high-explosive bombs (attack missions).

7. AGM-65 Maverick (on triple launchers) plus Rockeye or . . .
8. SUU-25 flares (armed reconnaissance missions).
9. LAU-8 launchers for unguided rockets (on triple launchers), plus Rockeyes and a centreline tank (combat rescue escort missions).
10. Maverick (on triple launchers), SUU-25 flares and a centreline tank (maritime strike missions).
In all cases, a single ALQ-119 jamming pod is carried on the port outboard hardpoint for self-protection.

bound to attract further political controversy, and its future is far from secure.

ARMAMENT

Most important weapon carried by the A-10 is the General Electric GAU-8/A seven-barrel 30mm cannon. This is a rotary-barrelled weapon of the Gatling type able to fire its 1,170 rounds of ammunition at a rate of 70 rounds per second, some three times the rate possible with rotary-breech weapons such as the 30mm ADEN and DEFA. The weapon is intended to deal with enemy armour, so fires discarding-sabot projectiles (manufactured from depleted-uranium) at muzzle velocities 3,500ft/sec (1,066m/sec). A one second burst should be sufficient to deal with most main battle tanks, and the ammunition drum carried by the A-10 has enough ammunition for more than 15 such bursts. The gunsight has no air-to-air modes, but any pilots managing to get a MiG in the sight are unlikely to be deterred from trying a quick burst.

Eleven hardpoints are fitted as standard—four under each wing and three beneath the fuselage. In practice however, all three of the latter cannot be used at the same time. Ordnance must be fitted either to the centreline pylon, or to the flanking pylons. A maximum load of 16,000lb (7,260kg) may be carried, including Mk 82 or Mk 84 "iron" bombs or their laser-guided equivalents, BLU-1 or BLU-27/B incendiary bombs, CBU-52/71 or Rockeye

Above: Practice firing with the GAU-8/A 30mm cannon. Many A-10 pilots regard this as the primary anti-tank weapon, claiming that each well-aimed one-second burst would be enough to knock out a Soviet main battle tank.

Below: An A-10 at the beginning of a training sortie. The photo exaggerates the bulk of the engine pod and the degree to which the ALQ-119 jamming pod protrudes ahead of the starboard wing. (It is carried on either wing.)

Left: Pilots assigned to the A-10 after flying the F-4 must have wondered where all the instruments and displays had gone. The most exotic item of kit visible in this cockpit view is the CRT display for Maverick (at upper right of instrument panel).

Stand-off Maverick launch

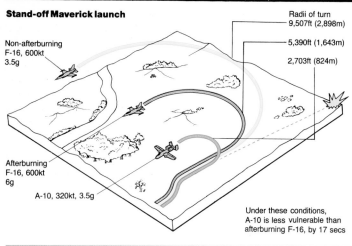

Non-afterburning
F-16, 600kt
3.5g

Afterburning
F-16, 600kt
6g

A-10, 320kt, 3.5g

Radii of turn
9,507ft (2,898m)

5,390ft (1,643m)

2,703ft (824m)

Under these conditions, A-10 is less vulnerable than afterburning F-16, by 17 secs

Left: The lower speed and tighter turning circle of the A-10A minimise the distance which the aircraft must fly towards its target after releasing a Maverick missile. The three flight paths shown are those for (in increasing size) a 320kt (590km/h) A-10 pulling 3.5g, a 600kt (1,110km/h) F-16 pulling 6g, and a 600kt F-16 pulling 3.5g. Turn radii are 2,700ft (824m), 5,400ft (1,643m) and 9,500ft (2,898m), respectively. In these circumstances, the A-10 would appear to be less vulnerable.

cluster munitions, SUU-23 gun pods, or AGM-65 Maverick missiles. Countermeasures systems such as the ALQ-119 jamming pod and the ALE-40 chaff/flare dispenser may also be carried.

PERFORMANCE

Top speed of an A-10 at sea level and in clean condition is a mere 380kt (705km/h) while "never-exceed" speed is only 450kt (835km/h). By modern standards, these figures may seem unimpressive at first sight, but detailed reading of the A-10 specification shows that the aircraft is well matched to its intended role. Heavily loaded, few fighters will do much in

excess of 450kt under similar conditions, even if their top speed is Mach 2, but with two TF34s pushing, the A-10 driver knows that his maximum speed is available even when carrying a heavy warload. Flying at 5,000ft (1,500m) with a load of six Mk 82 bombs, the aircraft can still make its nominal 380kt.

At maximum take-off weight, the aircraft can get airborne from 4,000ft (1,200m) strips and land in half that length. At a forward-airstrip weight of 32,770lb (14,865kg)—four Mk 82 bombs, 750 rounds of ammunition, plus 4,500lb (2,040kg) fuel load—the A-10 needs only 1,450ft (440m) of take-off run, and 1,300ft (395m) on landing. Assuming a 1.7hr

loiter and a 20min fuel reserve, the aircraft has a range of 250nm (463km), rising to 540nm (1,000km) for a deep strike mission against a known target. Ferry range against a 50kt (90km/h) headwind is more than 2,100nm (3,950km).

Like the dedicated attack aircraft of yesteryear such as the Ju-87 Stuka, Il-2 Stormovik and Henschel Hs-129, the A-10 relies on air superiority having been won by its air force's fighters. Jumped by MiGs or other agile fighters, it could be badly mauled. But the job of the A-10 is not to play Red Baron but to get ordnance on target, come home, reload, and fly off to repeat the performance again and again until the battle is won.

Several years ago, the author discussed A-10 survivability with one of the first USAF pilots to be assigned to the type—a Vietnam veteran. The A-10 was no "bulletproof airplane" he insisted. "If a Shilka gets a good sight on you, it could saw the wing clean off with 23mm fire— no airplane can take a large number of hits and survive. But most of the aircraft downed in action just get a few rounds ... and we lost a lot of good guys in Vietnam to those 'few round' kills. Sure, you'd lose of lot of guys in a Central Front battle—but a large number of A-10s and their pilots would be able to come home after hits which would have downed a lesser airplane."

Left: As the aircraft turns away, note how the tail fin and fuselage begin to screen the hot jetpipes of the TF34 turbofans, a precaution against heat-seeking air-defence weapons.

Right: Some A-10 "drivers" claim that their massive mount "makes military flying fun again". The pilot performing for the camera makes rolling this 20-ton Maverick-armed warplane seem effortless.

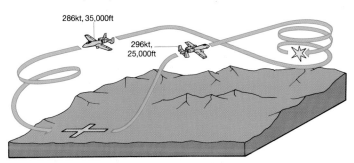

Close air support design mission
Mission radius 250nm (463km)

286kt, 35,000ft

296kt, 25,000ft

Left: Close support mission with a payload of 18 Mk82 bombs. The aircraft would cruise out at 296kt (25,000ft (548km/h, 7,600m), loiter in a combat area 250nm (463km) from the take-off point for 1.88hr at 174kt/ 5,000ft (322km/h, 1,500m), drop its ordnance during 10 minutes of sea-level combat at 300kt (555km/h), then return home at 286kt/35,000ft (530km/h, 10,670m).

Battlefield support mission
Mission radius 252nm (467km)

Sea level penetration and exit

Cruise out and back at 5,000ft

Left: Battlefield support mission with six AGM-65, an ALQ-119 jammer plus full internal fuel and ammunition. Allowing for a 5,000ft (1,500m) cruise to and from the target area, a 40nm (75km) sea-level run into and out of the target area, and a 30 minute period of combat at full power, the A-10A has a tactical radius of 252nm (467km). Maximum airspeed on such a mission would be 368kt (680km/h).

Low angle gun power

Short exposure above terrain masking, and during attack

Very low egress and manoeuvre for re-attack

Left: In combat, the A-10 would fly pop-up manoeuvres to locate targets for gun attack, then dive to bring the GAU-8/A to bear. This simple diagram exaggerates the aircraft's operating height – for most of the time, the A-10 would fly as low as possible in order to avoid being tracked by radar or engaged by enemy gun or missile systems.

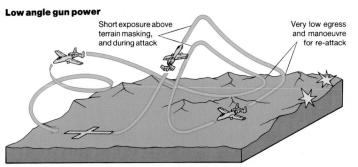

F-16 FIGHTING FALCON

DEVELOPMENT

Early in the morning of June 7, 1981, eight Israeli jet fighters carried out a daring low-level air attack against Iraq's Osirak nuclear reactor at Twartha near Baghdad. Due to become operational within months, this installation could in theory have produced sufficient plutonium to allow Iraq to construct up to five 20kT nuclear weapons by the mid-1980s.

Despite the reported presence of Thomson-CSF/Matra Crotale firing units, Soviet SAMs and radar-guided anti-aircraft guns, the attackers were able to land several 2,000lb (900kg) Mk 84 bombs on the 105ft (32m) diameter concrete cupola covering the reactor with an accuracy initially ascribed to "smart" bombs or other guided weaponry. A few minutes later, the attackers headed for home, leaving the reactor badly damaged and buried in rubble—a highly successful if politically embarrassing combat debut for the F-16 Fighting Falcon.

The raid highlighted just two of the features of this small but highly-combat-effective warplane. Its long range and high navigation accuracy had allowed a strike to be mounted at a long range from the nearest Israeli base, while the pinpoint weapon delivery had allowed the attack to be carried out using only a handful of aircraft. The lessons of this raid will not be lost on future customers for high-performance multirole fighters, and augur well for future sales of the type, which promises to become the F-4 of the 1980s and 1990s.

The first contract for what was to become the F-16 was awarded to General Dynamics early in 1972, when the company received $38 million to develop two YF-16 prototypes which would be test-flown against the rival Northrop YF-17. The Lightweight Fighter programme was intended to explore the military usefulness of small fighters weighing about 10 tonnes fully loaded, and to assess the advantages of new technology such as relaxed-stability.

The goal of the new designs was optimum performance at the speeds and altitudes thought likely to form the arena for future air combat—30,000 to 40,000ft (9,140 to 12,190m) and speeds of Mach 0.6 to 1.6. A high priority was placed on parameters such as turn rate, acceleration and range. Although intended as technology-demonstration programmes, both designs were drawn up with the possibility of a follow-on production model very much in mind. High-technology features adopted by the GD team included relaxed stability, fly-by-wire control, wing/body blending and strakes, variable camber and a reclining seat intended to improve the pilot's resistance to g loads.

First "official" flight of the YF-16 took place on February 2, 1974, although the aircraft had already carried out a six-minute circuit and landing two weeks before when GD test pilot Phil Oestricher

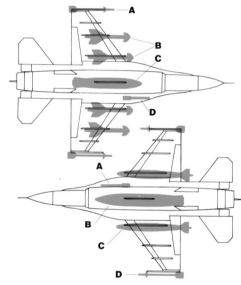

Above: As an F-16A pulls up to a high angle of attack during a test flight, local condensation shows the position of the vortexes created by the leading-edge extensions. Streaming back over the wing surface, these keep the local boundary air energised, delaying the point at which the wing will finally stall. This technique allowed the F-16 designers to reduce the size and aspect ratio of the wing. Structural weight of the Fighting Falcon thus ended up 570lb (260kg) lighter.

Typical weapons:
Top: For maritime missions, Norwegian F-16s will carry up to four indigenous Penguin Mk3 anti-ship missiles (**B**) plus Sidewinders (**A**) for self-defence. The 20mm internal cannon (**D**) would be effective against air or ground targets. The stores loading shown here includes an external fuel tank (**C**) on the centreline. Penguin Mk3 uses mid-course inertial guidance plus a terminal homing IR seeker.

Above: Israel's daring raid against Iraq's Osirak nuclear reactor was carried out using Mk84 2,000lb (910kg) "iron" bombs rather than LGBs. Each aircraft carried two Mk84s (**C**) probably on the inner underwing hardpoints, plus a large external tank (**B**) to give the range needed to reach the target area deep inside Iraq; the F-16s had no need to use their AIM-9 Sidewinder missiles (**D**) or 20mm internal cannon (**A**).

Below left: The apparently simple lines of the F-16 give no hint of a design intended to offer high performance while being easy to build and maintain. This view shows the wing and its leading-edge extensions (note the gun port on the port side), the definitive pattern of horizontal stabiliser and the airbrakes located on each side of the afterburner. The skin of the aircraft incorporates large numbers of access panels to help ground crews service the avionics, hydraulics, fuel pumps and lines, and other on-board systems. As a result, Fighting Falcon should be easier to maintain than the F-4.

Above right: The F-16 will be progressively updated in the mid-to-late 1980s. It will be the first USAF fighter to carry the new Hughes AIM-120A AMRAAM, seen here just inboard of the wingtip-mounted Sidewinders. The aircraft shown here carries a Westinghouse ALQ-131 jamming pod on the centreline, but a later retrofit programme will replace this with the internally-mounted Advanced Self-Protection Jammer (ASPJ).

Below left: By the time that the F-16 closes to gun range, its AIM-9 (wingtip) and AIM-120A (underwing) missiles could have despatched four enemy aircraft. Having dealt with the airborne opposition, this multi-role aircraft will be free to attack ground targets with its "iron" bombs.

opted to lift off after allowing an excessively high speed to build up during a taxi trial.

Following the fly-off against the YF-17, the GD aircraft was selected for service as an operational fighter, flight trials having shown the YF-16 to be "significantly better", particularly at supersonic and near-supersonic speeds. Acceleration, endurance and turning capability were all superior to those of the YF-17.

The production aircraft was slightly scaled-up from the YF-16 design, incorporating a longer and wider nose able to house a multi-mode radar, an additional pair of hardpoints beneath a wing of slightly increased area, a horizontal tailplane of increased size, and a modified F100 engine with a jet starter.

Four NATO nations—Belgium. Denmark, the Netherlands and Norway—all

needed a replacement for ageing F-104 Starfighters. Following an evaluation of the YF-16, YF-17, Saab-Scania Draken and an M53-engined Mirage F1, choice of the GD warplane was announced on June 7, 1975.

Under an agreement signed in that year, a total of 348 F-16s for the European partners will be assembled in Europe— 184 at the Fokker plant at Schiphol in the Netherlands, and 164 by SABCA at Gosselies in Belgium. Follow-on orders have now raised this total to 414. Under an offset agreement, European companies involved in the project also work on USAF aircraft and F-16s destined for Third World operators.

The first full-scale development aircraft flew at Fort Worth in December 1976, and formal authority for full-scale production was given the following October, leading

to the first flight of a production aircraft in August 1978. Deliveries started in early 1979. A year later, the air arms of the USA, Belgium, Denmark, Israel, the Netherlands and Norway were all taking delivery of the new aircraft.

The Multi-Stage Improvement Programme (MSIP) is intended to add further refinement to the basic aircraft. The MSIP Phase 1 standard (often referred to as F-16+) incorporates structural changes and new wiring required by Hughes AIM-120 AMRAAM missiles, electro-optical nav/attack systems, internal ECM and other new avionics, plus a modified horizontal tailplane of increased size. Phases 2 and 3 will see these new items of avionics being installed in the F-16C/D version of the aircraft.

Several F-16s have been modified for trials purposes. One of the YF-16 proto-

General Dynamics F-16C Fighting Falcon
1. Pitot tube.
2. Radome.
3. Incidence vane.
4. ILS glideslope aerial.
5. Radar warning aerials.
6. Cockpit pressurization and relief valves.
7. Rudder pedals.
8. Pilot's instrument displays.
9. Head-up display.
10. Fly-by-wire sidestick controller.
11. Canopy cover.
12. McDonnell Douglas ACES II zero-zero ejection seat.
13. Canopy rotary actuator.
14. Liquid oxygen converter.
15. Conditioned air distribution duct.
16. Blast suppression gun muzzle.
17. Forward fuselage fuel tank.
18. Cockpit and avionics air conditioning ducting.
19. Ammunition loading point.
20. Ammunition drum.
21. Emergency power unit.
22. Hydraulic reservoirs.
23. Hydraulic accumulator.
24. Leading edge manoeuvre flap drive motor and control unit.
25. Starboard leading edge manoeuvre flap.
26. Starboard wing integral fuel tank.
27. AIM-9L Sidewinder air-to-air missile.

28. Missile launch rail.
29. Static dischargers.
30. TACAN aerial.
31. Fuel system vent tank.
32. Starboard flaperon.
33. Centre fuselage fuel tank.
34. Flight refuelling ramp door and hydraulic jack.
35. Flight refuelling receptacle.
36. Jet fuel starter.
37. Hydraulic pumps.
38. Generator.
39. Rear fuselage fuel tank.
40. Pratt & Whitney F100-PW-100 (3) afterburning turbofan engine.
41. UHF/IFF aerial.
42. Starboard all-moving tailplane.
43. Flight control system hydraulic accumulators.
44. VHF aerial.
45. Anti-collision strobe light.
46. Tail warning radar.
47. Rudder.
48. Rudder hydraulic actuator.
49. Tail navigation light.
50. ECM power amplifier.
51. ECM aerial.
52. Variable area afterburner nozzle.
53. Nozzle control jacks.
54. Airbrake, upper segment.
55. Airbrake hydraulic jack.

56. Airbrake lower segment.
57. Port all-moving tailplane.
58. Tailplane pivot bearing.
59. Tailplane hydraulic actuator.
60. Formation light.
61. Chaff/flare dispenser.
62. Emergency arrester hook.
63. Flaperon hydraulic actuator.
64. Missile launch rail.
65. Port wing outboard stores pylon.
66. AIM-9L Sidewinder air-to-air missiles.
67. Port flaperon.
68. Port leading edge manoeuvre flap.
69. 500lb bombs.
70. Port wing intermediate stores pylon.
71. Port wing integral fuel tank.
72. Leading edge manoeuvre flap drive shaft.
73. Rotary actuators.
74. Engine fuel system.
75. Pressure refuelling connection.
76. Airframe mounted engine accessory gearbox.

77. Forward-retracting mainwheel.
78. Port wing inboard pylon.
79. Landing/taxying lamp.
80. Main undercarriage hydraulic retraction jack.
81. Manoeuvre flap drive shaft bevel gearbox.
82. External fuel tank.
83. Ammunition feed flexible drive.
84. Ventral fuel tank.

85. Air conditioning system.
86. M-61-A1 Vulcan 20mm rotary cannon.
87. Electrical system equipment.
88. Heat exchanger air intake.
89. Lantirn pod, radar and infra-red navigation and attack system.
90. Nose undercarriage hydraulic retraction jack.
91. Navigation light.

92. Nose undercarriage pivot bearing.
93. Aft retracting nosewheel.
94. Nosewheel steering unit.
95. Avionics equipment bays.
96. UHF/IFF aerial.
97. Avionics cooling air ducting.
98. Engine throttle lever.
99. Canopy emergency release.

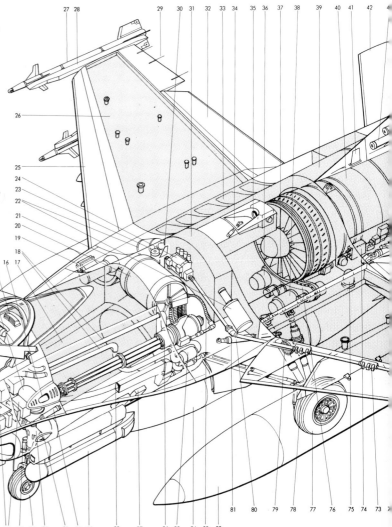

types was rebuilt in the mid-1970s for use as an experimental control-configured vehicle (CCV). Canard control surfaces were fitted beneath the air intake, the fuel system was modified to allow greater control over the aircraft's centre of gravity, and the flight-control system was modified to allow the aircraft to be manoeuvred in ways not possible with conventional controls. Aircraft movements were fully independent or "decoupled"—the F-16/CCV could rise or fall using direct lift, move laterally by direct side force, or yaw, pitch or roll independently of direction of flight.

To evaluate the concept further, the USAF is now flight-testing the AFTI/F-16 (Advanced Fighter Technology Integration). One of the original full-scale development F-16s has been rebuilt, receiving intake-mounted canard surfaces, a triplex digital flight-control system, plus a dorsal spine which houses the additional flight-test avionics.

Originally developed as a private-venture project known as SCAMP (Supersonic Cruise and Manoeuvring Prototype), the F-16XL project involved the third and sixth full-scale development F-16s being flight-tested with a "cranked" delta wing and a slightly stretched fuselage. Despite the extensive nature of these modifications, the rebuilt airframe has more than 70 per cent commonality with the standard pattern.

The first F-16XL flew on July 15, 1982, and was followed three months later by an F110-powered two-seater. A USAF evaluation began in the summer of 1982 to assess the type's suitability as a long-range strike fighter, but in February 1984 the Service selected the F-15E version of the Eagle to become its Dual Role Fighter. The F-16XL will be further evaluated, however, with a view to producing perhaps a single-seat advanced version.

The fuselage is built in three sections—forward, centre and aft—and is of semi-monocoque all-metal construction. The wing-body fairings are extended forward and aft of the wing, and act as leading-edge extensions. At high angles of attack, they create vortices which help to maintain airflow across the wing even beyond the stalling point.

The swept vertical fin and all-moving horizontal stabilisers have a conventional aluminium structure, plus skins made from composite materials. Engineering Change Proposal (ECP) 425 increased the size of the horizontal stabiliser, giving the greater authority needed when the aircraft cg is modified by heavy weapon loads. The original component used a titanium pivot shaft and sub-spar, but this expensive material was eliminated as part of the same modification.

Components such as the horizontal tail surfaces, wing flaperons, 80 per cent of the main landing gear components, and many of the actuator units are designed to be interchangeable between port and starboard, minimising the number of spares which must be stocked.

When drawing up specifications for the original YF-16, the USAF asked for the new aircraft to be stressed for a load factor of 7.33g while carrying 80 per cent internal fuel. With an eye on an eventual production version, GD decided design the airframe to cope with 9.0g with a full internal fuel load, and to have a service life of 8,000 hours—twice the specified figure. Some minor strengthening was needed in order to cope with cracks found during ground testing, but the structure has so far proven trouble-free.

The delta wing tested on the F-16XL is of multispar design. Leading-edge sweep angle varies from 50 to 70deg, while area is increased by 120 per cent for a weight increase of only 2,600lb (1,180kg). Carbon composite materials were used for the upper and lower skins, saving around 600lb (270kg) from the wing weight.

STRUCTURE

In designing the F-16, GD tried to keep the structure as simple as possible. Proven constructional techniques were used to keep the price down, and to create a design which could easily be manufactured and maintained, and was suitable for licence production in aircraft plants not equipped to the latest US standards. It is likely that the Fort Worth design team had their sights set on the lucrative European market from the start of the programme to replace the widely-deployed F-104 Starfighter

Most of the structure is manufactured

100. Fire control system electronics.
101. Radar equipment bay.
102. AN/APG-66 pulse doppler flat plate radar antenna.

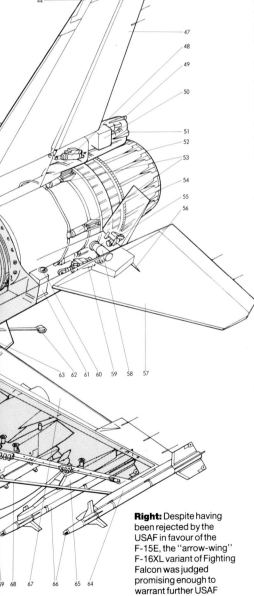

45
46
44
47
48
49
50
51
52
53
54
55
56
63 62 61 60 59 58 57
69 68 67 66 65 64

Right: Despite having been rejected by the USAF in favour of the F-15E, the "arrow-wing" F-16XL variant of Fighting Falcon was judged promising enough to warrant further USAF development.

from aluminium alloy. Around 60 per cent of the parts are made from sheet metal, while less than 2 per cent require chemical milling. Steel accounts for around 8 per cent, composites less than 3 per cent, and titanium only 1.5 per cent.

The design of the wing represented a trade-off between the conflicting demands of take-off and landing, subsonic cruise, combat manoeuvring at high g levels and supersonic flight.

The design finally adopted is of multi-rib construction, with a leading-edge sweep of 40deg, and an aspect ratio of 3.0. Wing skins are conventionally machined rather than chemically milled, a feature which eases production. A low aspect ratio and a thickness of only four per cent help to optimise drag-at-lift and thus transonic manoeuvring.

In order to maintain the handling qualities and performance at other parts of the flight envelope, particularly at between Mach 0.8 to 1.6 (the likely range of air combat speeds), variable camber is used.

Instead of the slotted pattern of leading-edge flaps often used in other aircraft, the F-16 wing incorporates plain flaperons (combined flap/aileron) surfaces. The leading edge is fitted with full-span manoeuvring flaps. Throughout the flight, the F-16 flight-control system adjusts the angles of the leading and trailing-edge surfaces to match the wing to changing Mach number and angle of attack. Drag is reduced, lift is thus maintained at high angles of attack, while directional stability is improved and buffeting minimised.

Near the wing root, the depth is increased to the point where the wing blends smoothly into the fuselage. This wing/body blending provides the internal volume needed to house the massive payload of fuel—some 31 per cent of the all-up weight—and makes the wing stiffer than that of other designs.

Above: To meet the needs of the air forces of Belgium, Denmark, the Netherlands and Norway, the F-16 is being built under licence in Europe and assembled on two lines. These aircraft are being completed at the Fokker plant at Schipol in the Netherlands. Some components built in the USA are used in the European aircraft, while offset agreements result in European-built parts being shipped back across the Atlantic to the GD line at Fort Worth, Texas, for incorporation into US-built aircraft.

Below: President Carter's idealistic attitude in the late 1970s towards arms exports saw the development of the J79-powered F-16/79 as an "FX" export fighter. The main result of installing its GE turbojet was to reduce the range of the aircraft. Sustained manoeuvrability was also reduced, but speed and instantaneous manoeuvrability were little affected. Customers have been reluctant to accept a deliberately downgraded aircraft, however, although Singapore is buying.

POWERPLANT

The P&W F100 medium bypass-ratio turbofan offered high thrust and good fuel economy, and had the advantage of already being in USAF service aboard the twin-engined F-15 Eagle. (A full description of this powerplant is given in the F-15 chapter.)

For the Fighting Falcon, P&W developed a modified F100-PW-200 optimised for the single-engined application. This incorporates a back-up fuel control system, plus an extended compressor inlet. Known as the proximate splitter, the latter is intended to prevent any pressure surges in the afterburner from travelling

forward along the bypass duct, and reaching the compressor. This modification was devised in the light of experience with the F-15 Eagle, which suffered a high rate of stagnation-stall failures early in the aircraft's career.

Two versions of the aircraft have flown with alternative powerplants. Intended for the Third-World export market, the F-16/79 is powered by a single General Electric J79 turbojet. The first flight of a re-engined aircraft took place on October 28, 1980, but customers for what is basically a downgraded aircraft have been slow to come forward. To date all export customers have received the standard F-16A, but in the spring of 1984 Singapore asked the US Government for permission to buy eight F-16/79s.

On December 19, 1980, another modified aircraft flew under the power of the General Electric F110 turbofan, an experimental engine based on the powerplant of the B-1 bomber and intended to maintain GE design expertise in the field of high-thrust afterburning turbofans. All trials objectives were accomplished in less than six months.

AVIONICS

The YF-16 prototypes carried only a simple avionics installation, but the design team sized the aircraft to be able to accept a more sophisticated equipment fit including a nose-mounted radar.

The aircraft's centre of gravity is located far enough aft to reduce longitudinal stability and increase manoeuvrability. This may be a plus in terms of air-combat performance, but no human pilot can cope with the task of flying an inherently unstable aircraft. A fly-by-wire stability augmentation and flight-control system is used to translate the pilot's control demands into movements of the aircraft control surfaces, effectively isolating him from the "raw" characteristics of his mount.

Original USAF planning had assumed that its new lightweight fighter would carry a small search radar similar in performance to the Emerson APQ-159 fitted to the Northrop F-5E, but the Westinghouse APG-66 finally chosen is a complex multi-mode pulse-Doppler radar. A medium-PRF set operating in I/J band, it weighs 296lb (134kg), and occupies a mere 3.6 cubic feet (0.1 cubic metres). It operates in conjunction with head-up and head-down displays, and all controls needed during air combat are located on the control "stick" and throttle.

Fighter-sized targets flying at low level can be located at ranges of more than 30nm (55km), though for targets at high altitude, the maximum range is around 40nm (70km). If the pilot can see the target in his HUD, and the range is less than 10nm (18km), the radar will automatically lock on. A "Designate" button on the sidestick controller allows the radar beam to be aligned accurately with one target in a formation. Using a slewable air-combat mode, the pilot can position the antenna

Above: Current powerplant of the F-16 is the Pratt & Whitney F100-PW-200 turbofan shown here – a modified version of the F-15's engine. The P&W engine has had a

troubled career, so the USAF has now decided to split its future F-16 engine buys between the F100 and the rival General Electric F110 power plant.

Below: The latest F-16C/D model introduces a revised cockpit featuring two head-down multipurpose CRT displays located just above the pilot's knees,

plus a wide-angle HUD. The latter was to have been a holographic unit developed in the UK by Marconi Avionics, but USAF decided to use a simpler HUD.

scan pattern to anticipate target manoeuvres.

Air-to-ground modes include ranging (used during continuously-computed impact point and dive-toss attacks), real-beam ground mapping, plus specialised sea-surface search modes. PPI imagery may be "frozen" on the display, and the radar transmitter is turned off so that the aircraft cannot be detected by passive ESM sensors. A moving symbol continues to indicate aircraft motion.

When maximum detail of ground features is required, expanded-beam mapping provides an ×4 magnification of a preselected area of the main display, while Doppler beam sharpened mode (usable at ranges of 10 or 20nm/18 or 36km) can provide a further ×8 magnification of target areas at angles of between 15 and 60deg off the aircraft's velocity vector.

The improved APG-68 radar was developed as part of the MSIP update programme, and is fitted to the F-16C/D. A modified version of the -66, this has a programmable signal processor, plus a dual-mode transmitter with low PRFs for air-to-ground modes and medium to high PRFs for use against air targets. Track-while-scan and raid-assessment modes improve capability against multiple targets, while resistance to ECM has been improved. Radar range against air targets is improved by at least 30 per cent.

Defensive electronic countermeasures (ECM) systems include a radar-warning receiver—normally an Itek ALR-69. This monitors all likely threat frequencies, probably from 2.0 to 18GHz, and is reported to have specialised facilities for the detection of missile-related radars. The choice of active jamming system depends on the user, and not all F-16 operators

Continuously computed release point attack

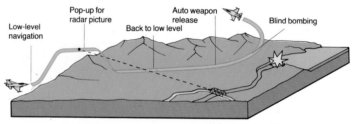

Continuously computed impact point attack

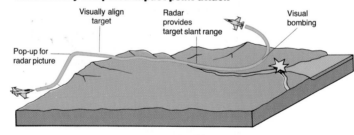

Radar range and field of view

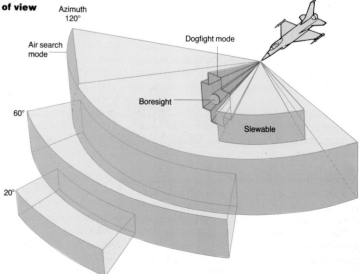

Left: During a continuously computed release point (CCRP) attack, the F-16 will "pop-up" to locate an offset aiming point by radar, then return to low level for the final attack run, following steering instructions on the HUD. The ordnance is released automatically.

Left: In a continuously-computed impact point (CCIP) attack, the pilot will fly a "pop-up" manoeuvre in order to acquire visually his target. As he dives, aligning the HUD aiming mark with the target, the APG-66 radar will provide the nav-attack system with range data.

Right: The Westinghouse APG-66 (F-16A) and APG-68 (F-16C) radars are advanced pulse-doppler sets which combine high performance, light weight and excellent reliability with the multiple operating modes, look-down ability and HOTAS procedures needed in modern air combat. Both sets offer the pilot one, two or four-bar scan search patterns covering 20, 60 and 120deg sectors. Air-combat modes include 20×20deg and 10×40deg patterns which may be slewed to follow movements of the target during a dogfight.

Left: Test-firing of an AGM-65 Maverick air-to-surface missile from an F-16 development aircraft. The test conditions look completely artificial, however. Any pilot attempting a combat launch at such a high altitude in a Central Front conflict would find himself at the receiving end of severe anti-aircraft artillery and missile fire.

Above: Most of the early F-16 training for USAF and foreign pilots alike was carried out by the 388th TFW at Hill AFB, Utah. The high accuracy of the nav/attack system means that fewer bombs need be carried – the configuration of the left-hand aircraft is probably similar to that of the Israeli aircraft which raided Iraq's reactor.

Above: USAF F-16s are deployed around the world as replacements for the earlier F-4 Phantom. Ground crew at Kusan Air Base in the Republic of Korea prepare to load iron bombs onto a Fighting Falcon. This is clearly a training exercise, since the aircraft is in a hangar rather than a hardened shelter.

plan to fit such equipment. The USAF and RNethAF both use the Westinghouse ALQ-131 ECM pod, a 570lb (260kg) modular system developed in the early 1970s. The system can monitor hostile signals, automatically allocating the power of its jamming transmitters according to the perceived threat, and using noise or deception-jamming modes as required.

The Belgian Air Force decided to adopt the Loral Rapport III internal ECM suite, an improved version of the Rapport II carried by its Mirage 5B force. Being internally mounted, Rapport does not tie up a hardpoint or impose a drag penalty, but has eaten into the internal avionics space—part of the system is carried in an extended fairing at the base of the tail fin. Rapport III has also been purchased by Israel for installation in IDFAF Fighting Falcons.

The USAF and US Navy are currently co-operating on the Advanced Self-Protection Jammer (ASPJ). Under development by Westinghouse and ITT, this is due to enter production in 1985. Internal holes and ducts required by the system's waveguides and wiring were added to the aircraft by Phase 1 of the MSIP programme.

MSIP Phase 2 introduces the F-16C/D build standard, with an improved APG-68 radar, Lantirn-compatible HUD, multifunction head-down CRT displays, uprated environmental control equipment and expanded "core" avionics including a revised fire-control computer. Production deliveries could start in December 1984 or early in 1985. MSIP Phase 3 will introduce further refinements such as the Lantirn nav/attack pods, Global Positioning System navigation aid, GE 30mm gun pod, a secure voice system, the ASPJ internally-

mounted jamming system and AIM-120 AMRAAM missile.

Final tests of the experimental AFTI/F-6 will see the installation and flight-test of an Automatic Manoeuvring Attack System (AMAS), incorporating a helmet-mounted sight, digital fire-control computer, Standard Avionics-Integrated Fuzing (SAIF) unit, and a Westinghouse pod-mounted FLIR and laser rangefinder.

The pod will be mounted in the port wing root, and will share the digital programmable signal processor of the APG-66 radar. Its electro-optical systems may be slaved to the radar or helmet sight, so that targets may be tracked passively. The integrated flight/fire-control system will use data from the FLIR to generate the commands needed to steer the aircraft automatically towards the target.

ARMAMENT

The aircraft was designed to handle an air-to-air armament of heat-seeking AIM-9 Sidewinder missiles plus an internally-mounted General Electric M61 cannon plus 500 rounds of ammunition.

Seven hardpoints are provided for ordnance—one on the centreline, and three under each wing, plus wingtip launch rails for Sidewinders. Under the MSIP Phase-1 modifications, the load capacity of the centre wing pylons was increased to 3,500lb (1,600kg) each. Payloads suitable for carriage include iron bombs, smart bombs, or guided missiles such as the AGM-65 Maverick. USAF F-16s may carry nuclear weapons.

The only missile specially designed for use with Fighting Falcon is the Penguin Mk III anti-ship missile. Developed by Kongsberg for installation on Norwegian

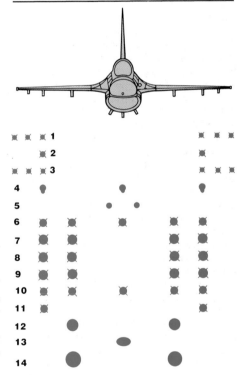

Possible weapons:
1. AIM-9 Sidewinder.
2. AIM-7 Sparrow or BAe Sky Flash.
3. AIM-120A AMRAAM.
4. ALQ-131 ECM pod.
5. Pod-mounted terrain-following radar, infra-red or electro-optical systems.
6. Up to 25 Mk82 1,000lb (450kg) bombs.
7. Mk84 2,000lb (910kg) bombs.
8. Paveway laser-guided bombs.
9. GBU-15 laser-guided bombs.
10. Up to 17 cluster bombs.
11. AGM-65 Maverick TV or IIR-guided missiles.
12. 370gal (1,400lit) external tanks.
13. 300gal (1,136lit) external tanks.
14. 600gal (2,270lit) external tanks.
Other USAF stores could include tactical nuclear weapons and dispensers for NBC agents.

F-16s, this is a development of the existing ship-launched versions of the weapon. Provision was made for the carriage of Sparrow-class missiles at a later date, although these would require the addition of a CW illuminator to the radar in order to provide the missile seekers with the reflected energy onto which they may home.

PERFORMANCE

Full details of the performance of the F-16A and C have not yet been released. During test flights the F-16 has been flown at speeds of greater than Mach 2, and at altitudes in excess of 60,000ft (about 18,300m). Thanks to the massive thrust of the F100, Fighting Falcon can climb at virtually any airspeed. A lightly-loaded F-16 with full internal fuel has a thrust-to-weight ratio of just over 1:1 in full afterburner. Acceleration is outstanding, and the Fighting Falcon should have no problem in outrunning current Soviet types, and should be able to match even the new MiG-29.

In high-speed cruise, the wing leading and trailing-edge flaps are positioned 2 deg above centre. Should the pilot attempt

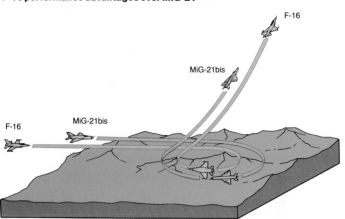

F-16 performance advantages over MiG-21

F-16

MiG-21bis

F-16

MiG-21bis

maximum-rate manoeuvres, the leading edge will move to 25deg down and the trailing edge will move to neutral. Hard manoeuvring at high supersonic speeds can result in some buffeting, according to GD, but for most of the performance envelope Fighting Falcon is buffet-free. Transition through the transonic region is smooth, with only a slight buffeting as speed is increased through Mach 0.95.

Few fighters will be able to out-turn the Fighting Falcon. Maximum instantaneous

Left: The F-16 enjoys a comfortable performance advantage over current Soviet types – it can out-turn the MiG-23 Flogger at sea level and out-turn and out-climb the third-generation MiG-21bis Fishbed at all altitudes. This era of superiority will be eroded in the second half of the present decade as the new MiG-29 Flanker enters service in growing numbers with the Soviet Air Force and is cleared for export. The F-16 might also one day have to face export models of the Mirage 2000.

turn rate is reported to be just over 20deg/sec—a figure 50 per cent greater than that of older fighters such as the Mirage III, F-4 Phantom and Northrop F-5E, and in the same class as the Grumman F-14 and Northrop F-20.

Its most likely opponents in air combat would be the MiG-23 Flogger and the smaller and more agile MiG-21bis third-generation development of the Fishbed. Even at sea level it is able to out-turn the latter aircraft, while the rate of climb,

acceleration and turning performance exceed those of the MiG-21bis at altitudes of up to 30,000ft (9,145m).

No matter how hard the pilot presses on his sidestick controller, the flight-control system ensures that he cannot over-stress the airframe. Angle of attack is limited to 25deg, and the load factor to 9g. In conventional cockpits, pilots often experience tunnel vision—often known as "grey-out"—at levels of around 6 or 7g, but the semi-reclining seat of the F-16 holds the pilot's legs in a raised position and extends his tolerance to 8 or 9g.

Despite having this level of air combat performance, the F-16 is a good weapons platform for ground attack. Even at high speed and low altitude, air turbulence does not create significant aircraft instability, while the nav/attack systems display high accuracy in weapon delivery. According to the USAF, 2,000lb iron bombs can be dropped within 30ft (10m) of a target, five times the accuracy typical of

the F-4 Phantom. Some crews of 8th TFW have managed CEPs of 9ft (2.7m) during 10deg dive attacks.

Substitution of the GE J79 turbojet in place of the F100 has inevitably given the F-16/79 export fighter some reduction in performance, but in some flight conditions the turbojet engine even has an advantage. At speeds above Mach 1.3 the turbojet actually produces more installed thrust than the F100, while in conditions such as low-speed flight at high angles of attack the J79 is more resistant to afterburner blow-outs.

The pilot of an F-16/79 must match aircraft speed and climb rate. Too much or too little speed can reduce climb performance. The lower thrust of the J79 forces him to select afterburner during some manoeuvres which the standard aircraft can manage in dry thrust. The aircraft can operate to the full g limits of the standard F100-powered versions, but cannot maintain them for so long during tight turns.

The need for greater use of the after-burner, and the higher specific fuel consumption of the GE engine cut into the endurance of the F-16/79. Range is some 30 per cent below that of the F100-powered aircraft.

OPERATORS

Belgium: 160 F-16A.

Denmark: 46 F-16A, 12 F-16B.

Egypt: 40 F-16A/B, 40 F-16A/B on order.

Israel: 67 F-16A, 8 F-16B, 75 F-16A/B on order.

Netherlands: 80 F-16A, 22 F-16B, 22 F-16A/B on order.

Norway: 60 F-16A, 12 F-16B.

Pakistan: 40 F-16A/B.

Singapore: 8 F-16/79 on order.

South Korea: 30 F-16A, 6 F-16B.

Thailand: 12 F-16A and 6 F-16B on order.

Turkey: 160 F-16C/D on order (all but 8 to be licence-built).

United States: 700+ F-16A/B in service, a total of 1,019 F-16s already on order to meet a planned requirement of 2,561.

Below: The pilot of this USAF F-16 would be ready for any kind of trouble in enemy airspace, having a multi-role mix of AIM-9s and iron bombs, plus external tanks to extend his endurance, and a centreline ALQ-131 jamming pod intended to deal with hostile radars.

Below: This vertical climb is effortless for the F-16, thanks to the greater than unity thrust-to-weight ratio given by the F100 turbofan. It is more stressful for the pilot who is leaning forward in his seat to hold his torso horizontal – his seat is tilted well below the horizontal.

In combat, the added impetus of the F-16's afterburner offers the pilot "brute force" solutions to any desired manoeuvre, while his opponent might have to conserve energy. The F-16 pilot could pull 9g, but this is probably close to the limit the human body can take.

DEVELOPMENT

If imitation is the sincerest form of flattery, General Dynamics must have been delighted by the emergence in the 1970s of the Soviet Su-24 "Fencer" swing-wing fighter-bomber. The USAF's F-111 had been a controversial programme since it started in the early 1960s, and was even considered a failure by some critics, yet the Soviet fighter shared many of the characteristics of the US warplane—variable-sweep high-mounted wings, twin engines, a two-seat side-by-side cockpit, plus the sophisticated avionics needed for all-weather attack missions at low level.

The F-111 programme began in 1960 in response to USAF SOR (Specific Operational Requirement) 183 which laid down guidelines for a new strike aircraft to replace the Republic F-105 Thunderchief. The USAF wanted to be able to carry two nuclear weapons in an internal bomb bay or a payload of around 10,000lb (4,500kg) of externally-mounted conventional ordnance over long ranges at a speed of Mach 1.2 at treetop height. What the service wanted was a light bomber, but the Thunderchief had been classed as a fighter, and its replacement was termed the Future Tactical Fighter.

The Department of Defense combined this Air Force requirement with a second requirement for a new shipboard interceptor for the US Navy, the joint programme being designated TFX (Tactical Fighter Experimental). A firm believer in the virtues of civilian control over the military, operational analysis of requirements, and standardisation/commonality, Defense Secretary Robert McNamara was sure that the use of variable geometry—a technique made practical by advances in research in the late 1950s—would allow the apparently conflicting requirements for a new interceptor and strike aircraft to be combined. When the services and aircraft companies pointed out that the two requirements could not be reconciled, McNamara had the arrogance

and power to dictate the compromises which both services had to accept.

Following an evaluation of rival designs, General Dynamics was given a contract in November 1962 to develop the new fighter. The company was to concentrate its efforts on the USAF F-111A fighter, while Grumman was tasked with creating the F-111B interceptor for the Navy. A rival Boeing design was adjudged superior in some respects by many USAF experts, but involved what were virtually two different aircraft for the USAF and USN with less of the commonality demanded by McNamara than the GD design.

In 1968, Congress finally cancelled the F-111B, leaving the F-111 strictly a USAF programme. Plans for a long-wing F-111K variant for the Royal Air Force had already been abandoned, so the US Air Force now had to fund the entire programme, leaving the USN to start planning its own specialised interceptor.

In creating the F-111, the GD design team were attempting a major step forward

in aircraft capability. Even without the US Navy's F-111B interceptor requirement, the specification would have challenged any aircraft design team in the world. A few aircraft projects seem to lead charmed lives, with the production hardware proving trouble-free and amply meeting performance requirements laid down in the specification. In most cases, technical troubles result in problems for the designers, but these are usually sorted out, and the production aircraft meets most of its specification. In the case of the F-111, the competence of the designers could not be questioned, but everything seemed to go wrong with the end product—structure, inlets, engine and avionics all displayed problems and required costly redesign, while some of the original and admittedly over-ambitious performance goals were never attained.

Given the wisdom of hindsight, it is easy to see that the production programme was mishandled. Instead of terminating F-111A production as soon as the problems

Above: An F-111D releases 12 Mk82 bombs during a training exercise. Back in 1972 when this photo was taken, the USAF was still content to train at unrealistically high attack altitudes, trusting to efficient ECM for combat survival.

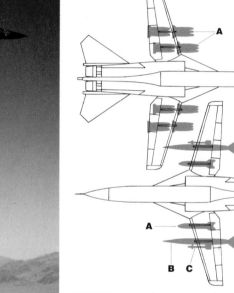

Typical weapons:
Top: On a conventional strike, the F-111 can carry large numbers of Mk82 "iron" bombs (**A**) on multiple ejectors. Payloads of this type were used to good effect during the Vietnam war, when the F-111 flew high speed, low-level

missions against targets in the North.
Above: On a nuclear strike mission, the aircraft would be much "cleaner". This example shows two B.61 nuclear weapons (**A**) on the inboard pylons, plus tanks (**B**) and self-defence AIM-9s (**C**).

Above: The F-111 was the world's first variable-geometry combat aircraft to see service. When the wing is swept fully to the rear, as shown here, its trailing edge is close enough to the horizontal stabiliser to form what is effectively a single large surface of delta planform. The form of the sweep control in the cockpit has been controversial, and is liable to misuse. Several aircraft have been lost in accidents when pilots attempted to land with the wing fully swept, only to stall short of the runway. The obvious logic of "control forward – wing forward" was ignored by GD.

Above: This underside view of an F-111F of the 48th Tactical Fighter Wing shows the wing in the swept-forward position. Note the four-section double-slotted flaps which occupy the entire wing trailing edge, and the full-span leading-edge slats. Also visible is the aircraft's advanced weaponry. The fairing on the centreline (mounted just ahead of the airbrake) is an AVQ-26 Pave Tack sensor, combining a FLIR and laser system with turret-mounted stabilised optics. This may be used to locate and designate targets for attack using laser-guided munitions. The stores on this aircraft are GBU-16B/B Paveway IIs based on 1,000lb (450kg) bombs. The swivelling pylons – another feature fielded for the first time in the F-111 – keep the centreline of the ordnance aligned in the direction of flight. The F-111 may be retrofitted with Paveway III.

Below left: A side view of the F-111F shown above gives a better impression of the steerable turret mounted at the rear of the Pave Tack fairing. The rearward-facing fairing at the top of the vertical fin houses the sensor for an infra-red warning system. The shape of the aircraft cockpit prevents either crew member from looking to the rear, so such a system is vital.

inherent in the basic design had been identified, returning the programme to the engineering development phase until an improved and definitive design could be created, the USAF purchased a series of versions. Each may have been superior to the version it replaced on the Fort Worth production line, but the end result was that all versions were ordered in small numbers, eliminating the savings which could have accrued from mass production and giving the USAF a severe logistical problem. A programme originally expected to result in the construction of more than 1,700 aircraft at a unit cost of

$3.4 million each, shrunk to an emasculated 562 aircraft production run between 1967 and 1976.

Production of the original F-111A (with Mk I avionics) ended after only 159 had been built. The F-111D introduced Mk II avionics, but was so expensive that only 96 were produced. Like the F-111A, the F-111E featured Mk I avionics, but had modified air inlets; only 94 were produced. By the time that the F-111F, complete with Mk IIB avionics and TF30-P-100 engines, was rolling off the line, the programme was virtually over. Only 106 were built.

This piecemeal approach to production resulted in high cost. Unit cost of the final F-111F version was $13.5 million.

The need to replace aging Douglas EB-66 electronic-warfare aircraft led to a 1974 decision to rework F-111A fighters as specialised jamming aircraft. Grumman was awarded a contract in 1975 to convert a total of 42 F-111As to the EF-111A Electric Fox Tactical Jamming System (TJS) configuration, adding an ALQ-99 standoff/escort jamming system in the weapons bay, plus an internally-mounted ALQ-137 self-protection ECM system. The first was delivered to the USAF in 1981,

General Dynamics F-111F

1. Radome.
2. Avionics equipment bay.
3. ADF sense aerial.
4. Pitot tube.
5. Rudder pedals.
6. Control column.
7. Instrument panel.
8. Head-up display.
9. Cockpit canopy cover.
10. Canopy latch/emergency release.
11. 2nd Pilot/Navigator/Weapons officer's seat.
12. Central switch panel.
13. Pilot's seat.
14. Escape capsule main parachute housing.
15. UHF/IFF aerial.
16. Self righting bag stowage.
17. Floatation bag stowage.
18. Drogue parachute housing.
19. Flight refuelling receptacle.
20. Crew escape capsule.

21. Forward stabilising fins.
22. Attenuation bags.
23. Self righting bags.
24. Floatation bags.
25. Starboard wing stores pylons.
26. Starboard wing integral fuel tank.
27. Leading edge slats.
28. Starboard navigation light.
29. Formation light.
30. Double slotted flaps.

31. Starboard spoilers.
32. Swivelling pylon bearings.
33. Boundary layer spill duct.
34. Wing sweep actuator.
35. Wing pivot bearing.
36. UHF/TACAN aerial.
37. Formation lighting strip.
38. Wing pivot box integral fuel tank.
39. Anti-collision light.

40. Central flap and slat hydraulic drive motor.
41. Inboard auxiliary flap.
42. Hydraulic reservoir.
43. Central main undercarriage wheel bay.
44. Engine bleed air ducting.
45. Main undercarriage breaker strut.
46. Hydraulic retraction jack.
47. Aft fuselage fuel tanks.
48. Tailplane control linkages.
49. HF aerial.

50. Starboard all-moving tailplane.
51. HF aerial.
52. Radar warning aerial.
53. Fin vent tank.
54. Formation lighting strip.
55. ECM equipment housing.
56. Detector scanner.
57. Static dischargers.
58. Rudder.
59. Rudder hydraulic actuator.
60. Fuel jettison.
61. Exhaust nozzle.
62. Exhaust blow-in doors.

63. Variable-area afterburner nozzle control jacks.
64. ECM aerial.
65. Tail warning radar aerial.
66. Wing fully swept position.
67. Port all-moving tailplane.
68. Tailplane pivot bearing.
69. Tailplane hydraulic actuator.
70. Afterburner duct.

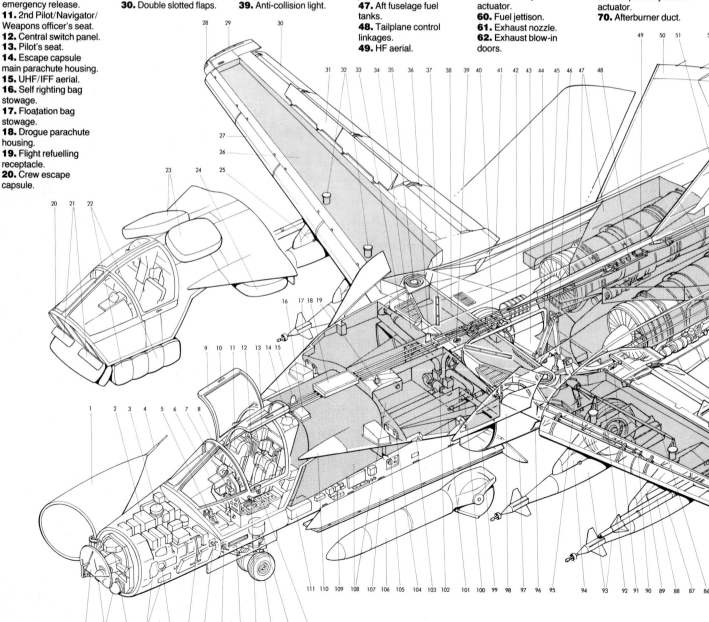

and aircraft were deployed to Western Europe in 1984. Total cost of the conversion work is estimated at $971 million.

No other major reworks are contemplated, plans considered in the late 1970s for a substantial enhancement programme having been abandoned. Several modification programmes are currently under way, but these are intended simply as "fixes" for known performance or reliability problems. The FB-111A is based on the F-111K planned for the RAF. Operated by SAC, this is a long-range nuclear bomber.

Following the UK decision to cancel its planned F-111K buy, the only other customer to adopt the aircraft was the Royal Australian Air Force which took delivery of 24. Four aircraft have since been modified to an RF-111C configuration, while an additional four ex-USAF F-111As have been transferred to make good attrition losses.

STRUCTURE

The F-111 was the first production aircraft to have variable-geometry wings. This method of matching a wing to changing flight conditions is no longer in fashion (at least in the West) and the news that the new Sukhoi Su-27 "Flanker" may have switched from variable to fixed geometry may suggest a growing Soviet disillusionment with the system. At the time, however, it seemed the only way of achieving the performance required at both high and low-speeds.

Basic features of the design adopted for the F-111 include fixed pivots mounted wide apart and well beyond the limits of the fuselage. To house the pivots, a fixed highly-swept centre section (known as a "glove") was provided. Sweep may be varied from 16deg to 72.5deg. Leading-edge slats and double-slotted flaps are

71. Ventral fin.
72. Pratt & Whitney TF30-P-100 afterburning turbofan engines.
73. Wing glove pneumatic seal.
74. Formation lighting strip.
75. Engine accessory equipment gearbox.
76. Formation light.
77. Port navigation light.
78. Slat drive torque shaft.
79. Port spoilers.
80. Spoiler hydraulic actuators.
81. Port wing integral fuel tank.
82. Flap drive torque shaft.
83. Flap screw jacks.
84. Port leading edge slat.
85. Slat guide rails.
86. Swivelling pylon control link.
87. AIM-9 Sidewinder air-to-air "self defence" missile.
88. Missile launch rail.
89. Outboard stores pylon.
90. Slat drive unit.
91. Auxiliary flap jack.
92. Inward retracting mainwheel.
93. GBU-10 laser guided bombs.
94. Inboard stores pylon.
95. Main undercarriage shock absorber strut.
96. Intake suction relief doors.
97. Main undercarriage wheel door/airbrake.
98. Rotating glove vane.
99. Engine air intake.
100. Intake centre-body control jack.
101. Conical intake centre-body.
102. Air conditioning plant.
103. Navigation light.
104. Escape capsule aft stabilising fin.
105. Pressure refuelling connection.
106. Pave Strike Laser Ranger and Marked Target Seeker pod.
107. Weapons bay doors.
108. Forward fuselage fuel tanks.
109. Electrical equipment bay.
110. Forward ECM aerial.
111. Pave Strike computer.
112. Wing sweep control lever.
113. Liquid oxygen converter.
114. Forward-retracting nose undercarriage.
115. Engine throttle levers.
116. Formation lighting strip.
117. Taxying lamp.
118. Angle of attack transmitter.
119. VOR localiser aerial.
120. Forward radar warning aerial.
121. Homing aerials.
122. Radar antenna controller.
123. Terrain-following radar antennae.
124. Attack radar.

Above: GD technicians check out the avionics and cockpit systems of a newly completed F-111. The entire nose section forward of the cockpit is crammed with electronic packages, but access for servicing is good. Such complex systems make great demands on ground crews.

Below: When flying at low level into hostile airspace, the F-111 can use terrain features such as hills and valleys to screen itself from radars.

fitted across the full span of the wing in order to increase lift at low speed, while part of the glove leading edge splits into two surfaces which are carefully positioned to control and guide the flow of air around the inboard end of the leading-edge slats. Wing and horizontal stabiliser are set at the same height. When the wing is fully swept, its trailing edge is close to the leading edge of the tail, creating what is virtually a single large delta wing. The stabilisers are of the all-moving type, controlling aircraft roll as well as pitch.

Since the F-111 was originally intended for carrier use, the maximum fuselage length was dictated by the size of the lifts on USN carriers. As a result, the fuselage had to be designed short and wide. Internal fuel is stored in tanks in the wing, gloves, centre fuselage and above the engine bay.

The inlets are located well aft and are of novel quarter-circle configuration with Dassault-style movable conical centre-bodies, while the ducts which carry the airflow to the engines are of relatively short length. As a result, the intake has to avoid ingesting boundary air disturbed by its long passage along the nose and fuselage, while the air flowing down the duct has little time to assume a distortion-free flow. Both features were to give rise to technical problems.

One novel feature of the F-111 fuselage is the use of an escape capsule. In the earlier B-58 Hustler bomber, GD had provided the crew with ejection seats which virtually encapsulated them before ejection into what could be a Mach 2 airflow, but for the F-111 the company decided to go a step further and turn the entire cockpit into a single unit which could be blasted free by explosive cutting chords, carried clear of a crashing aircraft by a 40,000lb (18,000kg) thrust rocket motor, then lowered to the ground by parachute. After touchdown, the capsule can act as a survival shelter or even as a liferaft. Despite its complexity, the system works well, and has saved the lives of many aircrew.

First structural problem to rear its head was weight. Target all-up weight had started at 45,000lb (20,400kg), but was later raised to 60,000lb (27,200kg). As finally delivered, the aircraft can weigh 100,000lb (45,000kg) or more at take-off. This weight growth was the main factor which killed the Navy's F-111B programme.

Several crashes early in the career of the F-111A revealed a series of structural problems. "Fixes" were devised, quality control was improved, but crashes continued. Eventually the entire fleet was grounded for inspection at the end of 1969, and a problem with the steel wing carry-through box was identified. The decision was made to proof-test all aircraft built to date. Two aircraft failed while on test, while the rest were given a clean bill of health.

Subsequent experience showed that the structure was sound, and the aircraft began what was to be a long and successful USAF career.

F-111 escape capsule:
1. Ejection handles (2).
2. Auxiliary flotation bag.
3. Chin flaps.
4. Auxiliary flotation bag pressure bottle.
5. Canopy internal emergency release handle.
6. Auxiliary flotation and recovery parachute deploy handle.
7. Recovery parachute release handle.
8. Severance and flotation handle.
9. Emergency oxygen bottles.
10. Right self-righting bag.
11. Emergency pressurization bottle.
12. Barostat lock initiator.
13. Emergency UHF antenna.
14. Aft flotation bag.
15. Pitch flap.
16. Stabilization brake parachute.
17. Left self-righting bag.
18. Quick rescue kit.
19. Recovery parachute.
20. Survival gear.
21. Left canopy detach handle.
22. Chaff dispenser control lever.
23. Impact attenuation bag pressure bottles.
24. Chaff dispenser.
25. Rocket motor.
26. Impact attenuation bag.
27. Bilge pump.
28. Automatic severance initiator.

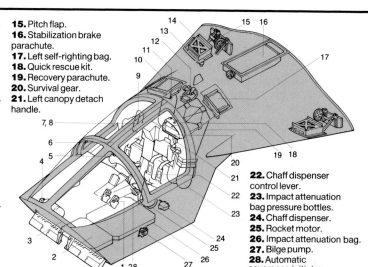

Above: The cockpit of the EF-111 is a hybrid of old and new technology. The left-hand side is virtually unchanged from the early 1960s F-111A; the EW operator's consoles (right) use 1980s technology.

POWERPLANT

Having decided that the engine of the new fighter should be a turbofan, the DoD was virtually forced to use the new Pratt & Whitney TF30. The rival Allision AR.166 was based on the Rolls Royce Spey, and was thus considered in many circles to be "foreign" (i.e. unacceptable), while General Electric's advanced MF-295 was only a proposed design and did not exist in hardware.

The TF30 is a two-shaft turbojet. The LP shaft carries the six-stage compressor and a three-stage turbine, while the HP shaft has a seven-stage compressor and single-stage turbine. Like many P&W engines, the TF30 was of slightly conservative design, the company traditionally believing that reliability was well worth a slight decrease in performance. Unfortunately for the F-111, the engine was to suffer its own share of problems. On the second flight of the original F-111A prototype, both engines stalled when the crew tried to take the aircraft past Mach 1. Tests showed that the compressor of the TF30 was operating uncomfortably close to the point at which

it was likely to stall, and that the air inlets on the sides of the F-111 fuselage were ingesting part of the disturbed boundary air.

Succeeding models of the F-111 introduced modified engines and revised intakes in a series of attempts to cure the problem. The F-111A, C and E were all fitted with TF30-P-3 engines with a modified inlet, revised blade angles and modified shaft speeds. This gave 18,500lb (8,390kg) of thrust in afterburner, but was still far from trouble-free. This was mated with a revised inlet design known as Triple Plow I which was positioned further away from the fuselage side, and contained additional facilities for diverting the boundary air. Introduced on the F-111A, it was also used on the E model. Since the EF-111 is a rebuilt F-111A, this aircraft retains the latter version's -3 engine.

The F-111D version was fitted with the improved -9 engine. Based on the -7 of the FB-111A strategic bomber, this has faster-turning shafts and a higher turbine-inlet temperature. For the F-111E, a further-modified Triple Plow II inlet was devised. Mounted still further away from the fuselage side and incorporating a series of suck-in doors positioned some 12in (30cm) behind the lip, this was better suited to high angles of attack, and could in theory allow the aircraft to reach the Mach 2.5 dash speed originally specified. What the F-111E lacked was a more powerful engine.

With the F-111F, the new intake was finally mated with a better engine—the TF-30-P100. A redesignd fan and compressor, a further increase in turbine inlet temperature and a new five-zone afterburner gave this model a massive 25,100lb (11,385kg) of thrust.

A further improved engine was proposed, but proved too expensive for the USAF and was never adopted for service. The engine remains in service in the forms listed above, and is still the subject of modification programmes. Under a programme designated Pacer 30, the reliability and durability of the engine is being improved.

AVIONICS

In order to fly at high speed at low height, locate and strike its targets, the F-111 requires reliable avionics. In specifying the original equipment fit, the USAF decided to stick with proven technology, accepting the fact that the complex systems required for the mission would as a result be large and heavy.

On the F-111A and C, the long nose radome contains two radars—the General Electric APQ-113 J-band multi-mode set for air-to-ground use (plus a limited degree of air-to-air performance for the aiming of AIM-9 Sidewinder missiles), plus the Texas Instruments APQ-110 terrain-following radar (TFR). Main navaid is the AJQ-20A INS. ECM systems include the ALE-28 chaff/flare dispenser, APS-109 radar-warning receiver (RWR), while the original internally-mounted jammer was the Sanders Associates ALQ-94 noise/deception set.

For the F-111D, the service succumbed to the attractions of solid-state digital technology. The Autonetics APQ-130 replaced the -113, the Sperry APQ-128 took over the TF role, while the IND system became the AJN-16.

The Mk 2 avionics were both costly and unreliable, so a less expensive Mk 2B fit had to be devised for the F-111F. The APQ-130 was replaced by the General Electric -144, the -128 TFR by the -146, while the Dalmo-Victor ALR-62 became the main RWR. The USAF is phasing out the earier ALQ-94 jammer, replacing it with the improved ALQ-137.

In developing the EF-111A EW aircraft, the USAF wisely decided not to attempt

Above: The EF-111A Raven is an EW rebuild of the original F-111A. The fintop and belly-mounted equipment fairings house part of the ALQ-99 suite.

Stand-off weapon for the future: Below: The Advanced Location/Strike System would rely on sensors carried in high-flying surveillance aircraft such as the TR.1 to locate enemy threat radars by observing the time of arrival of their radar signals. Attack aircraft such as the F-111 would fly in and release GBU-15 "smart" bombs: these would be guided by radio command to their targets.

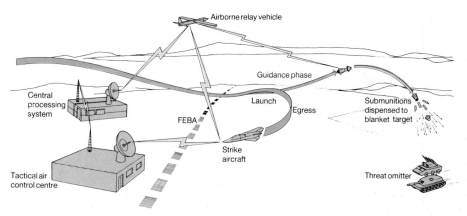

development of its own ECM suite, but adapted the ALQ-99 devised by the US Navy for its EA-6B Prowler project. Much of the USN system is carried in underwing pods, so the system required a degree of reconfiguration for installation in the EF-111 fuselage and ventral fairing. The F-111 lacks the four-man crew of the EA-6B, so a higher degree of system automation was required. Operational testing in 1978 highlighted a number of deficiencies in the modified system, but these were soon cleared up. Approval of full-scale production was given in 1979.

A series of update programmes are currently improving the F-111 avionics. The Weapons Navigation Computer is being replaced by a new system intended to improve reliability while providing better performance, while the VHF/UHF AM/FM

radio equipment is being given encryption facilities. The F-111D avionics have been specifically singled out for attention. Reliability of the integrated display set is being improved by the incorporation of modern digital logic and microelectronic components, while another programme is replacing all microelectronic components in the APQ-130 radar. The existing components have a high failure rate.

One recent electro-optical add-on has been the AVQ-26 Pave Tack, a belly-mounted all-weather target designator incorporating an AAQ-9 FLIR and AVQ-25 1.06 micron laser. This may be used to designate targets for attack by smart weapons such as the paveway laser-guided bomb. Australia adopted this system for its F-111C fleet, but high cost has forced the USAF to install it only on the F-111F.

Over the next six years the USAF expects to spend more than $1,000 million in further modifications to the F-111 navigation and bombing systems. The Service hopes to fit off-the-shelf systems such as the APG-67 radar and a modified version of the Texas Instruments LANTIRN electro-optical system. If the plan goes ahead, the first updated aircraft could be returned to service by late 1986.

F-111s have been used as a testbed for the experimental Pave Mover synthetic-

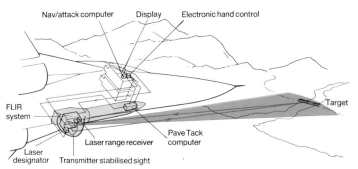

EO update for F-111: Left: Pave Tack combines a FLIR viewing system with a laser ranger and designator. Its own specialised computer is linked to the aircraft's nav-attack computer and to a display and hand controller operated by the right-hand crew member. High cost forced the USAF to adopt the equipment for the F-111F only.

aperture radars developed competitively by Hughes and Grumman/Norden. These radars use frequency-hopping and other spread-spectrum techniques to minimise the risk of their transmissions being detected and jammed. They would be used to designate targets for attack by long-range air to ground-launched missiles. Main task of such systems would be to blunt the impact of large armoured formations, a role explored by the experimental Assault Breaker programme.

ARMAMENT

The internal weapons bay is rarely used for conventional ordnance, although it can theoretically carry two 750lb (340kg) bombs. It is used for specialised payloads such as chaff, B43, B57 or B61 nuclear weapons, or—in the case of the RAAF's RF-111C's—reconnaissance equipment. A single 20mm M61 Vulcan cannon is normally carried only by the F-111D. The gun is mounted in the forward part of the

internal weapons bay, while the massive 2,084-round ammunition drum is carried just behind.

Most weaponry is carried on the under-wing hard points, the fuselage stations being largely used for ECM pods. Each outer wing has three pylons, but those nearest the wingtip lack the swivelling feature which, on the others, keeps stores aligned as the sweep angle varies. As a

Above: Four Royal Australian Air Force F-111Cs have been modified to RF-111C standard, receiving pallet-mounted recce sensors. The RAAF is the sole export operator of the F-111, fielding F-111C, RF-111C and ex-US Air Force F-111A aircraft.

Below: A UK-based F-111 of the 48th Tactical Fighter Wing flies over the English countryside with a warload of four Paveway LGBs and the belly-mounted Pave Tack system. One of the first units to receive this advanced weaponry, the 48th TFW is a potent long-range strike unit.

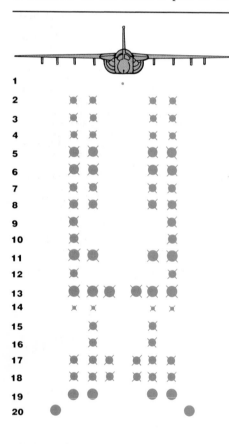

Possible weapons:
1. M61A1 20mm cannon module.
2. Mk82 500lb (230kg) bomb.
3. Snakeye low-drag bomb.
4. Snakeye high-drag bomb.
5. Mk84 2,000lb (910kg) bomb.
6. Mk84 laser-guided bomb.
7. Mk36 1,000lb (450kg) mine.
8, 9, 10. M117A1, D&R 750lb (340kg) general-purpose bombs.
11. M118 3,000lb
(1,350kg) bomb.
12. Cluster Bomb Units type CBU-24H/B, -29H/B, -49H/B, -52B/B, -58B/B, or -71B.
13. B43, B57 or B61 free-falling nuclear weapons.
14. AIM-9 Sidewinder for self-defence.
15. SUU-20 dispenser.
16. TDU-11/B.
17. BDU-8/B or -18/B practice bombs.
18. BDU-12/B, -19/B or -38/B practice bombs.
19, 20. 600gal (2,300lit) external tanks. FB-111 bombers can carry SRAM.

result, the outboard pylon is normally used only for external tanks.

The F-111 can carry most items of tactical ordnance. The individual wing pylons are stressed to accept loads of up to 5,000lb (2,250kg), so may carry weapon loads such as M117A1 bombs (quoted as "750lb" (340kg) but actually about 825lb (375kg)) or CBU-58 cluster bombs on multiple ejector racks, or single 2,000lb (900kg) Mk 82 and 3,000lb (1,350kg) Mk 83 bombs, plus their Paveway guided variants, or the Rockwell GBU-15 guided bomb. For attacks against airfields, the Matra Durandal anti-runway weapon could be used. The aircraft has the ability to carry AIM-9 Sidewinders for self-protection, but this is seldom done.

PERFORMANCE

The F-111 programme may at times have seemed little more than a catalogue of aeronautical disasters, but the end product was and still is the USAF's most effective

all-weather attack aircraft. Committed prematurely to combat in the Vientam War during the 1968 Combat Lancer programme, it was withdrawn after the loss of three of the six aircraft. Combat Lancer highlighted many early deficiencies, but also showed signs of just how effective the aircraft could be when fully developed. The three losses achieved much publicity, but during the other 53 sorties the aircraft flew into North Vietnamese airspace, reached their target, attacked it and came home without suffering combat damage or even being tracked by hostile radars. The F-111 concept worked; the problem was simply one of "wringing out the bugs"— including structural failures which had resulted in the loss of one (and perhaps all three) of the aircraft which failed to return.

With the North Vietnamese invasion of the South in 1972, the F-111A returned to Southeast Asia. Now a proven warplane, the aircraft remained in action for five months, with two squadrons striking deep into Vietnam and even into the flak and

missile-infested skies above Hanoi and Haiphong. Almost 4,000 low-level missions were flown for the loss of only six aircraft—a loss rate of 0.15 per cent. Given the loss rate of 2 per cent which some NATO planners envisage in any Central Front war in Europe, a similar effort would have seen the loss of 80 aircraft.

The F-111 can reach Mach 2 or more at a height of more than 35,000ft (10,700m), but in practice is more likely to cruise at 1,000ft (300m) or lower to avoid being detected by hostile radars and to hide among the radar ground clutter. During the final run-in to the target, the crew will probably select a cruise height of less than 300ft (90m). Speed at such height will normally be around 480kt (890km/h), but in a high threat area, the crew will push the aircraft to the speed limit dictated by its ordnance load, the height they are flying and the buffeting experienced.

Apart from the A-6, the F-111 remains the only true all-weather tactical aircraft in service today.

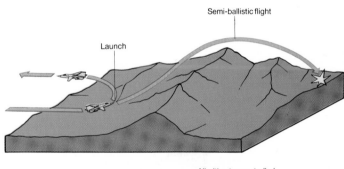

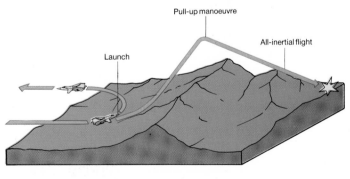

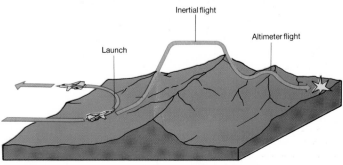

SRAM attack profiles:
Left: The most potent F-111 weapon is the Boeing SRAM stand-off missile carried by the FB-111 strategic bomber variant of the aircraft. The weapon has a range of up to 90nm (170km) and carries a W69, 200kT nuclear warhead. The simplest SRAM profile gives the missile a semi-ballistic trajectory.

Left: For attacks against the most heavily defended targets, SRAM can fly at low level. The on-board radar altimeter maintains clearance between the missile and the terrain. The radar cross-section is only a quarter of the specified figure, and in this flight mode SRAM is considered to be virtually immune from interception.

Left: SRAM has a rocket motor whose boost and sustain sections are separately initiated, time delays up to 80sec being possible between the two "burns". In the flight mode shown here, a ballistic pull-up boost phase is followed by a short aerodynamic coasting flight sustained by body lift. The sustainer is then lit for an inertially guided flight to the target.

Left: Flight at low level has a marked reduction on maximum range. This hi-lo flight profile represents a good compromise attack path, with an initial high-altitude flight being followed by a final low-altitude run to the target. SRAM weighs about 2,230lb (1,012kg) at launch and, with an overall length of 15.8ft (4.8m), is very compact.

A-6 INTRUDER

DEVELOPMENT

Probably one of the most unglamorous aircraft in current service, the Intruder is, by contrast, certainly one of the most combat-effective. It pioneered the low-level strike role since adopted for designs such as the F-111 and Tornado IDS, played a major part in the Vietnam War, and might still be in production in 1990.

Every air force dreams of having an aircraft able to land heavy ordnance loads accurately on small and/or mobile targets in all weathers by day or night. Even given present-day technology, this is not an easy task, but it must have seemed near-impossible back in 1956 when the US Marine Corps set out to procure such an aircraft. At a time when electronic technology still relied on vacuum tubes and when many aircraft required more than 100 man-hours of maintenance per flying hour, such a specification called for a degree of bravado (if not sheer recklessness) on the part of the USMC's planners. To complicate matters, the new aircraft had to be carrier-based, sized in the medium-attack category, yet able to lift the bombload of a

World War II heavy bomber. It was just the sort of challenge to which the US aerospace industry responds best. Eight firms submitted designs, and the Grumman G-128 was declared the winner late in 1957. The first of eight prototype A-6A Intruders flew in April 1960, production deliveries starting in February 1963.

The aircraft was a contemporary of the British Royal Navy's Buccaneer strike aircraft, entering service six months later but carrying a suite of complex avionics which made the fit of the Buccaneer seem crude by comparison—despite development having started some four years behind that of the British Aircraft.

As US Navy and USMC units converted to the new aircraft, they were assigned to the Vietnam War, where the type played a major part in supporting US ground forces and penetrating deep into the skies of North Vietnam to attack strategic targets. Almost inevitably, the aircraft's vacuum-tube avionics proved a technician's nightmare, with operational availability falling to around 35 per cent, and the maintenance workload rising to well above 100 manhours per flying hour.

But the design proved adaptable and able to meet more specialised later requirements, so a series of modified versions was fielded. The threat posed by North Vietnamese SAM systems resulted in the then 19 aircraft being modified to the AGM-78 Standard-armed A-6B anti-radar version. Three different configurations were deployed with varying degrees of strike capability. Attacks against small moving targets at night demanded another version, so 12 aircraft received FLIR and low-light TV (LLTV), in a detachable central turret under a programme known as TRIM (Trails, Road, Interdiction, Multi-

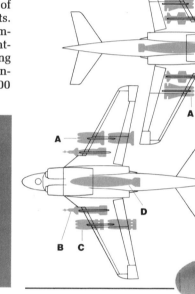

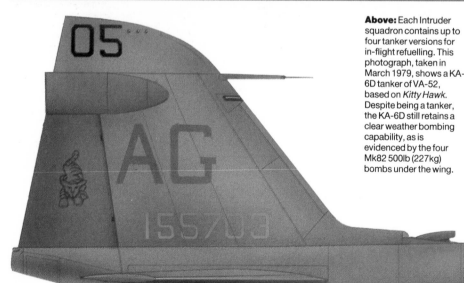

Above: Each Intruder squadron contains up to four tanker versions for in-flight refuelling. This photograph, taken in March 1979, shows a KA-6D tanker of VA-52, based on *Kitty Hawk*. Despite being a tanker, the KA-6D still retains a clear weather bombing capability, as is evidenced by the four Mk82 500lb (227kg) bombs under the wing.

Typical weapons:
Top: A, AGM-65 Maverick; **B**, AGM-84 Harpoon; **C**, external fuel tank. This is an anti-shipping load, and all weapons carried have a stand-off capability.
Above: A, Mk82 500lb (227kg) GP bombs; **B**, Paveway II laser guided bomb; **C**, Snakeye retarded bombs; **D**, external fuel tank. Note the tandem TERs.

Above: An A-6E Intruder of VA-65 Tigers. The Intruder does not look a very formidable attack aeroplane, but it proved its worth in the skies over Vietnam and, despite the attack capability of the F-18, looks set to remain in production, albeit on a small scale, for many years yet. The small protuberance under the nose is TRAM (Target Recognition Attack Multisensor), containing FLIR and a laser designator.

Above: In plan view, the Intruder, with its high aspect ratio wing, is strangely reminiscent of the German Me 262. Side-by-side seating is rare, but it reduces length at the expense of widening the body. The wings are full of fuel, even the sections outboard of the fold.

Left: The weapons load on this Intruder is six AGM-65 Mavericks, while two external tanks give extended range/loiter time. The first Mavericks were electro-optically guided, but later variants have laser or imaging infra-red guidance systems. The A-6 was designed to give a first pass blind attack capability on a fixed target. In the early days, the maintenance man hours/per flying hour (MMH/FH) figures were pretty horrific, but modern technology has reduced them to acceptable levels. During the Vietnam conflict, and until the arrival of half a dozen F-111s, the Intruder was the only tactical fighter that could work at night or in marginal weather. Intruders also took part in raids over the Lebanon in 1983; one was brought down by an air-to-ground missile.

sensor), and were fielded as the A-6C.

The much-improved A-6E was the second large-scale variant to be built, with production starting in 1970. This retained the airframe and power plant of the A-6A, but introduced a new suite of nav/attack avionics. Maintenance demands, although still high, were significantly reduced thanks to solid-state electronics, and aircraft availability soon passed the 80 per cent mark. The aircraft is expensive, costing more than $22 million a copy, but was just what the US Navy wanted. To supplement new-production aircraft 240 A-6As were updated to the -6E standard.

A US Marine Corps requirement for dedicated EW aircraft able to escort USN strike formations was met in the short term by the EA-6A. Introduced in 1963, this served as an interim design, with 27 being built (a mixture of 13 modified A-6As and 15 new-build aircraft). The EA-6A retains a partial strike capability, but its main task is to counter hostile radars and to gather electronic intelligence (ELINT) data. Deliveries were completed in 1969. Production deliveries of the more drastically modified EA-6B Prowler started in 1971 and around 100 examples have now been delivered, with production continuing at around six a year. Such jamming power is expensive—the price tag on a new EA-6B is around $40 million—but in combat each Prowler would protect a large number of $20 million A-6Es.

Procurement of the A-6E is scheduled to end in 1985, but the USN now hopes to switch to an improved A-6F version in the latter part of the decade, building at least 100 new aircraft. These would have up-graded radar and avionics, and be powered by a different engine—(see below).

The USN is currently studying its future requirements for strike aircraft, evaluating the rival merits of the A-6F, an improved version of the F/A-18, or the development of an all-new strike aircraft. A firm decision on the future of the A-6F is unlikely to be taken until late 1985 or 1986, but there are indications that the service has tentatively decided to proceed with the project.

The KA-6D is a tanker version intended for aerial refuelling. More than 60 early-production A-6As were rebuilt to this standard, the first flying in May 1966. Tankers still retain a daylight-bombing capability, and are able to act as control aircraft for rescue operations. Existing KA-6Ds are due to be upgraded under a

Grumman A-6E Intruder
1. Radome.
2. Fixed in-flight refuelling probe.
3. Search and terrain-following radar.
4. Radar power supply.
5. Refuelling probe floodlight.
6. Windscreen rain dispersal duct.
7. Rudder pedals.
8. Pilot's instrument display.
9. Control column.
10. Optical sight.
11. Pilot's Martin-Baker ejection seat.
12. Navigator/Weapons systems Officer's Martin-Baker ejection seat.
13. Inboard wing fence.
14. Starboard wing integral fuel tanks.
15. Leading edge slat.
16. Outboard wing fence.
17. Radar warning antenna.
18. Starboard navigation light.
19. Split trailing-edge speed brakes.
20. Fuel jettison.
21. Single slotted Fowler flap.
22. Canopy jack.
23. Starboard roll control spoilers.
24. Electrical system equipment.
25. Pratt & Whitney J52-P-8B powerplant.
26. Fuel system piping.
27. Fuselage fuel tanks.
28. Flap drive motor and gearbox.
29. Emergency ram air turbine.
30. Wing folded position.
31. Fuel venting air intake.
32. Avionics racks.
33. Tailplane control rods.
34. Cooling air intake.
35. Tailcone venting air intake.
36. Starboard all-moving tailplane.
37. Tailplane hydraulic actuator.
38. Remote compass transmitter.
39. Pitot tube.
40. Anti-collision light.
41. VHF aerial.
42. Tail warning radar and ECM transmitting aerial.
43. Rudder.
44. Rudder hydraulic actuator.
45. Tail navigation light.
46. Fuselage tank fuel jettison.
47. Tail bumper and tie-down.
48. Port all-moving tailplane.
49. Tailplane pivot bearing.
50. Tailplane control horn.
51. Auxiliary hydraulic pump motor.
52. ECM equipment.
53. Avionics equipment air conditioning system.
54. Arrester hook.
55. Directional gyro.
56. Arrester hook lateral damper.
57. Hook hydraulic jack and vertical damper.
58. Avionics pallet.
59. Liquid oxygen converter.
60. Port roll control spoilers.
61. Port single slotted Fowler flap.
62. Wing tank fuel jettison.
63. Split trailing edge speed brakes.
64. Formation light.
65. Radar warning power amplifiers.
66. Speed brake hydraulic jack.
67. Port navigation light.
68. Radar warning antenna.
69. Leading edge slat guide rail and rotary actuator.
70. Slat drive shaft.
71. Port leading edge slat.
72. Spoiler control rod.
73. Flap drive shaft and screw jack.
74. Outboard spoiler actuator.
75. Wing fold hinge joint.
76. Wing fold hydraulic jacks.
77. Port wing integral fuel tanks.
78. Inboard spoiler actuator.
79. Outboard stores pylon.
80. Hydraulic retraction jack.
81. Main undercarriage pivot bearing.
82. Forward retracting main undercarriage.
83. External fuel tanks.
84. Inboard stores pylon.
85. ECM transmitters.
86. Engine accessory equipment gearbox.
87. Hydraulic reservoir.
88. Wing root fixed spoiler.
89. Generator cooling air intake.
90. Ground test panel.
91. Ballistics control panel.
92. Boarding steps/handgrips.
93. Retractable boarding ladder.
94. Canopy emergency release.
95. Engine throttle levers.
96. UHF aerial.
97. Temperature probe.
98. Nosewheel bay avionics equipment.

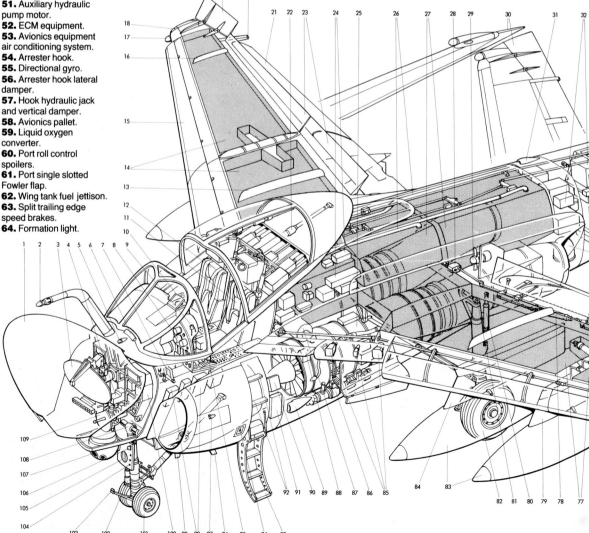

planned modification programme, and six more A-6As may be converted into tankers.

STRUCTURE

The Intruder is conservative in both general configuration and structure. Advanced technology was kept for the "black boxes" rather than the aircraft which would carry them. The wing seems large at first sight, but reflects the high weight of the aircraft—wing loading can be as high as 123lb/sq ft (600kg/sq m). It has 25deg of sweep on its leading edge, contains integral fuel tanks, and has folding outer sections. Leading and trailing edge flaps are fitted to most of the span, minimising stalling speed. Lateral control is by means of spoilers mounted just forward of the

trailing-edge flaps, while the wingtips incorporate unique split-section speed-brakes.

The tadpole-shaped fuselage has a wide front end which provides sufficient space for the large radome and array of antennas needed by the avionics, plus a side-by-side two-seat cockpit with a large rearward-sliding canopy. The navigator sits on the starboard side, slightly behind and below the pilot.

For the EA-6B Prowler, the nose section was extended 54in (137cm) to allow the installation of a four-man cockpit. Two extra seats are provided in the rear for operators of the ALQ-99 jamming system.

POWERPLANT

The twin engines are mounted low in the

fuselage, and have twin jetpipes just aft of the wing and angled 7deg downwards. The original design specified pivoting jetpipes—a crude form of vectored thrust. For low-speed flight conditions such as the approach for landing, these would have been deflected downwards by 23deg, but studies showed that the reduction in stalling speed would be negligible. The concept has recently been revived, however, and an experimental A-6 fitted with a two-dimensional vectoring nozzle was due to fly in October 1984.

The US Navy selected the P&W J52 two-shaft turbojet for the A-6; it is a reliable engine originally developed for Naval applications. Early A-6As were fitted with the 8,500lb (3,855kg) J52-P-6A, but from 1962 onwards aircraft were delivered with the uprated 9,300lb (4,218kg) J52-P-8A.

99. VHF aerial.
100. Palletised avionics equipment racks, port and starboard.
101. Aft-retracting nose undercarriage.
102. Nosewheel steering unit.
103. Catapult launch strop.
104. Approach lights.
105. Landing/taxiing lamp.
106. TACAN aerial.
107. Target recognition and attack multi-sensor (TRAM) infra-red and laser rangefinding.
108. Nose undercarriage pivot bearing.
109. Tracking radar antenna.

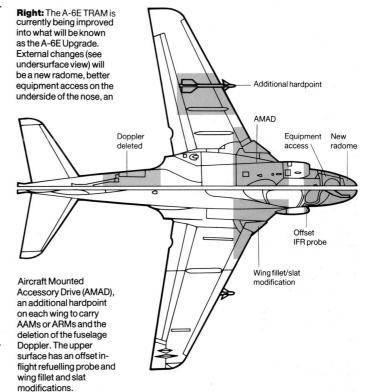

Right: The A-6E TRAM is currently being improved into what will be known as the A-6E Upgrade. External changes (see undersurface view) will be a new radome, better equipment access on the underside of the nose, an Aircraft Mounted Accessory Drive (AMAD), an additional hardpoint on each wing to carry AAMs or ARMs and the deletion of the fuselage Doppler. The upper surface has an offset in-flight refuelling probe and wing fillet and slat modifications.

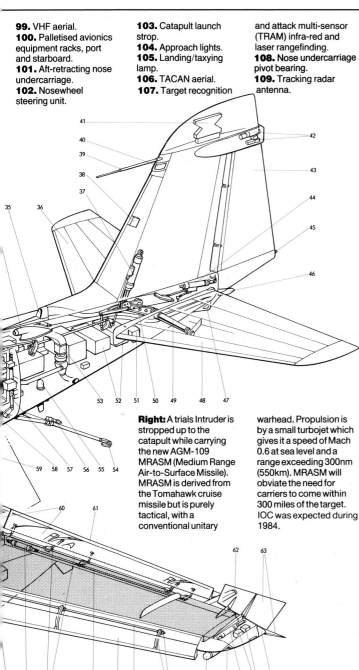

Right: A trials Intruder is stropped up to the catapult while carrying the new AGM-109 MRASM (Medium Range Air-to-Surface Missile). MRASM is derived from the Tomahawk cruise missile but is purely tactical, with a conventional unitary warhead. Propulsion is by a small turbojet which gives it a speed of Mach 0.6 at sea level and a range exceeding 300nm (550km). MRASM will obviate the need for carriers to come within 300 miles of the target. IOC was expected during 1984.

The interim EA-6A EW variant used the J52-P-6A, but for the heavier four-man EA-6B the J52-P-408 rated at 11,200lb (5,080kg) was required.

The planned A-6F will have a more modern engine. This is likely to be a non-afterburning version of the General Electric F404 turbofan used in the F/A-18, but a modernised and uprated version of the J52 is also being considered.

Internal fuel is carried in tanks in the wings and fuselage—a total of 15,940lb (7,230kg). For long-range missions, this can be supplemented by up to four 300 US gallon (1,136 litre) underwing tanks. A removable flight-refuelling probe is mounted on the aircraft centreline just forward of the canopy—a somewhat clumsy installation for such a well-thought-out aircraft.

AVIONICS

The heart of the A-6A avionics suite was the Digital Integrated Attack Navigation Equipment (DIANE). This used two radars—the Norden APQ-92 search set and the smaller APQ-88 for target tracking—combined with an APN-141 radar altimeter for terrain following, plus inertial and Doppler navigation systems. This equipment was all linked to a Litton ASQ-61 digital computer and to the flight-control system. When it all worked, the A-6A could fly over any terrain by day or

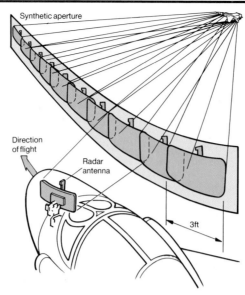

Synthetic aperture

Direction of flight

Radar antenna

3ft

Above: The synthetic aperture radar antenna, although only 3ft (0.91m) wide, operates as though it were far wider by collating a series of returns from a target within 10-15deg of the Intruder's track – which gives a very detailed radar picture – then analysing differing return angles on left and right halves of the antenna and converting data to relative position.

Below: The most complex and expensive A-6 is the EA-6B Prowler. A dedicated electronic warfare aircraft, packed full with "black boxes", it carries a crew of four – three EWOs and the pilot. This example, from NAS Lemoore, is configured with two fuel tanks and three ALQ-99 tactical jamming pods. Each pod is fitted with a windmill generator to power its transmitters.

night, deliver ordnance on known or unexpected targets, then return home. In some cases, the crew might never have to look at the ground between take-off and landing.

Approximately 20 A-6As have been modified to accept the Target Identification and Acquisition System (TIAS) and Mod 1 Standard Anti-Radiation Missile, these aircraft being redesignated A-6Bs.

In an attempt to inject greater reliability into the DIANE system, the track radar was redesigned, but the resulting APQ-112 was no great improvement. Rather than attempt to juggle two radars, many crews relied on the APQ-92 only. The obvious long-term solution was to combine the functions of the two sets in a single more modern design.

With the definitive A-6E, the two earlier radars were replaced by a single APQ-148 multi-mode track-while-scan set, and an IBM ASQ-133 navigation/attack system was installed in place of the earlier ASQ-61. An update programme in the early 1980s added MTI (Moving Target Indication) facilities to the radar.

Late-production E models were also fitted with the Target Recognition and Attack Multisensor (TRAM), which has since been retrofitted to earlier Es. This features a steerable chin turret containing an infrared sensor for target classification and identification, a laser ranger/designator and a laser marked-target detection

system. When modified for use with TRAM, the APQ-148 becomes the APQ-156. The Carrier Aircraft Inertial Navigation System (CAINS) replaced 1950s-vintage equipment carried by earlier A-6s, while more modern communications, TACAN and IFF systems were also installed.

The improved radar and avionics proposed for the A-6F would have the same capability as the systems in the -6E, but would have commonality with the computers and displays used on the F/A-18, F-14D and AV-8B. Radar under consideration include the Hughes APG-63 and APG-65 (used in the F-15 and F/A-18 respectively), the Westinghouse APQ-68 (from the F-16C/D), the existing Norden APQ-156 and the APQ-164.

Intruder carries a complex suite of ECM systems for self-protection, and this has been constantly upgraded to cope with new threats. These units include the Magnavox ALR-50, a radar-warning receiver intended to detect radar signals associated with target tracking and missile guidance, warning the crew that a missile launch has taken place. Simplest countermeasure system carried by the A-6 is probably the Goodyear ALE-39 dispenser for chaff, flares and miniature jammers. This can operate under manual or automatic control, ejecting payloads singly or in pre-programmed combinations, depending on the tactical situation. The EA-6B Prowler uses the Lundy ALE-32 dispenser system.

Most important item of jamming equipment originally carried was the Sanders Associates ALQ-100, an internally-mounted system used for noise and deception (track-breaking) jamming over several frequency bands. It has since been superseded by the same company's ALQ-126 deception jammer which, like the -100, was designed to cope with Soviet anti-aircraft weaponry—particularly surface-to-air missile systems. It is understood to cover E/F, G/H band and I/J band. AIL's ALQ-130 operates not by jamming radar transmissions, but by disrupting the communications links on which a modern air-defence system depends.

The Prowler also carries a specialised suite of jamming equipment intended for stand-off or escort jamming missions. The ALQ-99 is a complex and sophisticated array of jamming equipment, and was created by an industrial team headed by AIL, and including AEL and IBM. It exists in two versions for USAF (EF-111) and USN (EA-6B) use. On the Navy aircraft, the system is packaged in five external pods each containing two transmitters, a receiver and the associated antennas for these. Other equipment is located in the fuselage and in a fin-top fairing. The system can operate in automatic mode with the operators acting as monitors, or in manual mode.

Litton Industries' Amecom Division has been awarded a contract for full-scale development of an Advanced Capability (ADVCAP) EW system for the EA-6B. Delivery of six prototype systems is due to begin in 1986, and a production contract could follow three years later.

ARMAMENT

Most ordnance is carried on underwing hardpoints (four on the A-6A, and six on the -6E). Each is stressed to carry 3,500lb (1,600kg). The lower fuselage is contoured to allow a store to be carried in this location. Typical bomb loads might be 20 750lb (340kg), 15 1,000lb (450kg) or five 2,000lb (900kg) iron bombs, or 28 500lb (225kg) retarded bombs. All would be carried on multiple or triple ejector racks. Aircraft tasked with anti-radar strikes may carry ARMs such as Shrike, Standard ARM or the new HARM. In the nuclear-strike role, the A-6E would carry a single "nuke" plus external tanks.

One of the latest weapons to equip the Intruder squadrons is the AGM-84 Harpoon anti-shipping missile. First deployed in 1982 with VA-165 Boomers, Harpoon gives a very necessary stand-off capability.

PERFORMANCE

High speed is not necessarily an important qualification in an aircraft designed to operate at low level. An A-6E would normally cruise at about 413kt (765km/h) at medium altitude in order to save fuel, but is capable of up to 560kt (1,037km/h) at low level during the run-in to the target.

The original specification called for a minimum cruise height of 500ft (150m) but an A-6E would probably fly at around half that height over land and as low as 100ft (30m) over water. In the strike game, reduced altitude equals reduced vulnerability: the time during which the aircraft is exposed to a ground-based radar or weapon is reduced, whereas the aircraft's ability to use uneven terrain and ground "clutter" as a screen from threat systems is increased.

On a typical close-support mission, an A-6E might carry 30 500lb (225kg) Snakeye retarded bombs to a combat area some 300nm (560km) from the take-off point, loitering for up to an hour at low level before heading for home. With maximum ordnance load, the "one-way" range is 880nm (1,613km).

Lightly-loaded, an A-6E can get airborne in a take-off run of 1,800ft (549m). At full flap, stalling speed is only 98kt (182km/h) touching down in only 1,520ft (463m). Despite its portly lines, the Intruder can climb at 9,400ft/min (2,865m/min) at sea level, and reach a service ceiling of 47,300ft (14,415m).

The bulky ECM pods of the EA-6B reduce maximum level speed of this version to 533kt (987km/h), while service ceiling is reduced to 41,000ft (12,500m). Maximum range, allowing for 20 minutes at low level, is 955nm (1,769km).

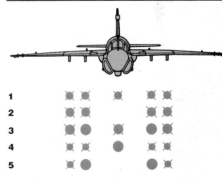

1				
2				
3				
4				
5				

Possible weapons:
1. Mk82 500lb (227kg) GP bombs carried in tandem triples, 30 total. **2.** M117 750lb (340kg) bombs. **3.** Mk84 2,000lb (907kg) bombs, 3 total, with two external tanks. **4.** AGM-84 Harpoon, 4 total plus C/L tank. **5.** AGM-65 Maverick, 6 total on TERS, plus two fuel tanks.

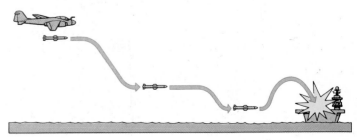

Right: AGM-84 Harpoon is a stand-off anti-ship missile with a range of 50nm (92km). Launched at medium altitude, it is programmed to dive to low level. Active radar homing is used for the final guidance phase at very low level, with a final pop-up and dive onto the target

F-14 TOMCAT

DEVELOPMENT

In long-range firepower and in price, the F-14 Tomcat is unsurpassed. At a flyaway cost of around $38 million it has a price tag which few nations could contemplate, but it packs enough firepower to deal with up to six targets flying some 80nm (148km) away, despatching them near-simultaneously using AIM-54 Phoenix missiles.

In the mid-1970s one problem facing the Shah of Iran was the Soviet Air Force's habit of sending MiG-25 Foxbat fighters on reconnaissance missions over his oil-rich country. When the Imperial Iranian Air Force's Tomcats were delivered, starting in 1976, the Service immediately started planning a demonstration of its firepower. A single test shot of Phoenix turned out to be enough to prove the weapon's operational status with the IIAF. Foxbat overflights promptly ceased.

The goal of the F-14 programme was to develop a new naval interceptor using the engines and technology of the unsuccessful F-111B naval version of the GD multi-role fighter. The conflicting requirements for the new aircraft—high speed, high manoeuvrability and good handling at low speeds, plus long range, virtually dictated the use of variable geometry, while the complex payload of avionics and long-range missiles made a two-man crew highly desirable.

Grumman received the development contract in February 1969, and flew the first prototype on December 21, 1970. It had a brief life, crashing during its second flight only eight days later. Both crew members ejected safely, and an investigation showed that fatigue failures of the pipes in both hydraulic systems had led to a partial failure of the flying controls. On May 24, 1971, the second prototype took to the air, and from that point onwards the programme went like a dream from the technical point of view, with only minor aerodynamic problems being experienced. On the financial side, the situation was far from satisfactory.

The initial contract, signed in 1969, covered 12 prototypes, but included options for 429 production fighters at an agreed price. This sort of fixed-price contract was very much in vogue at the time, but was almost to drive Grumman out of business. Escalating costs resulted in the company making a heavy loss on the initial batches of aircraft, and the price was finally renegotiated.

The USN deploys two Tomcat squadrons on each of its major aircraft carriers, and production is still under way. More than 400 are currently in service, some of which have been equipped with the Tacti-

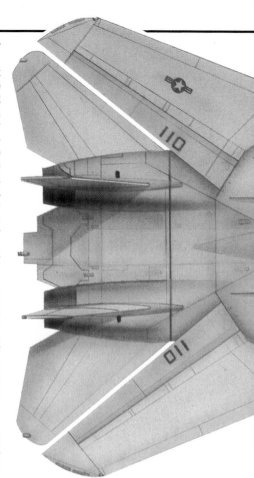

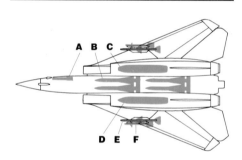

Above: Big fighter, big missile. An F-14A of VF-211 Fighting Checkmates launches an AIM-54 Phoenix: the combination is deadly at unprecedentedly long ranges. The NG tail code indicates CVW-9, of USS *Constellation*.

Typical weapons: Above: A, M61 20mm cannon; **B**, AIM-54A Phoenix; **C**, TARPS reconnaissance pod; **D**, external fuel tank; **E**, AIM-120 AMRAAM, **F**, AIM-9 Sidewinder. Phoenix mounted under the fuselage are carried on pallets, while AMRAAM (which is interchangeable with Sparrow) is carried semi-recessed. The TARPS (Tactical Air Reconnaissance Pod System), equipped with cameras and IR linescan, is carried by 49 Tomcats.

Left: Variable geometry combines the benefits of a low aspect ratio swept wing (for high speed) with the good manoeuvring and handling qualities of a high aspect ratio straight wing. The vanes which extend from the fixed wing glove at full sweep are in effect retractable canards. Twin vertical tails provide the aircraft with the required stability during high speed flight.

Above: The heart of a modern naval task force is its carriers. The Coral Sea and Midway battles of 1942 had set the pattern which made surface action outmoded. At the same time, the carriers became prime targets for an enemy and, with advances in weapons technology, had become increasingly difficult to protect, especially against an air arm with long range stand-off weapons. The Tomcat was conceived primarily as a fleet defence fighter, able to kill targets at great distances from the carrier. For this, the prime requirement was the ability to remain on station for long periods 200nm (370km) out from the carrier while armed with the highest possible number of on-board kills. The F-14A shown here has eight – four AIM-54 Phoenix, two AIM-7 Sparrows, and two AIM-9 Sidewinders – while the internal M61 cannon rounds out the armament options.

Below: The brightly coloured markings of most USN units have now given way to low-visibility grey; this F-14 of VF-143 Pukin' Dogs is no exception. In this side view, the pallet carriage of the Phoenix missiles is shown, as are the ventral strakes (with the squadron number) which give stability at high AOA when the fins are blanketed and thus less effective.

Grumman F-14A Tomcat

1. Pressure sensor.
2. Radar target horn.
3. Radome.
4. Flight refuelling probe.
5. ADF sense aerial.
6. Windscreen rain dispersal air ducts.
7. Incidence probe.
8. Rudder pedals.
9. Pilot's instrument displays.
10. Head-up display.
11. Control column.
12. Wing sweep control.
13. Throttle levers.
14. Pilot's Martin-Baker "zero-zero" ejection seat.
15. Naval Flight Officer's instrument console.
16. "Kick-in" boarding step.
17. Radar hand controller.
18. Cockpit canopy cover.
19. Naval Flight Officer's ejection seat.
20. Canopy jack.
21. Glove vane hydraulic jack.
22. Starboard glove vane.
23. Navigation light.
24. UHF/TACAN aerial.
25. Forward fuselage fuel tanks.
26. Intake spill door and hydraulic jack.
27. Leading edge slat.
28. Starboard wing integral fuel tank.
29. Starboard navigation light.
30. Formation light.
31. Spoilers.

32. Outboard manoeuvre flaps.
33. Flap sealing vane.
34. Wing pivot box integral fuel tank.
35. Inboard high-lift flap.
36. Manoeuvre flap and slat drive motor and gearbox.
37. Emergency hydraulic generator.
38. UHF/IFF aerial.
39. Wing sweep actuating screw jack.
40. Inflatable wing seal.
41. Engine bleed air ducting.
42. Flight control rod linkages.
43. Wing fully swept position.
44. Wing "overswept" position (carrier storage).
45. Aft fuselage fuel tanks.
46. Starboard all-moving tailplane.
47. Rudder hydraulic actuator.
48. Airbrake hydraulic jack.
49. Airbrake, above and below.
50. Tail navigation light.
51. ECM aerial.
52. Starboard rudder.
53. Fully variable convergent/divergent afterburner nozzle.
54. Anti-collision light.
55. Formation lighting strip.
56. ECM aerial.
57. Port rudder.
58. Fuel jettison.
59. ECM aerial.
60. Deck arrester hook.

61. Chaff and flare dispensers.
62. Afterburner nozzle control jacks.
63. Radar warning receiver.
64. Port all-moving tailplane.
65. Tailplane pivot bearing.
66. Tailplane hydraulic actuator.
67. Arrester hook dashpot.
68. Pratt & Whitney TF30-P-412 afterburning turbofan engines.
69. Formation lighting strip.
70. Hydraulic system filters.
71. Oil cooler air intake.
72. Formation light.
73. Port navigation light.
74. Manoeuvre flap rotary actuators and pushrods.
75. Port leading edge slat.
76. Port wing integral fuel tank.
77. Spoiler hydraulic actuators.
78. Slat drive shaft.
79. Flap drive shaft.
80. Slat rotary actuators and guide rails.
81. Hydraulic reservoir.
82. Engine accessory equipment gearbox.

83. Inboard flap hydraulic jack.
84. Main undercarriage hydraulic retraction jack.
85. Undercarriage leg pivot bearing.
86. Forward retracting mainwheel.
87. Wing pivot bearing.
88. Sparrow missile adaptor.
89. AIM-7 Sparrow air-to-air missile.

90. Wing glove pylon.
91. AIM-9 Sidewinder air-to-air missile.
92. Flap and slat bevel drive gearbox.
93. Telescopic drive shaft.
94. Variable area intake ramps.
95. External fuel tank.
96. Hydraulic brake accumulators.
97. Intake ramp hydraulic actuators.

98. Air conditioning system heat exchanger.
99. Air data computer.
100. Electrical relay panel.
101. Avionics equipment bays.
102. Electrical system equipment.
103. AIM-54A Phoenix air-to-air missile (4).
104. Phoenix missile pallet.

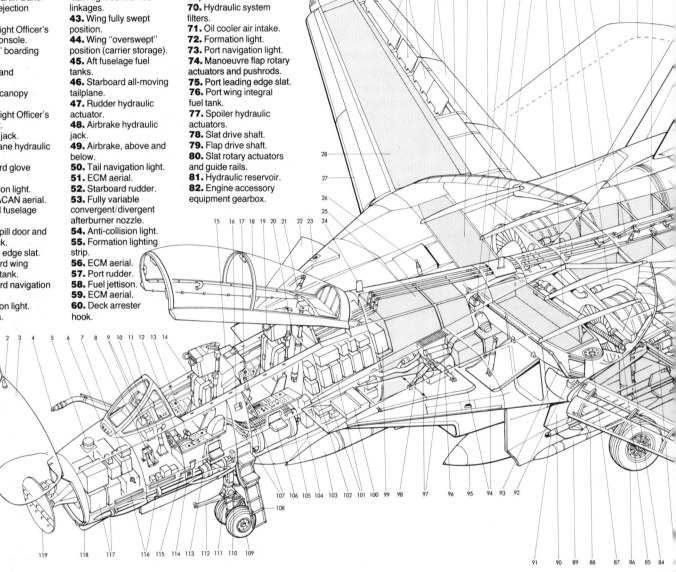

cal Air Reconnaissance Pod System (TARPS), allowing them to act as interim reconnaissance aircraft to meet the USN RFX requirement.

Modification programmes are also being carried out to maintain the effectiveness of existing aircraft. The USN has a total requirement for 899 aircraft, and plans that the final 306 will be the new F-14D model with General Electric F110 engines plus improved digital avionics. Deliveries of this version will begin in 1988. The possibility of retrofitting the F-14A with -14D avionics has been studied, but no funds have been allocated. Earlier plans for improved models designated F-14B

(new P&W F401 engines) and F-14C (upgraded avionics and improved TF30 engines) were abandoned.

Only a handful of the 80 Tomcats supplied to Iran are still operational, and there have been no authenticated reports of the Phoenix being used in the current war with Iraq. The role of the F-14 seems to have been that of airborne early warning, with the AWG-9 being used in an attempt to detect Iraqi strike aircraft.

STRUCTURE

A top speed of Mach 2.3 to 2.4 imposed no particular problem with materials, allow-

ing conventional aluminium alloys to be used for much of the structure. The variable sweep wings are mounted on a wide fixed centre section, and have upper and lower skins made from titanium. Wing sweep may be varied from 20deg to 68deg, but a special 75deg position which overlaps the tailplane is provided for use on the ground in order to minimise parking space. Sweep angle is automatically controlled by the air-data computer, to optimise the lift/drag ratio. This is particularly effective between Mach 0.6 and 0.9, the range of speeds most likely to be met in air-to-air combat.

The moving section of the wing has

105. Ammunition drum.
106. Boarding step.
107. Ammunition feed and link return chutes.
108. Boarding ladder.
109. Forward retracting nosewheels.
110. Nosewheel steering actuator.
111. Carrier approach lights.
112. Catapult launch strop.
113. M-61-A1 20mm six barrel rotary cannon.
114. Canopy emergency release.
115. Pitot head.
116. Formation lighting strips.
117. Radar equipment bay.
118. ECM antenna.
119. AWG-9 pulse doppler flat plate radar scanner.

Above: An F-14 over solid cloud cover shows off its unique lines to advantage. Photo distortion makes the nose look more bulbous than it is, but the widely spaced intakes and engines which give a central tunnel in which to hang four AIM-54s are clearly apparent, and the tail fins can be seen to cant slightly outward. Armament shown is two Sidewinders and two Sparrows; up to six AIM-54 Phoenix could be carried in addition, giving a total of ten on-board kills and a broad spectrum of ranges.

Below: Let it all hang out! With wheels, flaps, and hook dangling, an F-14A approaches the deck of *Constellation*. This is yet another area where variable geometry pays off: the approach is made at a comparatively flat angle and low speed – and stowage is eased.

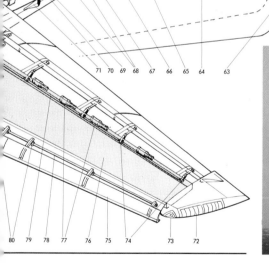

leading-edge slats, three-section flaps, plus spoilers mounted on the upper surface. To improve combat manoeuvrability, the slats and outboard flap sections may be deployed while the wing is in the fully-forward position.

The wing box had given trouble in the F-111, and Grumman was determined that their fighter should be an improvement in this respect. The wing box is a single-cell structure made from titanium, and also serves as a fuel tank. Titanium alloy is also used for the wing pivots, intakes, rear fuselage skins and the hydraulic lines, accounting for some 25 per cent of the empty weight of the Tomcat.

Two small triangular-shaped vanes are mounted in the leading edge of the gloves. These are extended at high speed to generate additional lift ahead of the aircraft's centre of gravity, helping to compensate for the nose-down pitching moment which occurs at such speeds, while maintaining manoeuvrability by overcoming the sluggishness in pitch control which would otherwise be experienced.

Like the designers of the contemporary F-15, the Grumman team opted to use twin fins on Tomcat, supplementing these with strakes fitted beneath the rear fuselage. Shorter than a single vertical surface would have been, the twin fins of the

Tomcat do not require to be folded for hangar storage aboard ship. The horizontal stabilisers were the first load-bearing structures in a Western military aircraft to be made from composite materials.

The intakes of the F-111 have been plagued with problems, so Grumman used a much more conservative design on Tomcat. The two engines were mounted as far apart as possible within the wide rear fuselage, and given straight ducts fed by variable-geometry multi-ramp intakes of wedge configuration. For the jetpipes, a convergent/divergent iris system was employed to contour the nozzle for the demands of dry and afterburning thrust. An engine may be changed in only three hours by a four-man crew.

A story dating from the mid-1970s tells how the Israeli Air Force evaluated Tomcat as a possible F-4 replacement before settling for the F-15 Eagle. After flying the aircraft, one Israeli pilot conducted his own walk-round inspection. "I counted all the aerodynamic surfaces which moved, then decided that I'd prefer to go to war in something simpler," he is reported to have said. Despite this complexity, the F-14's structure has been generally satisfactory. Fatigue testing has identified potential trouble spots, but these will be modified under a current $500 million structural improvement programme to be completed in the 1990s.

PROPULSION

USN safety requirements dictated the use of two engines. Current aircraft are powered by a pair of Pratt & Whitney TF30-P-412 or TF30-P-414 turbofans, developing a maximum of 20,900lb (9,480kg) of afterburning thrust. These are navalised derivatives of the TF30 engine originally used on the USAF's F-111 (see that entry for full details of the engine).

The USN has always considered the aircraft to be underpowered, and had planned to switch to the 27,000lb (12,250kg) Pratt & Whitney F401 turbofan—a navalised version of the F100 used on the F-15. This would have powered the F-14B, due to replace the -14A on the line in the eary 1970s. Problems with the F100 and its F401 derivative (which failed its preliminary flight-rating tests and was cancelled in 1975) effectively axed the F-14B, so all production Tomcats to date have been TF30-powered F-14As.

More than 1,000 TF30-P-414A engines are to be modified to reduce the possibility of engine stalls and to improve engine life, reliability and maintainability. This work is due for completion by the end of the decade.

Within days of the USAF announcement in early 1984 that its next engine buy for the F-16 would be split between the

Above: The canopy of a Tomcat of VF-1 gets a good pre-flight polish. A spotless canopy is as important today as it was back in 1940. In the background is the tail of a VF-2 Tomcat; both units are based on the carrier *Enterprise*.

P&W F100 and the GE F110, the USN selected the latter engine to power future versions of Tomcat, starting with the F-14D. There are no plans to retrofit the F110 in the existing F-14A fleet.

AVIONICS

The Hughes AWG-9 pulse Doppler radar was originally developed in the 1960s along with the AIM-54 Phoenix missile as the armament of the ill-fated F-111B interceptor. Despite the relative age of the basic set, it still has the longest range of any known air-interception radar—more than 110nm (210km), plus the ability to carry out simultaneous missile attacks on up to six targets while continuing to track others.

Look-down shoot-down attacks may be made against low-level targets while the Tomcat cruises at medium altitude. Operating modes of the AWG-9 include track-while-scan; range-while-search; single target tracking; air-to-ground mapping; ranging and weapons delivery; and dogfight.

In normal operation, a radar must trans-

mit at a low enough PRF to allow each pulse sufficient time to make the trip out to the target and back before the next is transmitted, but range-while-search encodes the pulses of a high-PRF Doppler waveform so that range information can be extracted by means of signal processing techniques. Range data obtained in this way is less accurate than that derived directly from a low-PRF waveform, but is accurate enough for the tracking of long-range targets.

This was the technical breakthrough which made it possible for a single radar simultaneously to track a number of targets. As each is detected within the volume of sky under surveillance, the radar determines the range and angular position, then passes the information to a central computer, where it can be compared with the predicted positions of targets already detected. If the newly-detected target can be corellated with an existing track file, then the latter is updated to show current position. If it cannot, a new track file is established for what is assumed to be a fresh target.

As part of an upgrading programme associated with the planned introduction of the improved AIM-54C Phoenix missile, the AWG-9 is being fitted with a programmable digital signal processor. Once this is done, the set is largely software-controlled, making future upgrades largely a matter of modifying software rather than hardware. Modified radars will also incorporate improved ECCM capabilities and medium-PRF waveforms for improved search and track capability, and provide the Tomcat crew with expanded missile launch zones.

A portion of the fleet is equipped with chin-mounted Northrop Television Sight Units, long-range electro-optical viewing systems which allow the pilot to identify positively targets at long ranges by day and in clear weather. Cost seems to have prevented a more widespread fitment, but the unit will probably be a standard feature of the F-14D.

Left: The cockpit of the F-14A dates back to 1968. The large central screen is the VSI, with the HSI just below, behind the stick. A move towards modernity is the three vertical tape instruments to the left, which show engine rpm, temperature and fuel flow; dials are nevertheless few.

In addition to these major updates, the Tomcat avionics are being improved in a number of other ways. Existing aircraft are being retrofitted with the new ARC-182 radio system. This operates in VHF/FM, VHF/AM, and UHF/AM modes and offers secure voice communications.

ARMAMENT

Like all fighters of its vintage, the F-14 carries a single 20mm M61 Vulcan cannon, but its real air-to-air firepower is provided by missiles—four AIM-7 Sparrow or AIM-54 Phoenix missiles carried on hardpoints under the fuselage and two AIM-9 Sidewinders under each wing.

Sidewinder and Sparrow are widely used on other US fighters, but Tomcat is the only platform for the long-range Hughes AIM-54 Phoenix. This may be expensive (even the original AIM-54A had a unit cost of $750,000), but offers fire-and-forget performance at ranges of 80nm (150km) or more. More than 2,500 AIM-54A rounds had been delivered by the end of 1980, when production finally ceased.

The new AIM-54C replaced the -54A on the production line, with the first evaluation rounds being delivered in October 1981. The modified weapon is partly a result of the original having been compromised as a result of the Iranian revolution. Changes are largely confined to the guidance system, and include a solid-state

Above: An F-14A of VF-41 Black Aces makes a perfectly judged approach to the wires of USS Nimitz during Exercise "Teamwork 80" off Norway. Despite its size, the Tomcat is easier to recover than the Phantom.

Like all US warplanes, Tomcat carries an array of ECM equipment, including radar-warning receivers, chaff/flare dispensers, and jammers. For the carriage and deployment of chaff, flares and miniature jammers, the aircraft is fitted with the Goodyear ALE-39 dispensing system. This operates under manual or automatic control, ejecting payloads singly or in pre-programmed combinations.

Several patterns of internally-mounted jamming equipments have been installed on the Tomcat. The Sanders/Magnavox ALQ-91 is intended to jam communications links, while the Sanders Associates ALQ-100 is used for noise and deception jamming over several frequency bands. Probably developed as an anti-SAM system, it uses track-breaking techniques when operating in deception mode. Another track breaker reported to have been fitted to the aircraft is the ITT ALQ-129. As part of an update programme, the Tomcat fleet is being fitted with the new Itek ALR-67 RWR and the Westinghouse/ITT ALQ-165 ASPJ (Advanced Self-Protection Jammer).

Below: Wings fully swept, an F-14A banks away from the camera to show a comprehensive load of four Phoenix, two Sidewinders and two Sparrows, plus a pair of external fuel tanks. Careful examination reveals a most unusual paint job. Few details are evident, but the white underside is supposed to counteract the dark silhouette when up-sun. This of course presupposes that fighters only fly wings level, and at high noon. It was not adopted.

Right: A simulated raid of three QT-33s and three BMQ-34 augmented target drones, flying at speeds between Mach 0.6 and 1.1 and at altitudes between 22,000 and 24,000ft (6,700-7,300m) was met by a single Phoenix-armed F-14, flying at Mach 0.78 and 28,400ft (8,650m). In the space of 38 seconds, all six targets had been tracked and a Phoenix launched against each, from ranges between 50 and 31nm (92-57km). Four hits were scored, one no test, and a miss.

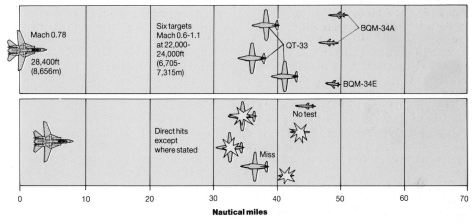

transmitter/receiver assembly for the seeker head, a programmable digital signal processor, and a new digital autopilot. The weapon also has a new pattern of proximity fuze.

Improved performance features of the AIM-54C include enhanced ability in beam attacks and pursuit attacks against receding targets, better ECCM capability, and increased ability to pick out small targets at low level, discriminating between the victim and chaff. The new missile has a top speed of Mach 5.0 rather than 4.3, and a maximum range of 80nm (148km), a 10 per cent improvement over the AIM-54A. Maximum target height is increased from 81,400ft (24,800m) to 100,000ft (30,500m).

Left: A Tomcat in the camouflage scheme and colours of the Imperial Iranian Air Force. Iran was the only overseas customer for the F-14. A handful are believed to be flyable, operating in the AEW role, though their Phoenixes must be inoperable.

Below: The Tomcat is an outstanding example of an integrated weapons system, able to track up to 24 targets and engage six of them simultaneously. This VF-32 Swordsmen aircraft could ripple-fire all its missiles in seconds.

The AIM-54C will remain the main long-range weapon of Tomcat during the 1990s, but the USN is already looking at potential replacements which could cope with threat systems likely to be fielded in the 1990s. These would be similar in performance to the -54C, but would be smaller and would have a higher speed.

PERFORMANCE

Even in its current TF30-powered F-14A form, the Tomcat is an impressive fighter. Maximum speed at height is Mach 2.34, while at low level the aircraft can manage Mach 1.2/792kt (1,468km/h). Under normal circumstances the cruising speed would be 400 to 500kt (740 to 930km/h).

Tests have shown that, with the wings fully forward, the F-14 is difficult to stall. With full wing sweep the aircraft's nose can be lifted to 90deg angle of attack, or depressed by up to 45deg. Stalling speed is 103kt (191km/h), and test flights have shown that control may be maintained at speeds down to 105kt (195km/h).

The sea-level climb rate of more than 30,000ft/min (9,100m/min) is far below that of the F-15, F-16 or Mirage 2000, but a naval fighter will generally have good warning of the approach of any attacker, thanks to the surveillance radars of the E-2C Hawkeye AEW aircraft and of surface ships of the task force.

Once at patrol height, the aircraft will be able to use its Phoenix missiles to pick off

attackers flying at virtually any altitude. Once the combat closes to short range, the Sparrow or Sidewinder armament may be used as combat develops. Despite being somewhat underpowered, the F-14 is a dangerous and agile adversary in a dogfight, as two Libyan Su-22 fighters learned during a clash with Tomcats in the Gulf of Sirte in 1982. Attempted Atoll shots against the F-14s failed, but both Sukhois fell to Sidewinder hits.

On carriers, Tomcat is launched by catapult, but a land-based aircraft can be airborne in a run of as little as 1,300ft (400m). Landing speed with the wings swept forward is 115kt (213km/h), and at a land base the aircraft needs a landing run of at least 2,700ft (820m).

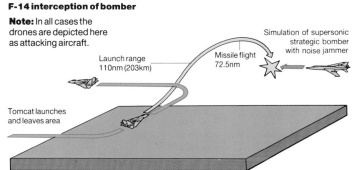

F-14 interception of bomber

Note: In all cases the drones are depicted here as attacking aircraft.

Launch range 110nm (203km)

Missile flight 72.5nm

Simulation of supersonic strategic bomber with noise jammer

Tomcat launches and leaves area

Left: A BMQ-34E drone with augmented radar cross-section, flying at Mach 1.5 and 50,000ft (15,250m) and emitting noise jamming, was shot down by a single Phoenix launched from a range of 110nm (203km). The F-14 flew at Mach 1.5 and 44,000ft (13,400m). The missile followed a high trajectory to a maximum of 103,500ft (31,550m) before arcing down onto the target.

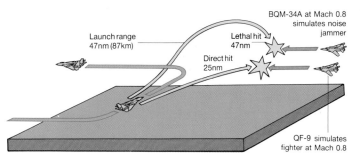

Interception of multiple target

Launch range 47nm (87km)

Lethal hit 47nm

Direct hit 25nm

BQM-34A at Mach 0.8 simulates noise jammer

QF-9 simulates fighter at Mach 0.8

Left: A raid using ECM was simulated by a QF-9 drone at 30,600ft (9,300m) covered by a BQM-34A drone equipped with a jammer at 35,500ft (10,800m). The speed of both drones was Mach 0.8 and their horizontal separation 25nm (46km). A Phoenix was launched at the QF-9 from a range of 25nm (46km) and, nine seconds later, another against the jammer. Both made hits.

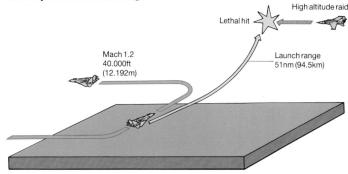

Interception of overhead target

High altitude raid

Lethal hit

Mach 1.2 40,000ft (12.192m)

Launch range 51nm (94.5km)

Left: A radar-augmented BOMARC missile simulated a high altitude, high speed raid at Mach 2.8 and 72,000ft (21,950m). From head-on, a Tomcat at Mach 1.2 and 41,000ft (12,500m) launched a Phoenix from 51nm (94km) away. Climbing over five miles in vertical distance, the Phoenix passed within lethal distance of the drone. Other, similar interceptions have been demonstrated.

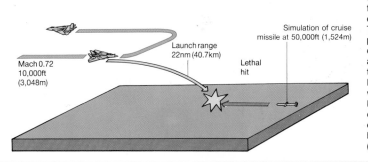

Interception of low-level cruise missile

Mach 0.72 10,000ft (3,048m)

Launch range 22nm (40.7km)

Lethal hit

Simulation of cruise missile at 50,000ft (1,524m)

Left: One of the most dangerous threats to the fleet is the sea-skimming cruise missile. The Tomcat/Phoenix has proved a successful combination even against such small targets as these. On test, BMQ-34, skimming the waves at 50ft (15m) and Mach 0.75, has been detected and knocked down by an AIM-54 launched from 22nm (40km).

KFIR AND NESHER

DEVELOPMENT

The product of a crash engineering programme, aided and abetted by some timely espionage by the Israeli Secret Service, Kfir is the cheapest Mach 2 fighter available from a non-communist supplier, and much more manoeuvrable than the Mirage 5 on which the design is based. An effective warplane, proven in Middle East combat, it has only two defects—the use of a delta wing and the fact that it is made in Israel.

In the late 1960s, the Israeli Government finally accepted that the batch of 50 Mirage 5J fighters embargoed by General de Gaulle were unlikely to be delivered. The temporary suspension of deliveries of spares for the Mirage IIICJ fleet had further highlighted the danger of relying on a foreign supplier. Although the USA had taken over as Israel's supplier of warplanes, delivering Phantoms and Skyhawks, Israel decided to develop its own aircraft industry.

The first problem was to prolong the service life of the existing Mirage IIICJ fleet. Some spares could be manufactured in-country, but a major breakthrough was provided by Israeli intelligence, who "liberated" the drawings of the Atar turbojet from Switzerland. The degree to which the engine may have been built by Bet-Shemesh engines is not clear—Israel also proved adept at obtaining French-built engines in defiance of the French embargo. aircraft delivered before the French arms embargo in 1968.

Another intelligence coup resulted in Israel obtaining most, if not all, of the manufacturing drawings of the Mirage, allowing unlicenced copies of the embargoed Mirage 5Js to be built in Israel. These aircraft were designated Nesher. Production deliveries started late in 1972, and early examples saw action in the 1973 Yom Kippur War.

Under a project known as Black Curtain, later renamed Salvo, IAI engineers attempted to mate the Mirage airframe with the General Electric J79 turbojet used in the Phantom. A trials aircraft was constructed and test flown in September 1971. This was probably a French-built two-seat Mirage, although some sources report that a Nesher prototype was used. In practice, early Nesher prototypes were rebuilt Mirages, so the distinction is largely academic.

Matching the US engine to the airframe and cooling the modified engine bay proved more difficult than the Israeli engineers had anticipated, but production of the definitive aircraft started in 1972. The first was flying by the time of the Yom Kippur War in October 1973.

Official "unveiling" of the type took place on April 14, 1975, when several Kfir 1 fighters were publicly displayed. The aircraft on show were in fact not the latest model, production of the improved Kfir C2 having started the previous year. Kfir 1 was intended for the ground-attack role, but had a secondary air-to-air combat capability. For Kfir C2, the priorities were reversed, the aircraft structure being modified with a revised wing, new canard foreplanes and nose strakes. A two-seat Kfir TC2 version flew in February 1981 and is now in service. Latest variants are the Kfir C7 single-seater and TC7 two-seater. Externally similar to the C2 and TC2, these have revised avionics.

Current production rate is around four or five per month, and delivery of about 300 to the Israeli Air Force has almost

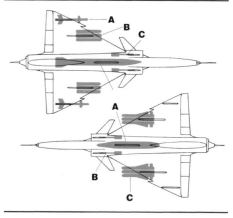

Above: The Mirage IIIC ancestry of the Kfir C-2 is clearly shown in this head-on view, although the canard foreplanes and the strakes on each side of the nosecone are the main identification clues. The nose itself is slimmer and longer than that of the Mirage, and carries ranging-only, rather than multimode, radar.

Typical weapons:
Top: A, Python 3 air-to-air missile; **B,** TAL cluster bomb unit (CBU); **C,** 30mm DEFA cannon; **D,** external fuel tank. This configuration is for a strike behind the lines on airfields, supply dumps, or supply route choke points where air opposition is likely to be encountered. The Python 3 is to replace the Shafrir series of air-to-air missiles.

Above: A, SUU-23A gun pod; **B,** 30mm DEFA cannon; **C,** AGM-65 Maverick air-to-ground missile. This configuration is for a battlefield strike, using the electro-optic or laser-guided Maverick against small targets such as armour, while the SUU-23A pod, housing a 20mm Vulcan GAU-4 gun supplements the two DEFA cannon in the strafing role.

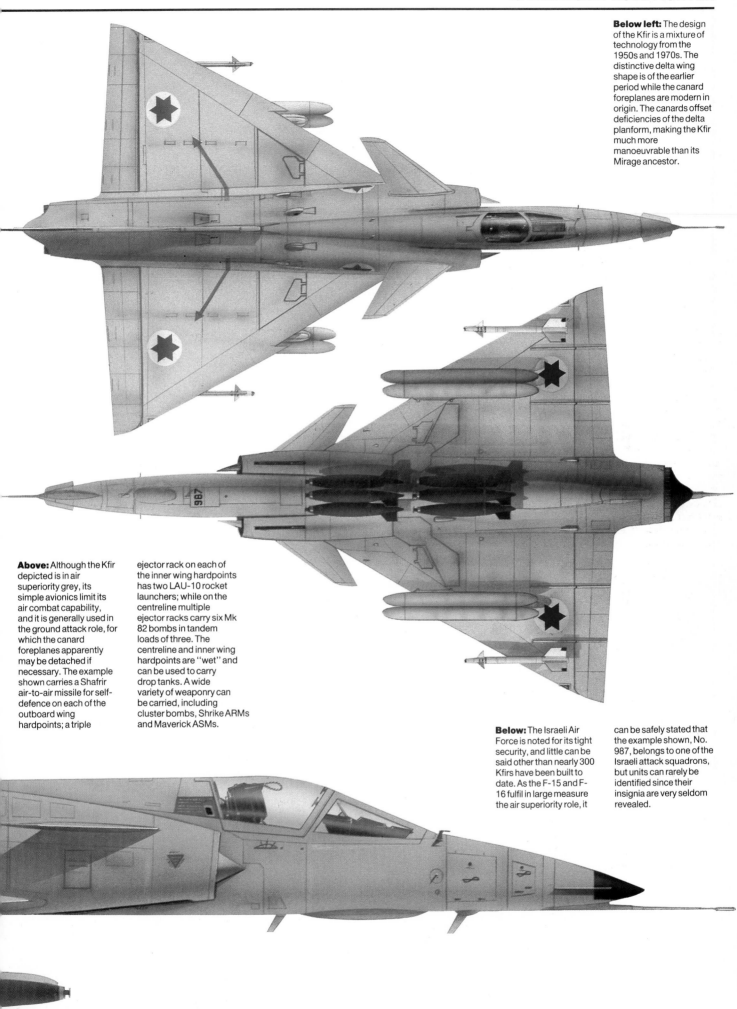

Above: Although the Kfir depicted is in air superiority grey, its simple avionics limit its air combat capability, and it is generally used in the ground attack role, for which the canard foreplanes apparently may be detached if necessary. The example shown carries a Shafrir air-to-air missile for self-defence on each of the outboard wing hardpoints; a triple ejector rack on each of the inner wing hardpoints has two LAU-10 rocket launchers; while on the centreline multiple ejector racks carry six Mk 82 bombs in tandem loads of three. The centreline and inner wing hardpoints are "wet" and can be used to carry drop tanks. A wide variety of weaponry can be carried, including cluster bombs, Shrike ARMs and Maverick ASMs.

Below: The Israeli Air Force is noted for its tight security, and little can be said other than nearly 300 Kfirs have been built to date. As the F-15 and F-16 fulfil in large measure the air superiority role, it can be safely stated that the example shown, No. 987, belongs to one of the Israeli attack squadrons, but units can rarely be identified since their insignia are very seldom revealed.

been completed. The first attempt to export the aircraft came in 1976 with a proposed sale of 24 to Ecuador. At first the US Government embargoed the export of Israeli-built J79 engines, thus effectively crippling plans to export the type, but this restriction was lifted in 1981. Ecuador and Colombia became the first customers, each ordering 12 aircraft.

Attempts were made to sell the aircraft to Austria in the late 1970s. Arab political pressure is reported to have caused the Austrian Air Force to reject the type. In the event, shortage of defence funds caused the planned procurement of new fighters to be shelved.

Despite a price tag of a mere $6 million (cheap by Mach 2 standards) for a single-seat Kfir, few nations have been prepared to risk the wrath of the Arab world by purchasing so conspicuous an item of Israeli military hardware. No nation ordering Kfir draws attention to the deal, but reports claim that Haiti has ordered 24, and that Honduras will receive an unspecified number. Attempts have been made to sell 50 or more Kfirs to Taiwan,

but this is likely to be embargoed by the US Government, which is determined to limit that nation's air arm to the Northrop F-5E. Latest potential customer for the Kfir could be the US Navy, which needs a batch of 24 aircraft to replace the F-5Es currently used as "MiG-simulators" during dissimilar air combat training.

The earlier Nesher is being phased out of IDFAF service, most of the surviving examples having been reworked to an export standard known as Dagger and supplied to Argentina. Many of the "Mirage" kills claimed by the British during the 1982 Falklands War were in fact Daggers. Further deliveries of Israeli aircraft have since been reported, so the possibility of Kfir entering Argentinian service seems likely.

STRUCTURE

Since Kfir is based on the Mirage 5, full details of the basic structure may be found in the entry for that aircraft. The most obvious feature added by Israeli engineers is a shortened rear fuselage of greater

diameter, an air intake at the base of the vertical fin and, in the case of the C2 version, canard foreplanes. The GE engine is some 25in (60cm) shorter than the Atar it replaces, so the aft fuselage has been cut back to suit. On the Mirage, the rear fuselage protrudes beyond the tail fin, but on Kfir the fin slightly overhangs the jetpipe.

The J79 can create severe heating problems within an engine bay unless an adequate supply of cooling air is provided. In the case of Kfir, this is admitted via the fin-base air scoop and other smaller inlets on the rear fuselage. The main air inlets have been increased in size to cope with the higher airflow demands of the new engine.

Although visually similar to the Mirage 5, Kfir embodies much aerodynamic refinement. Inspection of the forward fuselage shows that the underside is flatter than that of the French original, while the C2 model also has small strakes close to the tip of the nose. Most spectacular new feature on the C2 are the new foreplanes mounted near the top of the air intakes.

IAI Kfir C.2
1. Total pressure heads.
2. Rudder pedals.
3. Radar (head down) display.
4. Pilot's instrument display.
5. Head-up display.
6. Martin-Baker ejection seat.
7. Cockpit canopy cover.
8. Canopy jack.
9. Canopy emergency release.
10. Fuel filler cap.
11. Forward fuselage fuel tank.
12. Detachable canard foreplane.
13. VHF aerial.
14. Oxygen bottles.
15. Fuel system inverted flight accumulator.
16. Air system filter.
17. Temperature probes.
18. Bleed air ducting.
19. Starboard wing integral fuel tanks.
20. Engine starter housing.
21. Starboard navigation light.
22. Hydraulic reservoir.
23. Bleed air pre-cooler.
24. Cooling air intake.
25. Engine accessory equipment.
26. General Electric J79-J1E engine.
27. Fuselage ventral fuel tank.
28. Afterburner nozzle jacks.
29. Rudder artificial feel unit.
30. Rudder hydraulic jack.

31. Anti-collision light.
32. VHF aerial.
33. Tail navigation lights.
34. Tail radar warning receiver.
35. Rudder.
36. Brake parachute housing.
37. Tailcone vortex generators.
38. Parachute release link.
39. Variable area afterburner nozzle.
40. Afterburner duct.
41. Auxiliary fuel tank.
42. Infra-red jammer.
43. Elevon compensator hydraulic actuator.
44. Elevon compensator.
45. Inboard elevon.
46. Outboard elevon.
47. Port navigation light.
48. Outboard elevon hydraulic actuator.
49. Elevon control rod.
50. Outboard stores pylon.
51. Inboard elevon hydraulic actuator.
52. Missile launch rail.

53. Shafrir air-to-air missile.
54. Port wing main fuel tanks.
55. Leading edge dog-tooth.
56. Pylon mounting.
57. Inboard stores pylon.
58. Main undercarriage pivot bearing.
59. Hydraulic accumulator.
60. Inward retracting mainwheel.
61. Hydraulic retraction jack.
62. Hydraulic lock strut.
63. Airbrakes.
64. SUU-23A gun pod.
65. Leading edge fuel tank.
66. Airbrake hydraulic jack.

67. Generators.
68. Fuselage fuel tanks.
69. Port detachable canard foreplane.
70. Wing root stores pylon.
71. CBU 59/B cluster bomb.
72. Electrical system equipment.
73. DEFA 30mm cannon.
74. Intake suction relief door.
75. Ventral gun pack ammunition magazine.
76. Intake variable half cone screw jack.
77. Intake half cone centrebody.
78. Air conditioning system equipment.
79. Elevon artificial feel unit.

80. Nose undercarriage hydraulic jack.
81. Aft-retracting nosewheel.
82. Landing/taxiing lamps.
83. Engine throttle lever.
84. Control column and linkages.
85. Doppler navigation radar.

86. Incidence probe.
87. UHF aerial.
88. Forward radar warning receiver.
89. Avionics system equipment.
90. Nose strake.
91. Elta EL/M-2021 radar.
92. Radome.
93. Pitot head.

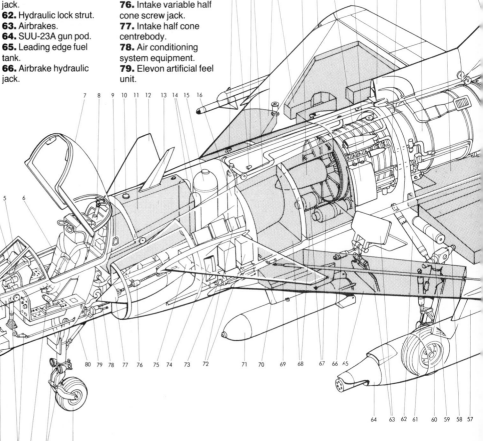

These may be detached if necessary (a move probably carried out only if the aircraft has been assigned to a ground-attack mission).

On the C2, the wing has an extended leading edge on its outer section, giving a prominent dog-tooth notch. Some aircraft

Above: A busy scene "somewhere in Israel" as the two nearest Kfirs are prepared for a training mission. The three furthest Kfirs appear to have unidentifiable unit markings on the fin.

Below: The cockpit of the Kfir reflects the austere design approach. Even the dials are few. Forward visibility is poor, although much less cluttered than that of the MiG-21.

have been seen with a small wing fence, but according to IAI this was only fitted to a few and not adopted for general service.

Training aircraft have an extended forward fuselage, a 33in (84cm) plus providing space for the second seat. The nose is drooped to improve the forward view.

PROPULSION

For Kfir, IAI selected the J79-J1E turbojet, a modified version of the General Electric J79-GE-17 engine fitted to the F-4E. This is built under licence by Bet-Shemesh. A full description of this powerplant appears in the F-4 entry. Most Israeli engines probably incorporate "combat Plus"—a facility which allows the engine to deliver 5 per cent extra thrust for a few minutes—a total of 18,790lb (8,525kg). Maximum internal fuel load is 5,670lb (2,572kg).

AVIONICS

An Elta EL/M-2001B bombing/navigation radar is carried behind a small radome at the tip of the nose. This is the most

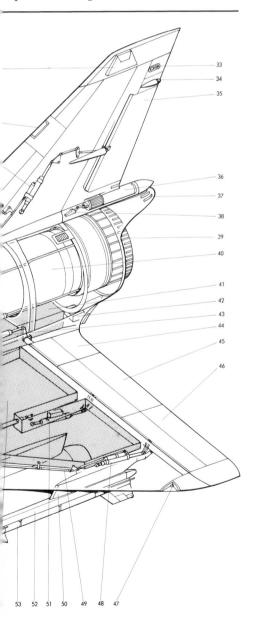

common installation, although some Kfirs are reported to carry the more advanced EL/M-2021, a multi-mode set similar in size to the Cyrano of the Mirage III, but of greatly-improved capability. The normal nav/attack system is either a Rafael Mahat or IAI WDNS-141, working in conjunction with an Elta S-8600 central digital processor. Data is presented to the pilot during combat by an Israeli-developed HUD.

The MBT flight-control system is of Israeli design, incorporating an ASW-41 control-augmentation, an ASW-42 stability-augmentation system, and a Tamam two-axis gyro. Other items of locally-developed avionics include a Taman central air-data processor, the IFF system, communications equipment, radar-warning receiver and ECM. The newer Kfir C7 carries improved weapons-delivery and navigation avionics, but full details are not yet available.

Although officially intended as a two-seat trainer, the TC2 and TC7 may have a specialised mission role. Israeli reports mention the installation of specialised equipment in the rear cockpit. This has led to suggestions that the type may be intended for anti-radar operations, but none of the available photographs shows evidence of the additional antennas which would be needed for such a role.

ARMAMENT

Seven hard points are provided—two under each wing and three beneath the fuselage. The outer wing pylons are lightly stressed and can carry only air-to-air missiles such as Shafrir or the newer Python 3 "dogfight" missile. Using the remaining five, Kfir C2 can tote an impressive 9,500lb (4,300kg) of ordnance, while the C7 can lift a maximum of 13,400lb (6,085kg). Typical payloads include 500lb (230kg) or 1,000lb (460kg) bombs, napalm tanks, cluster munitions such as the indigenously-developed TAL-1, launchers for unguided rockets, or Shrike, Maverick or HOBOS air-to-ground missiles. Reports that an Israeli-developed missile (Luz) with TV guidance may be carried beneath the fuselage should be treated with reserve until evidence for the existence of this long-rumoured weapon appears. Two DEFA 553 30mm cannon are carried in the lower sides of the air intakes—the location also used by the Mirage III and 5.

PERFORMANCE

Thanks to its US powerplant, the Kfir has a performance well in excess of that of the Mirage 5. Top speed at altitude and in clean condition is officially given as Mach 2 sustained, but the C2 can probably touch Mach 2.3. At sea level, a clean C2 can manage 750kt (1,390km/h). Sea level rate of climb is 45,950ft/min (14,000m/min), and a fully fuelled C2 carrying two Shafrirs can make 50,000ft (15,250m) in just over 5 minutes. Normal ceiling is 58,000ft (17,680m), but this can be increased to 75,000ft (22,860m) in a zoom climb.

High-altitude interception
Mission radius 419nm (775km)

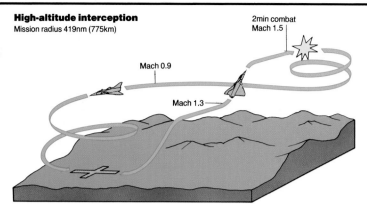

2min combat
Mach 1.5

Mach 0.9

Mach 1.3

Left: Armed with two Shafrir or Python 3 AAMs, the Kfir can intercept high flying targets far from base. To do this, it must carry extra fuel in two underwing 286gal (1,300lit) tanks with a further 180gal (825lit) on the centreline. The climb-out is typically followed by a transit at Mach 1.3, two minutes combat commencing at Mach 1.5, followed by egress at Mach 0.9. Radius in this configuration is 186nm (346km).

Combat air patrol
Mission radius 476nm (880km)

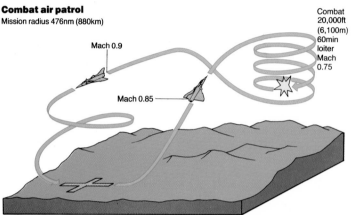

Combat 20,000ft (6,100m) 60min loiter Mach 0.75

Mach 0.9

Mach 0.85

Left: The combat air patrol mission, flown with two 374gal (1,700lit) wing tanks and a 286gal (1,300lit) centreline tank gives an hour on station at a radius of 476nm (877km) from base. The outward transit is flown at Mach 0.85 and the patrol at Mach 0.75. Two minutes of combat at 20,000ft (6,100m) are possible, followed by a high level Mach 0.9 egress. The patrol speed of Mach 0.75 would not be realistic; full military power would be far more likely.

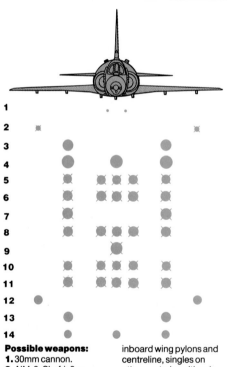

Possible weapons:
1. 30mm cannon.
2. AIM-9, Shafrir 2 or Python 3 missiles.
3. 130gal (500lit) tanks.
4. 340gal (1,300lit) tanks.
5. Mk82 500lb (230kg) bombs (triple ejector racks on centreline and inner wing pylons, singles on other ventral positions).
6. Mk83 1,000lb (450kg) bombs (two on each inboard wing pylon, singles under fuselage).
7. Mk84 2,000lb (910kg) bombs.
8. M117 820lb (370kg) high-drag bombs (2 on inboard wing pylons and centreline, singles on other ventral positions).
9. M118 3,000lb (1,360kg) bomb.
10. CBU-24 and -49 cluster bombs (as **8**).
11. 80gal (300lit) napalm stores (as **8**).
12. LAU-32 rocket launchers.
13. LAU-3A or -10A rocket launchers (two in each location).
14. SUU-25 flare dispenser (2 on each inboard underwing hardpoint, 1 on centreline).

Ground attack (hi-lo-hi)
Mission radius 640nm (1,185km)

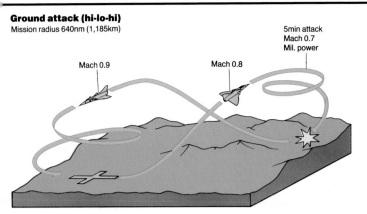

Mach 0.9

Mach 0.8

5min attack
Mach 0.7
Mil. power

Left: The range of ground attack missions is very sensitive to altitude. The hi-lo-hi profile shown here is the optimum and is flown with the same external fuel tanks as combat air patrol to achieve a radius of action of 640nm (1,185km), carrying a load of two M117 and two Mk82 bombs, plus two AAMs for defence. The entire mission is planned to be flown at subsonic speeds against a low threat target.

Left: Two Kfirs set out on a training mission configured for combat air patrol, with "jugs" and AAMs. The Kfir is a remarkable example of updating an elderly design, and will see service into the 1990s.

Below: The Kfir C7 is the most recent variant. Its Mach 2 capability will avail it little, as it takes three minutes to accelerate there from Mach 0.9. The sustained turn performance is 9.6deg/sec at 15,000ft (4,615m), Mach 0.68.

Being a delta, Kfir shares the Achilles' heel of the Dassault deltas—a long take-off run. A fully-loaded Mirage 5 needs 5,250ft (1,600m) to get airborne, and a fully-loaded Kfir C2 shows only a slight improvement at 4,750ft (1,450m). In more typical combat conditions, the Israeli aircraft can get airborne in only 2,300ft (700m), but this is no real improvement on the Mirage figure. Combat radius in the interceptor role ranges from 200 to 285nm (370 to 530km) depending on weapon load and flight profile, while ground-attack range varies from 350 to 700nm (650 to 1300 km).

The biggest gain comes in combat, where a Kfir C7 with 50 per cent internal fuel and two Shafrirs has a combat thrust: weight ratio of 0.91 when the engine is run in Combat Plus, and a wing loading of 6,098lb/sq ft (257kg/sq m). This may not match the figures for highly-agile dogfighters such as the F-15 or F-16, but is more than enough to deal with most opposition which Kfir is likely to face.

OPERATORS

Israel (c.300 planned), Argentina (32 Daggers), Colombia (12), Ecuador (12, plus option for 12 more), Haiti (24 on order), Honduran order reported.

AV-8B HARRIER II

DEVELOPMENT

First studies of a follow-on aircraft to the Harrier and AV-8A took place in 1973, when British Aerospace and McDonnell Douglas started preliminary work which was to result in a series of "paper" aeroplanes. Most technologically important of these was the AV-16A. As its designation suggests, this was meant to be twice as effective as Harrier/AV-8, offering twice the payload/range performance of the existing aircraft. It would have had a long-span supercritical wing and a 25,000lb (11,350kg) Pegasus 15 engine. One thing it sadly lacked was a firm customer.

The US Navy needed a new fighter for use on the projected Sea Control Ship light carriers, but had decided to explore an alternative approach to VTOL in what was to become the singularly unsuccessful Rockwell XFV-12A (quietly shelved when ground-running tests showed that thrust was not equal to weight). The USMC wanted an efficient close-support aircraft; the RAF wanted an improved Harrier built to a standard to which existing GR.3s might be updated; the RN was firmly wedded to the Sea Harrier. The British Government added to its endless list of nonsensical defence decisions by announcing in March 1975 that there was not enough common ground between the UK and USA to justify a joint programme with the USA. (They really wanted to cut defence spending yet again.)

UK withdrawal from the AV-16A virtually handed the long-term future of the Harrier/AV-8 family to the USA. Even faced with the built-in headwind created by supporters of the F/A-18A (who see the AV-8 programme as a useless diversion of funding from the Hornet), the future of the aircraft cannot be handled any more incompetently than was its fate in the hands of the UK Government.

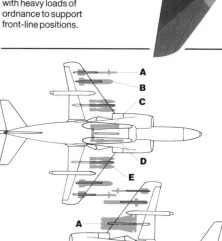

The USMC still wanted its new fighter, so McDonnell Douglas pressed ahead with what was to become the AV-8B. The expensive attractions of the proposed Pegasus 15 were ignored as the St Louis designers tried to design the best aircraft they could, using the standard Sea Harrier engine. Key elements in the new design were refined aerodynamics and the large-scale use of carbon composites.

To save time and money, the first two YAV-8B prototypes were converted from AV-8As. Fitted with the new wing, these retained the standard AV-8A forward fuselage, cockpit, inlets, tailplane and internal systems. The first flew on November 9, 1978. Flight demonstrations were completed during 1979, with the two prototypes having flown more than 170 test hours successfully.

In April of that year, McDonnell Douglas was awarded a contract for four full-scale development aircraft and initial preparations for production. The main problems proved to be political, with AV-8B still regarded in some US circles as a "foreign" aircraft. The Carter Administration made it clear that the USMC could proceed with the programme only if a major foreign customer could be found—a pointed reference to the UK.

Above: The USMC ordered the AV-8B and the earlier AV-8A as V/STOL "bomb trucks" – aircraft capable of flying missions at short notice with heavy loads of ordnance to support front-line positions.

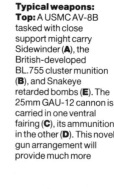

Typical weapons:
Top: A USMC AV-8B tasked with close support might carry Sidewinder (**A**), the British-developed BL.755 cluster munition (**B**), and Snakeye retarded bombs (**E**). The 25mm GAU-12 cannon is carried in one ventral fairing (**C**), its ammunition in the other (**D**). This novel gun arrangement will provide much more effective firepower than the slower-firing ADEN of the AV-8A.
Above: Aircraft ranging deeper inland to suppress enemy air attacks could carry AGM-65 Mavericks on triple launchers (**A**), French-built Durandal anti-runway weapons (**B**), plus the inevitable AIM-9 Sidewinders for self-defence on the outboard pylons (**C**).

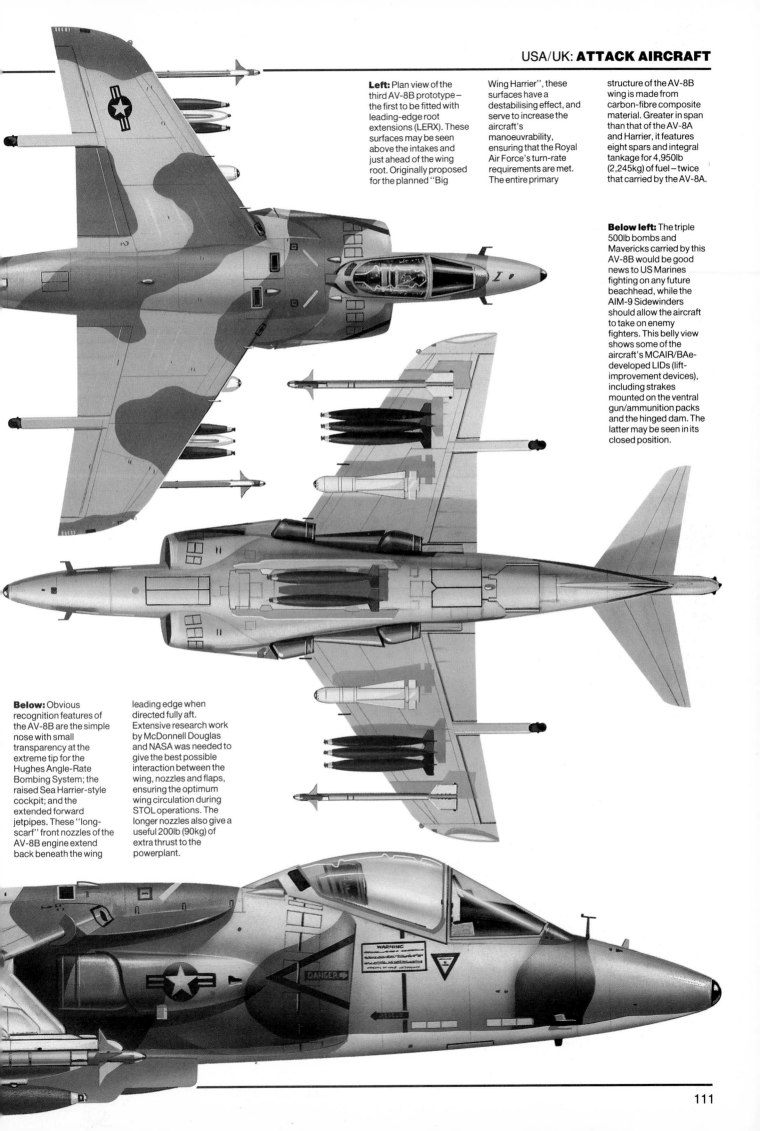

Left: Plan view of the third AV-8B prototype – the first to be fitted with leading-edge root extensions (LERX). These surfaces may be seen above the intakes and just ahead of the wing root. Originally proposed for the planned "Big Wing Harrier", these surfaces have a destabilising effect, and serve to increase the aircraft's manoeuvrability, ensuring that the Royal Air Force's turn-rate requirements are met. The entire primary structure of the AV-8B wing is made from carbon-fibre composite material. Greater in span than that of the AV-8A and Harrier, it features eight spars and integral tankage for 4,950lb (2,245kg) of fuel – twice that carried by the AV-8A.

Below left: The triple 500lb bombs and Mavericks carried by this AV-8B would be good news to US Marines fighting on any future beachhead, while the AIM-9 Sidewinders should allow the aircraft to take on enemy fighters. This belly view shows some of the aircraft's MCAIR/BAe-developed LIDs (lift-improvement devices), including strakes mounted on the ventral gun/ammunition packs and the hinged dam. The latter may be seen in its closed position.

Below: Obvious recognition features of the AV-8B are the simple nose with small transparency at the extreme tip for the Hughes Angle-Rate Bombing System; the raised Sea Harrier-style cockpit; and the extended forward jetpipes. These "long-scarf" front nozzles of the AV-8B engine extend back beneath the wing leading edge when directed fully aft. Extensive research work by McDonnell Douglas and NASA was needed to give the best possible interaction between the wing, nozzles and flaps, ensuring the optimum wing circulation during STOL operations. The longer nozzles also give a useful 200lb (90kg) of extra thrust to the powerplant.

The AV-8B had been designed to meet USMC payload/range requirements, but in 1980 the Royal Air Force studied the aircraft to see if it would meet Air Staff Requirement 409 for a Harrier replacement. This placed a strong emphasis on manoeuvrability and survivability in air-to-air combat. The RAF had given some thought to a "Big Wing" Harrier GR.5 which would have had a larger wing, extended intakes and front fuselage, and would have been optimised for increased manoeuvrability and high-speed flight. This was proposed by BAe, but the RAF was not initially convinced that the AV-8B would be suitable. In practice, the main deficiency turned out to be turn rate, which was below the 20deg/sec which the UK thought desirable in a fighter intended to be able to defend itself against air-superiority fighters. To increase the turn

rate, a leading edge wing root extension (LERX) was devised, clearing the way for the UK to announce its adoption of the aircraft and thus removing the final hurdle standing in the way of full production.

Under the joint programme formalised in the summer of 1981, the UK agreed to buy at least 60 AV-8B fighters—to be known as Harrier GR.5 in RAF service—and to participate in the development programme, contributing an initial $80 million to general development plus a further $200 million for the development of RAF-related features of the design. Harrier GR.5 will enter RAF service in 1986.

Having operated the earlier AV-8A, Spain was a natural customer for the AV-8B, and intends to buy 12. These will presumably be deployed aboard the new aircraft carrier *Principe de Asturias*.

The first full-scale development aircraft

flew on Novembr 5, 1981, and all four were flying by the following summer. On August 29, 1983, the first production aircraft flew, and by the end of that year the AV-8B fleet had clocked up more than 1,400 flying hours and testing was 75 per cent complete.

Procurement of the first 12 production aircraft was covered by the FY82 defence budget, and the first flew in August 1983. Initial follow-on orders were for 21 aircraft in FY83 and 27 in FY84. Production will continue to build up over the following years, reaching four a month for the USMC by the end of the decade. The first USMC AV-8B squadron will become operational in 1985, and the Service intends to buy a total of 336 aircraft. These will replace five A-4 squadrons and three AV-8A squadrons. Initial Operational Capability (IOC) is scheduled for June 1985. Unit cost of the

McDonnell Douglas AV-8B Harrier II

1. Angle rate bombing system receiver (ARBS).
2. All weather landing system receiver (Awls).
3. IFF aerial.
4. ARBS signal data converter.
5. Yaw vane.
6. Rudder pedals.
7. Control column.
8. Cockpit displays.
9. One piece 'wrap-around' windscreen.
10. Pilot's head-up display (HUD).
11. Stencel lightweight ejection seat.
12. Boundary layer air exhaust ducts.
13. Cockpit air conditioning system.
14. Starter/generator.
15. Formation lighting strips.
16. Engine accessory gearbox.
17. Auxiliary power unit (APU).
18. Leading edge root extension (LERX).
19. Starboard wing pylons.
20. Starboard wing integral fuel tank.
21. Aileron hydraulic actuator.
22. Radar warning receiver.
23. Starboard navigation light.
24. Roll control reaction air valve.
25. Formation light.
26. Fuel jettison.
27. Starboard aileron.
28. Water-methanol tank.
29. Flap slot door.
30. Anti-collision light.
31. Single slotted flap.
32. Water-methanol filler cap.
33. Flap hydraulic jack.
34. Fire extinguisher bottle.
35. Rear fuselage fuel tank.
36. Avionics equipment racks.
37. Electrical system distribution panel.
38. Equipment bay air conditioning system.
39. Rudder hydraulic actuator.
40. Starboard all-moving tailplane.
41. Formation lighting strip.
42. Total temperature probe.
43. Upper broadband communications and navigation antenna fairing.
44. Radar beacon antenna.
45. Rudder.
46. MAD compensator.
47. Rudder tab.
48. Yaw control reaction air valves.
49. Rear radar warning antennae.
50. Radar warning receivers.
51. Pitch control reaction air valve.
52. Port all-moving tailplane.
53. Tail bumper.
54. Lower broadband nav/comm antenna.
55. Tailplane hydraulic jack.
56. Tailplane control linkages.
57. IFF aerial.
58. Electrical system generator panel.
59. Airbrake hydraulic jack.
60. Airbrake.
61. Port single slotted flap.
62. Outrigger wheel housing.
63. Outrigger leg doors.
64. Aileron hydraulic actuator.
65. Aileron/roll control valve mechanical linkage.
66. Fuel jettison.
67. Formation light.
68. Roll control reaction air valve.
69. Port navigation light.
70. Radar warning receiver.
71. Bleed air ducting.
72. AIM-9L Sidewinder air-to-air missile.
73. Missile launch rail.
74. Outboard wing pylon.
75. Port outrigger wheel.
76. Outrigger retraction jack.
77. Port wing integral fuel tank.
78. 300-US gal drop tank.
79. Wing centre pylon.
80. Wing inboard pylon.
81. 750lb retarded bombs.
82. Bomb ejector rack.
83. Rear (hotstream) swivelling exhaust nozzle.
84. Main wheels.
85. Pressure refuelling connection.
86. Main undercarriage hydraulic jack.
87. Hydraulic reservoir.
88. Fuselage flank fuel tank.
89. Forward "zero-scarf" (fan air) swivelling exhaust nozzle.
90. Cushion augmentation strakes, port and starboard,

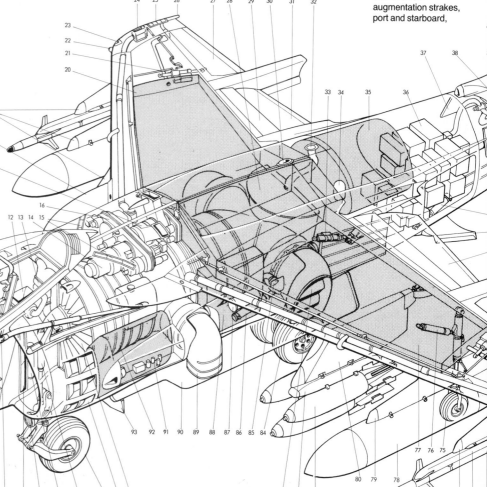

USMC aircraft is just over $20 million.

A two-seat trainer is planned. Two TAV-8B aircraft will be ordered in FY84, followed by six per year until all 27 currently planned for US service have been built. The first should be handed over to the USMC in 1986.

STRUCTURE

Based on the Whitcomb supercritical wing, the new wing of the AV-8B is of greater span and thickness than that on the AV-8A/Harrier. It carries three hardpoints on each side and has integral fuel tanks almost twice the volume of those of the original aircraft. Leading-edge sweepback has been reduced from 40deg to 36deg, and the outrigger landing gears have been moved closer to the fuselage. They are now located between the aileron and the

trailing-edge flap. The latter is of double-slotted form and may be deflected at angles of up to 62deg, reacting with the wing surface and nozzles to improve the local airflow and to provide increased lift. The entire primary structure of the wing is made from carbon fibre, resulting in a weight saving of 330lb (150kg).

The fuselage also makes extensive use of carbon fibre; this material is used for the forward section, upper panels on the centre section, horizontal stabiliser, and rudder. A Sea Harrier-style raised cockpit canopy gives good all-round visibility. Two large strakes known as LIDs (lift-improvement devices) are fitted beneath the fuselage. These operate in conjunction with a hinged airbrake-like dam to increase lift and reduce reingestion of hot efflux gas by the intakes.

Under the agreed work-sharing arrange-

ment, manufacture of aircraft for the USMC and RAF will be split, with approximately 60 per cent going to McDonnell Douglas and 40 per cent to BAe. On third-country sales the split would be 75:25 in favour of McDonnell Douglas. RAF aircraft will be assembled on a UK line, with components such as the wings, forward fuselage, and horizontal tail surfaces and some items of avionics being imported from the USA. BAe would manufacture the centre and rear fuselage, the centreline pylon and the reaction control system. Fin and rudder assemblies may also be included.

POWERPLANT

Having considered a number of proposals ranging from the standard Sea Harrier Mk 104 engine to the Pegasus 11D offering 21,800lb (9,890kg) of thrust, the US Navy opted for the F402-RR-404. Based on the Mk 104, this featured a revised fan able to run at higher RPM, a higher-output gearbox and modified pick-up points to match the AV-8 airframe. Maximum thrust rose to 21,700lb (9,840kg). YF402-RR-404 development engines for YAV-8B were sent to the USA in August 1978.

This version was rapidly supplanted by the F402-RR-404A, a derivative of the Mk 104 incorporating new zero-scarf cold nozzles, a revised swan-neck intermediate casing, plus modifications intended to increase maintainability and reliability. This is used in full-scale development and early production versions of the AV-8B. Deliveries started in April 1983.

The definitive F402-RR-406 (Pegasus 11-21E/F) used in production aircraft passed its 150hr qualification test in late 1982. It has a new shrouded LP turbine, improved seals, a forged combustion chamber and better HP turbine cooling. It will have 22,000lb (9,980kg) of thrust plus a 2 per cent improvement in SFC.

AV-8B engines are to be fitted with a

interchangeable with 30mm Aden gun packs.
91. Hydraulic ground connectors.
92. Forward fuselage fuel tank.
93. Cushion augmentation retractable cross-dam fence.
94. Rolls-Royce F402-RR-405 Pegasus vectoring thrust turbofan engine.

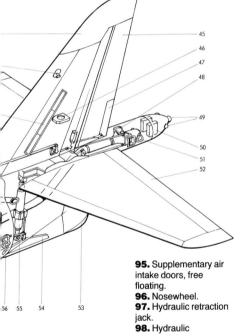

45
46
47
48
49
50
51
52

56 55 54 53

95. Supplementary air intake doors, free floating.
96. Nosewheel.
97. Hydraulic retraction jack.
98. Hydraulic accumulator.
99. Landing/taxying lamp.
100. Boundary layer bleed air duct.
101. Retractable in-flight refuelling probe.
102. Engine throttle and exhaust nozzle angle control levers.
103. OEAS concentrator.
104. Formation lighting strips.
105. Control system linkages.
106. Inertial navigation system.
107. Airdata computer.
108. Pitot head.
109. Pitch feel and trim actuators.
110. Pitch control reaction air valve.
111. ARBS heat exchanger.

62
63
64
65
66

69 68 67

Above: AV-8B is not just a close-support aircraft. Its ability to carry heavy ordnance loads makes it an effective short-range tactical fighter.

Below: This head-on view shows the transparency for the Hughes Angle Rate Bombing System, plus gun/ammunition pods.

full-authority digital electronic fuel control system developed by Dowty and Smiths Industries Controls. Some 60lb (27.2kg) lighter than the current electromechanical system, it gives better control of compressor stall margins, making the engine easier to handle at altitude and at high angles of attack. Flight-testing of the system started in May 1983 on a Harrier testbed and it is due to be installed in production AV-8B aircraft from late 1985 onwards. For the future, the USMC is interested in obtaining even more powerful engines. In the spring of 1984 Rolls-Royce was asked to study ways of increasing the thrust to up to 28,000lb (12,700kg). First results suggest that a Pegasus variant developing around 25,000lb (11,300kg) may be possible.

AVIONICS

No radar will be installed, but all aircraft are expected to have the Hughes Angle Rate Bombing System (ARBS), which features a nose-mounted electro-optical sensor package—a combined laser spot tracker and TV contrast tracker. This may be used for auto-release, CCIP (continuously-computed impact point) or depressed sightline attacks with unguided munitions, or to aim guided weapons. Prime navaid is the ASN-130 INS.

A large multi-function CRT display is mounted at the left-hand side of the instrument panel. The HUD for all aircraft will be made by Smiths Industries, and will be a modern design with twin combiner glasses, minimum structure to restrict vision, and a wide field of view.

Throttle and nozzle controls are being integrated into a single cockpit control to allow HOTAS (hands-on-throttle-and-stick) operation in combat. Unlike the pilot of a normal fighter such as the F-18A, the AV-8B "jockey" will include "viffing" (vectoring in forward flight) combat manoeuvres in his HOTAS repertoire. This already includes control of the manoeuvring flaps sensor selection, cage/uncage, slewing and target acquisition, gun firing and weapon release, plus control of the stability and attitude-hold system (SAAHS). USMC aircraft will carry an ALR-67 radar-warning receiver, plus an ALE-39 chaff/flare dispenser mounted in the rear fuselage.

The avionics fit of RAF aircraft has yet to be fully announced, but will be broadly similar to that of the standard AV-8B. One addition will be a head-down moving map display to be located on the right-hand side of the instrument panel. The aircraft will probably be fitted with the Zeus internally-mounted ECM system.

ARMAMENT

The AV-8B has carried payloads of up to 9,200lb (4,200kg) of ordnance on trials. Service loadings are likely to include conventional ordnance such as the Mk 81, Mk 82 and Mk 83 bombs, Rockeye retarded bombs, Durandal anti-runway bombs, Paveway and other "smart" bombs, and

Above: This mock-up was used to plan the cockpit of the Royal Air Force Harrier GR.5. Obvious features include the HUD, multi-function head-down CRT display (left) and the moving-map display (right). The CRT is displaying the aircraft's stores configuration.

Right: The two YAV-8B development aircraft were converted from existing AV-8A airframes. The new carbon-fibre wing was fitted (although not manufactured using production methods), along with the new main inlets and LIDs (lift-improvement devices).

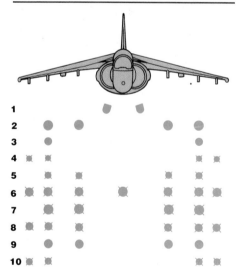

Possible weapons:
1. GAU-12 25mm cannon (right) plus ammunition pack (left).
2. 300 US gal (1,300lit) external tanks.
3. Externally-mounted gun pods in calibres such as 30mm.
4. AIM-9 Sidewinder air-to-air missiles. Several versions are currently in the USMC inventory.
5. AGM-65 Maverick air-to-ground missiles, including the TV-guided A and B versions and the USMC's new laser-guided E model.
6. "Iron" bombs,

including retarded weapons.
7. Laser-guided bombs, probably the Paveway II and III.
8. Cluster bomb units (CBUs) on US aircraft, or the improved version of the Hunting Engineering BL.755 cluster bomb on RAF aircraft.
9. Launchers for unguided rockets. The proposed Vought Hypervelocity Missile (HVM) or laser-guided Zuni, now under development, might be adopted in the future.
10. Flare dispensers.

missiles such as the AIM-9 Sidewinder and AGM-65 Maverick. Plans to carry tactical nuclear weapons, known as "special stores" in US Service parlance, have been reported but not confirmed.

AV-8A and Harrier GR.3 use a pair of single-barrelled 30mm ADEN cannon. USMC AV-8Bs will probably be fitted with the five-barrelled General Electric GAU-12/U 25mm cannon. The installation devised for the AV-8B would mount a single gun in one ventral pod, and the ammunition supply in the other. RAF aircraft may be fitted with a pair of ADEN cannon, perhaps of 25mm calibre.

PERFORMANCE

Since development of the AV-8B has not yet been completed, details of performance are still sketchy. Figures released so far reflect the aircraft's design role as a close-support/strike carrier of ordnance.

Top speed of the AV-8B in level flight at sea level is Mach 0.88/580kt (1,075km/h), well below the 638kt (1,185km/h) of the Harrier GR.3, while the maximum speed in a dive remains subsonic at Mach 0.93

(Harrier, Sea Harrier and the AV-8A/C are all supersonic in a dive).

In the field, the aircraft will have to operate from short strips, and McDonnell Douglas reports a typical STOL take-off run at full all-up weight of 29,750lb (13,500kg) of only 1,200ft (365m). Even the most zealous attacker would find it hard to mine or crater a runway to the point where a run of this length could not be obtained. Given a load of 12 Snakeye bombs plus full internal fuel, an AV-8B could get airborne with a 1,000ft (300m) run, fly for more than 150nm (280km) to a target area, then loiter for up to an hour. Tasked with a strike mission requiring no loiter in the target area and given external tanks, the aircraft could take off from the same short strip and deliver seven Snakeyes on a target 600nm (1,110km) away. Unrefuelled ferry range with four 300 gallon external tanks is 2,460nm (4,550km)

OPERATORS

USMC (336 planned); UK (60 Harrier GR.5 planned); Spain (12 planned).

Sea-based close support operations

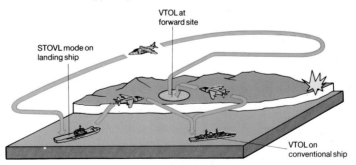

Harrier II using "ground loitering" sites

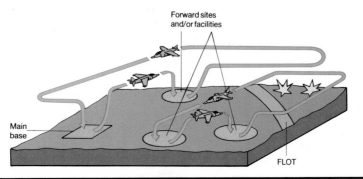

Left: When deployed in the close-support role as part of an amphibious operation, AV-8B could take off in STOVL mode from a *Tarawa* class landing ship, then land vertically on the helicopter pads of conventional warships or at shore-based forward sites until required for a mission. This technique of "ground loitering" saves fuel and provides fast-reaction support.

Left: When operating from land sites, the AV-8B can take off in vertical mode from its airfield, then fly to forward "ground loitering" sites close to front-line positions, or to a centralised support facility serving several airstrips. Such a system would be hard to knock out – an airfield would remain operational even if its runways were "taken out", and could carry out basic maintenance.

A-4 SKYHAWK

DEVELOPMENT

"Any of you who want out, you know where the door is", Douglas designer Ed Heinemann told his assembled design staff one morning in January 1952. The task that they were being invited to "want out" of was that of building a lightweight attack bomber for the US Navy—the aircraft which was to become the A-4 Skyhawk. The specification was a challenging one—the US Navy wanted a 30,000lb (13,600kg) aircraft, but Heinemann planned to deliver the required level of performance in a 12,000lb (5,440kg) package. If any of the team thought that their boss had bitten off more than they could chew, they kept their doubts to themselves. No-one left the room.

The Skyhawk has now become an aeronautical legend. Built in some 17 different configurations over a production run spanning a quarter of a century, the A-4 became a widely-exported strike aircraft. By the time the last example left the line in February 1979, a total of 2,960 had been built, while aerospace journalists and writers had virtually run out of superlatives with which to describe it.

No aircraft packs so much punch in so small a package, and its ability to take battle damage and come home remains legendary. Ground crews who maintain the aircraft praise its ability to keep flying.

In combat operations, the A-4 has flown 90 hours per month. Even in the difficult art (for a bomber) of air-to-air combat, the Skyhawk has earned laurels. Higher in performance than a MiG-15, it has downed the agile MiG-17. On the only campaign in which the type took a severe mauling, it was being flown in appalling weather against modern missile-equipped defences. It may lack the glamour associated with many jet fighters, but the Skyhawk—often dubbed "Heinemann's Hot Rod", "The Bantam Bomber" or "The Scooter"—must be one of the all-time "greats".

Above: The A-4 Skyhawk was originally developed as an ultra-lightweight attack bomber for the US Navy. Designed at a time when the life of a small jet was only reckoned to be a few years, the Skyhawk will have had an operational life of more than three decades by the time it finally ceases service. The USMC A-4M pictured here shows some of the developments that have been incorporated over the years, notably the lengthened nose, and the avionics "hump" behind the cockpit.

The first prototype XA4D-1 had its maiden flight in June 1954, and production deliveries started in October 1956. Originally known as the A4D-1, it was later redesignated A-4A. The A-4B introduced a navigation computer for automatic dead-reckoning, plus flight-refuelling capability, a dual hydraulic system, and Bullpup missiles.

These early aircraft carried very austere avionics, but the era of the simple day-only aircraft was clearly coming to an end. Later models saw the number of "black boxes" grow steadily. All-weather per-

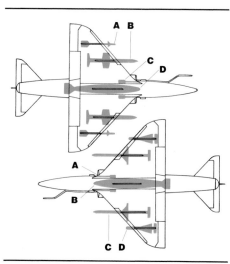

Typical weapons: Top: A, AIM-9 Sidewinder AAM; **B**, Gabriel 3 ASM; **C**, 30mm DEFA cannon; **D**, external fuel tank. The configuration here is for an anti-shipping strike using the latest version of Israeli Aircraft Industries Gabriel anti-shipping missile. Gabriel 3 is a sea-skimmer after the style of Exocet, and has been developed from earlier surface-launched versions of Gabriel.

Above: A, 20mm Mk 12 cannon: **B**, external fuel tank: **C**, AGM-88A Harm; **D**, AGM-65 Maverick. This is a stand-off weapon for use against pin-point targets, while Harm is carried for self-defence against enemy radar-guided or controlled ground-to-air weapons, homing on emitted radiation. The Mk 12 cannon have 200 rounds each compared with the 150 rounds of the 30mm DEFA.

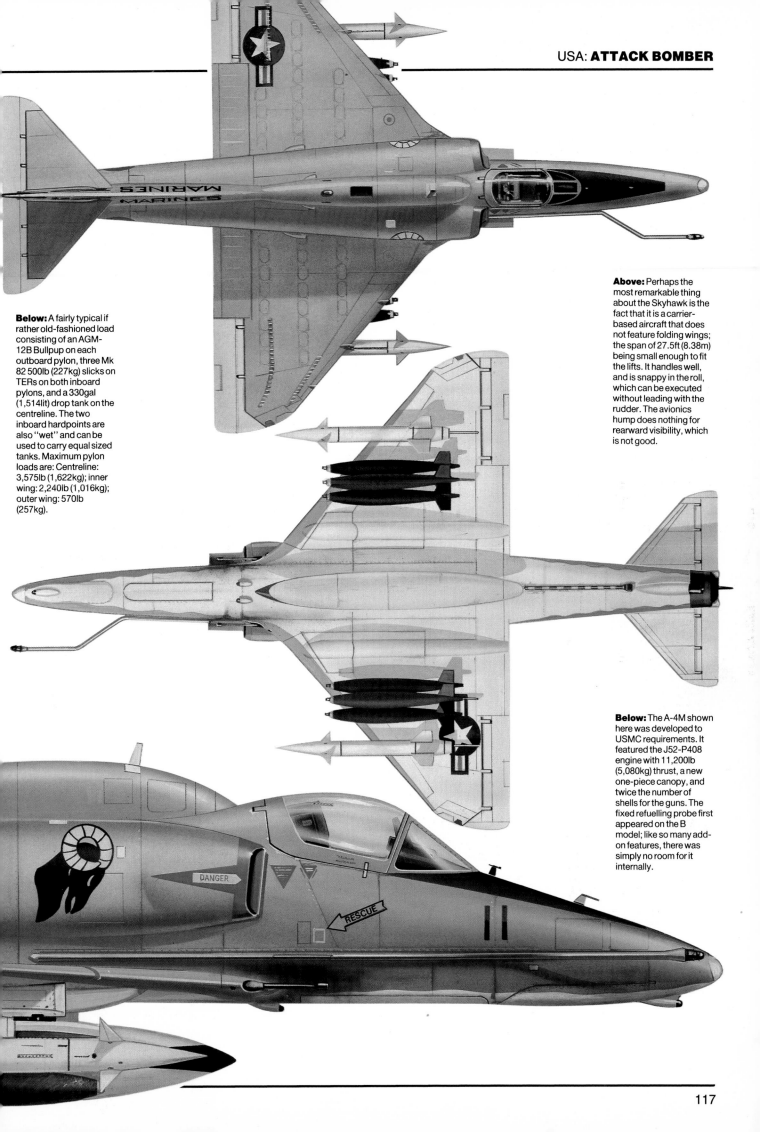

Below: A fairly typical if rather old-fashioned load consisting of an AGM-12B Bullpup on each outboard pylon, three Mk 82 500lb (227kg) slicks on TERs on both inboard pylons, and a 330gal (1,514lit) drop tank on the centreline. The two inboard hardpoints are also "wet" and can be used to carry equal sized tanks. Maximum pylon loads are: Centreline: 3,575lb (1,622kg); inner wing: 2,240lb (1,016kg); outer wing: 570lb (257kg).

Above: Perhaps the most remarkable thing about the Skyhawk is the fact that it is a carrier-based aircraft that does not feature folding wings; the span of 27.5ft (8.38m) being small enough to fit the lifts. It handles well, and is snappy in the roll, which can be executed without leading with the rudder. The avionics hump does nothing for rearward visibility, which is not good.

Below: The A-4M shown here was developed to USMC requirements. It featured the J52-P408 engine with 11,200lb (5,080kg) thrust, a new one-piece canopy, and twice the number of shells for the guns. The fixed refuelling probe first appeared on the B model; like so many add-on features, there was simply no room for it internally.

formance was introduced by the A-4C, while the -4E and -4F saw the installation of uprated powerplants and a consequent boost in payload-carrying capability. The A-4E could carry a total of 8,200lb (3,700kg) of ordnance on five hardpoints.

Better take-off and landing performance was the goal of the A-4F model, which had a further-uprated engine plus lift spoilers on the wings. This model carved some 1,000ft (300m) from the take-off run. A TA-4F two-seat trainer version was also built. Using the A-4F as a baseline, McDonnell Douglas was able to produce a series of specialised models to meet the needs of export customers.

Heinemann designed the Skyhawk to be a bomber but the next model was deployed as a carrier-based naval fighter. The Royal Australian Navy's A-4G was a modified A-4F armed with Sidewinder missiles. Only eight were built, along with two TA-4G two-seat trainers, for service on the carrier *Melbourne*. Next model was another A-4F variant, this time for Israel. The A-4H was delivered to the IDFAF

between 1967 and 1972, along with 10 TA-4H two-seat trainers. USN training needs were met by rebuilding most TF-4F two-seaters to the TA-4J standard, while the ten A-4K and four TA-4K trainers built for the Royal New Zealand Air Force rounded off the "family" of A-4F variants.

The A-4L was simply a modification of early A-4C with an uprated engine and

Above: The A-4G Skyhawk operated by the Royal Australian Navy was an A-4F modified to carry AIM-9 Sidewinders as shown here. Only eight were built, plus two twin-seat trainers. This was probably the only use of the A-4s as a dedicated fighter.

Right: The Skyhawk as opponent; a formation of VA-127 Cylons, based at NAS Lemoore, Ca. This squadron provides adversary training and their A-4s are fairly similar in performance to the MiG-17. The buzz numbers on the nose are the giveaway.

McDonnell-Douglas A-4M Skyhawk

1. Fixed in-flight refuelling probe.
2. Laser target seeker.
3. Avionics cooling air intake.
4. Pitot head.
5. Nose avionics equipment bay.
6. Communications system equipment.
7. Cockpit pressurisation valve.
8. Temperature probe.
9. Temperature sensor.
10. Rudder pedals.
11. Angle of attack sensor.
12. Head-up display.
13. Pilot's instrument display.
14. McDonnell-Douglas Escapac ejection seat.
15. Stand-by compass.
16. Cockpit canopy cover.
17. Canopy spring strut.
18. Fuselage fuel tank.
19. Gravity fuel filler cap.
20. Avionics cooling air intake.
21. Starboard leading edge slat.
22. UHF aerial.
23. Starboard navigation light.
24. Starboard wing integral fuel tank.
25. TACAN aerial.
26. Ammunition loading door.
27. Compressor bleed air spill duct.
28. Dorsal avionics pack.
29. Engine oil tank.
30. Anti-collision light.
31. Pratt & Whitney J52-P-408 powerplant.
32. Firewall.
33. Rear fuselage break point.
34. Flap hydraulic jack.
35. Pressure refuelling connection.
36. Inertial platform.
37. Arrester hook jack and damper.
38. Remote compass transmitter.
39. Tailplane pivot bearing.
40. Tailplane sealing plate.
41. Elevator hydraulic actuator.
42. Rudder hydraulic actuator.
43. Rudder spring feel strut.
44. Pitot tube.
45. ECM aerial fairing.
46. Externally braced rudder.
47. Fixed rudder tab.
48. ECM aerials.
49. Tail navigation lights.
50. Tailplane trim actuator.
51. Port elevator.
52. One-piece all-moving tailplane.
53. Radar warning antenna.
54. Tailpipe shroud.
55. Parachute door.
56. Brake parachute housing.
57. Engine tailpipe.
58. Parachute release link.
59. Port airbrake.
60. Airbrake hydraulic jack.
61. Liquid oxygen converter.
62. Arrester hook.
63. Spoiler hydraulic jack.
64. Split trailing edge spoiler.
65. Split trailing edge flap.
66. Port aileron.
67. Aileron tab.
68. Port navigation light.
69. Formation lights.
70. Trim tab actuator.
71. Port wing integral fuel tank.
72. Aileron control rod linkage.
73. Outboard stores pylon.
74. Missile pylon adaptor.
75. AGM-12 Bullpup air-to-ground missile.
76. Slat guide rail.
77. Automatic leading edge slat.
78. Inboard stores pylon.
79. Hydraulic retraction jack.
80. Main undercarriage leg pivot bearing.
81. Forward retracting mainwheel.
82. External fuel tank.
83. Undercarriage leg breaker strut.
84. Catapult strop hook.
85. Engine accessory equipment gearbox.
86. Marker beacon antenna.
87. Aileron servo actuator.
88. Cartridge case ejector chute.
89. Approach lights.
90. Mk.12 20mm cannon.
91. Electrical system equipment.
92. Ground intercom socket.
93. Ammunition feed drum.

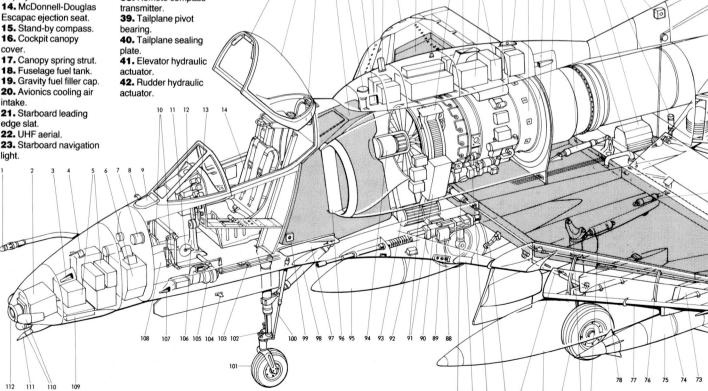

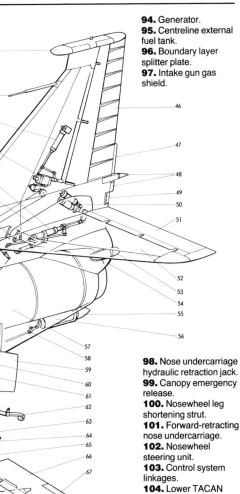

94. Generator.
95. Centreline external fuel tank.
96. Boundary layer splitter plate.
97. Intake gun gas shield.

98. Nose undercarriage hydraulic retraction jack.
99. Canopy emergency release.
100. Nosewheel leg shortening strut.
101. Forward-retracting nose undercarriage.
102. Nosewheel steering unit.
103. Control system linkages.
104. Lower TACAN aerial.
105. Air conditioning system.
106. Control column.
107. Heat exchanger air intake.
108. Nosewheel housing.
109. Doppler navigation radar.
110. Radar warning antennae.
111. ECM aerial.
112. Laser target seeker glazed aperture.

When Singapore ordered 40 ex-USN A-4Bs, these were updated to the A-4S standard by Lockheed. The three TA-4S operated by the same customer are a Lockheed rebuild of A-4B single-seaters. A separate bubble transparency has been added for the second cockpit. Late in 1983 McDonnell Douglas and Singapore Aircraft Industries discussed the possibility of opening a Skyhawk production line in Singapore, but the chances of such a development are slim as long as there are ample stocks of second-hand aircraft.

One of the biggest second-hand deals involves Malaysia, which was offered 88 USN/USMC-surplus aircraft—25 A-4Cs and 63 A-4Ls from stocks held at Davis-Monthan AFB. The original plan was that 68 of these would be reworked by a US contractor, who would be responsible for refurbishing the airframe and engine and installing new avionics including an inertial-navigation system, HUD, and laser rangefinder under a programme valued at an estimated $460 millon. In practice, a less ambitious scheme was chosen, with Grumman receiving a $120 million contract to refurbish 40 of these aircraft, and train Malaysian pilots and ground crews.

In 1980, deliveries of 14 A-4E and two TA-4E aircraft to Indonesia began. These were ex-Israeli aircraft. As newer types enter the IDFAF inventory, the Skyhawk is being phased out, so the next decade could see some 200 being released onto the market. To avoid political problems, they may be returned to the USA before being transferred to new owners.

improved avionics, but the A-4M was a very different breed. Developed for the USMC, this introduced the J52-P-408 engine of 11,200lb (5,080kg) thrust, a new pattern of one-piece upward-hinging canopy, doubled ammunition stowage for the 20mm cannon, and a more powerful electrical generator. Like the -4F, the -4M formed the basis for a family of export variants. The A-4N was supplied to Israel, while the A-4KU single-seater and TA-4KU two-seater were developed for Kuwait.

The US Navy and Marine Corps plan to keep the A-4 in service through the current decade, and are spending tens of millions of dollars per annum to upgrade the remaining examples in order to maintain their combat effectiveness. A-4Y is the USMC designation for A-4Ms retrofitted with the Hughes Angle Rate Bombing System (ARBS), while the OA-4M is a specialised Forward air control (FAC) aircraft flown by the USMC. Some USN aircraft will be given a new pattern of "buddy pack" airborne-refuelling system currently being developed by Sargent Fletcher, and due to enter service in 1986.

Relatively few A-4s were built as export aircraft. The only nations ordering new-production Skyhawks were Australia (10 A-4G), Israel (271 A-4E/H/N), Kuwait (36 A-4KU), and New Zealand (14 A-4K). All other export customers received second-hand aircraft either from US stocks or aircraft being phased out by Israel.

Many of these "hand-me-downs" have been refurbished for service with their new owners. A total of 70 US Navy A-4Bs have been modified for the Argentinian Air Force (as the A-4P), and 16 were supplied to her Navy as A-4Qs for service on the carrier 25 de Mayo. The A-4P played a major role in the Falklands War, suffering heavy losses. These early-model Skyhawks simply lacked the sophisticated avionics needed for all-weather attacks against missile-defended targets.

STRUCTURE

The primary structure of the A-4 is built in three major sections—forward fuselage, aft fuselage and wing. The wing has three spars, continuous from tip to tip. The rearward pair are straight, eliminating a load-concentration point found in most swept-wing aircraft. All access panels are in the upper surface, eliminating most cutouts in the lower skin.

A large part of the structure is manufactured from standard sheet metal and extruded stock—there are few forgings or machined parts. As a result, many repairs can be made at squadron level using the available tools and manpower.

The basic shape was designed to fit on the lifts of USN carriers without the need for folding wings. This configuration stood the test of time, but had to be modified to create more internal volume for avionics items which did not exist when the design was first drawn up. The A-4C introduced an extended nose section designed to house the additional avionics required by the USN, while the A-4F featured lift spoilers, nose-wheel steering, and the distinctive dorsal "hump" aft of the cockpit—another avionics bay.

POWERPLANT

Early aircraft such as the A-4A, B and C were powered by the Curtiss Wright J65-W-16A turbojet of 7,700lb (3,492kg) thrust. This proved unreliable, so all subsequent models used the Pratt & Whitney J52 two-spool turbojet. First model to be used was the 8,500lb (3,855kg) thrust J52-P-6A, which was installed in the A-4E and TA-4J. This allowed the aircraft to carry a higher payload. Further engine improvements were made with the A-4F, G, H, and K, which used the 9,300lb (4,218kg) J52-P-8A. For the A-4M and N, the J52-P-408A gave 11,200lb (5,080kg).

In line with his philosophy of keeping the A-4 as simple as possible, Heinemann used only two fuel tanks, a self-sealing fuselage tank and an integral wing tank fitted with anti-slosh baffles. A sump in the fuselage tank allowed the aircraft to be flown inverted for 30 seconds.

AVIONICS

The original A-4 had very little in the way of avionics. In order to save weight, Heinemann even combined the radio, navaids and IFF into a single 58lb (26kg) sealed unit with only one electrical connector. Such simplicity could not last; later versions carried an ever-growing array of "black boxes".

The A-4C featured an all-weather capability with advanced autopilot, terrain-avoidance radar, and a low-altitude bombing system. The A-4L is a modified version of the -4C with a new bombing computer, and relocated electronics.

By the time the A-4M entered service, the aircraft had been equipped with navigation and weapon-delivery systems ranging from a simple system with pilot dead-reckoning and a depressible fixed-reticle gunsight to advanced avionics suites incorporating an inertial platform, digital weapon-delivery computer, HUD and active ECM.

To keep the current fleet combat capable, newer systems are being retrofitted. The Hughes Angle Rate Bombing System (ARBS) will provide the US Marine Corps' A-4Ms with improved bombing accuracy and first pass acquisition capability. Aircraft with this system are designated A-4Y.

Other items of avionics being retrofitted to US aircraft include the APR-43 and ALR-45F radar warning receivers, and the ALQ-162 jammer being retrofitted to A-4M and OA-4M aircraft. Further modifications will add aircraft-mounted sub-units for the Maverick missile.

ARMAMENT

The maximum ordnance load varies from model to model. The A-4A, B and C could carry 5,000lb (2,250kg), while most subsequent versions could manage a maximum of 8,200lb (3,700kg). With the A-4M and N

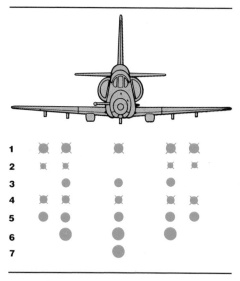

and their derivatives, maximum ordnance load was 9,155lb (4,153kg).

These loads could be made up of high-explosive or nuclear bombs, unguided rockets, or guided missiles such as the AIM-9 Sidewinder or AGM-12 Bullpup. AGM-65 Maverick is being retrofitted, and AGM-88 HARM seems a likely prospect for the future. External ordnance is normally carried on Aero 7A ejector bomb racks (centreline) or the Aero 20A (underwing). To increase the number of stores carried, these may be fitted with triple- or multiple-ejection racks.

Most aircraft carry two internally-mounted Mk12 20mm cannon, each with 200 rounds of ammunition, but some export customers (such as Israel) specified two 30mm DEFA (each with 150 rounds). The heavier projectile fired by this weapon is more effective against ground targets. A small number of A-4Ms can also carry an external 20mm GPU-2 gun pod.

Possible weapons:
Left: 1. High explosive bomb.
2. Air-to-air missile.
3. Multiple store rack.
4. Air-to-surface missile.
5. Rocket launcher.
6. External fuel/napalm.
7. In-flight refuelling store (buddy pack).
Most versions mount two 20mm Mk 12 cannon in the wing roots with 200 rounds each, although some export A-4s have two 30mm DEFA cannon with 150 rounds per gun. Compatible ASMs include the Gabriel 3, AGM-12 Bullpup, AGM-62A Walleye glide bomb, and AGM-65A Maverick. The D704 "buddy pack" holds 1,625lb (737kg) of transferable fuel.

Right: The TA-4J is the standard US Navy trainer. This example is from training squadron VT-125. To accommodate the second seat, the overall length was increased by nearly 2.5ft (76.2cm) and internal fuel reduced. Trainer versions have simplified avionics.

Below: Another VA-127 Cylons Skyhawk, this time an A-4F, sports its low visibility grey finish. The A-4 is a small aeroplane and is difficult to see at any distance. The A-4F features uprated engine and lift spoilers for a much improved short field performance.

Sea level strike
Mission radius 350nm (640km)

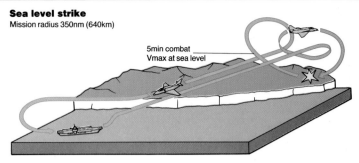

5min combat
Vmax at sea level

Left: The Skyhawk has a respectable radius of action at low level of 350nm (640km) using two 300gal (1,140lit) drop tanks and carrying a 2,000lb (907kg) bomb load, made up of one 1,000lb (454kg) bomb on the centreline and two 500lb (227kg) bombs on the outboard pylons. This radius allows 5 min combat at full throttle.

Sea level dash (hi-lo-hi)
Mission radius hi 475nm (880km)
lo 54nm (100km)

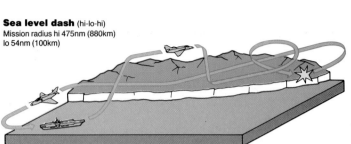

Left: Configured for the low level mission, the radius of action extends to 475nm (880km) by adopting a hi-lo-lo profile, the final 54nm (100km) approach flown at full throttle and at very low level, with a further low level dash back to the carrier after mission completion.

PERFORMANCE

Skyhawk is easy to handle, and the pilot is free to manoeuvre as required in combat without fear of over-stressing the structure. The combination of high thrust-to-weight ratio and low wing loading gives good manoeuvring capability. Roll rate of the A-4M is 100deg/sec at low or supersonic speeds, 300deg/sec at moderate speed. The only manoeuvring restriction placed on this model is that roll rate must not exceed 180deg/sec with a load of more than 2,800lb (1,260kg) on the fuselage centreline, or 1,800lb (810kg) on the inboard wing station. Stall warning is good, and the aircraft will spin only if deliberately forced to do so.

Best turning performance is at between Mach 0.3 and 0.4 (depending on altitude).

At low level such speeds can give a radius of around 1,700ft (500m) in a near-clean aircraft carrying 60 per cent internal fuel plus two Sidewinders. Sea-level climb rate of the A-4M with the same loading but full fuel tanks approaches 20,000ft/sec (6,000m/sec). At 35,000ft (10,600m) with 60 per cent internal fuel the aircraft can comfortably exceed Mach 0.9.

OPERATORS

Argentina (70 A-4P, 16 A-4Q), Australia (8 A-4G, 2 TA-4G), Indonesia (14 A-4E, 2 TA-4E), Israel (43 A-4E, 108 A-4H, 10 TA-4H, and 110 A-4N originally delivered—most now in storage), Kuwait (24 A-4KU, 6 TA-4KU), Malaysia (25 A-4C, 63 A-4L), New Zealand (10 A-4K, 4 TA-4K), Singapore (40 A-4S, 3 TA-4S), USA (600).

Close air support
Mission radius 535nm (990km)

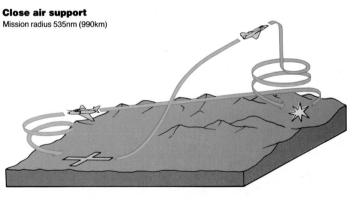

Left: The close air support mission often entails patrolling in wait for a suitable target. Configured as for the previous two missions, but using an optimum altitude cruise out and back, the A-4 has a mission radius of 535nm (990km), including 45 minutes loiter time in the target area at 5,000ft (1,500m). Air superiority is needed to fly this mission profile successfully.

Long-range interception
Mission radius 395nm (730km)

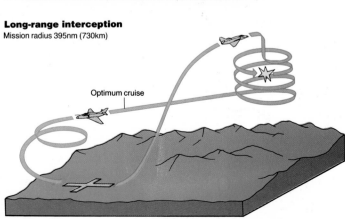

Optimum cruise

Left: Interception at long range is hardly a task for which the Skyhawk would be used today unless pitted against a low-tech adversary. With a 400gal (1,520lit) tank on the centreline and two air-to-air missiles on the inboard pylons, the Skyhawk has a radius of action of 395nm (730km). Transit both ways is at optimum cruise and height, followed by 20 minutes combat at full throttle at an altitude of approximately 20,000ft (6,000m).

MCDONNELL DOUGLAS
F-4 PHANTOM II

DEVELOPMENT

"Jack of all trades—master of none" is a proverb which might be regarded with some amusement at the St Louis design office which created the F-4 Phantom. The concept of a multi-role fighter is no longer as fashionable as it was in the 1960s, but the fact remains that, although many aircraft can match the F-4 in some performance areas, few can cap its all-round capabilities.

For the Warsaw Pact, the F-4 must have been—and still is—a major threat. Only the Su-27 Flanker offers F-4-style long-range air combat capability, but this new fighter, which is only just entering service, is unlikely to offer much in the way of air-to-ground attack performance.

Design of what would eventually become the F-4 started in 1953 with the aim of creating a carrier-based single-seat attack aircraft designated F3H-G. Rejected by the USN, the design was kept alive by McDonnell, which drew up revised versions designated F3G-H and AH-1. When

the Navy unveiled a new requirement for an interceptor able to fly combat air patrols more than 200nm (350km) from a carrier, engaging intruders using all-missile armament, the AH-1 proposal was reworked, given AIM-7 Sparrow missiles and GE J79 engines, then offered as a fighter.

The USN signed for three prototypes—two for flight test and a third for static trials—and the resulting F4H-1 flew in May 1958. A first production contract was awarded in December 1958, and production Phantoms were handed over to the Navy in December 1960.

Only a small batch of F-4A preproduction aircraft were built, the definitive initial model being the F-4B. The latter formed the basis of the DF-4B drone-director aircraft, the QF-4B target drone conversion and USMC RF-4B reconnaissance version.

The USAF adopted the Phantom as the F-4C, a variant with modifications such as larger wheels and slightly customised engines to suit Air Force practice. From this

were developed the EF-4C Wild Weasel interim anti-radar version, and the RF-4C reconnaissance aircraft.

Next USAF version was the F-4D, but this was in turn replaced by the definitive F-4E multirole fighter. This was widely exported and was built under licence in Japan as the F-4EJ. It in turn formed the basis of the RF-4E export reconnaissance version and the F-4F air-superiority fighter for the West German Luftwaffe. Some F-4Es were modified to the F-4G Wild Weasel standard to replace the earlier models used in this role.

By developing the F-4B naval interceptor along similar lines, the USN was able to field the improved F-4J, many of which were later rebuilt as F-4S, with extended airframe life. Some F-4Bs were reworked to the improved F-4N standard.

The UK adopted the Phantom, but decided to replace the J79 engine with an afterburning version of the Rolls-Royce Spey. The F-4K was built for service aboard Royal Navy aircraft carriers, while the F-4M was for the RAF.

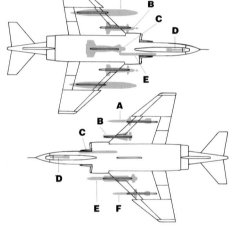

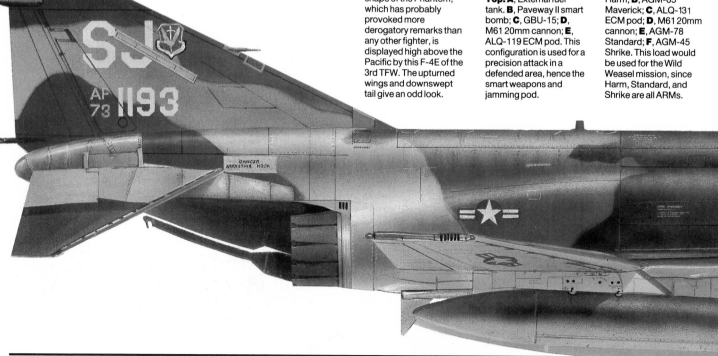

Above: The angular shape of the Phantom, which has probably provoked more derogatory remarks than any other fighter, is displayed high above the Pacific by this F-4E of the 3rd TFW. The upturned wings and downswept tail give an odd look.

Typical weapons:
Top: A, External fuel tank. **B**, Paveway II smart bomb; **C**, GBU-15; **D**, M61 20mm cannon; **E**, ALQ-119 ECM pod. This configuration is used for a precision attack in a defended area, hence the smart weapons and jamming pod.

Above: A, AGM-88A Harm; **B**, AGM-65 Maverick; **C**, ALQ-131 ECM pod; **D**, M61 20mm cannon; **E**, AGM-78 Standard; **F**, AGM-45 Shrike. This load would be used for the Wild Weasel mission, since Harm, Standard, and Shrike are all ARMs.

Left: In plan form, the F-4E Phantom retains much of the sleekness which distinguished the original mock-up. It is only from other angles that its apparent aerodynamic oddity is obvious. Like most of the swept-wing aircraft of its day, it suffers from dihedral effect; in the rolling plane the stick must be kept central and the aircraft rolled with the rudder at quite small angles of attack. By modern standards it is not very manoeuvrable, but despite this it is one of the great fighters of all time.

Below: The F-4E shown here is the definitive fighter version of the Phantom, armed with four AIM-7 Sparrows, carried semi-recessed under the fuselage, four AIM-9 Sidewinders under the wings, and an M61 20mm cannon capable of firing 6,000 rounds per minute. The slatted wings improve high AOA capability, and the tanks would be jettisoned before combat.

Below: This particular F-4E belongs to the 4th TFW at Seymour Johnson AFB. The F-4, designed originally as a carrier-based interceptor, was adopted by the USAF, and filled a multitude of roles. It is as an all-rounder that it will mainly be remembered, although it has proven very successful as an air combat fighter, in USAF and foreign service.

**McDonnell Douglas
F-4E Phantom II**
1. Radome.
2. Radar disconnect unit.
3. Pitot head.
4. ADF sense aerial.
5. Windscreen rain dispersal duct.
6. Ammunition drum.
7. Pilot's instrument display.
8. Lead computing sight and indicator.
9. Engine throttle levers.
10. Pilot's Martin-Baker ejection seat.
11. Forward cockpit canopy cover.
12. Weapons Systems Officer's instrument panel.
13. Boundary layer spill ducts.
14. Weapons Systems Officer's Martin-Baker ejection seat.
15. Rear cockpit canopy cover.
16. IFF aerial.
17. Avionics equipment bay.
18. Upper fuselage light.
19. Leading edge wing fence.
20. Starboard wing integral fuel tank.
21. Leading edge manoeuvre slat.

22. Radar warning antenna.
23. Wing tip formation light.
24. Retractable in-flight refuelling receptacle.
25. Rearward identification light.
26. Two-segment spoilers.
27. Fuel jettison.
28. TACAN aerial.
29. Drooping aileron.
30. Fuselage fuel cells.
31. General Electric J79-GE-17 powerplant.
32. Fuel system piping.
33. Ventral airbrake.
34. Airbrake hydraulic jack.
35. Flap hydraulic jack.
36. Tailcone cooling air intake.
37. Arrester hook jack and damper.
38. Tailplane artificial feel system unit.

39. Tailplane control linkages.
40. Anti-collision light.
41. Artificial feel system pressure head.
42. Formation lighting strip.
43. VHF aerial.
44. Tail navigation light.
45. Radar warning antenna.
46. Rudder mass balance.
47. Rudder.

48. Fuel jettison.
49. Brake parachute housing.
50. Parachute door.
51. Rudder hydraulic actuator and damper.
52. Tailplane hinge mounting.

53. Tailplane hinge sealing plate.
54. All-moving tailplane.
55. Fixed leading edge slat.
56. Tailplane hydraulic actuator.
57. AIM-7 Sparrow air-to-air missile.
58. Port plain flap.
59. Afterburner nozzle control jack.

60. Afterburner duct.
61. Port drooping aileron.
62. Variable-area afterburner nozzle.
63. Arrester hook.
64. Fuel jettison.
65. Rearward identification light.
66. Port wing tip formation light.
67. Port navigation light.

STRUCTURE

Design of the Phantom resulted in new techniques and materials being applied for the first time to a production aircraft. In order to save weight, the design team opted to use titanium for eight to ten per cent of the airframe, and to use integral machining and chemical milling.

The nose section of the F-4 is the area most affected by subsequent development. The F-4D has a larger radome, and initial deliveries lacked the chin-mounted IR sensor. The extended recce nose first appeared on the RF-4C, later on the RF-4E. Installation of an internal gun on the F-4E saw the cannon housed in an extended chin fairing, while a slimmed-down radome housed the new APQ-120 radar.

Internal fuel is carried in tanks located behind the cockpit, above the engine bays, and in the wings. Later models from the F-4E onwards have an extra tank located in the rear fuselage.

Ten nations currently operate more than 1,000 F-4s, while the US still fields more than 2,000. Although the latter are being phased out by the F-16 and F-18, they will be in the inventory for some time yet. Foreign Phantoms could have even longer lifetimes; some Israeli and West German examples could serve into the next century.

Several modification and upgrading programmes are under way. The most ambitious proposal to date is a joint Boeing/Pratt & Whitney scheme which would retrofit the aircraft with new avionics—the Westinghouse APG-66 radar, Marconi HUD and air-data computer, Honeywell INS, Sperry cockpit display, Teledyne avionics processors, a new cockpit-management system—as well as new PW 1120 engines. Likely cost of such extensive modifications would be between $7 million and $9 million per aircraft. But there is some USAF reluctance to extend the lives of 20-year-old airframes.

The folding wing is of low aspect ratio, and the outer sections have 12deg of dihedral to improve lateral stability. A dog-tooth in the wing leading edge helps control the flow of air across the wing. Ailerons are used for roll control, working in conjunction with spoilers on the upper wing surface. In the F-4J, the ailerons may be deflected 16.5deg downwards at take-off and landing in order to increase the available lift. Airbrakes are mounted on the underside of each inboard wing section.

The boundary-control system bleeds hot air from the compressors of the engines in order to "blow" the leading-edge droop flaps and trailing edge flaps to improve lift. F-4Es built from 1972 onwards feature leading-edge slats. At high angles of attack, these are automatically extended to increase lift, allowing the aircraft to pull tighter turns, and cutting some 12kt (22km/h) off the approach speeds. Under a modification programme, earlier F-4Es

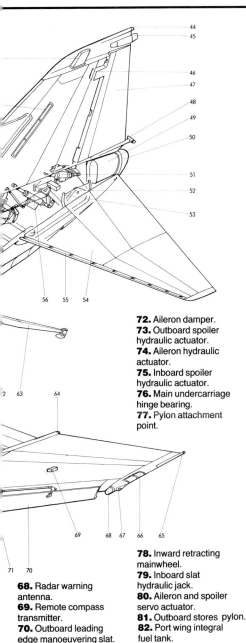

84. Inboard leading edge manoeuvring slat.
85. Systems ground connections.
86. Hydraulic accumulator.
87. Hydraulic reservoir.
88. External fuel tank.
89. Inboard pylon attachment.
90. Engine accessory equipment gearbox.
91. Radar ranging antenna.
92. Engine driven generator housing.
93. Inboard stores pylon.
94. Missile launch rail.
95. AIM-9 Sidewinder air-to-air missiles.
96. Starter cartridge container.
97. Lower avionics equipment bay.
98. Variable-area intake ramp.
99. Intake ramp actuator.
100. AIM-7 Sparrow air-to-air missile.
101. Boundary layer splitter plate.
102. Rear cockpit secondary flight controls.
103. Boarding steps.
104. Retractable boarding ladder.
105. Formation lighting strip.
106. Control column and mechanical linkage.
107. Equipment air conditioning system, crew system on starboard side.
108. Rudder pedals.
109. Aft retracting nosewheels.
110. Nosewheel steering control unit.
111. Landing and taxiing lamps.
112. Heat exchanger ram air intake.
113. M.61 Vulcan 20mm cannon.
114. Ammunition feed chute.
115. Radar equipment unit.
116. Cannon muzzle.
117. Radar scanner dish.

72. Aileron damper.
73. Outboard spoiler hydraulic actuator.
74. Aileron hydraulic actuator.
75. Inboard spoiler hydraulic actuator.
76. Main undercarriage hinge bearing.
77. Pylon attachment point.
78. Inward retracting mainwheel.
79. Inboard slat hydraulic jack.
80. Aileron and spoiler servo actuator.
81. Outboard stores pylon.
82. Port wing integral fuel tank.
83. Main undercarriage hydraulic jack.

68. Radar warning antenna.
69. Remote compass transmitter.
70. Outboard leading edge manoeuvering slat.
71. Outboard slat hydraulic jack.

Above: Mock-up of the "Super Phantom" proposed by Boeing and Pratt & Whitney. It would have new avionics and the PW 1120 engine.

Below: For many years the Phantom formed the backbone of fighter defence in Europe. This F-4E of the 86th TFW based at Ramstein is one of the diminishing number of USAF units to retain the type. The RAF and the Luftwaffe are the other major European F-4 operators.

had wing slats retrofitted. Similar slats were retrofitted to the naval F-4J when this model was rebuilt as the F-4S.

The stabilisers are angled downwards at 23deg to keep them clear of wing wake at high angles of attack, and to compensate for the aerodynamic effects of the upward-cranked outer wing sections. On the F-4E and F-4J, a fixed inverted slat was fitted to the stabiliser, to maintain its effectiveness at high angles of attack.

The variable engine inlets were the first to be fitted to a production fighter. In the Spey-powered F-4K and -4M, these had to be increased in size to match the greater airflow demands of the British engine. The rear fuselage also required significant re-design.

The basic design was sound, but the fact that some F-4s are being flown for longer than designers anticipated has resulted in the need for a series of minor structural "fixes". Under current programmes USN F-4S fighters are to be structurally up-graded to extend their service life, while USAF Phantoms are to have their outer wings reworked to repair fatigue cracks.

PROPULSION

The General Electric J79 single-shaft turbojet has clocked up more supersonic flying time than any other Western military powerplant, having been used in the F-104 Starfighter, IAI Kfir, A-5 Vigilante and B-58 Hustler. More than 17,000 have been built, 11,000 of which are still in active use.

The XF4H-1 Phantom prototype first flew with J79-GE-3A engines, but these were soon swapped for the more powerful YJ79-GE-2A fitted to all prototypes. For the USN F-4B, the J79-GE-8 gave enough thrust for Mach 2.4 flight—10,900lb (4,944kg) dry, rising to 17,000lb (7,710kg) in full afterburner.

In a conventional single-spool engine, all the stages of the compressor and the turbine which powers it are mounted on a common shaft, and rotate at the same speed. As the number of compressor stages is increased in search of greater efficiency, this simple configuration can result in problems with surges and stalls, since all the moving parts rotate at a single compromise speed. Instead of moving to the complexities of a two-shaft engine, the GE designers devised a novel high-pressure compressor whose later stages were fitted with variable-incidence stator blades.

The J79 is just over 17ft (5m) long, slightly more than 3ft (0.9m) in diameter, and weighs between 3,600 and 3,800lb (1,633 and 1,724kg). (Exact dimensions and weights vary from model to model.) The compressor has 17 stages and is driven by a three-stage turbine. The combustion chamber is of the 10-section cannular type. A modulated (fully-variable) afterburner and a variable-area exhaust nozzle are fitted.

The J79-GE-15 devised for the F-4C is similar to the -8, but features a self-contained cartridge starting system, and other minor modifications to suit USAF practice. The US Navy's F-4J introduced the 17,900lb (8,120kg) J79-GE-10, and the USAF soon developed the similarly-rated J79-GE-17 for use in the F-4E.

The Rolls-Royce Spey turbofan used by British Phantoms is a two-shaft turbofan whose first military application (in non-afterburning form) was the Buccaneer Mk2. It has 3,500lb (1,587kg) more afterburning thrust than the J79-GE-8 of the F4-B, 2,600lb (1,180kg) more thrust than the J79-GE-10 which was to power later USN F-4Js. Being of turbofan type, it has a lower fuel consumption in dry thrust than the GE engine.

Flight trials of the F-4K and -4M soon showed problems with afterburner stability, and compressor stalls, so delivery of production aircraft was delayed until "fixes" could be devised. The Spey cannot match the performance of the J79 at high Mach numbers, aircraft being limited to a maximum of Mach 2.1—the compressor of the British engine cannot accept the levels of heat associated with higher speeds.

The Pratt & Whitney PW1120 now being proposed as an update of export Phantoms is a twin-shaft turbojet derivative of the F100 turbofan. Compatible with the existing inlet system, it offers 25 per cent more dry thrust and 30 per cent greater output with full afterburner. Aircraft range would be increased by up to 18 per cent, thanks to the lower fuel consumption of this late 1970s design.

The J79 has always been a "smoker" emitting dark trails which betray its position to an enemy fighter pilot. To cure this problem the USN is replacing surviving J79-GE-8 engines by the J79-GE-10B, while the USAF is fitting smoke-free engines to its F-4 fleet.

AVIONICS

The avionics suite of the F-4 is extensive, and could well be the subject of a book in its own right. Standard features are normally a radar, nav/attack system, dedicated navaids such as inertial navigation systems, communications and flight-control equipment, and a radar-warning receiver. Many aircraft carry electro-optical viewing systems, pod-mounted jammers and target acquisition/designation systems.

The Westinghouse APQ-72 radar formed the heart of the F-4B avionics suite, but the USAF adopted the APQ-100 for the F-4C. For the F-4D, the improved APQ-109 offered air-to-ground ranging capability. The AWG-10 adopted for the F-4J is a pulse-Doppler set offering a limited degree of look-down capability. The broadly-similar AWG-11 and 12 were used in UK Phantoms. Under a USN/USMC retrofit programme, the F-4J was equipped with the improved AWG-10A radar, featuring digital data processing, built-in test equipment, and a servoed optical sight. Obsolete components in the AWG-

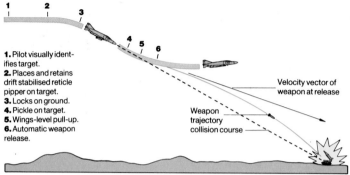

1. Pilot visually identifies target.
2. Locks on ground (A-G radar range displayed on sight reticle).
3. Tracks and fires when pipper on pre-planned aimpoint.
4. Pulls up in escape manoeuvre.

Line of sight through reticle image

Fuselage reference line

Depression angle

Left: The direct weapons delivery mode is used only as a last resort when incorrect data is fed into the weapons release computer via a faulty INS or other malfunction. The pilot visually identifies the target, locks on the radar in the air/ground mode, which gives the slant range, pickling when the pipper reaches the pre-planned aim point in the target area.

1. Pilot visually identifies target.
2. Places and retains drift stabilised reticle pipper on target.
3. Locks on ground.
4. Pickle on target.
5. Wings-level pull-up.
6. Automatic weapon release.

Velocity vector of weapon at release

Weapon trajectory collision course

Left: Dive toss release gives improved accuracy and permits almost continuous jinking to be carried out during the attack. The pilot places the stabilised reticle pipper on the target and keeps it there, aligning his ground track vector through the target. With radar locked on, he then performs a wings-level pull-up. Weapon release is carried out automatically.

1. Pilot visually identifies target.
2. Dives, tracking target with drift-stabilised optical sight.
3. Depresses bomb release button and begins pull-up to slightly decreased dive angle
4. Maintains glide angle.
5. Ripple release of weapons by computer.
6. Begins escape.

Left: Dive glide release is used for depositing ordnance on area targets such as supply dumps. The target is tracked through the optical drift-stabilised sight. The pilot then hits the pickle button and noses up to reduce dive angle, then maintains a constant descent angle. Weapons are released by computer and evasive action is taken.

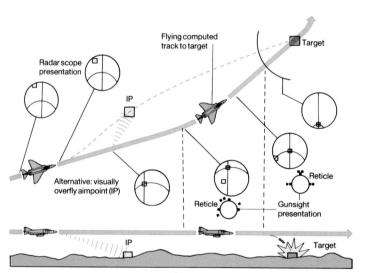

Flying computed track to target

Target

Radar scope presentation

IP

Alternative: visually overfly aimpoint (IP)

Reticle

Reticle

Gunsight presentation

IP

Target

Left: Offset bombing permits attacks to be made on targets that are not visible on the radar. This is done by selecting an aim point (IP) which has a known position in relation to the target. The IP is acquired by radar and a cursor is placed over the radar return and "frozen". The target insert button is then depressed, and the radar display then shows the course to steer. This course is maintained and the pickle button held down. This procedure should take the Phantom over the target, and weapons release is automatic.

10 are now being replaced to ensure that the set can continue to serve into the early 1990s.

The APQ-120 solid-state radar in the F-4E has a 27.5in (69.8cm) antenna instead of the earlier 32in unit (81.2m), and is mounted in close proximity to the 20mm cannon. A set using thermionic tubes (valves) would have been badly affected by the vibration resulting from gunfire. The USAF is currently upgrading these radars.

A small APQ-99 forward-looking radar is carried in the extreme nose of recce

Phantoms to aid the pilot in low-level flight. This set is quite old, and those fitted to 26 RF-4Bs are now being updated.

Most Phantom models carry an electro-optical sensor to back up the radar. On early aircraft such as the F-4B and -4C, this was the AAA-4 infra-red sensor, which allowed targets to be tracked by the heat emissions from their engine exhaust and airframe. The infra-red sensor was deleted from some F-4Ds, but was later re-introduced.

As an aid to long-range target identification, late-production F-4Es are fitted with

Above: Probably the most expensive Phantom of all is the F-4G Wild Weasel, which is packed with special gadgetry and operates in the defence suppression role. The ordnance load, reading near to far, consists of AGM-45 Shrike, AGM-65 Maverick, AGM-78 Standard, and AGM-88 Harm. Weasel birds normally carry a mix of missiles.

Left: Front panel layout of an F-4E, looking less complicated than that of the austere F-5E. The screen beneath the HUD combiner glass is a CRT multi-function display. Immediately beneath this is the attitude director indicator, while the pairs of instruments to the right are: top to bottom, fuel flow, tachometer, and exhaust gas temperature gauges. The interesting-looking switch to the left, set in a striped yellow and black panel, is the master arm switch, and below this is the weapons selector panel. Layout is dated compared to 1980s designs.

Major avionics updating programmes maintain the operational effectiveness of several nations' F-4 fleets. In 1979, West Germany began to convert its RF-4E reconnaissance aircraft to provide a secondary strike capability with up to 5,000lb (2,270kg) of external stores. Other changes upgraded the optronics equipment, infrared linescanner, and EW suite.

The Japanese Air Self-Defense Force is modifying its F-4EJ fleet to extend the service life through the late 1980s and even into the early 1990s. The existing radar is being replaced by a new set—a variant of the APG-66 carried by the F-16. This will provide the 10 JASDF F-4 squadrons with a look-down capability and the ability to fire AIM-9L and AIM-7F missiles.

ARMAMENT

Most air-launched guided and unguided missiles in the US inventory can be carried by the F-4, with the exception of specialised items of weaponry such as the SRAM nuclear missile, the long-range AIM-54 Phoenix, and the heavy strategic weapons toted by the B-52.

For air-to-air combat, the AIM-9 Sidewinder is used at short range, the AIM-7 Sparrow against radar targets. Sidewinder played a major role in the Vietnam War, gradually supplanting the traditional "gun kills". The only Phantom to mount an internal gun is the F-4E, which carries a single 20mm M61 in an under-nose fairing. Other models must make do with "draggy" external gun pods.

If Sidewinder emerged from Vietnam combat with an enhanced reputation, the same cannot be said for Sparrow. When this medium-range guided weapon worked it proved deadly, but many combat reports of the time described how rounds failed to guide after launch. These early Sparrows were probably pushing

the Northrop TISEO (Target Identification System Electro-Optical) a system able to show a high magnification stabilised image on a cockpit display. The seeker is mounted in a small fairing on the leading edge of the port wing. USN F-4S fighters are being retrofitted with the Phantom Eye target-magnification telescope.

Some USAF F-4D and -4E aircraft carry the AVQ-23A Pave Spike television/laser designator pods, while others are fitted with the Pave Tack FLIR/laser designator.

Aircraft EW systems require continual updating. The F-4 has carried ECM pods

such as the ALQ-101, -109 and -131, while its RWR facilities are regularly updated to maintain effectiveness against new threats. The USAF is currently fitting the F-4E fleet with the new ALR-74 radar warning receiver.

The extensive EW suite of the F-4G Wild Weasel must also be kept abreast of the latest threats. The frequency coverage of the APR-38 radar-detection and homing system is currently being extended under a $200 million contract awarded to E-systems, and the aircraft is also receiving a new inertial navigation system.

miniature thermionic tubes to the limits of obtainable reliability; the newer Sparrows such as the AIM-7F use solid-state electronics and are likely to be a significant improvement.

Some users fit the F-4 with indigenously-developed weaponry. Israel's F-4Es have been seen with the Rafael Shafrir, and could be retrofitted with the new Mk III version of the Gabriel anti-ship missile. UK Spey Phantoms now carry the BAe Dynamics Sky Flash missile—a modern radar-guided weapon which combines the proven aerodynamics and propulsion system of Sparrow with an all-new guidance system of advanced design and high accuracy. During development trials of warheadless weapons, many targets were downed by direct hits from Sky Flash rounds.

PERFORMANCE

In the early stages of the air war over North Vietnam in the 1960s, the opposing MiGs made great efforts to seek out and attack F-105 fighter-bomber formations, the workhorses of the USAF bombing campaign. US archives contain a tape recording of the commands given by the officer leading one such attack on an incoming strike. On radar, its speed and height had suggested an F-105 formation, but as the range closed the US radio-monitoring stations detected a cry of surprise as the attack . leader recognised the cranked wings and tailplanes of the fighters which were increasing speed to meet him—not the heavily-loaded F-105 but the high-performance F-4 Phantom.

In the years that followed, Phantoms and MiGs were to clash again and again in the skies above Vietnam and the Middle East. When the US and its allies needed fighters able to tangle with the MiGs or get ordnance onto ground targets, the Phantom was available in quantity and could deliver the goods.

Top speed of around Mach 2.2 is strictly a brochure figure, relating to a clean aircraft. Carriage of four Sparrows trims this figure to Mach 2.04, while the drag imposed by external tanks will bring the top speed down to Mach 1.5.

Normal service ceiling is around 55,000 to 57,000ft (16,765 to 17,373m) in supersonic flight at full power, but zoom climbs can take the aircraft to more than 70,000ft (21,335m). (By this point the engines will have flamed out, the aircraft rising thanks to the energy built up during a high speed run prior to pulling up into the climb.)

Take-off from land bases usually involves half-flaps. The elevators become effective at around 110 to 115kt (204–213km/h), and the aircraft is rotated at 130 to 135kt (240–250km/h). Lift-off speed varies with air temperature and altitude, but is typically around 140 to 150kt (256–278km/h).

Subsonic handling at medium altitudes (30,000 to 40,000ft/9,145–12,190m) is comfortable, provided that the airspeed is kept above 300kt (556km/h). In high-speed subsonic flight at low altitude a

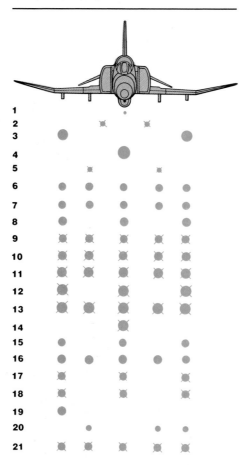

Possible weapons, F-4E:
1. M61 20mm cannon with typically 639 rounds.
2. AIM-7 Sparrow or AIM-120 AMRAAM.
3. 370gal (1,400lit) tank.
4. 600gal (2,275lit) tank.
5. AIM-9L Sidewinder.
6. LAU-3A, 32A rocket pod.
7. LAU-10 rocket pod.
8. SUU-16A, 23A, gun pod.
9. Mk81. 10. Mk82.
11. Mk83. 12. Mk84.
13. M117. 14. M118 general purpose and/or retarded bombs (as are items 9 to 13).
15. SUU-25A dispenser.
16. SUU-21A practice bomb dispenser.
17. CBU-2A cluster bombs.
18. CBU-24, -29 ditto.
19. A/A37U-15 tow target.
20. ECM pods.
21. MLU-10B land mine.

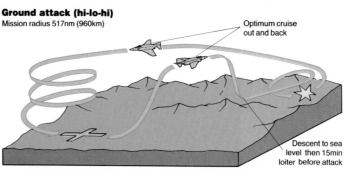

Ground attack (hi-lo-hi)
Mission radius 517nm (960km)

Optimum cruise out and back

Descent to sea level then 15min loiter before attack

Combat air patrol
Time on station at 250nm (460km) 1.58hr

Optimum cruise out and back

2min combat at Mach 1.5 40,000ft (12,190m)

Left: In the ground attack mission, carrying six M117 bombs, total weight 4,920lb (2,232kg), armed with four AIM-7F Sparrows for defence, plus 1,340gal (5,070lit) of fuel in external tanks, the F-4E has a mission radius of 517nm (953km) using high level optimum cruise for outward and return flights, 15 minutes loiter time, and attack at ground level.

Left: The combat air patrol mission is what the original Phantom was designed for. Using optimum cruise out and back, it can remain on station for 1.58 hours at a distance of 250nm (460km), accelerating to Mach 1.5 at 40,000ft (12,200m) for 2 minutes combat, while carrying four AIM-7F Sparrows. To do this it carries 1,340gal (5,070lit) of fuel externally.

Above: A Phantom FGR 2, MCAIR designation F-4M, of No 111 Squadron, RAF, configured for the long range fighter mission with Sparrows, Sidewinders and tanks.

Below: The F-4 operated extensively as a fighter bomber in Southeast Asia. An F-4E, wing slats fully extended, delivers a salvo of Mk82 slicks.

combination of high aircraft response and low stick forces requires careful handling by an inexperienced pilot, otherwise over-control may lead to pilot-induced oscillations.

Phantom is generally easy to fly, and tolerant of the shortcomings of a tyro pilot, but it does have one great weakness. At low speed and low altitude, spinning and stalling accidents have been frequent, especially under the stress of combat. Careful training has helped, but the best solution proved to be the use of a slatted wing. On the unslatted aircraft, buffeting starts soon after the nose is lifted above the normal cruise angle of attack. The slats have a marked effect on the handling characteristics of the F-4E, F-4F and F-4S. Onset of buffeting is delayed, while optimum turning performance comes at higher angles of attack.

F-4 stability increases at transonic speeds, but manoeuvrability remains good. As the speed picks up, the engines become more efficient. Starting from just below Mach 1.0 at 36,000ft (11,000m), an F-4C or -4D can reach Mach 1.2 in less than a minute once afterburner is selected. As Mach number continues to build up, the effectiveness of the horizontal stabiliser slowly decreases, roll rate decreases, and stick forces become high above Mach 2, limiting the manoeuvrability—but never to unacceptable values.

OPERATORS

The following figures refer to the number of aircraft delivered. Australia (24 F-4E on loan in early 1970s); Egypt (35 F-4E); West Germany (10 F-4E, 88 RF-4E, 175 F-4F); Greece (56 F-4E, 6 RF-4E); Iran (32 F-4D, 177 F-4E, 16 RF-4E); Israel (204 F-4E, 12 RF-4E); Japan (15 F-4E as kits, 125 F-4EJ built by Mitsubishi, 14 RF-4E); South Korea (36 F-4D, 37 F-4E); Spain (40 F-4C, 4 RF-4C); Turkey (87 F-4E, 8 RF-4E); UK (52 F-4K, 118 F-4M, 15 F-4J from US Navy); US Air Force (583 F-4C, 2 YRF-4C, 503 RF-4C, 793, F-4D. 993 F-4E); US Marine Corps (651 F-4B, 46 RF-4B, 522 F-4J); US Navy (47 F-4A).

F-15 EAGLE

DEVELOPMENT

The world's "hottest" fighter is the F-15 Eagle. Other types may climb faster, carry swing wings, longer-ranged missiles and more modern avionics, or use more exotic materials, but none can match the McDonnell Douglas aircraft at close-in air combat. The Eagle may be bigger than some pilots would like; it is undoubtedly too expensive for many potential operators; but on the Central Front between NATO and the Warsaw Pact the Eagle is a weapon which must feature in the nightmares of many MiG pilots, even those converting to the new MiG-29.

The F-15 owes its origins to a USAF FX (Fighter Experimental) requirement drawn up in the eary 1960s. Until the Soviet Union revealed its MiG-23 Flogger and MiG-25 Foxbat fighters during the 1967

Domodedovo air show, USAF's FX studies remained low-key. A glimpse of the next generation of Soviet warplanes sent the USAF scurrying to re-examine its future fighter plans. A revised Request for Proposals was issued to the US aerospace industry in August 1967, drawing bids from Boeing, Fairchild, General Dynamics, Grumman, LTV and North American.

At first the USAF seemed unsure of what sort of fighter it really needed, specifying a top speed of Mach 3. The resulting submissions included fixed wing and variable-geometry designs. The final shortlist drawn up late in 1968 consisted of designs by Fairchild, McDonnell Douglas and Rockwell. By this time McDonnell Douglas had settled on a single-seat design with a delta wing, horizontal stabiliser and twin verticals. In its final form, this

was accepted by the USAF on December 23, 1969. The initial contract covered the production of 18 F-15A single-seat and two TF-15A two-seat development aircraft.

First flight of an F-15A took place on July 27, 1972, with the two-seater (now redesignated F-15B) following a year later. Production deliveries started in November 1974 and the first squadron was declared operational in January 1976.

Production was switched in mid-1979 to the improved F-15C and D models. These are equipped with conformal fuel tanks developed under the Production Eagle Package 2000 (PEP-2000) programme. The additional 2,000lb (907kg) of internal fuel extends aircraft endurance, increasing ferry range by around 20 per cent.

Production is currently running at

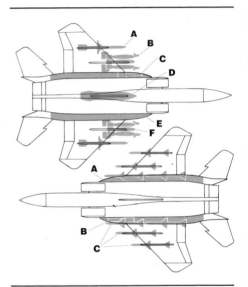

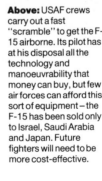

Above: USAF crews carry out a fast "scramble" to get the F-15 airborne. Its pilot has at his disposal all the technology and manoeuvrability that money can buy, but few air forces can afford this sort of equipment – the F-15 has been sold only to Israel, Saudi Arabia and Japan. Future fighters will need to be more cost-effective.

Typical weapons:
Top: The USAF has now adopted the F-15E as its next multi-role fighter. A typical strike payload might be HARM anti-radar missiles (**A**); AIM-9L Sidewinders (**B**) for self-protection; the internal gun (**C**); a Pave Tack designator pod (**D**) on the centreline; FASTpack conformal fuel tanks (**E**) to extend the range; plus smart or "iron" bombs (**F**) on multiple ejector racks.
Above: With the phasing out of the veteran F-106 Delta Dart, the F-15 is now tasked with defending US airspace. A possible future payload for this task could be the new Hughes AIM-120A AMRAAM "fire-and-forget" missile (**C**) on all hardpoints, and FASTpacks (**A**), plus the 20mm gun (**B**).

Below left: The layout of the F-15 combines a simple high lift wing with a pair of massive and hot-running F100 turbofans, a combination giving good acceleration and manoeuvrability. All the lessons of last-generation fighters and Vietnam War combat experience were embodied. The engines are widely spaced to prevent a single hit from knocking out both, while the intakes provide a near straight-through airflow to the engines. The horizontal stabiliser is smaller than might be expected.

Above: An underside view of the F-15 shows the location of the AIM-9 Sidewinders on the underwing hardpoints, and the AIM-7 Sparrows mounted on the sides of the conformal fuel tanks. The latter allow the aircraft to carry an additional 10,000lb (4,500kg) of fuel, increasing the internal capacity by 85 per cent, while having minimal effect on drag. Also visible is the large area of the upper side of the "nodding" intakes, a part of the airframe which acts in a manner similar to that of a canard foreplane, helping to control the pitch of the aircraft.

Below left: Not since the days of the late-1940s F-86 Sabre have USAF pilots had a raised cockpit canopy giving the good all-round view needed in air combat. An additional watch on the vital rear sector is maintained by RWRs.

McDonnell Douglas F-15C Eagle

1. Radome.
2. Radar flood horn.
3. Pitot head, port and starboard.
4. Avionics bay door.
5. ADF sense aerial.
6. Forward avionics equipment bay.
7. Frameless windscreen panel.
8. Rudder pedals.
9. Instrument display.
10. Head-up display.
11. McDonnell Douglas ACES II ejection seat.
12. Hand hold/step.
13. Cockpit canopy cover.
14. Canopy jettison strut.
15. Tactical electronic warfare system (TEWS) equipment.
16. Canopy actuator.
17. Cockpit air conditioning system.
18. Heat exchanger air exhaust.
19. Intake spill door and hydraulic jack.
20. M61A-1 20mm six-barrel rotary cannon.
21. Ammunition drum.
22. Upper UHF/IFF aerial.
23. Ammunition feed chute.
24. Starboard wing integral fuel tanks.
25. Fuel vent compartment.
26. ECM antenna.
27. Starboard navigation light.
28. Formation light.
29. Aileron hydraulic actuator.
30. Airbrake.
31. Airbrake hydraulic jack.
32. Flap hydraulic actuator.
33. Starboard aileron.
34. Hydraulically driven emergency generator.
35. High band tuner.
36. Intake duct bleed air supply to heat exchanger.
37. Plain flap.
38. Engine bleed air ducting.
39. Pratt & Whitney F100-PW-100 afterburning turbofan engines.
40. Starboard all-moving tailplane.
41. Starboard fin.
42. Forward facing ECM aerial.
43. Aft facing ECM antenna.
44. Anti-collision light.
45. Starboard rudder.
46. ECM antenna.
47. Afterburner nozzle control jacks.
48. Fore and aft radar warning pod.
49. ECM antenna.
50. Tail navigation light.
51. Port fin.
52. Port rudder.
53. Rudder hydraulically operated rotary actuator.
54. Variable area afterburner nozzle.
55. Tailplane hydraulic actuator.
56. Tailplane pivot bearing.
57. Port all-moving tailplane.
58. Formation lighting strip.
59. Emergency arrester hook.
60. Primary heat exchanger, port and starboard.
61. Port aileron.
62. Fuel jettison.
63. Aileron hydraulic actuator.
64. Formation light.
65. Port navigation light.
66. ECM antenna.
67. Fuel jettison valve.
68. Flap hydraulic actuator.
69. Fuel vent compartment.
70. Outboard wing stores pylon.
71. Westinghouse ECM equipment pod.
72. Port wing integral fuel tanks.
73. Hydraulic accumulators.
74. Engine driven accessory gearbox.
75. Inboard wing stores pylon.
76. Jet fuel starter.
77. Main undercarriage pivot bearing.
78. Forward-retracting main undercarriage.
79. Hydraulic system reservoir.
80. Main undercarriage hydraulic jack.
81. Missile launch rail.
82. Anti-collision light.
83. AIM-9L Sidewinder air-to-air missile (4).
84. In-flight refuelling receptacle.
85. Refuelling receptacle door hydraulic jack.
86. Fire control system missile launch units.
87. AIM-7F Sparrow air-to-air missile.
88. Air system ducting.
89. Variable area intake ramp doors.
90. Ramp hydraulic actuator.
91. Intake incidence control jack.

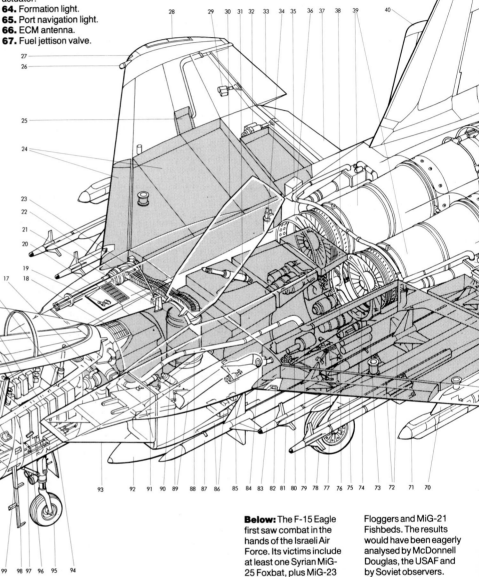

Below: The F-15 Eagle first saw combat in the hands of the Israeli Air Force. Its victims include at least one Syrian MiG-25 Foxbat, plus MiG-23 Floggers and MiG-21 Fishbeds. The results would have been eagerly analysed by McDonnell Douglas, the USAF and by Soviet observers.

around three aircraft per month. More than 750 have been delivered, out of a total order book of around 800. By the end of the decade, the USAF plans to purchase a further 372 F-15s, and hopes to take delivery of 1,376 aircraft by the time the programme ends in the early to mid-1990s. These will include 392 examples of a new model designated F-15E.

The original design was optimised as a dedicated air-combat fighter, but in February 1980 McDonnell Douglas began the task of converting one of the two-seat F-15B prototypes into the private-venture Strike Eagle night/all-weather ground attack fighter. The USAF had indicated an interest in aircraft of this type, and the company hoped to get a head start on its rivals, and to persuade the USAF to issue a formal requirement.

Design of Strike Eagle had started back in 1977 under a USAF programme designated Enhanced Tactical Fighter (ETF), which called for an existing fighter to be enhanced for night and all-weather attack missions. Although this requirement has resulted in submissions, including a Panavia offer of Tornado and the two-seat Night/Adverse Weather (N/AW) version of the Fairchild A-10, it was dropped by the Service.

McDonnell Douglas pressed ahead with

92. Centreline external fuel tank.
93. Variable incidence "nodding" air intake.
94. Flight control augmentation system equipment.
95. Forward-retracting nosewheel.
96. Canopy emergency release.
97. Landing and taxying lamps.
98. Retractable boarding ladder.
99. Boarding step.
100. Underfloor avionics equipment bay.
101. Formation lighting strip.
102. TACAN aerial.
103. Control column linkage.
104. Incidence probe.
105. Liquid oxygen converter.
106. Lower UHF aerial.
107. ILS glideslope aerial.
108. APG-63 pulse doppler antenna.

Strike Eagle, beginning flight tests in 1981. Early flights checked out the performance of the radar—a modified version of the Hughes APG-63 offering synthetic-aperture operating modes—and test firing of the General Electric GAU-8 gun. This was followed by a series of ordnance-release trials. This private-venture work paid off when the F-15 was adopted by the USAF in 1984 as a multi-role fighter, following a fly-off against the rival F-16XL. Production of the new F-15E should begin in 1986, with aircraft entering service in 1988.

The F-15E will be some $4 million more expensive than the current F-15, which already carries a $??? price tag. Changes to suit the aircraft to its new role include a synthetic aperture radar, advanced flight-control system and increased ordnance-carrying capability.

Export opportunities for such an advanced and expensive fighter are limited but, as part of a balanced Middle East arms package drawn up by President Carter, Israel was allowed to order 25 F-15s in December 1975, while Saudi Arabia was cleared to buy 60. By 1978 the IDFAF had received its aircraft, and the sale of a follow-on batch of 15 F-15s was approved by Congress in May of that year, leading to deliveries in 1981 and 1982. Israel is since reported to have ordered 11 more examples.

Delivery of the Saudi aircraft (all F-15C/D models) is due to be completed in 1984. After much debate, the Reagan Administration finally agreed to supply conformal fuel tanks and MER-200 bomb racks for these aircraft.

Japan is currently building at least 86 single-seat F-15DJ fighters for the Air Self-Defense Force (JASDF), and 12 two-seater trainers are being built for Japan in the USA. The McDonnell Douglas line also built the first two single-seaters for the JASDF, followed by kits of parts for the assembly of the first eight Mitsubishi-assembled aircraft. The remainder will be built under licence. A follow-on order for 23 further aircraft might be placed in the late 1980s. The first operational JASDF F-15DJ squadron was formed early in 1983.

Under a $360 million Multi-Staged Improvement Programme (MSIP), USAF F-15s will be given upgraded avionics designed to improve air-to-air and air

defence capabilities. This includes improved fire-control, EW and command, control and communications facilities. Future production aircraft could also be given the General Electric F110 turbofan in place of the current engine, following a USAF decision to adopt this engine as an alternative to the F100.

STRUCTURE

Slightly larger than the F-4 Phantom it is replacing, the F-15 Eagle tips the scales some 6,000lb (2,700kg) lighter at maximum take-off weight, partly as a result of the smaller fuel load made possible by high-efficiency turbofan engines, but also thanks to the use of weight-saving materials such as titanium and composites.

Titanium is extensively used in the rear fuselage skin, bulkheads, and inter-engine firewall, as well as the cantilever boom sections which pass outboard of the engines to carry the tail assembly, plus the internal spars of the fins. Composites are used in areas such as the skins of the wing flaps, ailerons, horizontal stabilisers, air brake and wingtips.

The wing is of multispar construction, the inner sections of the main three spars being of titanium, the outer of aluminium alloy. The strength of this assembly allows the Eagle to keep flying even if one spar in each wing is severed. The use of variable camber was rejected. The wing has a fixed leading edge (swept at 45 degrees), plus simple trailing-edge flaps and ailerons.

The fuselage is built in three sections—forward, centre and aft. Air inlets are of unconventional "nodding" design which can move 4deg above or 11deg below the horizontal to keep their "mouths" aligned with the airflow at high angles of attack. At high speeds they also act as control surfaces, and this allowed the F-15 designers to reduce the size of the horizontal stabilizers. A speed brake is located on the top surface of the fuselage, aft of the canopy.

Windscreen and canopy are made from acrylic, the latter being of the bubble type used on all recent US fighters in order to give a good rear view. Canopy size is the only external difference between the single- and two-seat models; in the latter, the second crewman takes up the space normally used for an avionics bay.

Many access panels are provided to help

Below: Since the late 1970s, the F-15 has been the ultimate air-superiority fighter, easily able to outfly the best that the Soviet Air Force could field. With the arrival in front-line service of the new MiG-29 Fulcrum and Su-27 Flanker, however, things will not be so easy in future.

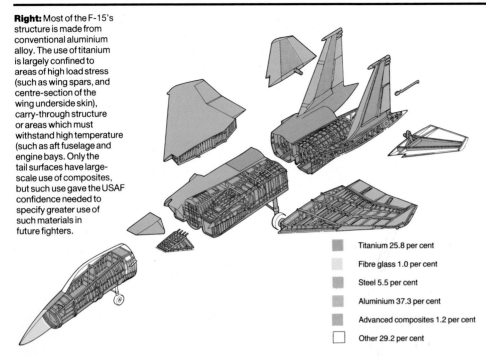

Right: Most of the F-15's structure is made from conventional aluminium alloy. The use of titanium is largely confined to areas of high load stress (such as wing spars, and centre-section of the wing underside skin), carry-through structure or areas which must withstand high temperature (such as aft fuselage and engine bays. Only the tail surfaces have large-scale use of composites, but such use gave the USAF confidence needed to specify greater use of such materials in future fighters.

Titanium 25.8 per cent

Fibre glass 1.0 per cent

Steel 5.5 per cent

Aluminium 37.3 per cent

Advanced composites 1.2 per cent

Other 29.2 per cent

with maintenance, while electrical connectors, plumbing connections, filters, and lubrication points have been kept to a minimum.

The structure has needed few changes in the light of either development or service flying. As a result of minor buffet problems experienced during flight testing, the wingtips were given raked tips, a dogtooth was added to the horizontal stabiliser, and the airbrake was increased in size. Some cracking of the vertical stabilizer has been noted in service, but this has been cured by a $130 million modification programme.

PROPULSION

The F100 is a two-shaft turbofan with a bypass ratio of 0.7:1. In creating it, Pratt & Whitney engineers pushed engine technology to the limits in order to obtain the high thrust:weight ratio demanded by the USAF. A three-stage LP fan is followed by a ten-stage HP compressor, an annular combustion chamber, a two-stage HP turbine, two-stage LP turbine and the afterburner. The engine develops 14,670lb (6,654kg) at full dry thrust, and 25,830lb (10,890kg) at full afterburner, impressive figures for an engine only 191in (485cm) long and weighing 3,068lb (1,391kg).

To achieve this level of performance, advanced technologies such as powdered metallurgy were used, while turbine inlet temperature was pushed well beyond the 2,000deg F (1,090deg C) of the best existing engines to a demanding 2,565deg F (1,400deg C).

Before being adopted for service, the new engine was put through a punishing series of ground tests, completion of which was delayed by persistent failures, not a good omen for the future. Given a highly agile fighter, USAF pilots pushed their new mount to the limits in simulated air combat, throwing the throttle open and closed at a rate never before attempted, and certainly never predicted by USAF.

This placed the engine under greater stress than had been expected, leading to reliability problems.

The most difficult engine problem was that of stagnation stalling. Any pressure surge experienced in the afterburner could travel forward through the bypass duct of the engine, reaching the compressor and being ingested by the engine. This could cause the compressor blades to stall, interrupting the flow of air through the engine. If undetected by the pilot, this situation could result in thermal damage to the turbine section. Several modifications were devised. A sensor was added to the afterburner section to detect any "light-up" failures—a common source of pressure pulses due to the unlit fuel suddenly exploding into flame on contact with hot metal—while an unused facility originally intended to adjust the engine to prevent the possibility of a stall due to the inges-

Below: The Eagle's Pratt & Whitney F100 turbofan gives brisk acceleration and a high climb rate, but runs much hotter than previous engines and has proved troublesome in service. Retrofitting of the rival General Electric F110 is unlikely, but this engine could be fitted to late production F-15s.

tion of efflux from missile launch was adapted to cope with afterburner pressure pulses.

When these and other modifications were installed on the F-15, the rate of stagnation stalling fell remarkably. A further modification (known as the proximate splitter) was devised to reduce the gap between the bypass duct and the rear of the fan. This has been adopted for F100s destined for the single-engined F-16, but is not fitted to F-15 engines. Modification work to rectify deficiencies revealed during operational service is continuing, and USAF spent more than $11 million on such work during Fiscal Year 1984.

The engine breaks down into five main modules – inlet/fan assembly, gearbox, fan drive, "hot" core section, and the afterburner. These may be interchanged between engines, simplifying repair jobs and minimising spares holdings. Each engine connects to the airframe with only ten connections, and may be slid backwards on integral rails and removed from the aircraft. The entire process takes less than 30 minutes.

Fuel is carried in tanks in the wings and fuselage centre section. Total capacity is 11,600lb (5,260kg), but this may be supplemented by conformal FastPack fuel tanks on the fuselage sides, each holding a further 5,000lb (2,268kg). The tanks are filled with foam, while the fuel lines are self-sealing. Fuel pumps are of plug-in design and may be changed in only 30 minutes.

AVIONICS

One of the boldest development moves in the creation of the F-15 was the elimination of a specialist back-seater tasked with operating the radar. USAF was confident that the power of modern digital electronics would allow a single crewman to cope with the workload shared by two men in the earlier F-4. This optimism is not shared by all air forces; when the Royal Air Force evaluated alternatives to the Tornado ADV interceptor, the F-15 was rejected because the British still believed that a two-man crew would be needed in the face of heavy ECM.

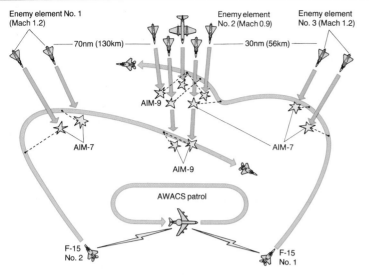

Enemy element No. 1 (Mach 1.2)

Enemy element No. 2 (Mach 0.9)

Enemy element No. 3 (Mach 1.2)

70nm (130km)

30nm (56km)

AIM-9

AIM-7

AIM-7

AIM-9

AWACS patrol

F-15 No. 2

F-15 No. 1

Left: This diagram showing how the F-15 can cooperate with the E-3A Sentry is based on an actual exercise carried out at the Air Combat Maneuvering range at USMC Air Station Yuma. Although outnumbered by nine to two, the Eagles should win such an engagement by picking off the attackers at long range using Sparrow, then closing for Sidewinder kills. During the Yuma test, one F-15 had a single AIM-9 left, the other had two AIM-9 and two AIM-7s. In combat, one or more missiles might fail, but firepower would still be available.

Below: The F-15 cockpit is dominated by the head-up display (centre) which will be the main information link between the pilot and his avionics during combat, and by the CRT displays of the radar (left) and TEWS electronic-warfare system (right). This photo seems to have been taken during a test of the warning lights. Any pilot seeing this number of lamps lit in combat is in real trouble – the top left indicator warns of a possible fire in the engine bay!

Above: The Eagle's high thrust:weight ratio makes vertical climbs easy, but the spectacle of such manoeuvres should not be allowed to conceal the fact that the Soviet Union swiftly recaptured all the time-to-height records won by the US fighter.

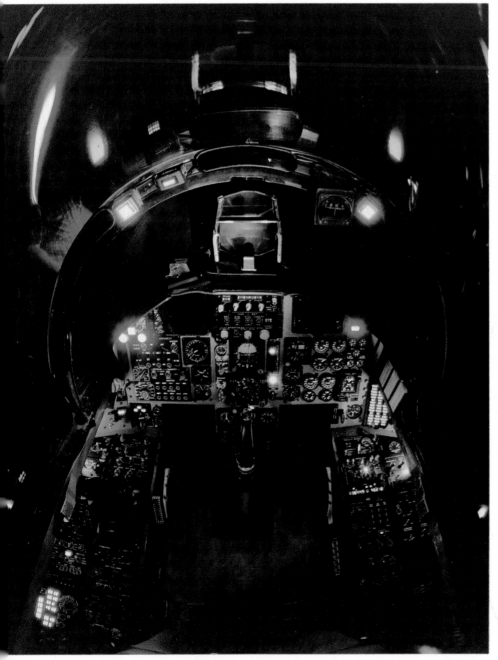

For the F-15, Hughes developed the APG-63 radar, a landmark in sensor technology. Operating in what used to be termed X-band (8 to 12GHz), now I-band and the lower part of J-band, this can acquire and track targets at long range, presenting clutter-free synthetic data to the pilot via two displays—a head-down CRT mounted on the upper left-hand side of the instrument panel, and a HUD.

Older radars such as the APQ-120 in the F-4E operate with analogue data, so the operator must be trained to interpret the raw video which appears on his CRT display. In the case of the APG-63 and other modern digital radars, the data is digitally processed, appearing on the screen as alphanumeric or other symbology, whose interpretation is less of a "black art". All controls needed during combat are located on the throttle, allowing the pilot to remain "head-up", keeping his attention on the external view.

Complex electronic circuitry allows the set to use high, medium and low pulse-repetition frequencies (PRFs) as required, giving all-altitude all-aspect target tracking and attack capability. Maximum detection range is greater than 100nm (185km). The radar in the F-4E is virtually blind when forced to operate in "look-down" mode against low-flying targets, but threat aircraft such as the Su-24 Fencer made such capability mandatory for the APG-63.

The F-15C/D introduces a modified radar incorporating a programmable signal processor. The earlier set had controlled its radar modes using hardware, but addition of the new processor has allowed this function to be transferred to software, facilitating modification and upgrading, should this become necessary.

For the F-15E, the signal processor allows the use of synthetic-aperture radar techniques to improve radar resolution. Early test flights with the Strike Eagle prototype showed that resolutions of less than 10ft (3m) could be achieved, yielding radar imagery detailed enough to allow streets, vehicles and parked aircraft to be detected. Another sensor tested on Strike Eagle was the Pave Tack pod-mounted FLIR, which could provide the TV-like detailed imagery needed for the final attack against targets screened by bad weather or darkness.

In the original F-15 build standard, a Litton ASN-109 inertial navigation system is backed up by traditional navaids such as TACAN and ADF. The running-up time of the inertial platform takes several minutes. This is acceptable on a peacetime mission, but in wartime might give a marauding Flogger enough time to dig up the runway or taxiways using an anti-airfield weapon, or even destroy the hardened aircraft shelter and Eagle.

Standard RWR is the Loral ALR-56, a digital system which monitors the spectrum from H-band to J-band (6 to 20GHz). For self-protection, a Northrop ALQ-135 jammer is carried internally.

The current F-4G Wild Weasel anti-radar aircraft are rebuilds, so will have a limited service life. There has been little public discussion of Wild Weasel F-15s, but the type seems the only logical replacement for the existing aircraft.

The Control Augmentation System (CAS) translates the demands made by the pilot using the control column and rudder into deflections of the control surfaces. Without this system, stick forces would be unacceptably high during manoeuvring flight. Even when manoeuvring at 6g, the Eagle can be flown with one hand.

All avionics are packaged in LRUs which incorporate built-in test facilities. If a system fails, the ground crew can tell which unit or units need to be replaced by consulting an indicator panel in the nose-wheel well. Problems with automatic test equipment used for base-level LRU faultfinding and repair have resulted in a high proportion of faulty LRUs being returned to the depot for repair, a factor which has resulted in increased utilisation of spares and degraded operational availability of the aircraft. This was well under 60 per cent in the late 1970s, but was gradually restored to more than 65 per cent, a figure significantly bettered by some F-15 units. In three years, availability at the 1st TFW rose from an abysmal 35 per cent to a near-perfect 98.6 per cent.

The Multi-Stage Improvement Program is intended to maintain the F-15's air-superiority against the numerically superior threat posed by future Soviet fighters. Three performance areas require upgrading—target acquisition, identification and destruction; command and control; and self protection (EW). The avionics must be integrated with the improved AIM-7M and AIM-120 missiles as well as the JTIDS data link.

A programme known as "All-environment ID" will provide the improved target-identification needed to allow these medium-range missiles to be used effectively against multiple targets in bad weather, at night, or in the face of heavy jamming.

ARMAMENT

Main air-to-air weapons carried by the Eagle are the well-proven AIM-9 Sidewinder and AIM-7 Sparrow. Both are also used on the F-4 which the Eagle is replacing, but the new aircraft will use the latest versions of these missiles.

The AIM-9L is a third-generaton Sidewinder designed to cope with highly-manoeuvring targets, and is the standard

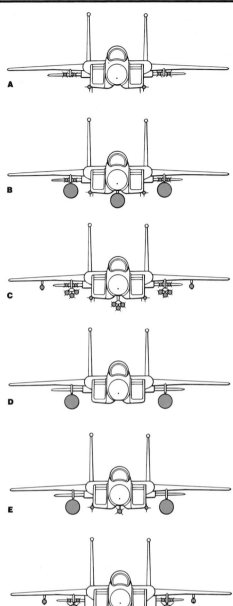

Below: Following a disappointing combat record in Vietnam, the Sparrow semi-active radar guided missile has been developed into the much more reliable and effective AIM-7F and AIM-7M forms to arm modern fighters such as the Eagle. Solid-state electronics and a larger warhead are among the new features.

Above: Alternative payloads for the F-15A and F-15C fighters show the versatility of the McDonnell Douglas design. New versions of the Eagle could result from future requirements for dedicated recce or "Wild Weasel" anti-radar aircraft.
(A) Standard air-superiority loading, with Sidewinders on the underwing hardpoints and Sparrows on the lower corners of the fuselage. In order to minimise drag, no external tanks are carried.
(B) For long-range interception duties, the same missile warload is carried, plus external tanks under the wings and on the centreline.
(C) The F-15A was never assigned to attack duties, but the use of the aircraft in the air-to-ground role has been much studied by McDonnell Douglas. Sidewinders and Sparrows could be retained in their current locations, with one or more triple clusters of "iron" bombs being added to each of the inner pylons and centreline. The outer wing pylons could carry AGM-88 HARM anti-radar missiles or jamming pods.
(D) Although no dedicated recce Eagles have been ordered, McDonnell Douglas studies have already shown that the aircraft could be a first-class platform for reconnaissance sensors. The current RF-4E fleet cannot last indefinitely.
(E) Availability of the AIM-120 AMRAAM missile in the second half of the 1980s will allow improved interceptors to be fielded.
(F) FASTpack conformal fuel tanks and a wide range of air-to-ground ordnance was tested on Strike Eagle, leading to USAF buying F-15Es.

short-range missile on all the latest US fighters. Used in combat in the Falklands and the Middle East, it has demonstrated a high kill rate.

The AIM-7F Sparrow is intended to cure many of the deficiencies noted when earlier models were used in combat during the Vietnam War. First fielded in 1977, it features solid-state guidance electronics, an improved rocket motor and a larger warhead, but its seeker is still potentially

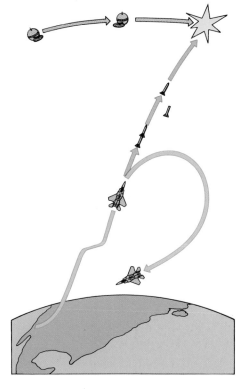

vulnerable to some types of deception jamming. The newer AIM-7M introduces an ECM-resistant monopulse seeker plus digital signal processing and a new autopilot, so promises to be very much better.

In the long term, the Eagle will carry the Hughes AIM-120 AMRAAM "fire-and-forget" missile, so the USAF will have to add the new missile launchers, weapons switches, avionics software and other equipment to the F-15. Not much larger than the Sidewinder, the AIM-120 will offer the performance of the Sparrow, which it will probably replace; at a later date it might also replace the AIM-9.

Having deployed the F-4 without an internal cannon, USAF was determined not to make the same mistake again. Plans to fit the F-15 with a 25mm GAU-7 cannon firing caseless ammunition had to be abandoned in 1973 when it became obvious that problems with jamming and inconsistent performance could not be overcome. The long-established General Electric M61A1 Vulcan 20mm gun fitted to early-production aircraft had to be retained as the standard cannon.

Instead of the chin location adopted for the F-4E Phantom, or the internal-fuselage location used in most other M61-armed aircraft, the F-15 design team opted for a location in the wing root, with the 940-round ammunition drum being mounted in the upper fuselage close to the centreline. The F-15E could be armed with the GAU-12/U, a new pattern of 25mm cannon (this time using conventional cased ammunition) which is being developed for use on the AV-8B.

The F-15E will be able to carry air-to-

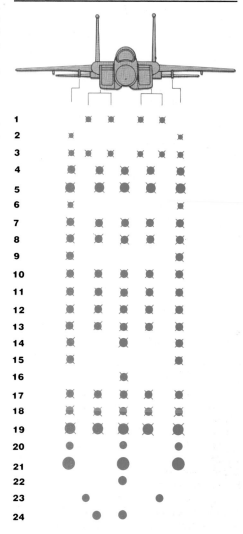

Above: The USAF plans to deploy two squadrons of F-15s equipped with the Vought ASAT anti-satellite weapon. The two-stage weapon (the first stage based on the Boeing SRAM missile, the second on an Altair III rocket motor) will be released after a zoom climb to around 80,000ft (24,000m) and will carry a non-nuclear warhead.

Below: The success of flight tests with heavy air-to-surface ordnance loads persuaded the USAF to order a multi-role version of the Eagle rather than the proposed arrow-wing F-16XL. The aircraft shown here carries no Sparrows but retains Sidewinders. Mounted on the side of the pylon, the latter leave the hardpoint free.

Possible weapons:
The F-15 was designed and initially deployed as a dedicated fighter carrying air-to-air weapons only, but will now be fielded in the new F-15E multirole form.
1. AIM-7 Sparrow (-7F or -7M version).
2. AIM-9J, -9L or -9M Sidewinder for short-range combat.
3. AIM-120A AMRAAM (one per fuselage station; two on each wing hardpoint).
4. Mk82 500lb (230kg) bombs (6 on centreline, 4 on all other locations).
5. Mk83 1,000lb (450kg) bombs
6. AGM-65 Maverick (triple-round launcher on each underwing hardpoint).
7. GBU-8/B or GBU-10A/B "smart" bombs.
8. GBU-12 "smart" bombs (3 on centreline, 2 in all other positions).
9. GBU-15 "smart" glide bomb.
10. Mk20 Rockeye cluster bomb (6 on centreline, 4 in all other positions).
11. CBU-52B/B 770lb (350kg) cluster munitions – 3 or 4 in each position.
12. CBU-58B 815lb (370kg) cluster munitions – 3 or 4 per position.
13. CBU-71B 815lb (370kg) cluster munitions – 3 or 4 per position.
14. LAU-3A cluster munitions (3 per position).
15, 16. JP233 anti-runway weapons (the USAF withdrew from this joint UK/US project, and no longer plans to field the system. Export F-15 users would be free to purchase the weapon from the UK).
17. SUU-20B/A bomb and rocket dispensers.
18. BLU-27 750lb (340kg) fire bomb – 3 on centreline, 2 in all other positions. Each has 100 gallons of napalm.
19. Free-falling nuclear weapons.
20. 30mm gun pods.
21. 610 US gall tank.
22. ALQ-119(V) jamming pod.
23. Targetting (starboard) and navigation (port) pods for the LANTIRN night/adverse-weather electro-optical system.
24. Pave Tack night/adverse weather electro-optical target acquisition and laser-designation system.

ground munitions such as iron bombs, retarded bombs, smart bombs, cluster munitions, and nuclear weapons. One likely load is the Matra Durandal, a French anti-airfield weapon recently adopted by the USAF. Air-to-ground missiles could include the AGM-65 Maverick and the Texas Instruments AGM-88 HARM anti-radar missile. The high cost of the HARM has forced the USAF to trim its planned procurement, but this high-speed passive-homing weapon is still expected to play a major role in suppressing enemy defences.

PERFORMANCE

When it comes to all-round performance, the F-15 has no peers. Specialised aircraft such as the MiG-25 or SR-71 may have a higher top speed, but the former is incapable of manoeuvring, while the latter is so lightly stressed that it must be flown virtually "straight and level" at high speed.

Top speed of the F-15 under normal conditions is a respectable Mach 2.3, but brief dashes at Mach 2.5 are possible. At sea level, the maximum speed is Mach 1.2. Approach speed is a handleable 125kts (232km/h).

On an interception mission, the F-15 can be airborne with a roll of only 900ft (275m). Landing run is longer, since the engines which blasted it into the air cannot be used as thrust reversers. A typical figure would be 2,500ft (760m).

Ferry range with full external tanks is more than 2,500nm (4,600km). If the conformal fuel tanks are also fitted, the range rises to more than 3,000nm (5,500km).

F-15 out-turns/out-accelerates Phantom

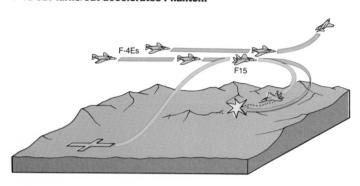

F-15 gains gun advantage within 360° of turn

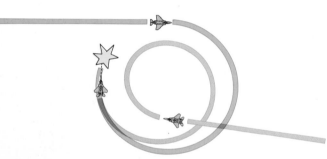

Left: The F-15 can out-turn and out-accelerate the F-4E Phantom. Even with the older aircraft starting 1,000ft (300m) behind the Eagle, and both travelling at 170kt (315km/h) at 12,000ft (3,650m), the F-15 can out-turn the Phantom within half a turn. As the older fighter attempts the tightest turn it can manage, the Eagle is able to reverse the situation—the Phantom overshoots, allowing the F-15 to kill.

Left: In combat, attacks often develop out of a head-on approach. In the instance shown here, an F-15 flying at 300kt (555km/h) at 10,000ft (3,000m) takes on an F-4E flying at the same speed and height, but on the opposite course. Both aircraft enter a tight turn in an attempt to get on the tail of its opponent, but before the F-4E has completed a single turn, the Eagle is in position to open fire.

Above: Turbulence associated with high-speed flight at this sort of altitude causes buffeting which is fatiguing to airframe and crew alike, while the radar and missile seeker heads must use the latest technology if they are not to be distracted by ground clutter etc.

Right: The missile firepower of the F-15 could in theory "take out" eight opponents by the time that combat closes to gun range. This is the sort of capability that the West needs to offset Warsaw Pact numerical strength, but the USSR will doubtless soon catch up.

Maximum mission endurance with conformal fuel tanks is more than 5 hours, but this can be stretched to 15 by means of airborne refuelling.

Wing loading under half-fuel combat conditions is 57lb/sq ft (333kg/sq m), while the thrust:weight ratio is 1.15:1. Both characteristics help give the high manoeuvrability for which the Eagle is renowned. Its pilot need give little thought to conserving energy during manoeuvres, since the sheer power of the two F100s will cope with most eventualities. The

F-15 can easily out-turn an F-4E, or climb by 7,100ft (2,160m) from 20,000ft (6,100m) while matching the Phantom's tightest 180deg turn. The airframe is stressed to accept from +7.33 to −3g.

Absolute ceiling is 100,000ft (30,500m), a figure unmatched by any other Western fighter. The F-15 was used to capture time-to-height records formerly held by the MiG-25 Foxbat, but its triumph was short-lived. The record was soon reclaimed by a Russian Ye-266M research aircraft—probably a MiG-25 being used to test the

upgraded engines of the MiG-31 Foxhound. It is probably unfair to compare the Soviet type with the F-15, since the former—being a pure interceptor—was probably designed for maximum speed and climb rate and very little else. The Eagle is intended to manoeuvre and fight. It remains the dogfighter par excellence, and the standard against which future designs must be measured. The next few years will see Soviet fighters such as the MiG-29 and Su-27 entering service as the Soviet Air Force attempts to match the Eagle.

MCDONNELL-DOUGLAS
F-18 HORNET

DEVELOPMENT

The F-18 is a multi-role fighter of considerable capability and promises to be one of the most reliable and mission-available in service. The design is based on that of the experimental Northrop YF-17 lightweight fighter. Following the selection of the rival F-16 by the USAF, the US Navy opted to take a developed and heavier version of the YF-17 under the designation F-18. This was to be powered by the new General Electric F404 engine, a development of the YJ101 powerplants used in the YF-17.

Northrop lacked experience in naval aircraft design, so the new aircraft—now designated Hornet—became a joint McDonnell Douglas/Northrop project. Since the St. Louis company was a long-established USN supplier, it was made responsible for the new naval fighter, while Northrop retained design leadership of the planned F-18L land-based export variant. The latter design has a non-folding wing, two extra stores stations, a lower empty weight, and a lighter undercarriage optimised for land use.

The Navy had no intention of replacing the F-14 Tomcat, since even today the big Grumman interceptor offers better long-range killing performance than any other aircraft. The F-18 was intended as a less-expensive complement to the F-14, and to be a replacement for the McDonnell Douglas F-4 Phantom and the Vought A-7 Corsair II attack aircraft. At one time, separate F-18A and A-18A variants were planned, but it proved possible to create a single dual-role model.

In drawing up the specification for Hornet, the USN placed great emphasis on reliability, rather than performance. Instead of offering the Mach 2.5 performance of the earlier F-4 Phantom, the Hornet is intended to give the USN and USMC an aircraft which will be easy to maintain. Engines, avionics "Black boxes" and other sub-systems are all designed for easy access and removal.

The first prototype flew for the first time on November 18, 1978, and was followed by 10 other development aircraft. Initial experience revealed a number of shortcomings in performance, requiring modifications to the structure, control system software and engine. Since the most urgent requirement was to replace the USMC's F-4s, initial acceptance testing of the F/A-18 concentrated on the fighter role. Clearance for this mission was achieved by the end of 1981, while evaluation in the attack role was completed in October 1982. Production of the F-18 got under way in the course of 1982, with deliveries to the US Navy starting late that year.

Approval for production of the attack version of Hornet was postponed late in 1982 following criticisms made by the USN operational-evaluation unit. Approval was granted for production of the fighter version only. In the following spring, go-ahead for the attack version was finally given, but the DoD kept an open mind on the number to be purchased.

A total of 700 attack Hornets was originally planned, but there is a possibility of a cutback to 300 (from the anticipated overall production run for the US of 1,366) to trim the escalating cost of the programme in the mid-1980s. An alternative possibility would involve holding down the annual production rate, thereby

Above: A Canadian CF-18 lets fly with air-to-ground practice rockets. Canadian Hornets differ from the US version in minor ways, one of which is the painting of a false canopy on the fuselage underside.

Typical weapons:
Top: A, AIM-9 Sidewinder; **B**, external fuel tanks; **C**, M61 20mm cannon; **D**, AIM-120 AMRAAM. It is here configured for beachhead air superiority, escort, or fleet defence duties.
Above: A, FLIR pod; **B**, Laser Spot Tracker; **C**, AGM-109 Harpoon; **D**, AGM-65 Maverick; **E**, AIM-9 Sidewinder. The F/A-18 is a true multi-role aircraft; both modes are shown, the F-18 at top.

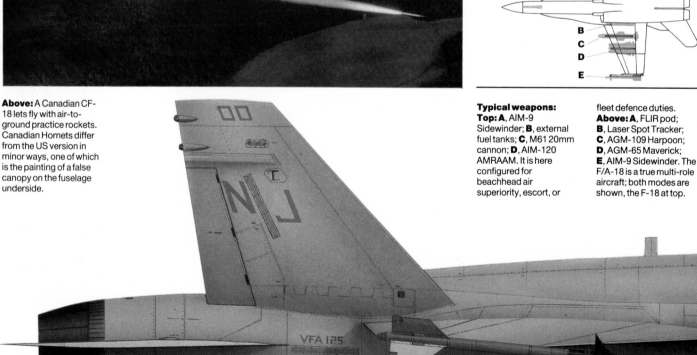

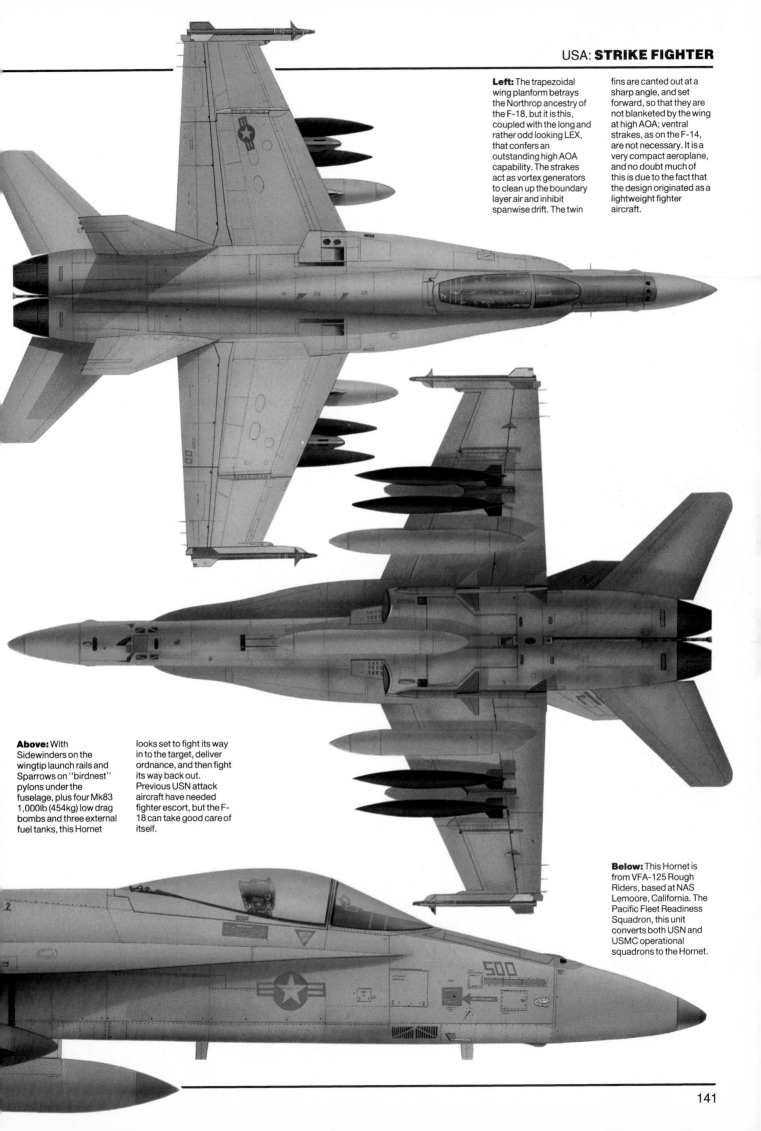

Left: The trapezoidal wing planform betrays the Northrop ancestry of the F-18, but it is this, coupled with the long and rather odd looking LEX, that confers an outstanding high AOA capability. The strakes act as vortex generators to clean up the boundary layer air and inhibit spanwise drift. The twin fins are canted out at a sharp angle, and set forward, so that they are not blanketed by the wing at high AOA; ventral strakes, as on the F-14, are not necessary. It is a very compact aeroplane, and no doubt much of this is due to the fact that the design originated as a lightweight fighter aircraft.

Above: With Sidewinders on the wingtip launch rails and Sparrows on "birdnest" pylons under the fuselage, plus four Mk83 1,000lb (454kg) low drag bombs and three external fuel tanks, this Hornet looks set to fight its way in to the target, deliver ordnance, and then fight its way back out. Previous USN attack aircraft have needed fighter escort, but the F-18 can take good care of itself.

Below: This Hornet is from VFA-125 Rough Riders, based at NAS Lemoore, California. The Pacific Fleet Readiness Squadron, this unit converts both USN and USMC operational squadrons to the Hornet.

141

stretching out the costs of this expensive and controversial programme. Unit flyway cost is currently just over $25 million.

In an attempt to replace the ageing RF-8 reconnaissance aircraft, the USN has asked for a dedicated reconnaissance version of Hornet, with an internally-mounted sensor pallet taking the place of the 20mm gun. A $3.8 million contract for the design, construction and flight testing of a prototype was awarded in 1983.

Hornet was strongly promoted as an export aircraft, beating the rival F-16 in several major competitions, and winning orders from Canada, Australia and Spain. In every instance, the customer adopted the standard McDonnell Douglas naval fighter rather than the proposed Northrop F-18L. Canada received its first CF-18 in October 1982, and deliveries of the entire batch of 138 will run until mid-1988. The Royal Australian Air Force ordered 75 as replacements for the elderly Dassault Mirage IIIO. These aircraft will be locally assembled, the first being due for delivery in October 1984.

Spain originally announced its selection

of the F-18 in 1982, but the evaluation was reconsidered following a change of Government. Confirmation of the order was finally announced in June 1983, but Spain may decide to cut the order from the planned 84 aircraft to only 72, retaining an option on the final 12. Deliveries will probably begin in early 1986.

STRUCTURE

Although now a McDonnell Douglas aircraft, the Hornet owes its birth and its physical configuration to a Northrop project of the late 1960s—the P.530 Cobra. Conceived as a higher-performance follow-on to the best-selling F-5 series, Cobra retained the traditional twin-engined configuration of the earlier aircraft, but featured a large unswept wing and long strakes—known as leading-edge extensions (LEXes)–which extended along the front fuselage. Now a familiar sight thanks to the General Dynamics F-16, these are intended to smooth the fuselage/wing airflow, a narrow slot between each LEX and the fuselage side allowing air to

pass through for boundary-layer control purposes. Because of these features, the Hornet may be flown at angles of attack of up to 60deg.

The wing itself is made from aluminium alloy and graphite composite material, and folds for carrier storage. The leading edge incorporates full-span manoeuvring flaps capable of being deflected down to 30deg, while the single-slotted trailing-edge flaps are capable of 45deg deflection. Operation of both is commanded by the digital flight-control system in order to create the optimum wing camber for cruise and combat flight conditions. Prior to landing, the ailerons are deflected 45deg downwards to act as flaps, thus minimising approach speeds.

Like the wing, the fuselage makes extensive use of composite materials for its external surfaces, metal being retained for the primary load-bearing structure. The engines are separated by a titanium firewall. The twin vertical fins and horizontal stabilisers are swept, the former being mounted in a novel location between the wing and stabiliser.

McDonnell-Douglas F/A-18 Hornet
1. Radome.
2. Planar array radar scanner.
3. Flight refuelling probe, retractable.
4. Gun gas purging air intakes.
5. Radar module withdrawal rails.
6. M61-A1 Vulcan, 20mm rotary cannon.
7. Ammunition magazine.
8. Angle of attack transmitter.
9. Hinged windscreen (access to instruments).
10. Instrument panel and radar 'head-down' displays.
11. Head-up display.
12. Engine throttle levers.
13. Martin-Baker MK.10L "zero-zero" ejection seat.
14. Canopy.
15. Cockpit pressurization valve.
16. Canopy actuator.
17. Structural space provision for second seat (TF-18 trainer variant).
18. ASQ-137 Laser Spot Tracker.
19. Leading edge root extension (LERX).
20. Position light.
21. TACAN aerial.
22. Intake ramp bleed air spill duct.
23. Starboard wing stores pylons.
24. Leading edge flap.

25. Starboard wing integral fuel tank.
26. Wing fold hinge joint.
27. AIM-9P Sidewinder air-to-air missile.
28. Missile launch rail.
29. Starboard navigation light.
30. Wing tip folded position.
31. Flap vane.
32. Leading edge flap drive shaft interconnection.
33. Starboard drooping aileron.
34. UHF/IFF aerial.
35. Boundary layer bleed air spill duct.
36. Leading edge flap drive motor and gearbox.
37. Engine bleed air ducting.
38. Aft fuselage fuel tanks.
39. Hydraulic reservoirs.
40. Fuel system vent pipe.
41. Fuel venting air grilles.
42. Strobe light.
43. Tail navigation light.
44. Aft radar warning antenna.
45. Fuel jettison.
46. Starboard rudder.
47. Radar warning power amplifier.

48. Rudder hydraulic actuator.
49. Starboard all-moving tailplane.
50. Airbrake.
51. ECM aerial.
52. Radar warning aerial.
53. Formation lighting strip.
54. Variable-area afterburner nozzles.
55. Afterburner duct.
56. Engine fire suppression bottles.
57. Arrester hook jack and damper.
58. Port all-moving tailplane.
59. Afterburner nozzle actuator.
60. Tailplane pivot bearing.
61. Arrester hook.
62. Tailplane hydraulic actuator.
63. General Electric F404 afterburning turbofan engine.

64. Engine digital control unit.
65. Formation lighting strip.
66. Engine fuel system equipment.
67. Port drooping aileron.

68. Single-slotted Fowler-type flap.
69. Aileron hydraulic actuator.
70. Wing fold rotary actuator and gearbox.
71. Port navigation light.

72. AIM-9P Sidewinder air-to-air missile.
73. Leading edge flap rotary actuator.
74. Port leading edge flap.
75. Airframe mounted

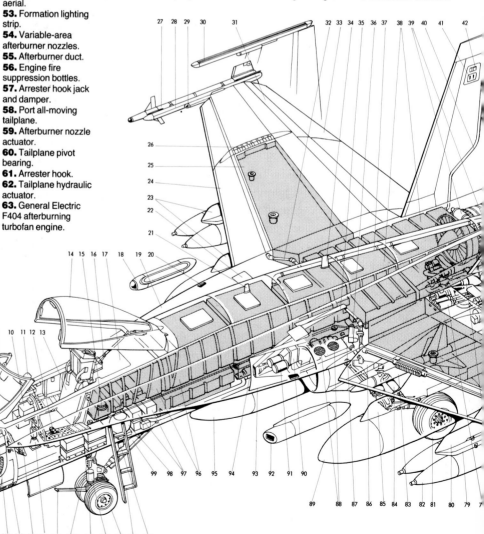

Following early flight-test experience, modifications were carried out to the structure. To improve roll rate, the outer wing sections were stiffened, the ailerons extended further outboard, and a differential flap system installed. Other modifications to the strakes and environmental control-system exhaust were devised to reduce drag.

POWERPLANT

GE deliberately "backed off" from the ultimate performance in developing the F404, believing that a reduction of five to ten per cent from the theoretically possible thrust-to-weight ratio and specific fuel consumption (s.f.c.) would make possible a major reduction in complexity, minimising hardware cost and maintenance requirements. This technical conservatism has paid off, the only major problem experienced being a result of the use of powdered-metal fabrication processes. One crash was caused by the in-flight disintegration of a turbine stage, but the problem was cured by changing the fineness of the powdered material.

The F404 is a two-shaft low-ratio turbofan with a dry thrust of 16–18,000lb (7,257–8,165kg) and 20,000lb (9,072kg) in full afterburner. Bypass ratio is 0.35, some 25 per cent of thrust being provided by the fan. Afterburning s.f.c. is reported to be five per cent lower than that of the F100 which powers the F-16 and F-15, while time from idle to full afterburning thrust is less than seven seconds.

Stall problems with the TF30 used by the F-14, plus knowledge of the USAF's problems with the F100 engine in the F-15, made the USN demand a reliable and stall-free powerplant. Experience has shown that the stall margin of the F404 is better than that of the GE turbojets used in earlier US fighters. Exact values vary with conditions under which the engines are being run, but at sea level an F404 running on the test bench has a 25 per cent stall margin, better than the 20 per cent figure of the J79. Compared with the J79, the F404 has 19,000 fewer parts, three fewer compressor stages and two fewer turbine stages, and a single-stage afterburner light-up rather than a five-stage system.

The engine is 158in (403cm) long, 34.8in (88cm) in diameter and weighs 2,000lb (907kg). It breaks down into six interchangeable modules and is fitted with 11 borescope ports. No trim testing is required if a module is replaced, says GE. This saves fuel and engine running time as well as reducing maintenance man-hours.

AVIONICS

The cockpit of the F-18 is probably the most advanced avionics data-display installation on any military aircraft. Three multi-purpose CRT displays, a HUD and an information-control panel replace much of the conventional instrumentation found in a normal cockpit. Throughout the flight, the data chosen for display is that required for the relevant phase of the mission. In air combat, for example, the HUD will be used as the main source of data at short range, while the right-hand CRT displays tactical data. On the left-hand CRT, a schematic diagram of the aircraft and its armament stations may be

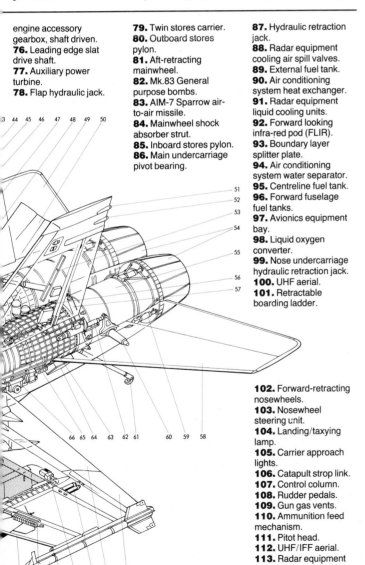

engine accessory gearbox, shaft driven.
76. Leading edge slat drive shaft.
77. Auxiliary power turbine.
78. Flap hydraulic jack.
79. Twin stores carrier.
80. Outboard stores pylon.
81. Aft-retracting mainwheel.
82. Mk.83 General purpose bombs.
83. AIM-7 Sparrow air-to-air missile.
84. Mainwheel shock absorber strut.
85. Inboard stores pylon.
86. Main undercarriage pivot bearing.
87. Hydraulic retraction jack.
88. Radar equipment cooling air spill valves.
89. External fuel tank.
90. Air conditioning system heat exchanger.
91. Radar equipment liquid cooling units.
92. Forward looking infra-red pod (FLIR).
93. Boundary layer splitter plate.
94. Air conditioning system water separator.
95. Centreline fuel tank.
96. Forward fuselage fuel tanks.
97. Avionics equipment bay.
98. Liquid oxygen converter.
99. Nose undercarriage hydraulic retraction jack.
100. UHF aerial.
101. Retractable boarding ladder.
102. Forward-retracting nosewheels.
103. Nosewheel steering unit.
104. Landing/taxying lamp.
105. Carrier approach lights.
106. Catapult strop link.
107. Control column.
108. Rudder pedals.
109. Gun gas vents.
110. Ammunition feed mechanism.
111. Pitot head.
112. UHF/IFF aerial.
113. Radar equipment module.
114. Formation lighting strip.
115. Forward radar warning antenna.
116. Radar scanner tracking mechanism.

Above: The cockpit of the Hornet has been described as "out of Star Wars". Frankly it looks better than Star Wars, and the remaining few old-fashioned dials are for back-up data. HOTAS (Hands On Throttle And Stick) is used so that everything needed in situations where time is critical is instantly at hand. The near absence of conventional instruments is startling at first. Almost all information can be called up on one of three CRTs. Top left is the Master Monitor Display, and the Multi-Function Display is on the right; between is the CNI panel, with the horizontal situation display below it. Control is via touch switches.

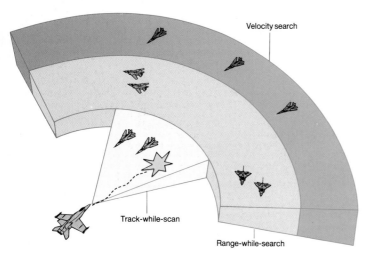

Velocity search

Track-while-scan

Range-while-search

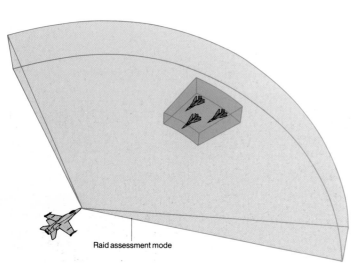

Raid assessment mode

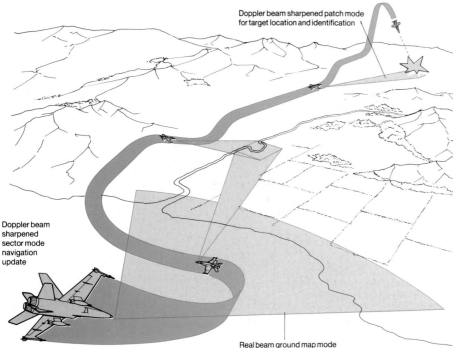

Doppler beam sharpened patch mode for target location and identification

Doppler beam sharpened sector mode navigation update

Real beam ground map mode

Above: Navigation and attack modes are also built into the APG-65. Large terrain features can be identified from considerable distances using the real beam ground mapping mode. This uses non-coherent pulse to pulse frequency agility to avoid glint, and long range is given through a combination of pulse compression and low prf. Further modes use Doppler beam sharpening to give better resolution over smaller areas. The sector mode uses a beam sharpening ratio of 19:1, while the patch mode gives first class resolution with a ratio of 67:1. The display presentation is computer-adjusted to give a plan view of the terrain under study.

drawn, showing the pilot the exact array of armament currently carried, and which rounds are prepared for firing. As missiles are expended, this electronic "tote-board" is automatically amended.

Following the current HOTAS (hands on throttle and stick) concept, the F/A-18 cockpit is designed so that all switches needed during air-to-air or air-to-ground combat are located on the control column (five switches) or throttle (10 switches).

The designers chose not to adopt the semi-reclining seat position used in the F-16. Such an installation would probably have increased the g-resistance limits of the pilot, but the use of a more conventional seating posture allows a deeper instrument panel to be fitted.

Like all modern fighters, Hornet relies on an advanced flight-control system. The system devised by General Electric is quadruple-redundant and incorporates two AYK-14 digital computers. Navigation data is provided by a Litton inertial-navigation system. Data from this is passed to the central CRT display unit—a combined projected-map/CRT unit developed by Ferranti and manufactured under licence by Bendix. Using this unit, the INS-controlled moving-map may be superimposed with digitally generated alpha-numerics or other navigation symbology.

Primary long-range sensor for air-to-air and air-to-ground use is the Hughes APG-65 multi-mode radar. Although smaller and lighter than the APG-63 set carried by the F-15 Eagle, the more modern APG-65 closely approaches the long-range target detection capabilities of the earlier equipment. Operating frequency is in I/J-band (8–10GHz).

Long-range detection of head-on targets is handled by a velocity-search mode, a range-while-search mode being used for targets at other aspect angles. Raid-assessment mode allows the pilot to examine an area around a target at greatly magnified scale, giving the high degree of discrimination needed to pick out individual aircraft in a formation at long range.

Three air-combat modes cover the needs of air-to-air combat. As its title suggests, HUD-acquisition mode automatically searches the volume of sky contained in the HUD field of view, locking on to the first target it finds within the specified range bracket. Boresight mode provides a stationary pencil beam aligned with the aircraft's fore-and-aft axis. The pilot can thus acquire a target simply by pointing his aircraft at it. To meet the demands of dogfighting, the APG-65 has a vertical-acquisition mode in which the antenna scans in a vertical pattern

Modes available for use during air-to-ground strikes include high-resolution surface mapping, terrain avoidance, sea-surface search and ground moving-target modes. By using a Doppler beam sharpening facility, the pilot can examine a small area of terrain at very high resolution, effectively "zooming-in" to obtain a detailed image which may easily be corellated with photo-reconnaissance data.

In order to cope with the "fire-and-

Three air combat manoeuvring modes of APG-65 radar

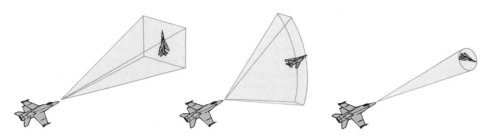

forget'' AMRAAM missile currently under development for the USAF and USN, the APG-65 is provided with a track-while-scan mode. This will allow the pilot to maintain a track on up to eight targets while continuing the search for others.

Two pod-mounted electro-optical aids are planned for use in air-to-surface missions. These are a Martin-Marietta ASQ-173 laser spot tracker/strike camera, and a Ford Aerospace AAS-38 FLIR (forward-looking infra-red) system. The latter incorporates a Ferranti Type 117 laser-designator/ranger.

The most basic item of ECM equipment carried by the Hornet is the Itek ALR-67 radar-warning receiver. This is designed to detect the signals from hostile radars, and to signal to the pilot that he is under observation. If the ALR-67 is the Hornet's EW "ears", the ALQ-165 Advanced Self-Protection Jammer (ASPJ) is its "teeth". Development of this joint USAF/USN system started as a competition between two industrial groups—Westinghouse and ITT defeating the Northrop/Sanders team. A production decision on ASPJ is due to be taken in 1984/1985. The specification was a bold one, calling for an ECM system capable of fitting into an avionics bay of little more than 2 cubic feet (0.05cu m). ASPJ is reported to cover the radar spectrum from 2 to 18GHz, responding to and jamming hostile signals in less than a quarter of a second. Like all modern ECM systems, the ALR-165 incorporates a computerised power-management system able to allocate the output of the jamming transmitters among the highest-priority threats.

ARMAMENT

Normal air-to-air armament of the F-18 is two AIM-9L Sidewinders on the wingtip launch rails, plus two AIM-7F Sparrows on the lower sides of the fuselage air inlets. This configuration might be typical of an aircraft assigned to the fighter-escort role. In the longer term, Hughes AIM-120 AMRAAM missiles will be carried once this advanced "fire-and-forget" missile becomes operational in the mid-1980s.

Hornet has a single 20mm GE cannon mounted in a Northrop-style upper-nose location. Although this places the gun muzzle in the pilot's field of vision, the F-18 designers had little choice of location. A lower-fuselage location could have resulted in gun gases being ingested by the engines, while the wing strake is too thin to house armament. The magazine holds 570 rounds of ammunition.

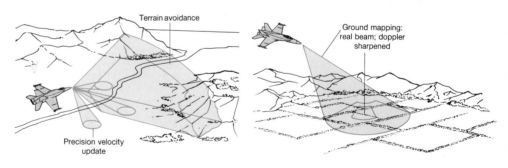

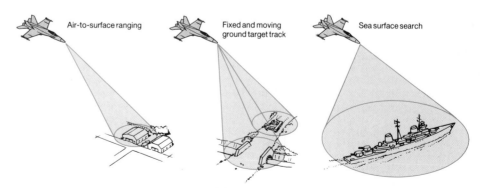

Above: The Hornet radar system has many modes available for air-to-surface strikes. Top left shows the terrain avoidance mode. This should not be confused with terrain following mode, as the pilot has to perform his own avoidance manoeuvres. Top right shows the two ground mapping modes, with a Doppler beam-sharpening segment in the centre. Above left is the air/surface ranging mode which provides target ranging information. Above centre shows both the fixed and moving ground target tracking modes, which use two-channel monopulse angle tracking. Above right is the sea/surface search mode.

This basic armament may be supplemented by additional missiles carried on nine external hardpoints—outboard and inboard underwing pylons plus a fuselage centreline station. The inboard underwing hardpoint is plumbed for external tanks.

Air-to-ground munitions can include Maverick or HARM missiles, launchers for unguided rockets and up to 27 Mk82 500lb (227kg) bombs on multiple ejector racks. In its attack role, Hornet will probably be cleared for the delivery of tactical nuclear weaponry. Total load-carrying capability of the nine hardpoints is 17,000lb (7,711kg), even at high g levels.

PERFORMANCE

Hornet has undoubtedly suffered from "bad press", and has been described by USN Chief of Operations Admiral James D. Watkins as "a somewhat maligned aircraft". During development and evaluation flight testing, a number of deficiencies were reported in the technical press. Several resulted in modifications to the aircraft, but others seem to have been more a reflection on the way that the aircraft was flown than to any faults in the design.

On paper, the Hornet's performance may look unspectacular in absolute terms. The top speed of just over Mach 1.85 and 50,000ft (15,240m) combat ceiling are well below the Mach 2.2+ and 55,000ft (16,764m) of the earlier F-4. In practice, such "ultimate" figures have little or no meaning in modern air combat.

In Hornet, the US Navy has obtained what it asked for—an aircraft able to hold its own with the best which the opposition may be flying, but designed to criteria which placed high emphasis on reliability and availability. Despite being almost a maintenance technician's dream, with mean times between failure some three times the USN average, Hornet is a first-class fighter.

When the design was approved for production as a fighter in 1981, the US Navy stated that it was superior to the F-4 "in all respects". During early service flight tests, Hornets were flown against the F-4, F-5, F-14 and A-4, demonstrating what the commander of VFA-125 (the first F-18 transition squadron) described as "superior air-to-air capability, both from the standpoint of manoeuvrability and weapon-system management". The modifications carried out to improve the roll rate have resulted in an aircraft which exceeds the time-to-bank and steady-state roll performance at low to medium subsonic speeds of all other USN fighters.

Hornet's performance in the attack role has come in for a greater degree of criticism, but care is needed in interpreting the offered evidence. Much of the best-directed "flak" has been fired by supporters of the A-7.

Hornet is required to have a range of 550nm (926km) radius of action with a warload of two AIM-9L Sidewinders, four 1,000lb (454kg) bombs plus laser and FLIR pods. This will almost certainly involve

flying an optimised hi-lo-hi flight profile. Although company flight tests with this payload demonstrated ranges of more than 600nm (1,112km), first reports from the USN evaluation units VX-4 and VX-5 suggested that the specification could not be met. Part of the problem seems to have been that the trials units, tasked with checking out the aircraft's ability to replace the existing A-7 Corsair II, flew the new aircraft on flight profiles better suited to the Vought aircraft. At the time the A-7 was developed. USN thinking favoured attack aircraft being subsonic low-altitude

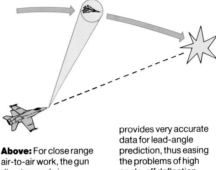

Above: For close range air-to-air work, the gun director mode is employed. This mode provides very accurate data for lead-angle prediction, thus easing the problems of high angle-off deflection shooting.

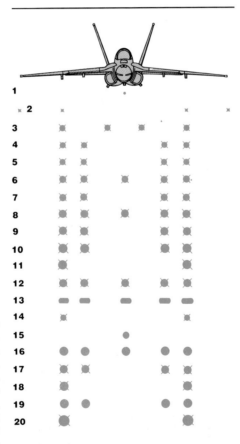

Possible weapons:
1. M61 20mm cannon with 570 rounds.
2. AIM-9G/L Sidewinder.
3. AIM-7F Sparrow.
4. AGM-65E Maverick.
5. AGM-88A HARM.
6. Mk82 LD/HD bomb.
7. Mk82 LGB.
8. Mk83 LD bomb.
9. Mk83 LGB.
10. Mk84 LD bomb.
11. Mk84 LGB.
12. Mk20 or CBU-59/B

Rockeye.
13. BLU-95 FAE II.
14. AGM-62 Walleye.
15. Walleye Data Link pod.
16. Mk76/106 practice bomb dispenser.
17. BDU-12/20.
18. BDU-36.
19. LAU-10D/A, -61A/A or -68B/A launchers.
20. B-57 or B-61. A total of three fuel tanks can be carried.

lifters of heavy ordnance loads.

The philosophy of the Hornet attack missions is very different. Being essentially a fighter, the aircraft has less to fear from hostile fighters, and can attempt to engage attackers in air combat. Its ordnance load for air-to-ground strikes will probably consist of "smart" bombs guided by the laser-designator pod, so the massive loads of "iron" bombs toted by the Corsair are simply not required.

Flown in an optimised mission, the F-18 can carry six 1,000lb (454kg) bombs, two AIM-9L Sidewinder and two AIM-7 Sparrow missiles, plus two 315gal (1,192lit) external tanks for the same distance that an A-7 can carry the six 1,000 pounders.

Reports from VX-4 and VX-5 that the aircraft has only a modest fuel capacity at maximum landing weight have also been criticised by the manufacturer. During the test sorties from the carrier *Constellation*, the landing wires had not been re-ten-

Below: A two-seater TF-18 Hornet of VFA-125 is lined up at the catapult ready for launching. The flimsy-looking launch bar on the front of the nose gear is placed in the shuttle on the catapult track (bottom left of picture), ready to go. Over 150 TF/A-18s are to be built.

sioned to accept the 33,000lb (14,970kg) landing weight for which the aircraft has already been cleared, so aircrew accepted a maximum landing weight some 800lb (363kg) lighter, reducing the amount of fuel available during landing.

Since Hornet can use anything from 500 to 900lb (227 to 408kg) of fuel during a single circuit and landing attempt, the evaluation pilots had virtually "thrown away" enough fuel for one landing attempt. By electing to divert to land bases once the remaining fuel fell to 3,500lb (1,587kg) instead of the 2,500 to 3,000lb (1,134 to 1,361kg) recommended by the manufacturer, the number of landing attempts allowable was cut back yet again.

These discouraging reports were not echoed by the USMC. During early operations by No. 11 Group at El Toro, California, USMC Hornets flew 20 hi-lo-hi strike missions over ranges greater than 500nm (926km). The aircraft landed with more than 3,000lb (1,361kg) of fuel remaining. According to the Marines, the fuel burn of the F-18 and A-7 are about the same, given a similar payload and mission. On arrival at the target area, the combat performance of Hornet far exceeds that of the Corsair II.

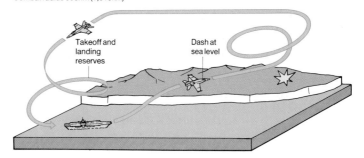

Interdiction mission
Combat radius 550nm (1,019km)

Takeoff and landing reserves

Dash at sea level

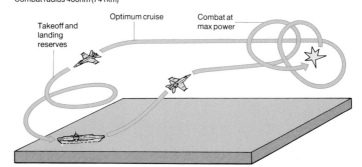

Interception mission
Combat radius 400nm (741km)

Takeoff and landing reserves

Optimum cruise

Combat at max power

Left: The lo-lo-hi interdiction mission – with three external tanks on the centreline and inboard pylons, LST/SCAM and FLIR pods on the Sparrow stations, four Mk83 GP bombs on the outboard pylons and self-defence Sidewinders on the wingtips – has a radius of over 550nm (1,013km). This includes a high speed low level dash into the target area.

Left: The Hornet is entering service to supplement the Tomcat in the US Fleet Air Defence role. With its standard complement of two AIM-9 Sidewinders and two AIM-7 Sparrows, it can make a deck-launched interception over 400nm (737km) from the parent carrier, engage in full throttle combat and return at optimum cruise speed and altitude with an adequate fuel margin.

F-5E TIGER II AND F-20 TIGERSHARK

DEVELOPMENT

The most widely-deployed Western supersonic fighter is not, in fact, an American frontline type, but the small and nimble F-5—a low-cost combat aircraft developed as a private venture by Northrop. Easy to fly, simple to maintain, able to match the performance of rival Soviet types, but low in cost (just over $5 million each, even at inflated 1984 prices), the aircraft has proved a commercial winner. The F-20 Tigershark follow-on design—another Northrop private venture—shares many features of the F-5 series, but offers the higher performance needed to cope with perceived future threats. The F-20 carries one of the most advanced multi-mode radars currently available, and its climb rate is better than that of any other US fighter, if not that of all fighters currently operational anywhere in the world.

In the three decades since starting the private-venture, NF-156F fighter project which led to the current Northrop designs, the US company and various foreign licencees have built more than 3,500 F-5A/B/E/F and T-38 aircraft. Production is still under way at a rate of around five aircraft per month in the USA. The F-20 has not yet attracted any orders.

Metal was cut on the first of three NF-156F prototypes back in May 1958, leading to a first flight in July 1959. The design was heavily based on that of the Northrop T-38 advanced trainer fielded by the USAF. The first order for the new fighter was placed in 1962 by the US Department of Defense, for some 170 aircraft to be supplied to friendly nations under the Military Assistance Program (MAP). The first production example flew in 1963, and a small number were taken into USAF service and sent to Vietnam for evaluation.

The type was also licence-built by Canadair (115 CF-5s for the Canadian Armed Forces, plus 105 NF-5s for the Netherlands), and CASA (70 SF-5s for the Spanish Air Force). Not all of Canada's CF-5s were kept operational, and a batch of 20 was supplied to South Vietnam in 1972. By the time that F-5A/B production ended in 1971, more than 1,000 had been built, including camera-equipped RF-5A reconnaissance aircraft.

Impressive as it was, this programme was only a preliminary to an even larger F-5E/F production run. Following the International Fighter competition held in 1969 and 1970 by the US DoD to find an F-5A/B replacement, orders were placed for the improved F-5E/F version powered by uprated engines.

Judged superior to rival types (such as a simplified version of the McDonnell Douglas F-4E, and new "paper" designs based on the Lockheed F-104 and Vought F-8), the Northrop F-5-21 was adopted as the new export fighter and designated F-5E. The first example flew in August 1972, and production deliveries to overseas recipients via the USAF started a year later.

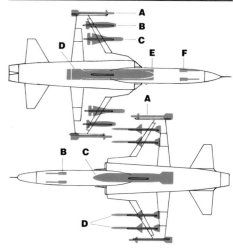

Above: An F-5A Freedom Fighter of the Kongelige Norske Flyvaapen flies over Norway, configured with drop tanks, and with empty Sidewinder launch rails. From this unpromising beginning, widely called the true air *inf*eriority fighter, came the F-5E Tiger II and the F-20 Tigershark. The F-5A is also a direct ancestor of the F-18.

Typical weapons:
Top: A, AIM-9 Sidewinder AAM; **B,** Mk83 bomb; **C,** AGM-65 Maverick; **D,** external fuel tank; **E,** AN/ALQ-171 ECM pack; **F,** 20mm M39 cannon. Designed as a low-cost fighter, the F-5 series was adapted to give a limited ground attack capability. The upgraded F-5E can carry a worthwhile load of munitions.

Above: A, AIM-9 Sidewinder; **B,** 20mm M39 cannon; **C,** external fuel tank; **D,** AIM-120 AMRAAM. The F-5E, a potent clear weather fighter, has since been developed into the F-5G, later redesignated as the F-20 Tigershark, shown here. With six on-board missiles plus two guns, the Tigershark will be a formidable opponent.

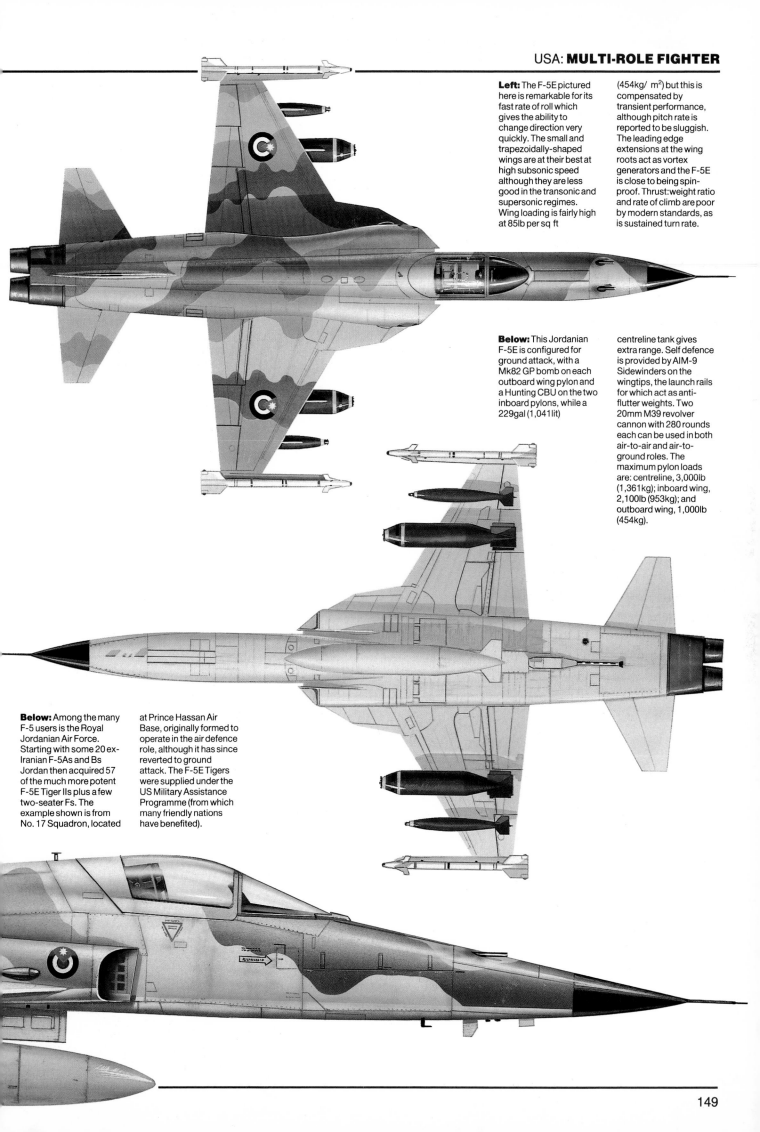

Left: The F-5E pictured here is remarkable for its fast rate of roll which gives the ability to change direction very quickly. The small and trapezoidally-shaped wings are at their best at high subsonic speed although they are less good in the transonic and supersonic regimes. Wing loading is fairly high at 85lb per sq ft (454kg/ m²) but this is compensated by transient performance, although pitch rate is reported to be sluggish. The leading edge extensions at the wing roots act as vortex generators and the F-5E is close to being spin-proof. Thrust:weight ratio and rate of climb are poor by modern standards, as is sustained turn rate.

Below: This Jordanian F-5E is configured for ground attack, with a Mk82 GP bomb on each outboard wing pylon and a Hunting CBU on the two inboard pylons, while a 229gal (1,041lit) centreline tank gives extra range. Self defence is provided by AIM-9 Sidewinders on the wingtips, the launch rails for which act as anti-flutter weights. Two 20mm M39 revolver cannon with 280 rounds each can be used in both air-to-air and air-to-ground roles. The maximum pylon loads are: centreline, 3,000lb (1,361kg); inboard wing, 2,100lb (953kg); and outboard wing, 1,000lb (454kg).

Below: Among the many F-5 users is the Royal Jordanian Air Force. Starting with some 20 ex-Iranian F-5As and Bs Jordan then acquired 57 of the much more potent F-5E Tiger IIs plus a few two-seater Fs. The example shown is from No. 17 Squadron, located at Prince Hassan Air Base, originally formed to operate in the air defence role, although it has since reverted to ground attack. The F-5E Tigers were supplied under the US Military Assistance Programme (from which many friendly nations have benefited).

Northrop F-20 Tigershark
1. Radome.
2. Radar system electronics.
3. Retractable gun blast deflectors.
4. Deflector actuator.
5. Avionics cooling air ducts.
6. Pitot head.
7. M39 20mm cannon.
8. Gun gas purging air ducts.
9. Air data computer.
10. Hinged windscreen access panel.
11. Pilot's instrument display.
12. Angle of attack transmitter.
13. Weapons system display.
14. Head-up display.
15. Engine throttle lever.
16. Lightweight ejection seat.
17. Cockpit canopy cover.
18. Starboard wing stores pylons.
19. Canopy actuator.
20. Engine monitoring and recording unit.

21. Fuel filler cap.
22. Air system ducting.
23. Avionics equipment bay.
24. Formation light.
25. VHF aerial.
26. Centre fuselage fuel tanks.
27. Starboard aileron.
28. ECM aerials.
29. Azimuth unit.
30. Fuel system piping.
31. Rear fuselage flank fuel tanks.
32. Fuel filler cap.
33. Auxiliary power unit/ gas turbine starter.
34. Cooling system air intake.
35. General Electric F404 powerplant.
36. Primary heat exchanger.
37. Hydraulic reservoir.
38. Engine bleed air ducting.
39. Autostabiliser yaw actuator.
40. Rudder hydraulic actuator.
41. Anti-collision light.
42. Tail navigation light.
43. UHF aerial.
44. TACAN aerial.

45. IFF aerial.
46. Fuel jettison.
47. Rudder.
48. Brake parachute.
49. ECM aerials.
50. Parachute door conic fairing.
51. Variable area afterburner nozzle.
52. Engine bay venting air exhaust.
53. Afterburner duct.
54. Afterburner nozzle actuator.
55. Radar warning antenna.

56. Radar warning power amplifier.
57. Port all-moving tailplane.
58. Tailplane pivot bearing.
59. Tailplane hydraulic actuator.

60. Engine electronic control unit.
61. Hydraulic accumulator.
62. Arrester hook.
63. Emergency hydraulic pump.
64. Engine accessory equipment gearbox.

65. Battery.
66. Flap electro-mechanical actuator.
67. Port single slotted flap.
68. Aileron cable control linkage.
69. Port aileron.
70. Port formation light.

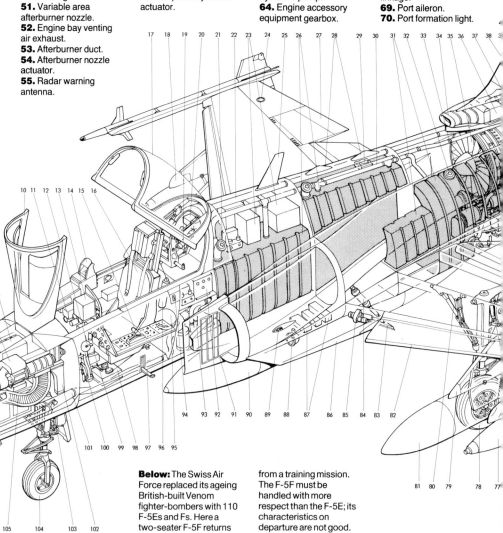

Below: The Swiss Air Force replaced its ageing British-built Venom fighter-bombers with 110 F-5Es and Fs. Here a two-seater F-5F returns from a training mission. The F-5F must be handled with more respect than the F-5E; its characteristics on departure are not good.

The official requirement was for only 325 aircraft, but Northrop soon found itself with a best-seller. More than 1,300 have now been sold to 30 operators (see table) and licence production or local-assembly programmes are under way in three nations. Northrop delivered the 3,500th member of the F-5/T-38 series in July 1981, and expects F-5E/F production to continue until the late 1980s.

Assembly of 66 F-5Es and six F-5Fs at the Swiss Federal Aircraft Factory had been followed by work on a further batch of 32 and six respectively, while Korean Airlines is currently assembling 68 F-5E/F aircraft for the South Korean Air Force. The Aero Industry Development Center (AIDC) in Taiwan has license-built 212 F-5E and 36 F-5F for the Taiwan Air Force and is now working on a follow-on batch of at least 60 aircraft.

To meet the demand for a low-cost reconnaissance aircraft to replace the earlier RF-5A, Northrop devised the RF-5E Tigereye. Ordered by the air arms of Malaysia and Singapore, this flew for the first time on December 16, 1982.

F-20 TIGERSHARK

To improve the performance of the aircraft, Northrop engineers devised the F-20 Tigershark. Powered by a single afterburning GE F404 instead of the twin J85s of the earlier models, this is recognisably a member of the F-5 series. It started life under the F-5G designation in an attempt to keep the project low-key, and to emphasise commonality with the F-5E. When the US finally abandoned the idealistic limita-

tions on military aircraft exports imposed by the Carter Administration, Northrop was able to acknowledge openly the new fighter's dramatically-increased performance by applying to the US Air Force for a new "F-series" designation.

A US Government decision to cut back on military support for Taiwan was a severe blow to the Tigershark programme, the largest single potential customer having been removed at the stroke of a presidential pen. The company simply

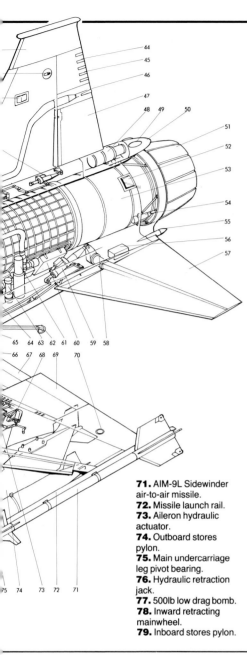

80. Undercarriage leg breaker strut.
81. External fuel tank.
82. Leading edge manoeuvre flap.
83. Ventral airbrake (2).
84. Airbrake hydraulic jack.
85. Leading edge flap electro-mechanical actuator.
86. Leading edge root extension (LERX).
87. External stores electronic management units.
88. Retractable landing/taxying lamp.
89. Navigation light.
90. Centreline external fuel tank.
91. Boundary layer bleed air louvres.
92. Inertial navigation system.
93. Air conditioning system.
94. Canopy external release.
95. Liquid oxygen converter.
96. Canopy counterbalance strut.
97. Fold-down boarding step.
98. Marker beacon antenna.
99. Control column.
100. Rudder pedals.
101. Avionics cooling air ducting.
102. Cartridge case ejection chute.
103. Nosewheel steering unit.
104. Forward retracting nose undercarriage.
105. Ammunition feed chute.
106. Temperature probe.
107. Ammunition tank.
108. UHF/IFF aerial.
109. Radar warning aerial.
110. TACAN aerial.
111. Radar scanner.

71. AIM-9L Sidewinder air-to-air missile.
72. Missile launch rail.
73. Aileron hydraulic actuator.
74. Outboard stores pylon.
75. Main undercarriage leg pivot bearing.
76. Hydraulic retraction jack.
77. 500lb low drag bomb.
78. Inward retracting mainwheel.
79. Inboard stores pylon.

Above: Best of breed! The F-20 Tigershark first prototype in its new grey finish. The two J85 turbojets of the F-5E have been replaced by a single General Electric F404 turbofan, and a redesigned nose, larger LEX and other features have produced a remarkable increase in performance in all parts of the envelope.

Below: The Aggressor Squadrons of the USAF use the F-5E to simulate the MiG-21 in air combat training. Here a Nellis-based Tiger II accompanies an F-15.

shelved its production plans for the type and concentrated on getting the prototypes into the air, and into the hands of foreign evaluation pilots.

Tigershark will not be the ultimate member of the Northrop private-venture family. Even before the first F-20 had flown, Lee Begin—former Northrop vice-president for advanced programmes—made no secret of the fact that his engineers were already sketching out future derivatives of the F-5 and F-20.

STRUCTURE

The wing of the F-5E is of multi-spar construction and made from aluminium alloy. Single-slotted trailing-edge flaps are fitted inboard of the ailerons, while the leading edge features manoeuvring flaps. Light alloy is also the main fuselage material, although small quantities of steel, titanium and magnesium are also used. Area ruling was critical to the success of such a small fighter, and gives the aircraft a distinctly waisted appearance. The jet-pipes protrude beyond the tail assembly—a single vertical fin with a conventional rudder, plus all-moving horizontal stabilisers. All control surfaces are hydraulically operated.

Much of the Tigershark structure is based on that of the earlier design, but embodies more refined aerodynamics. The larger leading-edge extensions (LEXs) on the wing account for only 6 per cent of the wing area but provide around 30 per cent of the total lift. Maximum wing lift on the Tigershark is 80 per cent greater at all subsonic Mach numbers than that of the basic configuration first used on the F-5A.

The horizontal stabilisers have 30 per cent more area and 3deg more travel than those on the F-5E, giving the additional margin of control needed at post-stall angles of attack. At high angles of attack (greater than 30 to 35deg), the flattened nose profile acts as an aerofoil, helping to maintain aircraft attitude. The new vertical is located further forward and higher on the fuselage than on the F-5E, so is more effective at high angles of attack.

All flying controls are hydraulically-actuated. The horizontal stabiliser is controlled via electrical signalling, while some control augmentation is provided on the rudder, though ailerons are unaugmented.

Unlike the F-5 series, the fuselage of the F-20 is not area-ruled. The high thrust: weight ratio of the newer aircraft is such that there is no need to minimise transonic drag. The single F404 has more than enough power to cope with the high rise in drag experienced at around Mach 1. The new intakes are of three-cell fixed-geometry design, and the ducting is sized to cope with the airflow demands of future engines.

The raised "bubble" cockpit transparency has 40 per cent more area than that of the F-5E, giving the pilot a good rear view. Allowed to try out the Tigershark cockpit in 1981, the author found that it was possible to see most of the horizontal stabiliser by looking over the shoulder.

Some 10 per cent of the F-20 structure is made from composites, but this portion may rise in future versions. Service life is planned to be 8,000 hours—some 26 years of normal flying operations.

POWERPLANT

When choosing an engine for the original T-38 and NF-156F projects, Northrop decided to use the General Electric J85, a small but reliable single-shaft turbojet. This was used in its J85-5 afterburning version in the T-38 trainer, but for the F-5A/B fighter, the J85-GE-13 was selected. This is rated at 2,720lb (1,234kg) in full afterburner. In this form, the aircraft was somewhat underpowered for supersonic flight, so the improved F-5E/F saw the adoption of the J85-GE-21A version delivering 3,600lb (1,633kg) of dry thrust, 5,000lb (2,268kg) in full afterburner. In this form the engine is 112.5in (2.68m) long, 21in (53cm) maximum diameter, and weighs 684lb (310kg). Specific fuel consumption in dry thrust is 1lb/lb/hr—(ie, 1lb of fuel must be burned to generate 1lb of thrust per hour)—high by present-day standards—rising to 2.13lb/lb/hr with afterburner.

The nine-stage compressor has variable-incidence blades in its first three stages, a conventional annular combustion chamber, and a two-stage turbine. This hardly counts as high technology by present-day standards, but the engine is extremely rugged and reliable. When studying the F-5G, Northrop was loath to part with the well-proven J85, at one point drawing up a scheme for a three-engined F-5 with the third powerplant carried in the base of the tail fin.

The favourable experience gained in the YF-17 and F-18 programmes convinced Northrop that a newer engine such as the F404 turbofan might give similar reliability in a single-engined design. The F404-GE-400 engine used in the F-20 offers 7 per cent more afterburning thrust than the F-18 powerplant, a result of increased airflow and turbine-entry temperature. These modifications increase afterburning thrust between Mach 0.6 and 1.3 where aircraft drag is highest. Future Growth 1 and Growth 2 versions will offer some 20 and 30 per cent more thrust than the current F-20 engine. Total internal fuel is 4,400lb (2,000kg), the same as carried in the F-5E.

AVIONICS

Although not as austere as the original F-5A/B series aircraft, the F-5E carries what is by modern standards a modest avionics fit. The most complex items normally fitted are the Emerson APQ-159 I/J-band target acquisition and tracking radar. This weighs only 140lb (64kg), but can detect targets at out to 23nm (37km). Optional equipment includes a Litton LN-33 INS, a radar-warning receiver, or aircraft-mounted equipment for the AGM-65 Maverick missile.

A small fighter cannot really afford the extra drag posed by an ECM pod, so Northrop has devised the ALQ-171 Conformal Jamming System. This is packaged in a canoe-shaped fairing which fits around—but does not occupy—the hardpoint on the fuselage centreline.

Above: A contrast in fighter styles. The nearest aircraft is an F-5A, noted for its transient manoeuvrabilty. Centre is the F-16, designed for sustained turn performance, and farthest from the camera the F-104 Starfighter which was originally designed for maximum speed and rate of climb. The Netherlands Air Force used all three.

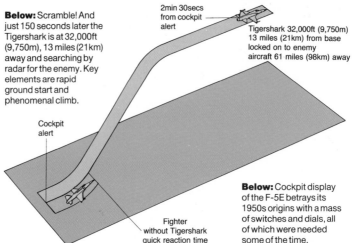

Below: Scramble! And just 150 seconds later the Tigershark is at 32,000ft (9,750m), 13 miles (21km) away and searching by radar for the enemy. Key elements are rapid ground start and phenomenal climb.

2min 30secs from cockpit alert

Tigershark 32,000ft (9,750m) 13 miles (21km) from base locked on to enemy aircraft 61 miles (98km) away

Cockpit alert

Fighter without Tigershark quick reaction time

Below: Cockpit display of the F-5E betrays its 1950s origins with a mass of switches and dials, all of which were needed some of the time.

Right: The display of the F-20 looks much simpler, and much of the required information is presented digitally on HUD and CR screens.

The newer F-20 Tigershark is an "all-digital" aircraft, and carries a General Electric GE-200 multimode coherent radar, Honeywell laser gyro INS, Bendix digital display and control set (DDCS), General Electric head-up display and a Teledyne Systems mission computer. All items of avionics communicate via a duplicated digital data bus.

Operating frequency of the GE-200 radar is in I-band (X-band) between 9.5 and 9.7GHz. Low pulse repetition frequencies (PRFs) will be used in air-to-air modes for look-up target detection and tracking. Medium PRFs will be used in look-down operations against low-flying targets and for air-to-ground operations. The use of high PRFs will be for techniques such as velocity search during air-to-air combat.

The radar offers three main air-to-air modes, plus real-beam ground mapping, high-resolution ground mapping using

Doppler beam sharpening, air-to-ground ranging, beacon, and Sea 1 and 2 for use against naval targets in calm or rough waters. All important radar and weapon controls are located on the control stick and throttle. Future options include track-while-scan capability against up to eight targets, a CW illuminator for semi-active radar missiles such as AIM-7 Sparrow, and the ability to handle the Hughes AIM-120 AMRAAM fire-and-forget missile.

The USAF believes that conventional instruments will help pilots convert to the more modern CRT and HUD displays, so early plans to fit the aircraft with a "glass cockpit" were abandoned. Provision of a radar-warning receiver (RWR), chaff/flare dispensing systems or the Northrop-developed ALQ-171 conformal ECM system is subject to US Government approval, although it seems unlikely that an operator cleared to receive a fighter in the F-20 performance class would be denied ECM equipment.

ARMAMENT

For its size, the F-5E can tote a heavy warload. Four underwing hard-points plus one on the fuselage centreline can carry up to 7,000lb (3,175kg) of ordnance, including 500lb (230kg) Snakeye retarded bombs, iron bombs as heavy as the 2,000lb

(900kg) Mk 84, CBU-series cluster bombs, BLU-series napalm stores, or launchers for unguided rockets.

Two M39 20mm cannon are carried in the upper fuselage just forward of the cockpit, each having 280 rounds of ammunition. These can be used for short-range air-to-air combat, along with AIM-9 Sidewinder missiles on wingtip launch rails. AGM-65 Maverick missiles or laser-guided bombs may be carried, but the US Government tends to be cautious in approving the export of such equipment.

Tigershark is designed to carry the same weaponry as the F-5E. In the long term the aircraft would be a highly effective platform for the Hughes AIM-120 AMRAAM fire-and-forget air-to-air missile, but supply of this item could raise political problems. Like the rival J79-powered ver-

Above: However dedicated a fighter may be to the air superiority role, sooner or later it will be required to have a strike capability. Here the prototype F-20 is seen launching an AGM-65 Maverick air-to-surface missile during trials.

sion of the F-16, Tigershark is intended to be an export fighter for sale to nations not having a requirement for (or not cleared to receive) the latest USAF aircraft or weaponry. Customers requiring a longer-ranged missile than the AIM-9 could be restricted to the AIM-7 Sparrow, at least for the next few years.

PERFORMANCE

The T-38 Talon trainer from which the F-5 series was derived has a reputation for being temperamental. The US astronauts used T-38s as flight-proficiency trainers

Possible weapons, F-5E:
1. Two 20mm M39 cannon (280 rounds each).
2. 150gal (568lit) tanks.
3. 275gal (1,042lit) tanks.
4. AIM-9J Sidewinders.
5. TDU-11/B target rocket.
6. M129E2 leaflet bombs.
7. Mk36D destructors (Mk82SE and mod. kit).
8. Mk82LD and Snakeye 500lb (227kg) bombs.
9. M117 750lb (340kg) bombs.
10. Mk83 1,000lb (454kg) LD bombs.
11. Mk84 2,000lb (907kg) LD bombs.
12. BLU-1B, -1B/B, -1C/B, 27B, 27A/B, 27B/B, 27C/B fire bombs.
13. BLU-32A/B, -32B/B, -32C/B fire bombs.
14. CBU-24B/B, -49B/B, -52B/B, -58A/B, -58B, -71B, -71A/B cluster bombs.
15. LAU-68A/A, -68B/A, 2.75in (70mm) rockets with Mk1, Mk5, M151, M156 or WDU-4 warheads.
16. LAU-3A, -3A/A, -3B/A, -60A, rockets in launchers as item 14.
17. Training pack for bombs and rockets, SUU-20A(M), A/A, B/A.
18. Flare dispensers SUU-25A/A, C/A, EA.
19. TDU-10B tow target.
20. RMU-10/A dart reel.
21. Multiple ejector rack for five Mk82 LD or Snakeyes.
22. AGM-65 Maverick.
23. GBU-12/BHS LGB.
24. GBU-12A/BLS LGB.
25. MXU-648 cargo pod.

Below: The F-5A at Mach 0.8 and 15,000ft (4,575m), can perform a sustained 4.2g level turn. The more powerful F-5E can gain 1,500ft (460m) while matching this turn, and the yet more powerful F-20 gains 7,500ft (2,290m).

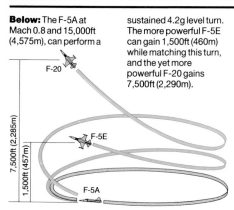

Below: While clearly an F-5 derivative, most of the external changes which distinguish the F-20 from the F-5E can be seen here. The shark nose, redesigned rear fuselage, and splitter plates on the intakes show clearly, as do the new LEX, although those on the later Tiger IIs were very similar. The single F404 turbofan was originally developed for the F-18 Hornet and has proved outstandingly reliable in service.

Below: The manoeuvrable opponent's turn without loss of speed, whereas the opponent depletes energy in the turn and dives away.

Right: The machine with the best thrust:weight ratio (F-20) can pull high to attain the advantage, enabling it to assume an enviable position for a kill.

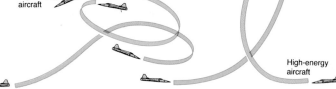

High-energy aircraft

High-energy aircraft

and general "hack" aircraft, and the memoirs of at least one US astronaut leave little doubt that the type was disliked. The F-5 fighter seems to have cast off this reputation, and has a fine reputation for good handling qualities and reliable performance. The original F-5A has a nominal supersonic capability, with an official top speed of Mach 1.4. In practice, few pilots will have clocked up much supersonic flying time.

With the arrival of the F-5E, top speed was increased to Mach 1.63 at 36,000ft (11,000m). Maximum cruising speed of the -5E is Mach 0.98, while economic cruising speed is nearer Mach 0.8. Maximum rate of climb at a combat weight of 13,300lb (6,000kg) is 14,500ft/min (10,516m/min), the service ceiling being 51,800ft (15,790m).

The F-5E proved itself a small and tricky adversary in combat, and was adopted by the US services as a "MiG-simulator" for dissimilar air-combat training ("Aggressor" squadrons). Flying against them, US aircrew were able to get first-hand experience of combating fighters in the MiG-21 performance class. The Northrop aircraft could often outfly larger opponents. On an RF-4C training sortie in the late 1970s,

Flight International's defence editor suffered the indignity of being "shot down" three times in three engagements, by an "Aggressor" F-5E.

The F-5A was designed to cope with the threat posed by the MiG-19, while the F-5E can match the first- and second-generation MiG-21s. The F-20 is intended to cope with the MiG-21bis, MiG-23 or even the new twin-engined MiG-29. Maximum speed at 15,000ft (4,600m) is Mach 2, and the aircraft is expected to have a service ceiling of 53,000ft (16,000m).

Able to match the fast acceleration of the MiG-23 Flogger series, it promises to be the fastest-climbing interceptor in the world. Sea level rate of climb is around 54,100ft/min (16,500m/min), time to 40,000ft (12,200m) being 2.2 minutes from brake release. Tigershark could be airborne at Mach 0.9 more than 10nm (18.5km) from base and ready to carry out an interception in less than three minutes. Turnaround time should be short: times of less than 10 minutes from engine stop to engine start have been demonstrated.

Acceleration time at 30,000ft (9,000m) from Mach 0.9 to 1.2 should be less than 30 seconds. Tigershark is stressed to withstand 9g rather than the 7g of the F-5E and this allows a 7 per cent improvement in turn rate over the current aircraft. The 4g manoeuvring envelope has been greatly extended over that of the F-5E, and now includes speeds of up to Mach 1.3 instead of Mach 1.0+. Sustained turn rate varies with height and Mach number, with typical values ranging from 5deg/sec at Mach 1.2/30,000ft (9,144m) to 11.5deg/sec at Mach 0.8/15,000ft (4,572m).

Air superiority
Mission radius:
F-5E 160nm (296km)
F-20 175nm (325km)

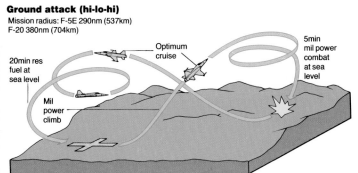

Left: Air superiority is the prime mission of the F-5E and F-20. Configured only with two Sidewinders, the radii of action are 160nm (296km) and 175nm (325km) for the F-5E and F-20 respectively. This is achieved with a military thrust climbout, cruise at Mach 0.8, acceleration at maximum thrust to Mach 1.2 at 30,000ft (9,145m) six 360deg turns at full power followed by an optimum cruise egress. This leaves sufficient reserve fuel for 20 minutes flying.

Ground attack (hi-lo-hi)
Mission radius: F-5E 290nm (537km)
F-20 380nm (704km)

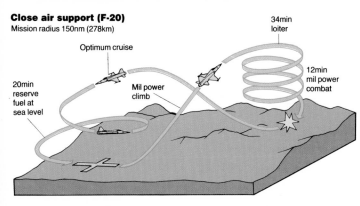

Left: In air-to-ground mission the hi-lo-hi profile gives the best radius of action, and in this example the entire mission is flown in military power. With two 275gal (1,042lit) tanks, a payload of seven Mk82 bombs, and two AIM-9s for defence, the radii of action are 290nm (537km) for the F-5E, and 380nm (704km) for the F-20. The drop tanks are retained.

Close air support (F-20)
Mission radius 150nm (278km)

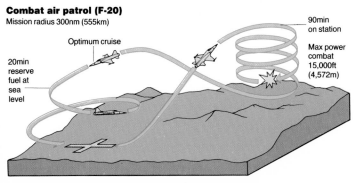

Left: Close air support is another role for the F-20. Configured as for the strike mission as described above, the mission radius for the F-20 is the 150nm (278km). This features a military power climb-out and cruise; 34 minutes time on station, 12 minutes combat at full military power; bombing and strafing, followed by an optimum cruise back to base. Once again, the tanks are retained.

Combat air patrol (F-20)
Mission radius 300nm (555km)

Left: Endurance is the feature most needed for combat air patrol. For this, the F-20 wears three 275gal (1,042lit) external tanks. This, at a radius of 300nm (555km), allows 90 min on station, acceleration to Mach 1.1 from Mach 0.8, and five maximum power 360 degree turns. Weapons are two Sidewinders. This capacity is insufficient to give true combat persistence.

F-5 OPERATORS

	F-5A	F-5B	RF-5A	F-5E	F-5F	RF-5E
Bahrain				2		
Brazil		6		36		
Canada	49	4				
Chile				15	3	
Ethiopia	12	2		8		
Greece	40	6	14			
Indonesia				12	4	
Iran				95	28	
Jordan	10	9		57	6	
Kenya				10	6	
Malaysia		2		15	4	4
Mexico				10	2	
Morocco	13	3		20		
Netherlands	66	18				
Norway	32	14	13			
Philippines	16	2				
Saudi Arabia		20		70	24	15
Singapore				24	3	
South Korea	37	30	12	162	55	
Spain	17	24				
Sudan				10	2	
Switzerland				98	12	
Taiwan	65	10		242	66	
Thailand	12	4	4	32	6	
Tunisia				6	6	
Turkey	80	10	20			
US Air Force		4		109	2	
US Navy				11		
Venezuela	15	4				
Yemen		4		12		

TORNADO F.2

DEVELOPMENT

Critical to NATO planning is the need to control what is known as the Greenland-Iceland-UK gap—the area of sea through which the surface warships, submarines and maritime patrol aircraft of the Soviet Navy's Northern Fleet must pass in order to reach the North Atlantic. The forces which monitor this vital area are receiving a new boost in capability with the entry into RAF service of the Tornado F.2, the finest interceptor in the world.

Also referred to as the Tornado ADV (Air Defence Variant), it is not an agile dogfighter, but a high-endurance interceptor able to patrol 500nm or more (over 800km) north of the UK, capable of dealing with mass enemy raids at low level in the worst conditions which darkness, bad weather or jamming can create.

Air Staff Target 395, issued in 1971, specified the performance required from the RAF's replacement for the Phantom and Lightning. The most obvious candidate for the task was a new version of the Panavia Tornado IDS strike aircraft. The original operational requirement for the Tornado, drawn up in 1968, contained many parameters which would be useful in an interceptor—good acceleration, climbing performance and specific excess power. As a result, the RAF was able to specify a minimal-change version of the Panavia aircraft. Almost inevitably, the original minimal-change design did not stand the test of time, but the fighter now being delivered to the RAF still has sufficient commonality with the existing IDS version to allow it to be built using the same trinational production facilities.

The new role required a different radar designed for air-interception. This had to be larger than the Texas Instruments set carried by Tornado IDS, and operated at different frequencies. To cope with these changes, the nose of the aircraft had to be stretched, and a new radome matched to the revised frequencies. When the latter component was designed, engineers replaced the relatively blunt shape used on the IDS with a more elongated design.

The first studies for the Tornado ADV assumed that the Sky Flash missiles could be carried on underwing pylons, but it soon became obvious that the drag imposed by such a scheme would cut the performance of the new fighter to below that of the Phantoms it was to replace. The obvious solution was to use the semi-flush method of carriage featured by the AIM-7 Sparrow armament of the Phantom, but the fuselage of Tornado was too short to accommodate four rounds beneath the belly. To overcome this problem, a further lengthening of the forward fuselage was needed. A new fuselage section was inserted just aft of the cockpit, a move which allowed the aircraft's internal fuel capaci-

Above: The prototype Tornado F.2. The ADV, or Air Defence Variant, is optimised for long range interception, and can remain on station at extended ranges for long periods. Like the much larger F-14, it has the capability of simultaneously engaging multiple targets from beyond visual range with its Sky Flash missiles.

Typical weapons: **A**, external fuel tank; **B**, AIM-9 Sidewinder; **C**, AIM-120 AMRAAM, **D**, 27mm Mauser cannon. This is the normal long-range interception configuration, with two tanks for extra endurance, a primary armament of four AIM-120 AMRAAM, Sidewinders as back-up, and the cannon for close range work. The AIM-120 is being produced to have a far higher performance and lethality than any update of Sparrow would have been able to give, but to be interchangeable with it. Inertial mid-course guidance means that it is a "launch and leave" weapon, and does not need radar illumination of the target after firing. Until AIM-120 enters service, Tornado will be armed with Sky Flash, a British development of Sparrow with vastly more accurate homing.

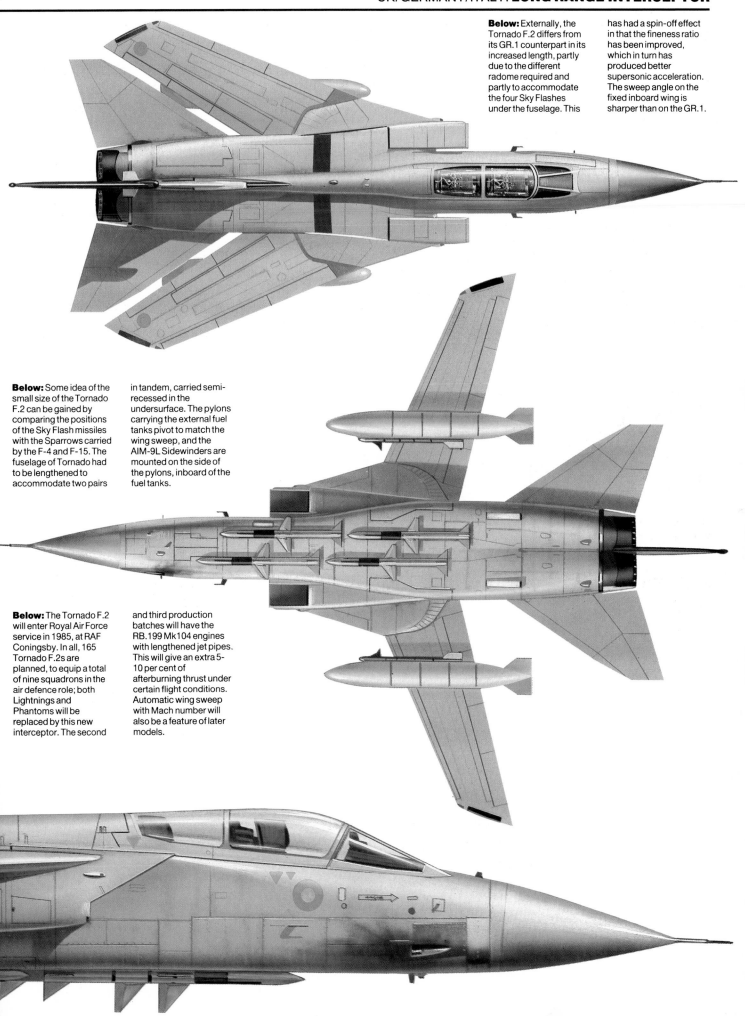

Below: Externally, the Tornado F.2 differs from its GR.1 counterpart in its increased length, partly due to the different radome required and partly to accommodate the four Sky Flashes under the fuselage. This has had a spin-off effect in that the fineness ratio has been improved, which in turn has produced better supersonic acceleration. The sweep angle on the fixed inboard wing is sharper than on the GR.1.

Below: Some idea of the small size of the Tornado F.2 can be gained by comparing the positions of the Sky Flash missiles with the Sparrows carried by the F-4 and F-15. The fuselage of Tornado had to be lengthened to accommodate two pairs in tandem, carried semi-recessed in the undersurface. The pylons carrying the external fuel tanks pivot to match the wing sweep, and the AIM-9L Sidewinders are mounted on the side of the pylons, inboard of the fuel tanks.

Below: The Tornado F.2 will enter Royal Air Force service in 1985, at RAF Coningsby. In all, 165 Tornado F.2s are planned, to equip a total of nine squadrons in the air defence role; both Lightnings and Phantoms will be replaced by this new interceptor. The second and third production batches will have the RB.199 Mk104 engines with lengthened jet pipes. This will give an extra 5-10 per cent of afterburning thrust under certain flight conditions. Automatic wing sweep with Mach number will also be a feature of later models.

ty to be increased by fully 10 per cent.

Before giving the go-ahead for development to begin, the MoD looked at alternative US designs. The F-14 probably came closest to what the RAF wanted; the F-15 offered attractive flight performance, but it was felt that its radar and single-seat cockpit were not able to meet the requirements of all-weather combat in the face of heavy ECM.

Three prototypes were built, with the first flying in October 1979. Flight trials went smoothly, and the first production aircraft were handed over to the RAF in the spring of 1984. An eventual fleet of 165 is planned, some of which will be dual-control trainers.

STRUCTURE

The stretching of the fuselage by a total of 4ft 5in (1.36m) to create space for the new radar and semi-flush-mounted missile armament forced other minor structural modifications. Since the aircraft's centre of gravity had been moved forward, the centre of pressure had to be moved to compensate. The sweep angle on the wing inboard fixed section was therefore increased, and the Kruger flap installed in this location on the IDS was deleted.

Wing sweep and flap/slat position are varied automatically by the flight-control system to match the aircraft's angle of attack. Four basic angles of wing sweep are normally used: 25deg at speeds of up to Mach 0.73, 45deg up to Mach 0.88, 58deg to Mach 0.9 and 67deg at higher speed. Flaps and slats are available only at 25deg, slats alone at 45deg. At all greater angles, slats and flaps are retracted.

The ADV will rely on tanker support to

PANAVIA Tornado F.2
1. Airborne Interception radar antenna.
2. Hinged radar equipment module.
3. Hinged radome.
4. Upper IFF aerial.
5. Windscreen rain dispersal air duct.
6. Pitot tube.
7. Hinged windscreen panel.
8. Retractable in-flight refuelling probe.
9. Pilot's instrument display.
10. Control column.
11. Head-up display.
12. Pilot's Martin-Baker Mk.10A "zero-zero" ejection seat.
13. Canopy jettison unit.
14. Cockpit canopy cover.
15. Tactical Navigator's instrument display.
16. Tactical Navigator's ejection seat.
17. Canopy actuator.
18. Starboard wing swivelling pylon.
19. Leading edge slat.
20. Obstruction light.
21. Wing tip antenna fairing.
22. Formation lights, upper and lower.
23. Air system ducting.
24. Spoilers.
25. Forward fuselage fuel tanks.
26. Double slotted flaps.
27. UHF homer aerials.
28. Wing sweep and high lift devices control units.

29. Anti-collision light.
30. Wing sweep actuating screw jack.
31. Wing pivot box integral fuel tank.
32. Rear fuselage fuel tanks.
33. Auxiliary Power Unit (APU).
34. Engine driven accessory gearbox, interconnected port and starboard.
35. Heat exchanger air intake.
36. HF aerial.
37. Starboard airbrake.
38. Primary heat exchanger.
39. Starboard all-moving tailplane.
40. Heat exchanger exhaust.
41. Fin integral fuel tank.
42. ILS glideslope and Localiser aerial.
43. Fuel jettison system.
44. Forward passive ECM pod.
45. VHF aerial.
46. Tail warning radar.
47. Rear passive ECM pod.
48. Tail navigation lights.
49. Obstruction light.
50. Fuel jettison.
51. Rudder.
52. Rudder hydraulic actuator.

53. Thrust reverser bucket doors.
54. Port airbrake.
55. Turbounion RB 199 Mk.104 afterburning turbofan engine.
56. Airbrake hydraulic jack.
57. Port all-moving tailplane.
58. Wing fully swept position.
59. Thrust reverser actuator.
60. Afterburner nozzle control jacks.
61. Tailplane pivot bearing.
62. Tailplane hydraulic actuator.
63. Hydraulic reservoir.
64. Engine fuel system.
65. Hydraulic filters.
66. Fuel vent.
67. Formation lights, upper and lower.
68. Wing tip antenna fairing.

69. Obstruction lights.
70. Flap drive shaft and screw jacks.
71. Slat drive shaft.
72. Structural provision for outboard swivelling pylon.
73. Spoiler hydraulic actuator.
74. Slat screw jack.
75. Wing integral fuel tank.
76. 1,500-litre external fuel tank.
77. Inboard pylon pivot bearing.
78. Inboard swivelling stores pylon.
79. Pylon angle control link.
80. Missile launch rail.
81. AIM-9L Sidewinder air-to-air missile.

82. Main undercarriage pivot bearing.
83. Mainwheel.
84. Wing pivot bearing.
85. Main undercarriage breaker strut.
86. Landing lamp.
87. Intake suction relief doors.
88. Intake ramp hydraulic jack.
89. Variable intake ramps.
90. Navigation light.
91. Cockpit air conditioning system.
92. BAe Skyflash air-to-air missile (4), semi-recessed ventral housing.
93. Ammunition magazine.
94. Liquid oxygen converter.

95. Heat exchanger air intake.
96. Ammunition feed chute.
97. Total pressure head.
98. Mauser M.27 cannon.
99. Engine throttle and wing sweep control levers.
100. Nosewheel steering unit.

extend its range and endurance, but cannot afford the drag penalty of the bolt-on flight refuelling probe used on the IDS. A neat retractable probe was devised, and fitted in the port side of the forward fuselage.

PROPULSION

When the Tornado was designed, no off-the-shelf European powerplant was available. Buying American powerplants was rejected, so the three nations were forced to mate a new engine with a new airframe—often a recipe for problems.

Early production aircraft are being delivered with the RB.199 Mk 103 turbofan fitted to the Tornado IDS, but the interceptor role requires more thrust, particularly at altitude. Turbo-Union has devised an uprated Mk 104 version of the engine. This has an afterburner extended by around 14in (36cm), giving up to 7 per cent more thrust than Mk 103 but having a slightly improved specific fuel consumption in afterburner.

Another feature of the Mk 104 is a digital engine control unit (DECU). A replacement for the current analogue mechanical system, this will give better control over the engine, be more reliable, and incorporate built-in test equipment. The new engine will be introduced on the production line in 1985, and will probably be retrofitted to earlier examples, while a further-developed RB.199 variant is already under study. Demonstration engines offering a 35 per cent increase in thrust have already been run, and some of this technology could find its way into a future ADV powerplant.

The RB199 is in the same thrust class as the US J79 turbojet and its F404 turbofan replacement. The veteran J79 is 208in (530cm) long and weighs 3,847lb (1,745kg). The use of modern technology on the later F404 brought the length of that engine down to 159in (403cm) and the weight to around 2,000lb (908kg). The Turbo-Union design team produced an even more compact engine only 127in (323cm) long, and managed to shave the weight down to 1,980lb (900kg). The initial service model was the Mk 101, which developed around 8,000lb (3,630kg) of dry thrust and more than 15,800lb (7,167kg) with afterburner.

The engine's compact lines are largely a result of the use of three shafts, each of which is free to rotate at the speed best suited to the section of the engine mounted on it. The outer shaft carries the three-stage LP fan and is driven by a two-stage turbine, while the intermediate shaft rotates in the opposite direction and carries a three-stage compressor and single-stage turbine.

The inner shaft rotates in the same direction as the outer, and has a six-stage compressor whose final stages are made from heat-resistant alloy rather than the titanium used for the earlier stages and the blades of the IP compressor and LP fan. The HP shaft is driven by a single-stage turbine able to withstand the 1,327 deg C gas from the annular combustion chamber.

The afterburner is very compact, having no section in which core gas and bypass air may mix—the two are burned concurrently. At the aft end are located the variable-area nozzle and twin-bucket thrust reverser.

101. Intake ramp controller.
102. Taxying lamp.
103. Nose undercarriage.
104. Electrical equipment bay.
105. Rudder pedals.
106. Canopy emergency release.
107. Incidence probe.
108. Lower IFF aerial.
109. Avionics equipment bay.
110. Marconi Avionics Airborne Interception Radar equipment.

46
47
48
49
50
51
52
53
54
55
56

65 64 63 62 61 60 59 58 57

75 74 73 72 71 70 69 68 67 66

Right: The technology of the Tornado F.2 cockpit instrumentation is not so advanced as that of the Hornet or Viggen, but it is still modern in concept, as a comparison with the F-16 reveals. On the other hand, comparisons with single seaters are probably unfair, as much of the workload is handled by the navigator in the rear seat. Forward visibility for the Tornado pilot is rather better than is suggested by this illustration.

Display for unplanned attacks

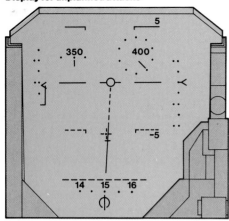

Air-to-air override

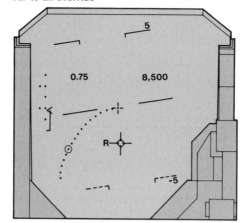

Medium-range air-to-air attack

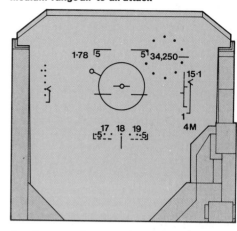

AVIONICS

Items of avionics not required for the air-defence mission were removed from the aircraft, while other units were either modified for the new role or replaced by new equipment. The Texas Instruments terrain following/ground mapping set was replaced by the Marconi Avionics AI.24, often referred to as Foxhunter. This is a coherent pulse-Doppler set using frequency-modulated interrupted continuous-wave (FMICW) modulation. A high PRF is available for use against head-on targets; a low-PRF for tail-chase interceptions, short-range combat and navigational ground mapping. Maximum detection range is around 100nm (185km), and track-while-scan facilities are provided for an unspecified number of targets, reported to be between 12 and 20.

Much attention had been given to maximising resistance to ECM. The radar antenna is of conventional inverse-Cassegrain type rather than the currently-fashionable planar array. The older technology gives more consistent performance over a wide range of frequencies, and has lower sidelobes (unwanted secondary "beams" which may be exploited by a hostile ECM system). Digital signal processing techniques were used to create a fast frequency analyser and correlator able to prepare spectra of all received signals, filtering out wanted target returns from natural interference such as clutter and man-made interference resulting from jamming.

AI.24 is an active radar system, but on occasions when the Tornado may not want to emit tell-tale radar transmissions which might alert its victim, or if the target is emitting a powerful jamming signal which makes radar-guided attacks difficult, the crew may rely on data from the Marconi Space and Defence Systems Hermes radar homing and warning receiver.

Other new items of equipment include a new HUD, Cossor IFF interrogator, Singer Kearfott secure data link, a second Ferranti FIN 1010 inertial platform, and a Smiths Industries/Computing Devices missile-management system. In the longer term the aircraft will be fitted with the planned NATO Identification System being developed to replace the current IFF system.

Above: Typical examples of HUD symbology are depicted here. At the far left is a display for attacking targets of opportunity on the ground, while in the centre is shown the air-to-air override, with guns and missiles being automatically armed. The right-hand display shows symbology typical of a medium range air-to-air missile interception by the Tornado.

Additional avionics mean additional heat to be dissipated, so the ADV is fitted with an extra heat-exchanger to cope with the thermal load imposed by the radar.

Existing equipment modified for use on the ADV includes the autopilot, triplex command stability augmentation system, and computer (increased from 32K of memory to 64K, with 128K planned for the long-term). One planned item of avionics which has been shelved for the moment is a long-range electro-optical viewing system for target identification. This was to have been installed in a retractable mounting just ahead of the canopy. The RAF still has a requirement for this equipment, and the main reason for its elimination was probably a need to trim costs.

ARMAMENT

Tornado IDS carries a pair of 27mm Mauser cannon, but studies of likely ADV operations suggested that a single cannon would be acceptable for the new role. One of the Mausers was duly deleted, freeing internal space for other systems.

For short-range combat the ADV carries AIM-9L Sidewinders. The original armament scheme called for these to be carried on the outboard pylons, but one change introduced during development was the addition of an extra pair of AIM-9s on the inboard wing pylons. AIM-9L will eventually be replaced by the planned ASRAAM.

The current long-range weapon is the BAeD Sky Flash originally fielded on the RAF's Spey-powered Phantoms and now being further developed for use on Tornado ADV. The missile is currently powered by a Sparrow-style rocket motor, and coasts to the target after an initial boost.

An improved motor incorporates a sustainer section which will improve performance against high-flying targets. A thermal battery will replace the current built-in generator, reducing pre-launch warm-up time.

Sky Flash is carried on a new pattern of launcher developed by Frazer-Nash. This is the first launcher able to fire missiles at any point in the launch aircraft flight envelope, a feat made possible by pyrotechnically actuated rams which apply a force of up to 4 tons to the round, forcing it away from the fuselage and through the airflow around the aircraft.

In the late 1980s the Tornado ADV will be retrofitted with the Hughes AIM-120 AMRAAM "fire-and-forget" missile. This modification will involve the installation of new missile launchers—also being developed by Frazer-Nash—and the addition of a US-style 1553 digital data bus to the avionics suite of the aircraft.

Right: One complexity of variable geometry is that the stores pylons have to swivel. The store also moves aft as the degree of wing sweep increases. The inboard wing pylon on Tornado has to be deep enough to allow the large external tanks to clear the tailplane when the wings are fully swept back, as seen here on F.2 prototype ZA254.

PERFORMANCE

Tornado F.2 shares most of the fine flying qualities of the IDS version, but adds one or two extra features of its own. Thanks to the use of a system known as SPILS (Spin Prevention and Incidence Limiting System), the pilot is free to demand maximum deflection of the aircraft's control surfaces without the risk of spinning or stalling. The only limit on manoeuvring then becomes the g limits on the aircraft and its crew.

The aircraft has already been flown to Mach 2.16 at height and 800kt (1,480km/h) indicated airspeed. Given a normal weapon and fuel load, it can get airborne in only 2,500ft (760m), while the touchdown speed of only 115kt (213km/h) allows the aircraft to land with a roll of just over 1,200ft (370m).

A typical combat air patrol might involve a two-hour loiter on station 300 to 400nm (550 to 750km) from base, with sufficient fuel for 10 minutes of combat. The capacity of the underwing drop tanks was increased from 396 to 660 US gall (1,500 to 2,500 litres) during development, in order to extend range and endurance.

Performance will be significantly increased when the Mk 104 engine enters service. The SEP of the aircraft will be improved by 15 per cent, time-to-intercept will be cut by 10 per cent, and sustained turn rate will icrease.

Most results of F.2 flight testing are still under security wraps, but early in 1984 *Flight International* pilot Joey Gough (a former Lightning 'driver') was allowed to fly the second prototype and tell the story. He found the aircraft easy to fly and was

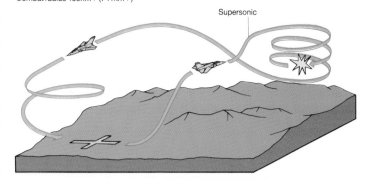

Point interception
Combat radius 400nm+ (741km+)

Supersonic

Combat air patrol
Combat radius 350nm (648km), 2 hours on patrol

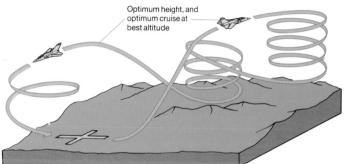

Optimum height, and optimum cruise at best altitude

Left: The Tornado Air Defence Variant, with its normal complement of six AAMs and two external tanks, has a point interception range of better than 400nm (737km) at high level. It achieves this with a stepped military power climb, followed by a full power supersonic dash to intercept, which also gives the missiles maximum launch energy. The return flight is made at optimum cruise speed and altitude.

Left: In the combat air patrol mission, configured as above, Tornado's performance is startling. It can spend more than two hours on patrol at 350nm (650km) from base at 30,000ft (9,150m) and still have fuel for ten minutes combat at full throttle. Part of this capability is conferred by very low fuel consumption, and part by the benefits derived from the fact that Tornado is equipped with variable geometry wings.

entranced by it's manoeuvrability—"the most exciting thing about the F.2 is that its manoeuvrability can be fully utilised without any heart-stopping moments.... It out-accelerates the Lightning. I am told it out-scissors a Hunter.... If the combat simulator is anything to go by, its ability to defeat the F-4 is as predictable as everything else about the Tornado F.2."

At one point in the flight, BAe F.2 project test pilot Peter Gordon-Johnson flew the aircraft in a 4g 360deg turn directly over the airfield, a manoeuvre which barely exceeded the field boundaries. The ADV may not have the agility of the dedicated "dogfighters", but it clearly has the ability to outmanoeuvre virtually everything else.

PANAVIA
TORNADO IDS

DEVELOPMENT

In the early 1970s, the Soviet Air Force must have been considerably agitated by the threat posed to its ground forces by almost 500 Tornado fighter/strike aircraft which would be available by the late 1980s—aircraft, indeed, which could fly well under the maximum height of the existing F-111 swing-wing and, while doing so, outrun every type of fighter in the Soviet inventory. Tasked with designing new warplanes with the ability to intercept such high-speed low-level targets, the Mikoyan and Sukhoi design bureaux would immediately have realised that many of the numerical specifications contained in the top-secret directive could be summed up in just two words—"Stop Tornado!"

But they would have known, too, that, with its advanced avionics and two-man crew able to share the demanding workload of low-level navigation and attack, the European aircraft would be difficult to stop. The only consolation faced by the Soviet designers as they developed the new MiG- and Su-series fighters was that slippages in the timescale of the Tornado programme would delay Tornado's deployment to the point where the intended counterweapons could be fielded on a near-compatible timescale. Had the European aircraft entered service in the late 1970s as originally planned, the technological gap between the Soviet and NATO air arms would have been impossible to close for the best part of a decade.

The days when strike aircraft could rely on speed and height to give immunity to interception are long since over. Only by flying just above the ground, so that it is exposed only fleetingly to defensive fire and its radar echo is swamped by returns from the ground, can a modern fighter hope to survive. This mode of flight was the key element in planning when the

nations of Western Europe considered their fighter requirements for the late 1970s and beyond.

When the air arms of Belgium, Germany, Italy and the Netherlands set out in the late 1960s to plan a successor to their F-104G Starfighter fleets, the United Kingdom at first showed little interest. Following the French decision in July 1967 to withdraw from the Anglo/French Variable Geometry Combat Aircraft (AFVG) pro-

Above: Third prototype Tornado IDS, with Sky Shadow ECM pods on the outer pylons, drop tanks inboard, and one of eight dummy Mk83 bombs peeping from underneath, skims low over a lake. Aircraft are easier to detect from above when over water.

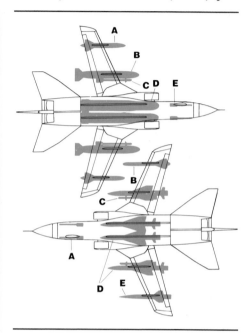

Typical weapons:
Top: A, Sky Shadow ECM pod; **B**, external tank; **C**, AIM-9 Sidewinders; **D**, JP.233 dispenser; **E**, 27mm Mauser cannon. This configuration is for an airfield attack. The JP.233 dispenser holds two types of sub-munition, one to crater the runway surface, one an anti-personnel device to inhibit repair work. Two Sky Shadow pods are to confuse the defences.

Above: A, 27mm Mauser cannon; **B**, Zeus ECM pod; **C**, Kormoran ASM; **D**, AIM-9 Sidewinder; **E**, chaff/flare dispenser. The main weapon here is Kormoran, which is an anti-shipping missile with a range of up to 20nm (37km), used by the Marineflieger and the Aeronautica Militare Italiana. The two ECM pods cover a wide range of threats: Zeus is an active jammer, the other pod for disposables.

Below: The small wing (particularly noticeable in the minimum sweep position), with its attendant high wing loading, gives excellent gust response at low level, where most of Tornado's work will be done, yet high lift devices give it what may well be the highest lift coefficient of any supersonic fighter, thereby ensuring excellent short-field performance.

Below: A fairly typical Tornado load of eight low drag 1,000lb (454kg) bombs, supplemented by two Sky Shadow ECM pods (a common RAF fit) and drop tanks on the inboard pylons. The IDS variant carries two 27mm Mauser cannon compared with one on the ADV. Maximum hard point loadings are: centreline 2,000lb (907kg); fuselage, four tandem twin pylons, 2,000lb (907kg) each; inner wing 3,000lb (1,361kg); and outer wing, 1,000lb (454kg).

Below: The elephant insignia on the fin denotes No 27 Squadron RAF, which back in the RFC days was the only unit to operate the Martinsyde Elephant. The camouflage scheme is standard European low level wrap-around, it having long been known that the flash of a light-coloured belly is an infallible MiG magnet. Tornado has been designed to carry almost every weapon in the NATO armoury, including laser and electro-optically guided weapons and anti-radiation missiles.

gramme, the UK attempted to salve its injured pride by pursuing a national project—the British Aircraft Corporation Advanced Combat Aircraft.

Given the UK political climate of the mid-to-late 1960s, the prospects for a national project were not good, so the UK eventually opted in July 1968 to join with the governments of West Germany, Italy, the Netherlands and Canada (the last two subsequently dropping out) in signing a Memorandum of Understanding on a new multi-role combat aircraft for service in 1975. In March 1968, the Panavia consortium was created to tackle the task of creating the new warplane. Two months

later, the UK, West Germany and Italy formally committed themselves to the definition phase of the project.

The Multi-Role Combat Aircraft (MRCA) was ambitious both in timescale and performance. Working to a timescale more typical of a US project, the partners hoped to create an advanced variable-geometry strike fighter able to engage and destroy targets in a single pass in any type of weather. Almost inevitably the timescale slipped badly, with Tornado squadrons not becoming operational until 1983. The high inflation rate of the early 1970s also played havoc with costs. Despite such problems, the project ran more smoothly

than many might have dared to predict, creating a combat aircraft able to fly under-the-radar missions at heights well below those possible in the USAF's F-111.

In addition to contributing the configuration of its own variable-geometry Advanced Combat Aircraft (ACA) design, the UK also added another vital component to the MRCA project—the lightweight and compact Rolls-Royce RB.199 three-shaft turbofan.

Project definition work was completed in April 1970, allowing the three governments formally to launch development of the aircraft a month later. By this time, the West German Luftwaffe had abandoned its

PANAVIA Tornado GR Mk.1

1. Ground mapping and target radar antenna.
2. Hinged radome.
3. Hinged radar equipment module.
4. Upper IFF aerial.
5. Retractable in-flight refuelling probe.
6. Windscreen rain dispersal air duct.
7. Pitot tube.
8. Hinged windscreen panel.
9. Pilot's instrument display.
10. Control column.
11. Head-up display.
12. Pilot's Martin-Baker Mk.10A "zero-zero" ejection seat.
13. Tactical Navigator's instrument display.
14. Canopy jettison unit.
15. Cockpit canopy cover.
16. Tactical Navigator's ejection seat.
17. Starboard wing swivelling pylons.
18. Leading edge slat.
19. Obstruction light.
20. Wing tip antenna fairing.
21. Formation lights, upper and lower.
22. Canopy actuator.
23. Spoilers.
24. Double slotted flaps.
25. UHF homer aerials.
26. Wing sweep and high lift devices control units.
27. Forward fuselage fuel tanks.
28. Anti-collision light.
29. Wing sweep actuating screw jack.
30. Wing pivot box integral fuel tank.
31. Air system ducting.
32. Rear fuselage fuel tanks.
33. Auxiliary power unit (APU).
34. Engine driven accessory gearbox, interconnected port and starboard.
35. Heat exchanger air intake.
36. HF aerial.
37. Starboard airbrake.
38. Primary heat exchanger.
39. Starboard all-moving tailplane.
40. Heat exchanger exhaust.
41. Fin integral fuel tank..
42. ILS glideslope and Localiser aerial.
43. Fuel jettison system.
44. Forward radar warning receiver.
45. VHF aerial.
46. Rear radar warning receiver.
47. Tail navigation lights.
48. Obstruction light.
49. Fuel jettison.
50. Rudder.
51. Rudder hydraulic actuator.
52. Thrust reverser bucket doors.
53. Port airbrake.
54. Turbounion RB 199 Mk.103 afterburning turbofan engine.
55. Airbrake hydraulic jack.
56. Wing fully swept position.
57. Port all-moving tailplane.
58. Thrust reverser actuator.
59. Afterburner nozzle control jacks.
60. Tailplane pivot bearing.
61. Tailplane hydraulic actuator.
62. Hydraulic reservoir.
63. Engine fuel system.
64. Hydraulic filters.
65. Fuel vent.
66. Formation lights, upper and lower.
67. Wing tip antenna fairing.
68. Obstruction lights.
69. Outboard pylon pivot bearing.
70. Outboard swivelling stores pylon.
71. Leading edge slat screw jack.
72. Flap drive shaft and screw jacks.
73. Marconi Skyshadow ECM pod.
74. Slat drive shaft.
75. Spoiler hydraulic actuator.
76. Engine oil tank.
77. Inboard pylon pivot bearing.
78. Inboard swivelling stores pylon.
79. Pylon angle control link.
80. 1,500-litre external fuel tank.
81. Wing integral fuel tank.
82. Main undercarriage pivot bearing.
83. Mainwheel.
84. Wing pivot bearing.
85. Main undercarriage breaker strut.
86. Wing glove Kruger flap.
87. Kruger flap hydraulic jack.
88. Landing lamp.
89. Intake suction relief doors.
90. Intake ramp hydraulic jack.
91. Variable intake ramps.
92. Navigation light.
93. Twin stores carrier.
94. Cockpit air conditioning system.
95. Fuselage shoulder pylon (2).
96. Mk.83 high speed retarded bomb (8).
97. Ammunition magazine.
98. Heat exchanger air intake.
99. Liquid oxygen converter.
100. Ammunition feed chute.
101. Total pressure head.
102. Mauser M.27 cannon.
103. Engine throttle and wing sweep control levers.
104. Nosewheel steering unit.
105. Intake ramp controller.
106. Taxying lamp.
107. Nose undercarriage.
108. Electrical equipment bay.
109. Rudder pedals.

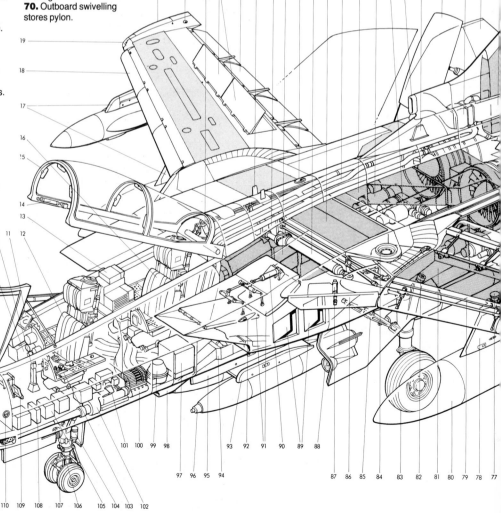

requirement for a single-seat variant, allowing the design effort to be focussed on the definitive two-seater.

The first of nine prototypes flew for the first time in August 1974, and an order was placed for the first batch of aircraft in July 1976. Pre-series aircraft began flying in February of the following year, and the first production British and West German examples flew in July 1979. A year later, delivery of production aircraft to the Tri-national Tornado Training Establishment had begun, and the user air arms could begin training on the new type.

Six production batches are planned—a total of 644 made up of 324 (West Ger-many), 220 (UK) and 100 (Italy). In order to keep annual costs within the national budgets of the partners, the annual production rate is being deliberately held to 44 (UK) 42 (W. Germany) and 24 (Italy). More than 300 Tornados have already been delivered, and the current order book should keep the line busy until the end of the decade.

The high cost of Tornado ($16.6 million flyaway cost for an IDS, according to German figures), has prevented adoption of this versatile aircraft by nations outside the original consortium. It was evaluated and subsequently rejected by Australia, Canada and Spain, all of whom purchased the F-18 Hornet. The last chance of another sale within Nato is the Greek Air Force, which has expressed a requirement for at least 60 new fighters. Greece has been offered a substantial offset deal including co-production, but a decision has been repeatedly postponed.

Studies of a dedicated ECM variant have been carried out since the late 1970s, but no decision seems likely in the near future. Only the West German Luftwaffe is reported to have a requirement for such an aircraft.

STRUCTURE

Production of the Tornado airframe is shared between the three member nations of the consortium. Main contractors are Aeritalia (outer wings), British Aerospace (front fuselage, rear fuselage and tail), and MBB (fuselage centre section, including the intakes and wing box).

The wing inboard section has a leading-edge sweep of 60deg, and incorporates a wing box manufactured from titanium using electro-beam welding techniques. This was a bold move—the earlier F-111 used steel for this critical component, a conservative choice which did not prevent problems due to cracking. A small Krueger flap is built into the leading edge. The outboard wing panels are made from aluminium alloy, and are pivoted hydraulically on Teflon-coated bearings through leading edge sweep angles ranging from 25 to 68deg. The outer wings have full-span leading-edge slats and full-span double-slotted trailing-edge flaps. There are no ailerons, but spoilers are provided to augment roll control by the tailerons, and to kill lift after touchdown.

Operating differentially, the all-moving horizontal tail surfaces (tailerons) provide control in roll, but act as elevators when operated together. The sheer size of the single vertical fin gives an indication of the control demands of a highly-manoeuvrable Mach 2 design. (US and Soviet designers currently favour twin vertical tails in order to provide the necessary area.) All control surfaces are hydraulically actuated.

The fuselage is of conventional design, and is made largely from aluminium alloy. The nose radome swings to starboard to give access to the radar during maintenance. To minimise drag, it is essential that the gap between the fixed inner and movable outer wing sections be closed over all sweep angles. This is achieved using elastic seals.

POWERPLANT

All versions of the Tornado, including the Royal Air Force's specialised Air-Defence Variant, are powered by the Turbo-Union RB.199. A full description of this revolutionary engine—the world's first three-spool military turbofan—is given in the Tornado ADV entry (see page 159).

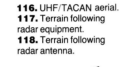

110. Canopy emergency release.
111. Incidence probe.
112. Lower IFF aerial.
113. Doppler.
114. Avionics equipment bay.
115. Ground mapping and target radar equipment.
116. UHF/TACAN aerial.
117. Terrain following radar equipment.
118. Terrain following radar antenna.

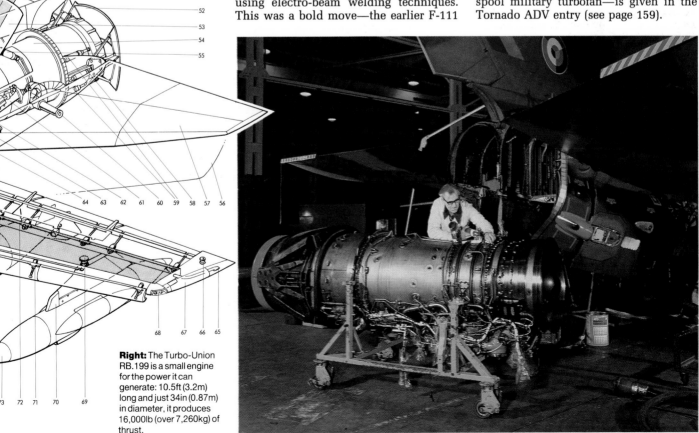

Right: The Turbo-Union RB.199 is a small engine for the power it can generate: 10.5ft (3.2m) long and just 34in (0.87m) in diameter, it produces 16,000lb (over 7,260kg) of thrust.

AVIONICS

Heart of the avionics suite is the navigation and terrain-following radar. This was designed by Texas Instruments, but is being produced under licence by a European industrial team headed by AEG-Telefunken and including Elettronica, Ferranti, FIAR, Marconi, and Siemens. In the final stages of an attack, this works in conjunction with a nose-mounted Ferranti laser-ranger and marked-target seeker.

Primary navaid is the Ferranti FIN 1010 three-axis digital INS, although the aircraft also carries a Decca Type 72 Doppler radar. All data is processed to improve navigational accuracy. The aircraft is fitted with a Litef Spirir 3 16-bit central computer. A large array of displays is needed to cope with the data from these systems. These include a Smiths/Teledix/OMI HUD of advanced design, and TV tabular displays developed by Marconi Avionics.

The flight-control system is complex, and the work of many companies. It includes a triplex command stability augmentation system (Marconi Avionics/Bodenseewerk), an autopilot and flight director (Marconi Avionics/Aeritalia), air data set (Microtecnica), and a standby attitude and heading reference system (Litef). Release of ordnance is handled by a Marconi Avionics/Selenia stores management system.

Very little information is available on the Tornado's self-protection ECM systems. The radar-warning receiver was developed by AEG-Telefunken, Elettronica, and Marconi Space and Defence Systems, and uses antennas mounted in a fairing near the top of the vertical fin.

The designation EL-73 has been reported for an EW system developed by AEG-Telefunken and Elettronica for use on Tornado. This is reported to be an internally-mounted jamming system.

British Tornados will be fitted with the Marconi Space and Defence Systems Sky Shadow—the most advanced self-protection ECM pod in the Western world, according to the RAF. Capable of operating in noise or deception modes, it can deploy its transmitters against hostile ground and airborne surveillance and tracking radars. Built-in receivers are used to "look-through" the jamming signals in order to assess the effectiveness of the current operating mode. If the systems under attack show no sign of being dis-rupted, Sky Shadow can automatically alter the type of jamming being used until the best result is obtained. Being software-controlled, it can be re-programmed to cope with advances in enemy equipment and tactics.

The proposed electronic-warfare version of Tornado being studied by MBB would carry a version of the ALQ-99 jamming system fitted to the Grumman EA-6B and EF-111A. The US company is collaborating with MBB on studies of this scheme.

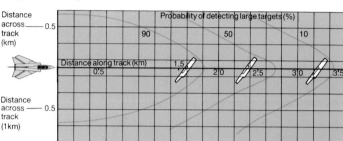

Right: The problems of target detection at high speed (Mach 0.9) and low level (200ft/60m) are illustrated here. Extreme accuracy in navigation is the key: a 50 per cent chance of acquisition at 2.5km reduces to just over 10 per cent with a 0.5km track error – a significant difference.

Possible weapons:
Left: 1. 27mm Mauser cannon, internal.
2. Four Mk13/15 1,000lb (454kg) bombs in tandem pairs, drop tanks, two ECM pods.
3. Two JP.233 dispensers, tanks and pods as **2**.
4. Eight Mk83 retarded bombs, two ECM pods.
5. Two CBLS-200 practice bomb dispensers and two drop tanks.
6. Four Kormoran ASMs.
7. MW-1 dispenser, two fuel tanks, ECM pod, and flare/chaff pod.
8. Eight BL.755 CBUs and two ECM pods. This weapons list shows only typical loads; the Tornado can carry a formidable array.

Below: Tornado GR.1 of No IX Squadron Royal Air Force, based at Honington. Replacing Vulcans in the long range interdiction role, the Tornado IDS is tasked with making deep penetrations of hostile air defences to strike at airfields, supply depots and communication "choke points". This can only effectively be done at very low level, by day or night, and in any weather that permits takeoff and recovery. Terrain-following radar is essential for this mission, and an ability to make a first-pass blind strike is similarly vital. Tornado has a low level ride quality unequalled by any other aircraft.

ARMAMENT

The range of stores which may be carried by Tornado is huge, varying according to the operator and the mission to which the aircraft is assigned. The aircraft's avionics allow high accuracy attacks to be carried out even with conventional free-falling or retarded bombs. During early weapon trials, bombs released at low altitude scored hits or near-misses against a 10ft (3m) diameter target. During toss-bombing attacks against similarly small targets some 3 to 4 miles (5 to 6.5km) away from release point, the ordnance impacted within 30ft (9m) of the aiming point.

Guided weapons available for use on the Tornado include the AIM-9 Sidewinder (for self-defence), the Texas Instruments Paveway LGB, Hughes AGM-65 Maverick, and Rockwell International GBU-15 glide bomb. Specialised anti-ship missiles include the MBB Kormoran and BAe Sea Eagle. Kormoran Mk 1 is used by the German Navy and Italian Air Force, and a Mk 2 model with an improved seeker is now under development.

Britain and West Germany have developed specialised sub-munition dispensers. The MBB MW-1 fires 112 individual submunitions in a sideways direction, the firing pattern and type of munition being selected according to the target. Anti-armour and anti-runway payloads are available. The Hunting Engineering JP-233 is specifically intended for anti-airfield use, and releases two patterns of submunition, one intended to break up the runway suface, and the other an anti-personnel grenade designed to deter attempts to repair the damaged strip.

These British and German weapons both involve flying close to or even over the target under attack, but the idea of attempting this in the face of new-generation point-defence systems in any aircraft—let alone in an aircraft as expensive as Tornado—seems ill-conceived. The USAF was originally a partner in the JP233 project but withdrew in the late 1970s, considering such attack patterns to be impractical.

PERFORMANCE

Low-altitude flight at high speeds imposes severe stress on the structure of an aircraft, but Tornado is built strong enough to cope with Mach 1.2 flight at low level. Any MiG-21 pilot lucky enough to locate the Panavia aircraft in ground-skimming flight at heights of down to 200ft (60m) will find that the NATO aircraft can outrun him with ease, maintaining a speed advantage of up to 100kt (185km/h) in clean condition. The more powerful MiG-23 might be able to maintain similar speeds, but if not within firing range would find it impossible to gain on the Tornado.

Handling qualities under other flight conditions were in no way compromised to gain this level of performance. Unlike some other "hot" aircraft, Tornado holds no terrors for the average squadron pilot. For take-off, the engines are run up to full dry thrust, then full reheat is selected. Lift-off is normally at around 150kt (280km/h), the nose being lifted to around 10deg angle of attack. Once airborne, the pilot can again select dry thrust; the twin RB199s have more than enough power to take the aircraft to the Mach 0.8/500kt (926km/h) maximum indicated airspeed for forward-swept wings.

The fly-by-wire system does much to maintain the handling qualities of Tornado over a wide range of flight conditions. Between Mach 0.5 and 1.0, for example, the maximum roll rate remains constant at 0 to 4g not only for all altitudes and wing-sweep positions, but also with all weapon loads. Stick forces are moderate, stiffening but remaining excellent even at supersonic speeds.

If the aircraft must be manoeuvred hard during combat, full afterburner would be selected, along with the intermediate (45deg) sweep angle. In this condition the aircraft can be taken to Mach 1.45/600kt (1,112km/h), although the full 67deg sweep gives better acceleration at transonic and supersonic speeds. Maximum speed with external stores is Mach 0.9, but in clean condition, pre-series aircraft have clocked up Mach 2.2 at altitude.

Full rudder may be used throughout the envelope, even at Mach 2, while the flight-control system progressively reduces the available roll and yaw as a precaution against spins. The pilot is thus free to manoeuvre in order to get the best out of his mount. There are no changes in trim resulting from changing the sweep angle or operating the airbrakes. The latter may be selected at any time; the maximum allowable airbrake angle is varied automatically according to airspeed.

Interdiction lo-lo-lo-lo
Mission radius 500nm+ (926km+)

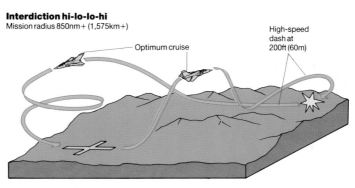

Left: Mission radius in the lo-lo-lo-lo profile with a typical weapons load exceeds 500nm (921km). The mission is flown at an altitude of 200ft (60m) at cruising speed, with a high speed dash from an unspecified distance into and out of the target area, cruising at 200ft (60m) back to base.

Interdiction hi-lo-lo-hi
Mission radius 850nm+ (1,575km+)

Left: The interdiction hi-lo-lo-hi mission profile with a typical weapons load gives the outstanding radius of action of over 850nm (1,566km). This profile involves an optimum altitude cruise out, then a high speed dash over an unspecified distance to and from the target at 200ft (60m). The "unspecified distance" is unlikely to be less than 100nm (185km).

Close air support
Mission radius 700nm+ (1,297km+)

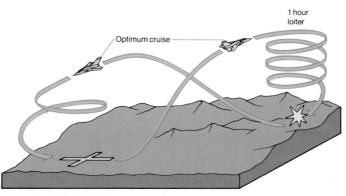

Left: For close air support, Tornado's performance is no less outstanding. Carrying a typical war load and using an optimum speed/altitude flight out and back, Tornado can remain on station for one hour at medium altitude at a radius of over 700nm (1,290km) from base. While the weapons loads in all these profiles are not stated, it is to be believed that they are worthwhile payloads and not token deliveries for the purposes of sales brochures.

Maritime attack hi-lo-lo-hi
Mission radius 700nm+ (1,297km+)

Left: The maritime attack profile of hi-lo-lo-hi carrying four anti-shipping missiles (Kormoran, Sea Eagle, or Harpoon) gives a mission radius of 700nm (1,290km) from base to the stand-off range of the missile. Optimum speed/altitude cruise out and back is once more combined with a high speed, low level dash to missile release.

SAAB-SCANIA
VIGGEN

DEVELOPMENT

If one programme had to be selected to serve as an example of how a West European military aircraft project should be run, Viggen would be the obvious contender. Despite her small size and limited wealth (compared with France, West Germany or the UK), Sweden is determined to maintain an aircraft design capability, and to equip its air force with national products. At a time when the UK was floundering through an apparently endless series of project cancellations, the Swedes sat down to determine the future armament of their air force, and decided that the best replacement for the Saab J35 Draken would be a fleet of 500 advanced multi-role jet fighters built to a specification which virtually combined the requirements of the Republic F-105 Thunderchief and Convair F-106 Delta Dart.

The new fighter was intended to cope with low-altitude strike and reconnaissance missions involving Mach 1 flight at sea level, while still being able to outperform the Draken in the high-altitude interception role. The latter part of the requirement demanded good acceleration and climbing ability, plus a Mach 2 top speed. As if determined to induce heart attacks in the Linköping design team, the Flygvapnet even specified STOL performance, so that the new aircraft could operate from short runways and strips of strengthened road.

Having drawn up a specification which

would have challenged the aerospace industries of even the superpowers, and decided to launch the project, the Swedes set to work to create the end product with a minimum of self-doubt or political wrangling. Inflation ruled out the planned buy of 500 but, by the time the line closes in the late 1980s, more than 300 aircraft will have been built—an impressive achievement for a nation of some eight million people.

First studies took place in 1961 and the first prototype took to the air in February 1967. The chosen design was a single-engine canard delta which, like the Dassault Mirage, has been developed into a family of customised variants. In a period when some governments traditionally funded military aircraft in tiny batches (a practice which was to continue until the era of collaborative programmes started in the mid-1960s), the Swedish Parliament was made of sterner stuff, and in 1968 duly authorised the production of the first 100 Viggens, took out an option on a further 75, and ordered development of the specialised reconnaissance versions. Money was clearly a problem for such a small nation attempting so large an undertaking, so the Swedes wisely opted to tackle Project 37 in stages. Priority was given early in the programme to the AJ37 attack version and the two-seat SK37 operational trainer.

The first AJ37 was rolled out in October 1970, and production deliveries to the

Flygvapnet started in July of the following year with deliveries to F7 at Satenas. The new aircraft replaced the subsonic Saab A32 Lansen fighter-bomber. A single-seat all-weather strike aircraft, the AJ37 was optimised for high-speed flight at low level, but offered some interceptor capability.

Typical weapons: A Viggen loading for long-range anti-ship missions over the Baltic (below) would consist of RB.04Es (**A**) and a centreline tank (**B**). For targets closer to Sweden's long coastline, the armament might be (bottom) RB.04Es (**D**) and rocket launchers (**A**), plus AIM-9s (**C**) and an AQ-31 jammer pod (**B**).

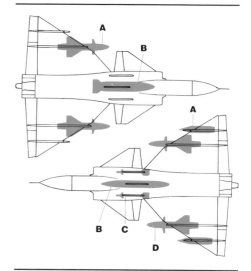

Right: When this spectacular head-on view of Viggen was first released, some aviation specialists suspected it of being the result of skilful trick photography. The camera vantage point was in fact the open tail ramp of a Swedish Air Force C-130 which acted as target for a Viggen interception.

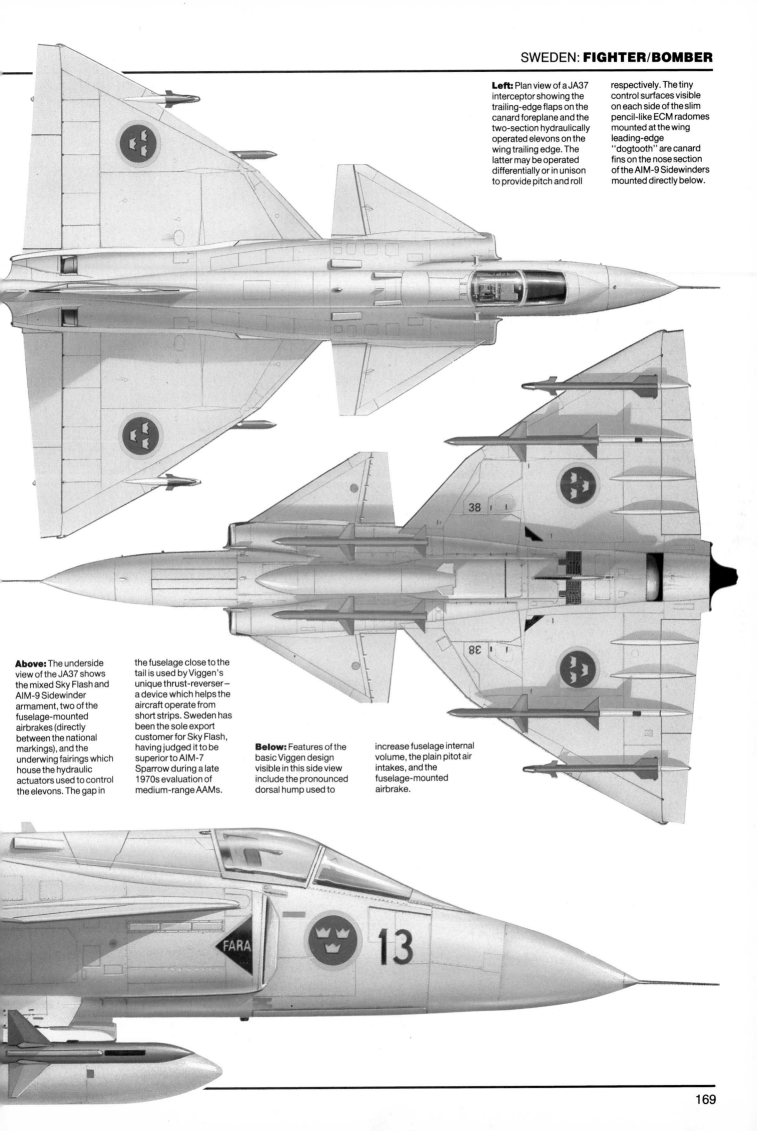

Left: Plan view of a JA37 interceptor showing the trailing-edge flaps on the canard foreplane and the two-section hydraulically operated elevons on the wing trailing edge. The latter may be operated differentially or in unison to provide pitch and roll respectively. The tiny control surfaces visible on each side of the slim pencil-like ECM radomes mounted at the wing leading-edge "dogtooth" are canard fins on the nose section of the AIM-9 Sidewinders mounted directly below.

Above: The underside view of the JA37 shows the mixed Sky Flash and AIM-9 Sidewinder armament, two of the fuselage-mounted airbrakes (directly between the national markings), and the underwing fairings which house the hydraulic actuators used to control the elevons. The gap in the fuselage close to the tail is used by Viggen's unique thrust-reverser – a device which helps the aircraft operate from short strips. Sweden has been the sole export customer for Sky Flash, having judged it to be superior to AIM-7 Sparrow during a late 1970s evaluation of medium-range AAMs.

Below: Features of the basic Viggen design visible in this side view include the pronounced dorsal hump used to increase fuselage internal volume, the plain pitot air intakes, and the fuselage-mounted airbrake.

These basic variants of Viggen were followed by more specialised SF37 and SH37 designs. Intended for general reconnaissance duties, the SF37 is equipped with high and low altitude cameras, an infrared line scanner, a night-reconnaissance pod, illumination equipment, and air-to-air missiles for self-protection. The SH37 is generally similar, but includes specialised maritime-reconnaissance equipment such as long-range cameras and a surveillance radar. Although primarily designed for over-water reconnaissance, it can also be used in the attack role against naval targets. Deliveries of the SH37 started in June 1975. These models may all be considered as first-generation Viggens. A total of 180 aircraft was delivered by the time that production ended late in 1980.

When the Flygvapnet considered its requirements for a new interceptor, the resulting JA37 was sufficiently different from the basic aircraft as to be the first member of the second-generation of Viggens. Studies of a Viggen interceptor started back in 1968, but were kept on back burner until the early 1970s by the workload imposed by the earlier models. Major development contracts for the interceptor were awarded in October 1972, and initial procurement funds for what was to become the JA37—often referred to as the JaktViggen—were authorised in 1974. Based on the newer and more powerful RM8B engine, the JA37 carries advanced avionics and a built-in Oerlikon 30mm cannon. Optimised for interception, it retains a secondary attack capability.

The first four prototypes were not true JA37s, but AJ37 prototypes re-assigned to the new programme. The first was used to explore stability and control systems, and flew in its new configuration on June 4, 1974, three months before the award of a contract for the first 30 production examples. First tests of the new RM8B engine to be used in the new fighter were carried out in this aircraft, but fuller development testing of this uprated and modified powerplant were assigned to second prototype. A third aircraft flight tested the avionics and radar system, while the fourth was used for electronics

Above: The efflux from the massive Volvo Flygmotor RM.8B military turbofan is clearly visible as this JA37 Viggen flies low over the Baltic. The engine also gives the type the unenviable reputation of being one of the noisiest participants at recent international air shows.

SAAB JA37 Viggen
1. Pitot tube.
2. Radome.
3. Radar scanner dish.
4. Radar equipment pack.
5. Forward avionics equipment bay.
6. Rudder pedals.
7. Control column and linkage.
8. Instrument panel.
9. Head-up display.
10. Pilot's "zero-zero" ejection seat.
11. Seat arming lever.
12. Cockpit canopy cover.
13. Boundary layer splitter plate.
14. Canopy jack.
15. Forward fuselage fuel tank.
16. Starboard canard foreplane.
17. Upper avionics equipment bay.
18. Air system distribution ducting.
19. Canard-flap.
20. Oxygen bottle.
21. Transponder aerial.
22. Venting air exhaust duct.

23. Air conditioning system.
24. Air turbine starter.
25. Anti-collision light.
26. Heat exchanger air exhaust.
27. Fuselage "saddle" fuel tank.
28. ECM aerial.
29. Fuel system recuperators.
30. ADF aerial.
31. Starboard wing integral fuel tanks.
32. Volvo Flygmotor RM8B afterburning turbofan engine.
33. Starboard navigation light.
34. Fuel system piping.
35. Artificial feel system pitot intake.
36. Airbrake.
37. Airbrake hydraulic jack.
38. Rudder auto stabiliser.
39. Yaw damper.
40. Rudder hydraulic actuator.
41. VHF aerial.
42. Rudder.
43. UHF/IFF aerial.
44. ECM aerial.

45. Thrust reverser actuator.
46. Afterburner nozzle control jacks.
47. Thrust reverser doors.
48. Variable area afterburner nozzle.
49. Fin folded position (manual folding for hangerage).
50. Tail navigation light.
51. Inboard elevon.
52. Elevon mechanical linkage.
53. Outboard elevon.
54. Port navigation light.
55. Elevon hydraulic actuators.
56. Outboard stores pylon.
57. Missile launch rail.
58. ECM aerial.

59. AIM-9L Sidewinder air-to-air missile.
60. Port wing integral fuel tanks.
61. Afterburner duct.
62. BAe Dynamics Sky Flash air-to-air missile.
63. Inboard stores pylon.
64. Main undercarriage hydraulic retraction jack.
65. Ventral airbrake.
66. Inward retracting main undercarriage.
67. Oil cooler.
68. Elevon artificial feel system linkage.
69. Air system pre-cooler.
70. Mainwheel door hydraulic jack.
71. Leading edge fuel tank.
72. Engine fuel system.

73. Formation lighting strips.
74. Ventral gun pack.
75. Ammunition tank.
76. Oerlikon KCA 30mm cannon.
77. Hydraulic reservoir.
78. Ammunition feed chute.
79. Canard-flap hydraulic actuator.

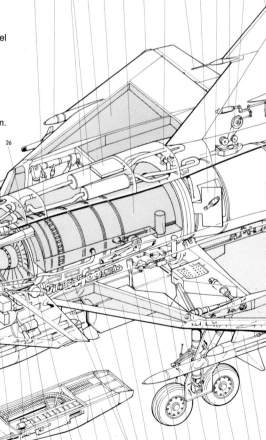

Above: By conventional wisdom, simple pitot air intakes were not regarded as suitable for speeds of Mach 2 plus, but Viggen's designers rewrote the rule book. A similar intake now flies on the US F-16. The light-coloured stripe on this Viggen's intake wall is a formation lighting strip.

80. Emergency ram air turbine.
81. Engine accessory gearbox.
82. Electrical equipment bay.
83. Fuselage stores pylon.
84. Pressure refuelling connection.
85. Temperature probe.
86. Missile launch rail.
87. AIM-9L Sidewinder air-to-air missile.
88. External fuel tank.
89. Avionics equipment cooling air intake.
90. Formation lighting strip.
91. Lower avionics equipment bay.
92. Forward-retracting nose undercarriage.
93. Nosewheel steering unit.
94. Landing/taxiing lamp.
95. Engine throttle lever.
96. Nose undercarriage hydraulic retraction jack.
97. Radar hand controller.
98. Canopy latch.
99. Radome withdrawal rails.
100. Angle of attack transmitter.

and weapon-system development. The engine-development aircraft was lost in a crash, so another AJ37 was modified to take its place in the autumn of 1976.

On December 15, 1975, the first true JaktViggen flew for the first time, complete with the RM8B engine and pre-production avionics. Production officially started in October 1977. Service trials were protracted, and the aircraft was not to become fully operational until the summer of 1980, two years behind schedule. First unit to operate the type was F13 at Norrköping.

Current production rate of the JA37 version is approximately one a month, and the Flygvapnet intends to procure a total of 149. A further domestic order is unlikely, and the type's chances on the export market are slim.

In the mid-1970s the JA37B was offered to the air forces of Belgium, Denmark, Norway and the Netherlands as an F-104 replacement. This version offered a higher gross weight, improved avionics, and an internal 30mm cannon, but was never built. The four NATO allies evaluated Viggen alongside the M53-powered Dassault-Breguet Mirage F.1E, the General Dynamics YF-16 and the Northop YF-17, but the Swedish aircraft was always seen as an "outsider".

The results of that evaluation are still classified, but despite the many fine qualities of the F-16, the Viggen would in many ways have been a better aircraft for European service. Designed to cope with the worst Swedish weather, offering its unique STOL capability, and able to carry a heavy avionics suite, it may have fallen victim to political rather than technical factors.

Sweden follows a strict policy of neutrality, and imposes severe export controls on its arms industry. The hoary joke told in defence circles that Sweden makes all purchasers of Swedish-built weaponry promise never under any circumstances to USE the kit may not be true, but captures the flavour of the situation.

In 1978 Viggen was locked into competition with the Mirage F1.C and SEPECAT Jaguar as India evaluated aircraft able to

meet its Deep Penetration/Strike requirement. The IAF needed some 170 new warplanes, and had been considering a Jaguar purchase for some time. Despite the pro-SEPECAT lobby, Viggen seemed to have a chance in this competition, and Saab-Scania was confident that modern production-technology such as numerically-controlled machines could allow the aircraft to be successfully built by Indian industry.

In August of that year the United States Government officially vetoed any possible deal by refusing to approve transfer of RM8 engine technology to India. The reason for the refusal has never been fully detailed, but the sense of outrage felt in some Swedish political and aerospace circles was intense. The core of the Swedish engine was the widely-exported JT8D civil turbofan used in many US civil airliners, so could hardly be considered a secret. Once again, politics rather than technical factors seemed to be dogging the Swedish aircraft.

Saab-Scania still offers an export version of Viggen. Designated 37X, this is based on the JA37, but has yet to attract an order. In the late 1970s the type was evaluated by the Austrian Air Force, but the chances of it being adopted were slim. Austria's current "interceptor" is the Saab 105 trainer, and the prospect of that nation suddenly finding the funds for a heavy all-weather fighter seemed remote. The Dassault Mirage 50 was eventually selected, but even this low-cost aircraft proved impossible to fund, and to date no order has been placed.

A third stillborn second-generation Viggen was the A20, an attack aircraft based on the JA37, and intended for service in the mid to late 1980s. Offered as an alternative to the design which eventually became the JA39 Gripen lightweight fighter, it was rejected in favour of the latter aircraft. Under current plans, the Viggen line will close in 1989 when deliveries of the JA37 are completed.

STRUCTURE

The logical way of meeting the Viggen specification would have been to use variable geometry, producing an aircraft in the class of the experimental Dassault Mirage G8. Having already displayed an ability to devise unique planforms tailored to national requirements—such as the double-delta layout of the Draken—the Linköping design team adopted an even more revolutionary concept for Viggen.

The key factor which influenced their choice was probably the requirement for STOL performance. Getting airborne from modest runways is a problem solved by a combination of high lift and a good thrust:weight ratio.

The Swedes turned to the long-neglected canard layout, taking advantage of the fact that on canards the forward-mounted elevators control pitch by applying lift to the nose, adding to the total lift. On a conventional design, the nose is lifted at take-off and landing by deflecting the elevators and pushing the tail downwards—sacrific-ing lift at the very time it is most needed.

At the time that the aircraft was designed, the only other jet-powered canard was the North American XB-70 bomber, but the Swedish design was subtly different from the US bomber in being close-coupled, with minimal spacing between the foreplane and wing. At high incidence, the foreplane acts like a strake, enhancing wing lift to a value some 20 to 30 per cent higher than that obtainable by the two surfaces working in isolation. Viggen has been described as being virtually a supersonic biplane.

The wing is of compound-sweep form, and incorporates hydraulically actuated elevons designed to work differentially or in unison. The smaller canard has trailing-edge flaps. Viggen was briefly grounded in 1976 following several in-flight wing failures, but the cause was swiftly determined, fully publicised, and the appropriate modifications were devised.

Most of the fuselage is made from aluminium alloy, the use of titanium being restricted to critical areas of the engine bay. Extensive use is made of honeycomb-bonded components in the fuselage, the same technique also being used in the moving surfaces of the wing, canard and fin, and also in the undercarriage doors.

Fuel is carried in six tanks (five in the SK37)—one in each wing, one above the engine, one on each side of the fuselage and one behind the cockpit. Total fuel capacity has never been revealed, but is probably about 1,250 gallons (5,700 litres).

The SK37 two-seat trainer has a modified structure, with the rear cockpit and second seat occupying space which houses the forward fuel tank and some avionics units in the standard aircraft. A taller tail fin is fitted to offset the effects of the bulged hood of the second cockpit.

Low-altitude interception missions place a greater strain on aircraft, so the JA37 has a strengthened structure. Fuselage length was slightly increased to cope

with the RM8B engine, and the tall tail fin originally devised for the SK37 trainer is fitted as standard.

POWERPLANT

Sweden has a long tradition of using British jet engines built under licence for its warplanes. The J35 used a Volvo Flygmotor-built version of the Rolls-Royce Avon, but Viggen required a powerplant with more than ten tons of thrust, ideally a turbofan. The only UK engine was the massive afterburning Olympus under development for TSR.2, while the only production engine in the correct thrust class was the Pratt & Whitney JT75 turbojet.

The Swedes bravely opted to create

Below: A prototype of the L.M. Ericsson UAP 1023 pulse-Doppler radar installed in a Viggen testbed. The heart of a suite of around 50 avionics "black boxes" – the most complex avionics array ever flown in a Swedish fighter – the UAP 1023 is controlled by software rather than hardware, with interchangeable programmes.

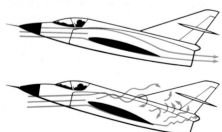

Above: In a conventional aircraft design with a wing and normal tail, the wing angle of incidence must be increased as speed decreases in order to maintain lift. At even moderate angles of incidence, the normal flow of air across the wing (upper drawing) can no longer be maintained, and the wing stalls (lower drawing). Lift is lost, and the aircraft nose drops sharply, leading to a loss of height until normal flying speed can be regained and the airflow returns to normal.

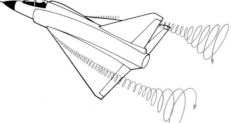

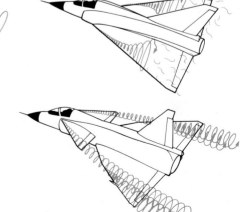

Above: In a delta design, vortexes generated by the wing leading edge keep the boundary layer air energised, maintaining the airflow and preventing a stall at high angles of incidence. If the incidence is further increased, the result is a "super stall" (above right). The addition of a canard foreplane can create a second set of vortexes (right). Given a suitable foreplane location, the new vortexes can help stabilise those from the wing.

their own Mach 2 turbofan in the thrust class of the P&W F100 and General Electric F101, but decided to cut corners by basing this on an existing civil engine. As a core Volvo selected the Pratt & Whitney JT8D, and set out to modify this for supersonic flight and to mate it with an afterburner of Swedish design. A licence was negotiated, and Volvo set to work on a project which was almost as great a technical challenge as the aircraft which it was to power.

In 1963/64 P&W supplied three JT8D engines to be fitted with Swedish designed afterburners. The first modified JT8D-22 ran in August 1964, and was followed by several development engines. In 1968, deliveries of production engines started, following some 4,000 hours of bench and flight testing with the prototypes.

Studies showed that the JA37 air defence mission required an engine of improved standard, particularly in terms of thrust and surge margin. Research on the resulting RM8B was carried out in conjunction with P&W, a task which was completed in 1971. The fan gained an extra stage, while the LP compressor lost a stage. Higher turbine-inlet temperatures needed in order to generate the extra thrust dictated modifications to the combustion system and HP turbine.

The RM8A is 242.2in (614cm) long, while the RM8B is slightly longer at 245.3in (623cm); diameter of both models is 55in (139.7cm). The basic RM8A weighs 4,630lb (2,100kg), while the B model is some 550lb (250kg) heavier. Front fan of the RM8A has two stages, while the RM8B has three. The four-stage LP compressor (three-stage in the case of the RM8B) leads to a seven-stage HP section and a cannular combustor with nine flame tubes. A single-stage HP turbine with air cooled blades drives the HP compressor, while a three-stage unit drives the fan and LP section.

Outer and inner walls of the afterburner are manufactured from titanium and special heat-resistant alloy respectively, the space between them acting as a duct for cooling air. The nozzle is fully variable, and actuated by fuel pressure.

All Viggen variants except the JA37 JaktViggen use the RM8A, which develops 14,750lb (6,690kg) of dry thrust, 25,990lb (11,790kg) in full afterburner. Equivalent ratings for the RM8B are 16,200lb (7,348kg) dry and 28,110lb (12,750kg) with afterburner. Specific fuel consumption is 0.63lb/lb/hr in dry thrust; 2.47lb/lb/hr with afterburner. Figures for the RM8B are marginally higher. Current TBO is greater than 500hr.

AVIONICS

The payload of electronics carried by the Viggen varies from version to version, but JaktViggen carries the most complex suite of avionics ever installed in a Swedish military aircraft—some 50 avionics units weighing a total of 1,300lb (600kg). Heart of the JaktViggen avionics suite is the L.M. Ericsson UAP 1023 (PS-46/A) radar, an

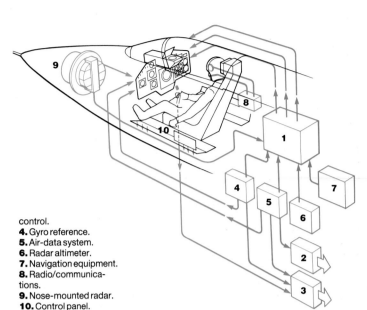

Right: Studies carried out by Saab-Scania showed that a computer-based avionics suite was a cost-effective substitute for a second crew member. For some tasks, a navigator was found to be better than "black boxes", while for others avionics proved superior. In the long run, the potential savings resulting from the elimination of the navigator – including the space, support equipment (such as an ejection seat and oxygen system), plus his salary and training – made the computer the optimum "back seater". This simplified block diagram of the Viggen avionics suite shows main sub-systems such as:
1. Central computer.
2. Automatic throttle control.
3. Automatic flight control.
4. Gyro reference.
5. Air-data system.
6. Radar altimeter.
7. Navigation equipment.
8. Radio/communications.
9. Nose-mounted radar.
10. Control panel.

Above: Pilot's eye view from the cockpit of a JA37 as it awaits permission to begin its take-off roll. The instrument panel has a clean and uncluttered look, with the conventional instrumentation on the left being supplemented by two multi-mode CRT head-down displays plus a modern HUD.

advanced pulse-Doppler set with a range of more than 26nm (50km) in look-down mode. Low PRF transmissions are used for look-up operation, and medium-PRF for look-down missions.

Operating parameters of the radar are software-controlled, and could be changed in wartime to confuse enemy ECM systems. The available modes include target search and acquisition, track or track-while-scan, target illumination, and air-to-ground ranging. Much attention was given

in the design to coping with the effects of ground clutter or deliberate jamming. Three displays present data to the pilot—a tactical display for navigation or status data, a head-down display for use during all-weather interception, plus a HUD.

A Singer-Kearfott CD107 computer replaces the Saab unit carried by earlier Viggens and the same company provides the rapid-alignment INS. System accuracy of the latter is 1nm (1.85km) per hour. JA37's Honeywell/Saab-Scania SA 07 digital flight-control system was the first to be adopted for a production military aircraft anywhere in the world.

The AJ37 carries an earlier radar designated UAP 1011 (PS-37/A) which used a simpler pattern of Cassegrain antenna and was optimised for air-to-ground use.

Operating modes include search, acquisition, air-target ranging, surface-target tracking, obstacle warning and terrain mapping.

ARMAMENT

For the attack mission, the AJ37 can carry up to 13,230lb (6,000kg) of stores on seven hardpoints, three under the fuselage and two on each wing. Weaponry can include iron bombs, launchers for unguided rockets such as the Bofors 135mm, or guided missiles. Sweden currently operates the Saab Rb04E anti-ship missile, the command-guided Rb05A air-to-ground missile, or the AGM-65 Maverick (known as Rb75 in Swedish service). No "smart" bombs are currently in the Flygvapnet inventory. AJ37 lacks an internal gun, but can carry external gun pods. The SK37 trainer can carry the full range of armament normally toted by the AJ37, and is able to fly attack missions.

For the JA37 interceptor, Sweden selected the BAe Dynamics Sky Flash semi-active radar homing missile. An evaluation of the AIM-7 Sparrow, Sky Flash and the air-launched version of Aspide being

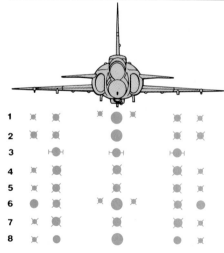

Possible weapons:
1. AIM-9, Skyflash and a centreline tank.
2. Four Skyflash plus centreline tank.
3. Three RB.04E anti-ship missiles.
4. Three RB.05s plus AIM-9s.
5. Three Mavericks plus AIM-9L.
6. Rocket launchers (outboard), Mavericks, AIM-9L and a centreline tank.
7. AIM-9s plus 1,100lb (500kg) bombs.
8. AIM-9s, Red Baron recce pod, SATT AQ-31 jamming pod, and centreline tank.

promoted by Selenia concluded that the Italian missile was superior on technical grounds, but full development of the weapon was being delayed by the Italian Air Force. The Flygvapnet opted to order the British missile, and has since placed a follow-on order.

For shorter-range combat, Jakt Viggen carries the Sidewinder missile (known as Rb24). The most modern version in Swedish service is the AIM-9L, but L.M. Ericsson is currently developing a new pattern of optical proximity fuze which could be retrofitted to older examples of the missile.

For close combat, a single Oerlikon KCA cannon is carried in a belly-mounted gunpack. Although its rate of fire is well below that of US Gatling-type weapons, the 30mm KCA is an impressive example of the gunmaker's art, with a firepower superior to that of ADEN/DEFA class weapons. The weapon throws 22 massive 13oz (0.36kg) projectiles every second, at a muzzle velocity of 3,445ft/sec (1,050m/sec). Each is 50 per cent heavier than those from the ADEN or DEFA, while muzzle velocity is almost double that of the older gun.

Left: Standard recce version of Viggen is the SF37. The modified nose section houses four vertical or oblique low-level cameras, one long-range vertical and one infra-red camera, plus a camera sight and ECM registration equipment. Pod-mounted sensors can include night-reconnaissance equipment such as the Red Baron infra-red line scanning system.

Left: Graphic proof that the invisible vortexes from the root of the foreplane and dogtooth on the wing maintain the airflow across the delta wing of Viggen at high angles of attack, delaying the point at which the wing stalls (see vortex diagram on page 172). This complex interaction between the wing and foreplane is the result of careful design and has given rise to the quip that Viggen is the world's first supersonic biplane.

Above: Sweden's traditional policy of armed neutrality is backed up by a defence force well enough equipped to make any non-nuclear attack on Sweden a costly operation for an invader.

This JA37 Viggen is just part of a planned force of more than 300 indigenously developed and very advanced Mach 2 warplanes which guards a nation of little more than eight million inhabitants.

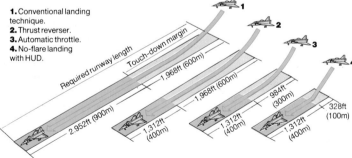

Right: Viggen uses several techniques to reduce the touchdown margin and the landing run since Sweden is unable to build large, well-defended air bases. From the 4,920ft (1,500m) needed for a normal landing, reverse thrust, autothrottle and a no-flare landing cut the total to only 1,640ft (500m).

1. Conventional landing technique.
2. Thrust reverser.
3. Automatic throttle.
4. No-flare landing with HUD.

Required runway length
Touch-down margin
1,968ft (600m)
1,968ft (600m)
984ft (300m)
328ft (100m)
2,952ft (900m)
1,312ft (400m)
1,312ft (400m)
1,312ft (400m)

The weapon has a four-round rotary breech, and all four chambers must be loaded before firing. This can be done in the air using pneumatic power, or pyro-technic cartridges. Twelve of the latter are carried, allowing the gun to be recocked several times in the event of stoppages.

PERFORMANCE

Viggen has a reputation of being a "pilot's aeroplane"—highly manoeuvrable and near-viceless in handling. Like all deltas, it can be tricky at high angles of attack, so pilots hold this below 15 degrees. Wing loading is approximately 65lb/sq ft (325kg/sq m) for a fully-loaded aircraft. This is higher than the optimum for a strike aircraft, but experience has shown that the gust response is low. High speed flight at low altitude does not place undue stress on the pilot.

Viggen was designed to operate out of 1,600ft (500m) airstrips. Landing on such short strips is a more difficult operation, particularly if snow or ice are present. The tactics used by Viggen would be familiar to any naval aviator—the Swedes simply treat the runway as an aircraft-carrier deck, touching down after a high-rate flareless approach. The undercarriage is stressed to accept sink rates of up to 16ft/ sec (5m/sec), and the aircraft is flown on to the ground. The pilot keeps the aircraft on the glideslope by movements of the control column, relying on the aircraft's autothrottle to control speed and attitude.

Carrier pilots rely on arrester wires, but Viggen carries its own built-in arrester system—a highly efficient thrust-reverser. After the main undercarriage touches down, the aircraft pitches forward and the nosewheels make contact with the runway. As the nosewheel strut is compressed, an automatic switch actuates the thrust reverser. The tail-mounted thrust-reverser doors close, deflecting air forward and through three annular gaps in the jetpipe.

Maximum speed at high altitude is greater than Mach 2, while at 300ft (90m) the JA37 can reach Mach 1.2. Time to 32,800ft (10,000m) for the JA37 is less than 1 min 40 sec from brakes off. Service ceiling has never been disclosed, but estimates have ranged from around 50,000ft (15,000m) to more than 60,000ft (18,000m). Tactical radius for hi-lo-hi sorties is greater than 540nm (1,000km), falling to half that figure for the more demanding lo-lo-lo profile.

SEPECAT
JAGUAR

DEVELOPMENT

When the Jaguar programme was started, it seemed at first sight that Britain and France were setting out to re-invent the Northrop F-5. In theory, the result should have been a modest design with marginally supersonic performance—a replacement for aging subsonic types used for training and light-strike duties. The aircraft finally built turned out to be a dedicated strike type which combines a wingspan slightly shorter than that of the wartime Messerschmitt Bf.109 with the range and payload-carrying capacity of the Lancaster bomber. In theory, every operator of the ubiquitous Canberra was a potential customer for the Anglo-French warplane. In practice, France chose to concentrate its marketing energies on all-French types such as the Mirage III and F1 families, leaving the promotion of Jaguar to the UK—a nation not renowned for its ability to sell modern military aircraft.

Further development by the British did give the aircraft a degree of multi-role capability, but a proposed "Big-wing version"—virtually a "poor man's Phantom"—was never built. The only major contract for the Jaguar was placed by the Indian Air Force, which plans to procure a total of 116.

Jaguar owes its origin to Royal Air Force and Armee de l'Air requirements of the early 1960s. Britain was in the market for new advanced trainers, while the French air arm also faced the need to replace outdated Dassault Ouragan and Mystere IV fighters used for attack and close-support missions. Initially, the two nations planned national programmes—the ECAT (Ecole de Combat et Appui Tactique) aircraft, and a British AST.362 project intended to replace the Hawker Siddeley Gnat and Hunter. Each nation produced its own design, France opting for the Breguet Br.121, while the UK pursued the v.g. British Aircraft Corporation P.45.

Discussions on possible collaboration started in the spring of 1964, with a joint requirement being hammered out during the winter of 1964/5. Combining the two requirements was a difficult task. The UK wanted a supersonic aircraft complete with advanced avionics, while France would have been content with a simple subsonic design with a minimum of "black boxes".

By the spring, a common approach had been agreed, and a Memorandum of Understanding signed on May 17, 1965, committed the two nations to work on a collaborative venture based on the Breguet Br.121 design. To handle the task of coordinating development and manufacturing by the two nations, an organisation with the cumbersome title of Societe Europeenne de Production de l'Avion ECAT (usually referred to as SEPECAT) was set up.

By November 1965 a basic design had been completed, and construction of a

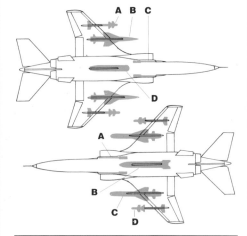

Above: For the last decade, the Jaguar A strike aircraft of the Armée de l'Air have been able to provide firepower to back up French foreign policy. Outside forces contemplating military action against former French colonies must face the possibility that Jaguars might be sent by France to help repel any attack. When the French Government decided in 1977 to support the Government of Mauritania the aircraft had its combat debut in operations against guerrilla forces. The avionics of the Jaguar A are simpler than those of RAF aircraft.

Typical weapons:
Top: The final 30 French Air Force Jaguars carry an ATLIS laser designator pod (**D**), and the new laser-guided version of the AS.30 missile (**B**). R.550 Magic "dogfight" missiles (**A**) are carried for self-defence in addition to the DEFA or Aden 30mm cannon (**C**).

Above: A centreline tank (**B**) would give Jaguar A sufficient range to penetrate deep into defended territory, attacking radars with Matra AS.37 Martel or ARMAT passive-homing missiles (**C**); Magics (**D**) and cannon (**A**) are for self-defence, so escorts are not needed.

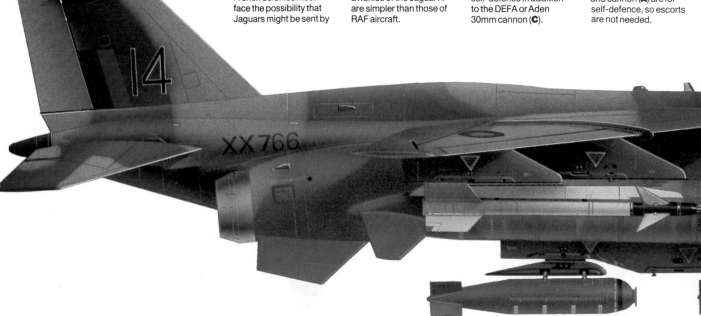

Below left: Beneath the simple lines of the Jaguar S lie a structure designed to cope with the stress of low-level flight and what was for its time a highly-sophisticated nav/attack system. This view shows the full-span trailing edge flaps, plus the leading-edge slats and roll-control spoilers on the outer wing panels. An "anti-Jaguar" faction within the RAF regards the type as less than a total success, and fought against a top-up order, a major mid-life update and a planned "Big Wing" version proposed by BAe in the late 1970s.

Above: RAF experience during Red Flag operations at Nellis AFB, Nevada, showed that the Jaguar could sometimes "jump" attacking F-5E Aggressors, turning the hunter into the hunted. The service took note of the lesson and has equipped its Jaguar S strike force with Sidewinder. The Hunting Engineering BL755 cluster bomb proved highly effective during the Falklands War, and is now to be replaced by a new version. Other RAF loadings include unguided rockets, iron bombs, Paveway Mk13/18 LGBs and the Green Parrot nuclear weapon.

Below left: This side view shows the spring-loaded supplementary doors on the sides of the intake, the retractable flight/refuelling probe (on the fuselage side near the front of the canopy), the 3deg anhedral on the wing, and 10deg anhedral on the horizontal stabiliser, and the "chisel nose" which houses the Ferranti laser ranger and marked-target seeker.

This aircraft is from 226 OCU/2 Sqn RAF based at Lossiemouth, and carries the tartan band on the ECM, in recognition of the "Scottish Air Force" designation conferred upon it.

prototype started the following summer. Flight testing began on September 8, 1968, with the first production example following in November 1971. In order to meet the various national requirements, four models were planned. Since the French requirement was more urgent and involved aircraft with simpler avionics, it made sense for the Armee de l'Air to take early-production aircraft, and for deliveries to the RAF to take place on a later timescale.

First production model to fly was the Jaguar E two-seat trainer for the French Air Force, becoming airborne on September 8, 1968. Jaguar A is the French tactical-support fighter version, and was first flown on March 23, 1969. Both partners had agreed to take 200 aircraft, the French split being 40 E and 160 A versions. A navalised Jaguar M version was planned for service aboard the carriers *Foch* and *Clemenceau*. A prototype was flown in November 1969, but the Aeronavale decided in 1972 to scrap the project.

The RAF tackled their versions in the opposite order. First to fly, on October 12, 1969, was the Jaguar S strike version (service designation Jaguar GR.1). The Jaguar B (Jaguar T.2) two-seat trainer followed on August 30, 1971. Early plans assumed that all RAF aircraft would be two-seaters. By 1967 the chosen mix was

Above: Although normally operated from fixed airfields, Jaguar has been test-flown from stretches of motorway. This technique could do much to improve the wartime survivability of the Royal Air Force, but is rarely practised. Trials

have confirmed that this type of operation poses no problem to a well-trained pilot, but badly-fatigued aircrew returning after wartime sorties might wish for greater familiarity with off-base operations than they probably have.

SEPECAT Jaguar GR.1
1. Pitot tube.
2. Ferranti Laser Ranger and Marked Target Seeker (LRMTS).
3. Total pressure probes.
4. Avionics cooling air duct.
5. Retractable in-flight refuelling probe.
6. Liquid oxygen converter.
7. Rudder pedals.
8. Control column.
9. Pilot's instrument panel.
10. Head-up display.
11. Martin-Baker Mk.9 "zero-zero" ejection seat.
12. Cockpit canopy cover.
13. Canopy strut.
14. Cockpit air conditioning system.
15. VHF homing aerials.
16. Cockpit air heat exchanger.
17. Starboard wing pylon.
18. IFF aerial.
19. Wing fence.
20. Leading edge slat.
21. Starboard wing integral fuel tank.
22. Starboard navigation light.
23. TACAN aerial.
24. Anti-collision light.
25. Spoilers.
26. Double-slotted flaps.
27. Heat exchanger air intake.

28. Primary heat exchanger.
29. Flap drive motor.
30. Hydraulic accumulator.
31. Hydraulic reservoir.
32. Heat exchanger exhaust ducts.
33. Fuel jettison control valve.
34. Rolls-Royce/Turbomeca Adour afterburning turbofan engine.
35. Starboard all-moving tailplane.
36. VOR/ILS aerial.
37. Forward passive ECM antenna.
38. VHF/UHF aerial.
39. Rear passive ECM aerial.
40. Recognition light.
41. Tail navigation light.
42. Rudder.
43. Fuel jettison.
44. Parachute release unit.
45. Parachute door.
46. Brake parachute housing.
47. Rudder hydraulic jack.
48. Tailplane hydraulic jacks.
49. Port all-moving tailplane.

50. Emergency arrester hook.
51. Tailplane pivot bearing.
42. Engine fire extinguisher bottles.
53. Rear fuselage fuel tank.
54. Afterburner nozzle shroud.
55. Ventral fin.
56. Afterburner nozzle control jacks.
57. Port navigation light.
58. Rocket pack.
59. Spoiler hydraulic jack.
60. Wing outboard stores pylon.
61. Flap screw jack.
62. Airbrake.
63. Flap drive shaft.
64. Engine accessory gearbox.
65. Slat screw jack.
66. Slat drive shaft.

67. Airbrake hydraulic jack.
68. Hydraulic ground connectors.
69. Twin-wheeled main undercarriage.
70. Main undercarriage pivot bearing.
71. Wing inboard stores pylon.

72. 264gal external fuel tank.
73. Roll control artificial feel system.
74. Port wing integral fuel tank.
75. Main undercarriage hydraulic jack.

76. Fuselage centreline pylon.
77. Leading edge slat drive motor.
78. Ground power socket.
79. Ammunition feed chute.

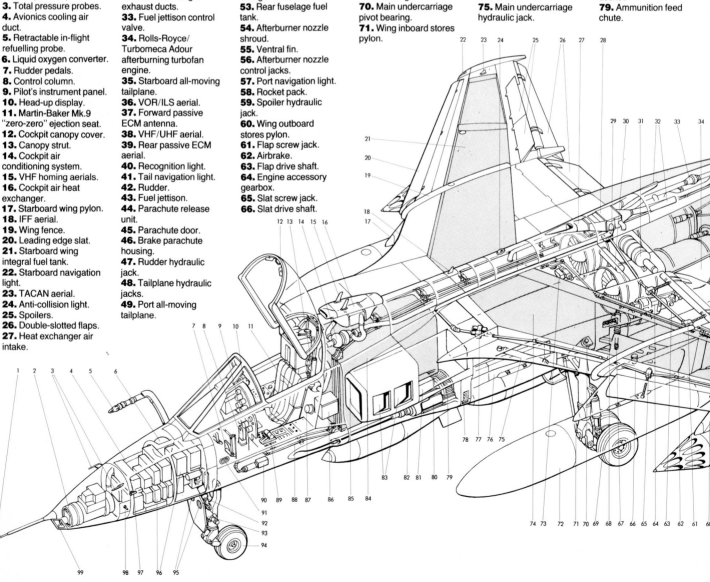

110 trainers and 90 strike aircraft, but a 1970 review by the contemporary Conservative Government resulted in Jaguar being assigned to the strike role. The final plan involved the purchase of 165 single-seaters and only 38 two-seat trainers to be used for operational conversion.

Production for France and Britain ended in December 1981 with delivery of the final Jaguar A to Armee de l'Air. All subsequent Jaguars have been for export. Designated Jaguar International, these are based broadly on the RAF-standard aircraft. First export customer was Oman, which ordered 24. The first flew on August 19, 1976. Ecuador ordered 12 aircraft to equip a single squadron, but the main export user is India.

Adoption of Jaguar by the Indian Air Force was a prolonged process. The service had a long-standing Deep Penetration and Strike Aircraft (DPSA) requirement, and made no secret of its desire to buy Jaguar. Shortage of funds repeatedly delayed the choice of a DPSA, but the selection of Jaguar was finally announced in 1979.

The first 40 aircraft were delivered from the UK production line, and Hindustan Aeronautics is currently assembling additional aircraft at its Bangalore plant using British-supplied parts. The first locally-assembled aircraft flew in March 1982. India originally planned to assemble 45 Jaguars from British kits, switching to full licence production. Plans for the latter option were cancelled early in 1983, and HAL will now assemble an extra 31 aircraft, bringing the total Indian production run to 76 examples. Production is reported to be running at more than one per month.

Despite a modest unit cost (by today's standards) of between $8 million and $10 million, Jaguar has not received the orders which might have been expected. Latest customer is reported to be Nigeria, which wants 18 aircraft to replace obsolescent MiG-17 and MiG-21 fighters. The original aircraft was a dedicated strike type, but the much-improved Jaguar International offers a degree of capability in the air-combat and air-superiority roles.

STRUCTURE

Dassault is responsible for the construction of the forward and centre fuselage, the forward fuel tanks and the undercarriage, while British Aerospace builds the rear fuselage, air inlets, wing and tail. In order to create the Jaguar, the original Breguet design had to be reworked, growing in length and being modified to use machined panels rather than the honeycomb construction originally proposed. Use of the latter material is confined to the cockpit area.

Most of the fuselage is made from aluminium alloy, but titanium is used in the engine bays. Airbrakes are mounted low on the fuselage sides, aft of the main undercarriage doors and directly below the wing trailing edge.

The wing is a one-piece unit with two main spars and 40deg of sweep. No aile-

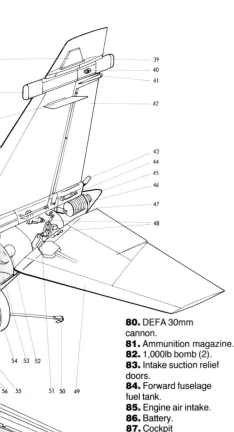

80. DEFA 30mm cannon.
81. Ammunition magazine.
82. 1,000lb bomb (2).
83. Intake suction relief doors.
84. Forward fuselage fuel tank.
85. Engine air intake.
86. Battery.
87. Cockpit pressurisation valve.
88. Control linkages.
89. Engine throttle levers.
90. Roll control artificial feel system.
91. Canopy emergency release.
92. Nose undercarriage hydraulic jack.
93. Nosewheel steering jacks.
94. Nose undercarriage.
95. Landing/taxiying lamps.
96. Avionics equipment bays.
97. Temperature probe.
98. Incidence probe.
99. Laser ranger wedge profile optical windows.

Above: After carrying out mock attacks on a bombing range in West Germany, an RAF Jaguar S and a Luftwaffe F-104G part company to head for their respective home bases. The British aircraft carries on its centreline an ML Aviation No. 200 Carrier Bomb Light Stores.

Below: Two-seat versions such as this Armée de l'Air Jaguar E advanced trainer have an extended nose section incorporating tandem accommodation and a revised canopy. Aft of the cockpit, the structure is identical to that of the single-seater. A total of 78 trainers were built.

Above: An over-wing launcher for the Matra R.550 Magic was developed for use on Jaguar International. This location for the carriage of air-to-air armament may be novel, but posed no problems during test firings. In combat, it gives the infra-red seeker head of the weapon an unrestricted field of view during manoeuvres which involve an attempt to out-turn an opponent.

Above: The twin-wheel main undercarriage of Jaguar minimises ground pressure. This taxiing run across rough grass at Boscombe Down was part of a series of rough-field trials, but has not led to any serious attempts to develop off-airfield front-line sites. Unlike the Warsaw Pact, NATO has no plans to operate fighters other than Harrier from grass strips – but is this wise?

Below: As Jaguars of 54 Sqn RAF fly towards the sunset, the falling light level allows the camera to capture the symbology on the aircraft's head-up display. Within a short time of entering service, Jaguar's navigation and weapon-aiming subsystem (NAVWASS) allowed the average squadron pilot – and "first tourists" – to obtain near miss distances of around 50ft (15m).

rons are fitted, roll control being by means of spoilers which operate in conjunction with the differential tailplane. Double-slotted flaps run the entire length of the trailing edge, while the outer sections of the leading edge are fitted with slats.

A total of 924 gal (4,200 litres) of fuel is carried in two wing tanks and four fuselage tanks, and critical elements of the fuel system are protected by armour. The only other part of the aircraft to be armoured is the cockpit transparency, which can resist small-arms fire.

POWERPLANT

Like the airframe, the powerplant is a collaborative Anglo-French venture. The RB.172 Adour afterburning turbofan was designed by Rolls-Royce and Turbomeca. Of modular design to ease maintenance, it is a two-spool design with a two-stage LP fan and five-stage HP compressor, both driven by single-stage turbines. The combustion chamber is annular with 18 fuel nozzles, while the afterburner is a compact but fully-modulated unit.

Standard powerplant on French and UK Jaguars was originally a pair of RB.172 (Mk 102) Adours. Each develops 5,115lb (2,320kg) of thrust, 7,305lb (3,313kg) in full afterburner. France was happy to retain this engine, but the RAF has always considered Jaguar to be underpowered. British aircraft are now fitted with the Mk 104, which offers an extra 205lb (93kg) of dry thrust and 735lb (333kg) with afterburner.

For Jaguar International, the initial powerplant was the RB.172-26 (Mk 804)—an export version of the MK 104—but aircraft destined for India and the second batch for Oman have the Mk 811 Adour developing 5,520lb (2,503kg) of dry thrust, 8,400lb (3,810kg) with afterburner.

Above: Spread out before the Jaguar International export model is the wide range of weaponry which the aircraft is cleared to carry. Note the parachute-retarded bombs for low-level attack, and the overwing-mounted Magic missiles (see opposite page). Not available for export are the powerful AN52 and Green Parrot tactical nuclear weapons.

AVIONICS

Britain and France developed their own avionics installations for Jaguar. The French opted for relative simplicity, while the RAF installed a more sophisticated system which has generally been adopted by export customers.

Main items of avionics in French Jaguar A strike aircraft include an EMD RDN 72 Doppler radar, CSF laser rangefinder, SFIM 153–6 twin-gyro inertial platform, Crouzet type 90 navigation computer, CSF Type 31 weapon-aiming computer, Dassault fire-control computer, and a radar-warning receiver. Some aircraft carry a Thomson-CSF/Martin Marietta ATLIS laser-designator pod.

UK Jaguar S aircraft are equipped with a Marconi Avionics digital/inertial navigation and weapon-aiming subsystem (NAV-WASS) based on an MCS 920M digital computer, a Marconi Avionics air-data computer, Ferranti Type 105 laser rangefinder and Type 106 marked-target seeker, Smiths Industries HUD, and a three-gyro inertial platform. A fairing in the tail fin houses the antennas for a Marconi Avionics radar-warning receiver.

When Jaguar entered service it was the most complex strike aircraft ever fielded by the RAF, but quickly earned the respect of its crews. Continuously-computed impact point (CCIP) attacks display an average miss distance of 50ft (15m). Parts of NAVWASS are currently being replaced by a new Ferranti FIN 1064 digital nav/attack system which started flight test in 1981.

India has specified an advanced suite of avionics for its Jaguar force. This includes a new HUD and weapon-aiming system similar to that in Sea Harrier, plus a Ferranti COMED combined map and electronic display. Eight aircraft will be fitted

out for maritime strike, with a Thomson-CSF Agave radar in a modified nose and a Ferranti laser ranger in a chin-mounted fairing.

The UK Ministry of Defence is using a single Jaguar to flight test a quadruplex fly-by-wire control system incorporating Marconi Avionics flight-control computers and control-surface actuators developed by Dowty Boulton-Paul. Flight tests started in 1982, gradually exploring high-angle-of-attack and relaxed stability. In the current stage and final stage of the programme, the wing planform has been modified to make the aircraft inherently unstable.

ARMAMENT

Five external hardpoints—one beneath the fuselage and two under each wing—allow Jaguar to carry up to 10,500lb (4,763kg) of ordnance. Normal loads can include 1,000lb (450kg) bombs, BL755 or Beluga cluster bombs, or launchers for 68mm SNEB unguided rockets. Two 30mm ADEN (UK) or DEFA 533 (France) cannon are mounted internally in the lower fuselage. Jaguar International can carry two Magic or Sidewinder air-to-air missiles on overwing pylons—a location which gives the IR seeker heads a clear field of view in air combat.

Specialised stores carried by French

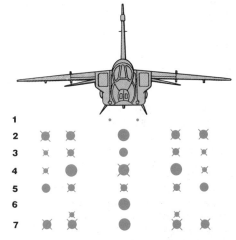

Possible weapons:
1. Two 30mm cannon (RAF, Adens; Armée de l'Air, DEFAs).
2. Harpoon ASM missiles outboard; 1,000lb (454kg) bombs inboard; 264gall (1,200lit) fuel tank on centreline.
3. Recce pod on centreline, with AIM-9B Sidewinders for self-defence.
4. BL755 cluster bombs outboard; short JP233 dispenser on centreline; 264gall (1,200lit) tanks inboard.

5. Durandal anti-runway weapons inboard; Beluga cluster dispenser on centreline; Matra 155 rocket launchers on outboard pylons.
6. AN52 nuclear store (on French aircraft).
7. BAe Dynamics Alarm anti-radar missiles outboard; Mk13/18 Paveway II smart bombs inboard (French Jaguars could carry overwing Magic missiles above this station); 264gal (1,200lit) tank on centreline.

Comparative maximum armament

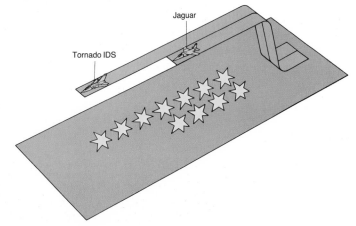

Tornado IDS

Jaguar

Left: Although the 10,500lb (4,760kg) maximum ordnance load of the Jaguar is well below that of the later Tornado, which can carry up to 18,000lb (8,150kg), this represents 30 per cent of the maximum takeoff weight – a similar fraction to that for Tornado. This impressive warload is carried on a total of six hardpoints – four underwing pylons rated at 2,500lb/1,130kg (inboard) and 1,250lb/570kg (outboard), plus tandem underfuselage locations each able to carry 2,500lb (1,130kg) of stores.

aircraft include the AS.37 Martel anti-radar missile, the new AS.30L laser guided missile (aimed using the ATLIS pod) or the AN52 tactical nuclear weapon. UK Jaguars can carry nuclear weapons, but no details have been released. Harpoon has been offered for anti-shipping use.

PERFORMANCE

Jaguar lacks the Mach 2 performance of rival types such as the Mirage F1, having a top speed of Mach 1.6 at 36,000ft (11,000m). At the low altitudes for which it was designed, a clean aircraft can

comfortably out-run first- and second-generation MiG-21 Fishbeds, and is marginally faster than the third-generation Fishbeds, managing Mach 1.1 at sea level.

The aircraft is in its element at low level. For most of the time, the Adours are running at more than 90 per cent of full rpm, operating at high efficiency. Under the same conditions, a Mach 2 type would be running its engines at a less efficient 70 to 80 per cent of full rpm. This feature, coupled with the low specific fuel consumption of the Adour, gives the Jaguar a long range—460nm (852km) hi-lo-hi, and 290nm (537km) lo-lo-lo. These figures

assume the use of internal fuel only. If underwing tanks are carried, range is increased by 65 to 70 per cent.

A tactical support aircraft needs to be able to operate from short strips. Given a payload of four 1,000lb (450kg) bombs, the Jaguar needs only 2,890ft (880m) of runway. Even with eight such bombs, take-off run is only marginally above the 4,000ft (1,200m) airstrip length assumed when the Fairchild A-10 was designed.

Some export customers operate Jaguar as a general purpose fighter, and its performance as an interceptor is acceptable. Aircraft fitted with the Adour Mk 804 can

Comparative maximum take-off weights

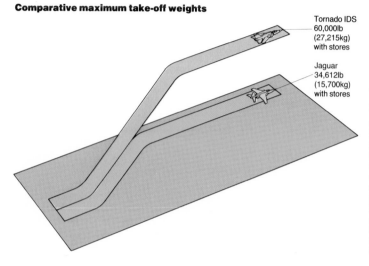

Tornado IDS
60,000lb
(27,215kg)
with stores

Jaguar
34,612lb
(15,700kg)
with stores

Left: Maximum takeoff weight of Jaguar is 34,600lb (15,700kg), just over half that of the 60,000lb (27,200kg) of a fully-loaded Tornado IDS. The Anglo-French aircraft is closer in size to the Mirage F1 and MiG-23 than to the swing-wing Tornado. Despite its small size it has the bomb-carrying capability and range to act as a replacement for much larger and heavier aircraft. The RAF uses it as a replacement for the F-4 Phantom, while in Indian Air Force service, Jaguar meets the Deep Penetration and Strike requirement, replacing the Canberra.

Comparative maximum speeds

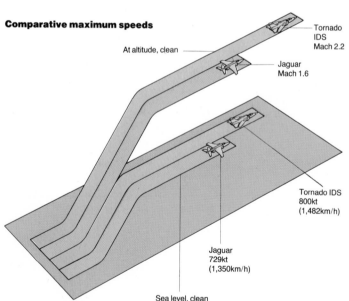

At altitude, clean

Tornado
IDS
Mach 2.2

Jaguar
Mach 1.6

Tornado IDS
800kt
(1,482km/h)

Jaguar
729kt
(1,350km/h)

Sea level, clean

Left: Jaguar's top speed of Mach 1.6 at altitude is well below the Mach 2.2 of Tornado, but sufficient for use by such nations as Oman which deploy it as a dual-role aircraft. At low level the speed difference between the two types is less marked. Jaguar can manage 720kt (1,350km/h) compared with the 800kt (1,480km/h) of Tornado. This lower speed will not represent any major disadvantage under most combat conditions – at low level, a Jaguar can outrun many Mach 2 types. Top speed of the MiG-21MF Fishbed J is only just over 700kt (1,300km/h) at low altitude, a figure exceeded by only the latest MiG-21bis and the MiG-23 Flogger.

Left: The high cruising altitude, large ventral fuel tank and clean configuration (no underwing stores) of this Armée de l'Air Jaguar A strike aircraft suggest the pilot is carrying out a long-range ferry mission.

Right: Although no major mid-life update is planned for RAF Jaguars, equipment such as the ALQ-101 jamming pod and Paveway laser-guided bomb will keep the aircraft combat-effective for some years.

reach 36,000ft (11,000m) in 2.5 minutes. The structure is stressed to accept +8.6g, so the pilot is free to throw the aircraft around in combat, as many a USAF fighter pilot has learned to his cost during Red Flag sorties.

OPERATORS

UK (165 Jaguar S and 38 Jaguar B), France (160 Jaguar A and 40 Jaguar E), Ecuador (12 Jaguar International), India (116 Jaguar International on order), Oman (24 Jaguar International), plus Nigeria (18 Jaguar International on order).

Comparative combat radii (hi-lo-hi)
(with 8,000lb/3,628kg of bombs)

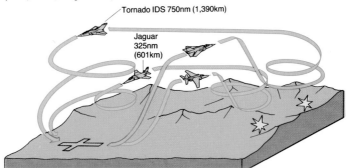

Tornado IDS 750nm (1,390km)

Jaguar 325nm (601km)

Left: Hi-lo-hi strike radius of a Jaguar with eight 1,000lb (450kg) bombs is 325nm (600km), just under half that of a similarly loaded Tornado IDS. The Jaguar hi-lo-hi radius with 4,000lb (1,800kg) of ordnance is 627nm (1,160km), and 770nm (1,425km) with a 2,000lb (900kg) warload. (Figures assume use of Adour Mk811 engines and that external tanks are jettisoned when empty. No combat allowance.)

VOUGHT
A-7 CORSAIR II

DEVELOPMENT

When the Corsair II first entered service, its pilots must have been endlessly faced with sarcastic enquiries from F-8 pilots as to whether the new aircraft had shrunk in the wash. One glance at the A-7 is enough to show its F-8 ancestry, but this subsonic attack aircraft has outlived its supersonic "parent" in the US inventory. Rugged and reliable, it played a major share in the Vietnam War, and recently saw action once more against Syrian missile sites in the Lebanon.

In 1963 the US Navy issued a requirement for a new ground attack aircraft to replace the supersonic A-5 Vigilante bomber and to supplement the McDonnell Douglas A-4 Skyhawk. The latter aircraft was still in production, but lacked the range which USN planners required.

Vought's design was declared the winner of a subsequent design competition, and received a development contract in March 1964. The specification was a tight one, with stringent penalty clauses covering areas such as performance, timescale and reliability. At a time when many aircraft needed 50 or more maintenance manhours per flight hour, the company was prepared to guarantee a figure of only 11.5.

Progress was swift, the first prototype flying ahead of schedule on September 27, 1965, and deliveries to Service units beginning little more than a year later, on October 14, 1966. Total time from start of design to operational service was only

three and a half years—impressive even by the fast-moving standards of the US aerospace industry.

The USAF was also looking for a new attack aircraft, in this case a replacement for the Douglas A-1 Skyraider and North American F-100 Super Sabre. Following a DoD evaluation of the new warplane, USAF decided to swallow its pride and "buy Navy". An order for the A-7D was placed in October 1966, but USAF specified that the type be given greater thrust to suit it to land-based combat, so the TF30 engine was replaced by an Allison/Rolls-Royce TF41-A-1 turbofan. Other features of the A-7D included an integrated nav/attack system, 20mm M61 Vulcan cannon, anti-skid brakes, and an internal engine starter. First flight of this version took place in September 1968.

The USN was taking its own action to boost what was generally accepted as lack of thrust. The A-7B, which flew for the first time in February 1968, used the more powerful P-8 version of the TF30 engine.

By this time, the Corsair programme was of massive size, spurred by the demand for attack aircraft for the Vietnam War. The production rate was to peak at three to four aircraft per day.

The A-7C started life as the A-7E, and

Above: An A-7D Corsair of the USAF lets go Snakeye retarded bombs in a shallow diving attack. Retarded bombs are used for low level delivery, and allow the aircraft to clear the explosion.

Typical weapons: Top: A, external fuel tank; **B**, Durandal ASM; **C**, AGM-65 Maverick; **D**, AIM-9 Sidewinder; **E**, FLIR pod; **F**, M61 20mm cannon. An airfield attack is indicated by the presence of Durandal.

Above: A, M61 cannon; **B**, 5in (12.7cm) rocket launcher; **C**, Rockeye cluster bombs; **D**, AGM-62 Walleye; **E**, external fuel tank. This load is tailored for battlefield or communication route interdiction strikes.

Left: The A-7 Corsair was derived from the F-8 Crusader, and the family resemblance is quite marked. The US Navy specification for which Corsair II was designed required great load carrying capacity, total 15,000lb (6,800kg), but subsonic speed only. Attack Squadron VA-147 introduced the Corsair to combat over Vietnam in December 1967, and it proved very effective in the close air support and ground attack roles. Its versatility is such that it has been calculated that more than 200 different combinations of stores are possible. It can carry the same payload over greater distances than the McDonnell Douglas F-18 which is scheduled to replace it.

Below: A very light attack load for an A-7 of two Mk82 low drag bombs (slicks) on the outboard hardpoints, two Mk82 Snakeye bombs on the central pylons, and 250gal (946lit) drop tanks inboard. The fuselage launching rails for the AIM-9L Sidewinders are its most unusual armament feature. The M61 Vulcan cannon has 1,000 rounds in its magazine, a lot by present standards. The white underfinish attracts attention in the air combat arena; and camouflage on the underside is more usual at the moment.

Below: An A-7D of the 366th TFW. The Corsair is an excellent aircraft in the low level attack role, and squadrons equipped with it have won many competitions. Corsair units are often deployed to Europe.

Vought A-7D Corsair II
1. Pitot tubes.
2. Windscreen rain dispersal ducts.
3. Radar equipment package.
4. Cockpit pressurization valve.
5. Pilot's instrument panel.
6. Head-up display.
7. Control column.
8. Engine throttle lever.
9. McDonnell-Douglas 'Escapac' ejection seat.
10. Cockpit canopy cover.
11. Starboard side cockpit air conditioning pack.
12. Angle of attack transmitter.
13. Canopy jack.
14. Electrical equipment compartment.
15. Starboard side emergency ram air turbine.
16. TACAN aerial.
17. Transformer rectifier unit.
18. Ammunition drum.
19. Air refuelling receptacle.
20. Anti-collision light.
21. Starboard stores pylons.
22. Flap hydraulic jack.
23. Inboard leading edge flap.
24. Starboard wing integral fuel tank.
25. Wing fold hydraulic jack.
26. Outboard leading edge flap.
27. Flap hydraulic jack.
28. Starboard navigation light.
29. Formation light.
30. Aileron hydraulic actuator.
31. Starboard wing folded position.
32. Starboard aileron.
33. Fuel jettison.
34. Plain flap.
35. Spoiler.

36. Spoiler hydraulic actuator.
37. Flap hydraulic jack.
38. Rear fuselage fuel cell.
39. Fuel filler cap.
40. Aileron feel trim control unit.
41. Hydraulic accumulator.
42. Hydraulic reservoir.
43. Rolls-Royce/Allison TF41-A-2 turbofan engine. engine.
44. Tailplane control linkage.
45. Tailplane autopilot controller.
46. Rudder autopilot controller.
47. Starboard all-moving tailplane.
48. VHF aerial.
49. VOR aerial.
50. UHF/IFF aerial.
51. Tail radar warning antenna.
52. Tail navigation light.
53. Radar warning antenna power amplifier.
54. Rudder.
55. Rudder hydraulic actuator.
56. Engine tailpipe.
57. Tailplane mechanical. interconnection.
58. Port all-moving tailplane.

59. Tailplane pivot bearing.
60. Tailplane hydraulic actuator.
61. Chaff/flare dispensers.
62. Arrester hook.
63. Engine accessory equipment gearbox.
64. Arrester hook hydraulic actuator and damper.
65. Port formation light.
66. Port navigation light.
67. Aileron hydraulic actuator.
68. Leading edge flap hydraulic jack.
69. Port leading edge flap.
70. Fuel jettison.
71. Aileron/spoiler interconnecting linkage.
72. Flap hydraulic jack.
73. Wing fold hydraulic jack.

74. Fuel vent mast.
75. Outboard stores pylon.
76. LAU-37 rocket launcher.
77. Port wing integral fuel tank.
78. Forward-retracting mainwheel.
79. Hydraulic retraction jack.

80. Main undercarriage leg pivot bearing.

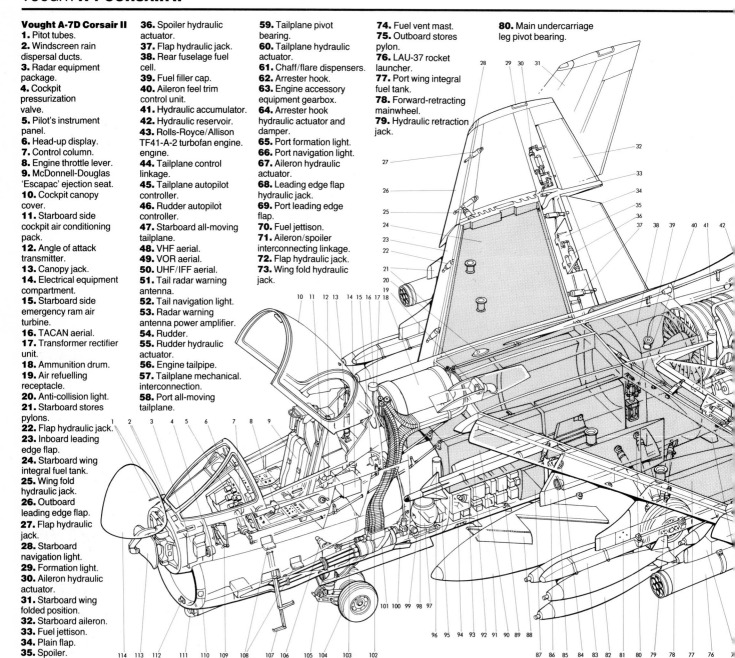

was powered by the TF30-P-408. Only 67 were built, and these were later reclassified as A-7Cs to avoid confusion with the definitive TF41-A-2-powered A-7E. First flight of this aircraft took place in November 1968 and it has been active in Navy service since July 1969.

The Corsair has attracted few export orders. This was hardly the fault of the aircraft, but is more likely to have been due to the availability of the A-4 Skyhawk, particularly from ex-US stocks. Greece has been the only export customer to order new-build aircraft, taking delivery of 60 A-7H, a model based on the USAF A-7E. Portugal was (and still is) desperately short of combat aircraft, and decided that its needs could best be met by purchasing 20 ex-USN A-7As and having these reworked to the A-9P standard by Vought under a $100 million contract. The first rebuilt aircraft flew in July 1981. Deliveries started in August and were completed by early 1982. Later that year, the US agreed to supply 30 more reworked

aircraft (24 single-seaters and six two-seat trainers) under a contract worth more than $200 million.

Several versions of the aircraft were proposed but never built. The A-7G was to be a modified A-7D equipped with the 15,000lb (6,800kg) thrust Allison TF41-A-3 turbofan, and proposed to Switzerland in the late 1960s as a Venom replacement. Having had their fingers badly burned by the Mirage IIIS programme, the Swiss seemed cronically incapable of making up their mind on what aircraft to procure, buying stop-gap batches of Hunters before eventually plumping for the Northrop F-5E. France also evaluated the aircraft—in this case for use on the carriers *Foch* and *Clemenceau*—but decided to back the indigenous Super Etendard project.

Other variants were drawn up in the hope of attracting US orders. The KA-7F would have been a dedicated tanker variant able to lift more than 30,000lb (13,600kg) of fuel in internal and underwing tanks, while other studies looked at

dedicated close-support aircraft literally built around the huge GAU-8/A 30mm cannon of the A-10 Thunderbolt II.

STRUCTURE

When the A-7 design was drawn up, much emphasis was placed—at least in public—on its being largely based on the existing Vought F-8 Crusader. Despite its external similarity to the earlier aircraft, the A-7 was virtually an all-new design.

The wing has the same 35deg sweep that was used on the F-8, but is thicker, housing a greater internal fuel load. Ailerons are located outboard of the wing fold, while spoilers are positioned just ahead of the large slotted trailing-edge flaps. Working in conjunction with full-span leading-edge flaps, the latter give sufficient lift to allow the design team to eliminate the unique variable-incidence wing fitted to the F-8. A total of 482 USN A-7B, A-7E and TA-7C aircraft are being retrofitted with automatic manoeuvring flaps—lead-

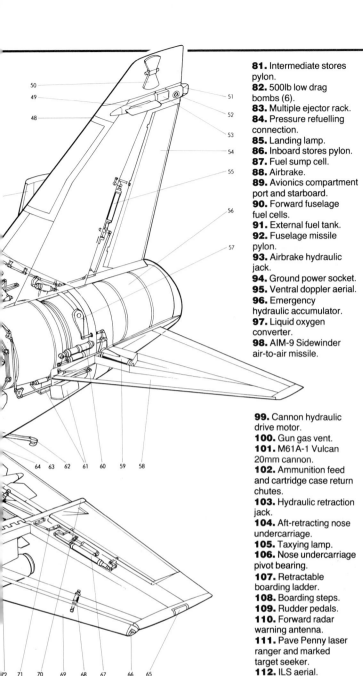

81. Intermediate stores pylon.
82. 500lb low drag bombs (6).
83. Multiple ejector rack.
84. Pressure refuelling connection.
85. Landing lamp.
86. Inboard stores pylon.
87. Fuel sump cell.
88. Airbrake.
89. Avionics compartment port and starboard.
90. Forward fuselage fuel cells.
91. External fuel tank.
92. Fuselage missile pylon.
93. Airbrake hydraulic jack.
94. Ground power socket.
95. Ventral doppler aerial.
96. Emergency hydraulic accumulator.
97. Liquid oxygen converter.
98. AIM-9 Sidewinder air-to-air missile.

99. Cannon hydraulic drive motor.
100. Gun gas vent.
101. M61A-1 Vulcan 20mm cannon.
102. Ammunition feed and cartridge case return chutes.
103. Hydraulic retraction jack.
104. Aft-retracting nose undercarriage.
105. Taxying lamp.
106. Nose undercarriage pivot bearing.
107. Retractable boarding ladder.
108. Boarding steps.
109. Rudder pedals.
110. Forward radar warning antenna.
111. Pave Penny laser ranger and marked target seeker.
112. ILS aerial.
113. Radar scanner dish.
114. Radome.

Above: Few Corsairs have been exported, although Greece's Elliniki Aeroporia has taken delivery of 60 A-7Hs.

Below: An A-7C Corsair of the USN comes aboard (believed to be USS *Forrestal*). Variable incidence wings had been a feature of the Crusader but, judging by the picture, the Corsair approach angle did not warrant them.

ing and trailing-edge surfaces whose extension and retraction will be controlled by the aircraft's flight-control system.

One surprising feature of the fast-moving A-7 programme was the length of time taken to create two-seat trainer versions. A prototype two-seat TA-7A flew as early as February 1962, but a production batch was never funded. The designation A-7C was originally applied to another planned two-seat configuration of the mid-1960s, but this too was never built. In 1971 the USN finally agreed to lend Vought an A-7E for conversion as a private-venture V-519 trainer prototype. This was flown the following August under the designation YA-7H, but no order was placed.

Deployment of trainers had to wait until the late 1970s when 40 A-7Bs and 41 A-7Cs were rebuilt with two seats for the use of replacement training squadrons. The original engines were retained, but the rebuild featured A-7E avionics, revised cockpit, and a new pattern of sideways-opening canopy.

Delivery of new-build trainers started with five TA-7H aircraft for Greece in 1980. Final model was the A-7K, a two-seat derivative of the A-7D. Built for the US Air National Guard, this has an extended fuselage 34in (86cm) longer than the standard pattern. Deliveries started late in 1980. Vought offered the type for export in a last-minute bid to keep the line open, but discussions with Thailand did not result in an order.

Having large inventories of A-7s, both the USAF and USN are now updating these aircraft. USN A-7s will be replaced by the F-18 Hornet, with the first two squadrons converting in 1984. Under present plans, the last A-7s will be retired in 1990.

The configuration of the semi-monocoque fuselage resembles that of the F-8, but is shorter and more compact, giving the aircraft the appearance which earned it the nickname SLUF (Short Little Ugly Fella). Armour was used to protect the cockpit and vital systems. This originally

took the form of steel and aluminium plating, but later models of the aircraft introduced lightweight but effective boron-carbide material.

Critical components are duplicated or even triplicated as an aid to combat survivability. The rudder has dual hydraulic systems, for example, while the all-moving horizontal stabiliser has triplicated hydraulics. A large speedbrake located beneath the fuselage has recently been the subject of modification work on US Navy aircraft.

Some 50 per cent of the total skin area of the A-7 is made up of removable panels intended to give the ground crews good access to the avionics and other systems. The structure was designed to have a service life of 8,000 hours.

POWERPLANT

The A-7A was fitted with the TF30-P-6 turbofan rated at 11,350lb (5,148kg) thrust, while the more powerful TF30-P-8 of

12,200lb (5,534kg) thrust was used in the A-7B, A-7C and TA-7C. The USAF's requirement for greater thrust would have pushed the TF30 to its limits, and consideration was given to using a limited degree of afterburning for use during take-off and combat.

The possibility of using the Rolls-Royce Spey turbofan as a powerplant for export aircraft had been studied, and problems with the TF30 led to suggestions that a US-built Spey could be used in place of the P&W powerplant. In 1965, Rolls-Royce and Allison proposed the Allison 912, a developed and uprated Spey, as a non-afterburning engine able to meet the USAF requirement. It was duly accepted for service and put into production by the US partner.

The A-7D is fitted with the TF41-A-1 of 14,500lb (6,577kg) thrust, while the USN A-7E has the slightly uprated TF41-A-2 offering up to 15,000lb (6,804kg). Greek A-7H aircraft have the TF41-A-2 offering up to 15,000lb (6,804kg). Greek A-7H aircraft have the TF41-A-400, similar in rating to the A-2.

Problems with the hot sections of the Allison engine resulted in a series of engine failures and the temporary grounding of the A-7D. Under an $83.1 million modification programme, the USAF is fitting the engine with redesigned blades and a new pattern of HP turbine. A USN Hot-Section Extended Life Programme for the TF-41 involves a redesign of the engine to improve reliability and reduce the risk of turbine failure. Another modification scheme upgrades the fuel-gauging system in order to increase reliability.

The Pratt & Whitney TF30 engine was to be installed in one final version of the aircraft, the A-7P (reworked A-7As) of the Portuguese Air Force. These are fitted with the 13,400lb (6,078kg) TF30-P-408.

For a once-planned A-7X twin-engined variant, Vought proposed to use either a single General Electric F110 (at that time known as the F101 DFE) or two GE F404 turbofans. Details of both engines may be found in the F-16 and F-18 entries.

AVIONICS

For the A-7A, a Texas Instruments APQ-116 multi-mode radar, a navigation computer, Doppler radar and roller-map display were fitted. For the A-7D, the USAF specified a more complex installation including an APQ-126 multi-mode radar, a British-built HUD, a projected-map display, a digital computer and inertial navigation. With the -7E, the USN adopted a similar avionics standard, but added its own navigation, ECM and communications equipment. Under a retrofit programme, a new pattern of digital scan converter and CRT replaces two existing line-replaceable units (LRUs) in the APQ-126 radar display of the A-7D, increasing MTBF from 80hr to 500hr.

Some 200 A-7Es will be equipped with Westinghouse Pave Penny Laser Search/Track (LST) sensors. FLIR systems were installed on late-production A-7Es, but the

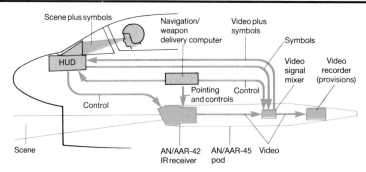

Labels on diagram: Scene plus symbols · Navigation/weapon delivery computer · Video plus symbols · Symbols · HUD · Video signal mixer · Video recorder (provisions) · Pointing and controls · Control · Control · Scene · AN/AAR-42 IR receiver · AN/AAR-45 pod · Video

Left: FLIR (forward looking infra-red) is used to detect and identify targets at night. The IR picture is displayed on the HUD.

Below: The final version of the SLUF: the two seater TA-7K, built for the Air National Guard. Note the wrap-around camouflage scheme of this aircraft.

USN is retrofitting 160 earlier A-6Es with wing-mounted FLIR pods and video recorders.

Retrofitting of Maverick to FLIR-equipped A-7Es requires the addition of a digital encoder/decoder to process the data needed in order to slew the missile seeker head, plus modifications to the TC-2A computer, APQ-126 radar, HUD, armament station control unit, and aircraft wiring. Basic RWR was the ALR-45/50, but another programme retrofitted the APR-43 Compass Sail/Clockwise, an RWR of advanced design. A-7C, A-7E and TA-7C aircraft were all fitted with the ALQ-126 internally-mounted jammer, but this is now being supplemented by the new ALQ-162.

Avionics standard of the Greek A-7H and Portuguese A-7P is similar to that of the A-7E. As part of the rework programme, the obsolete systems of the -7P were replaced by a new weapons aiming computer, inertial navigation system, and head-up display.

ARMAMENT

Three stores pylons are fitted to each wing, each having a built-in loading hoist, and two further hardpoints are located on the fuselage sides. The A-7D can carry two Sidewinder or Maverick missiles on its fuselage hardpoints, plus up to 15,000lb (6,800kg) of ordnance under the wings. Payload of the -7E is similar, but also includes Walleye "smart" bombs and Harpoon anti-ship missiles or HARM anti-radar missiles. HARM capability was introduced by the same package of modifications as was dictated by Maverick.

As internal gun armament, the USN selected a pair of Mk12 20mm cannon, each with 250 rounds of ammunition, but this relatively slow-firing weapon was replaced on the A-7D and -7E by a single 20mm M61 Vulcan rotary cannon located on the port side of the fuselage. This has 1,000 rounds of ammunition.

Possible weapons, A-7E:
1. M61 20mm cannon with 1,000 rounds.
2. GP bombs.
3. Chemical/fire bombs.
4. Cluster bombs.
5. Mines (land or naval).
6. Dispensers, ECM/IRCM.
7. Flares and sonobuoys.
8. External fuel tanks.
9. ECM jamming pods.
10. FLIR pod.
11. Special weapons.
12. Nuclear weapons.
13. AIM-9 Sidewinders
14. Air-to-ground missiles.
15. Smart bombs (EO/LGB).
16. Rocket launchers
17. Training weapons. Hardpoint capacities are as follows: outboard wing and centre wing, 3,500lb (1,588kg); inboard wing 2,500lb (1,134kg); fuselage points 360lb (163kg).

Right: Three A-7Ds of the 355th TFW set out from Davis Monthan AFB on a practice bombing mission. The small practice bombs can be clearly seen on the underwing pylons. The centre aircraft is a later production model.

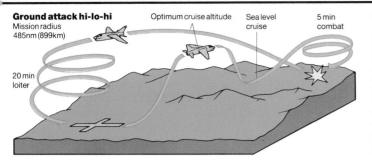

Ground attack hi-lo-hi
Mission radius 485nm (899km)

Optimum cruise altitude

Sea level cruise

5 min combat

20 min loiter

Left: An A-7E laden with 12 Mk82 bombs and two Sidewinders, using a hi-lo-hi profile at optimum height out and back, with a 50nm (92km) low level cruise to the target, has a radius of action of 485nm (890km). Fuel for 5 min combat at full throttle, and 20 min loiter time at sea level back at the parent carrier is allowed for.

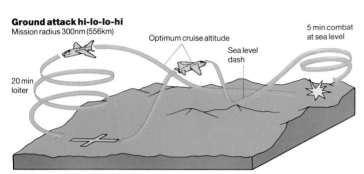

Ground attack hi-lo-lo-hi
Mission radius 300nm (556km)

Optimum cruise altitude

Sea level dash

5 min combat at sea level

20 min loiter

Left: Against defended targets, a hi-lo-lo-hi profile is safer, but reduces the mission radius. Configured as above, with the same loiter and full throttle combat allowances, but flying at low level at 500kt (920km/h), when within 120nm (220km) of the target, the mission radius is reduced to 300nm (550km). Low level flight is heavy on fuel.

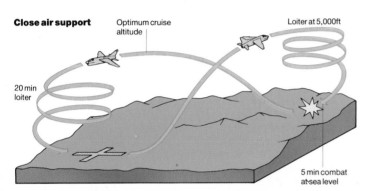

Close air support

Optimum cruise altitude

Loiter at 5,000ft

20 min loiter

5 min combat at sea level

Left: Close air support demands loiter time for target designation or marking by Forward Air Controllers, or from the ground. Flying at optimum cruise altitude both in and outbound, and with the same loiter and combat allowances, the A-7E can remain on station at 5,000ft (1,500m) for 100 min at 100nm (184km) radius, but only 20 min at a radius of 400nm (735km).

PERFORMANCE

Payload/range figures were the key aspects of the VAL specification to which the A-7 was designed. The USN wanted to be able to carry up to 3,600lb (1,630kg) of ordnance over a combat radius of 600nm (1,110km) from an aircraft carrier, or 7,500lb (3,400kg) of ordnance on a close-support mission up to 200nm (370km) from a land base.

Even the underpowered A-7A was a great improvement over the A-4 Skyhawk, demonstrating an ability to outperform the older aircraft by a factor of two, carrying either twice the payload or the same payload twice as far.

Top speed of the A-7 is 600kt (1,112km/h) at sea level, and the A-7E can maintain 562kt (1,040km/h) at 5,000ft (1,500m) when loaded up with 12 Mk 82 500lb (230kg) bombs. Tactical radius with this payload is 450nm (835km) in a hi-lo-hi flight profile. Given a 3,000lb (1,350kg) warload, it can get airborne from 4,000ft (1,220m) airstrips.

Combat ceiling is only 42,000ft (13,000m) but, like the larger F-111, the Corsair II is intended to spend its life at medium cruise altitudes, dropping to treetop height during attacks. In its element, the A-7 is a nimble opponent. Fighter pilots attempting to close with it in combat would do well to remember that at 500kt (925km/h) at 5,000ft (1,500m), a lightly-loaded A-7 has a turning radius of only 5,500ft (1,770m)—the Sidewinder missiles often carried on the fuselage hardpoints are not just for show!

ADVANCED TECHNOLOGY AIRCRAFT

With a new generation of Soviet fighters entering service and the first signs of a further generation to supplement them, the West cannot rely on the aircraft described in this volume if the balance of tactical air power is to be maintained in the 1990s.

But the main problem in creating tomorrow's fighters is that of cost. Most of the technical features which will be needed are already taking shape in the laboratories but, if sizeable numbers of new aircraft are to be taken into service, some attempt must be made to restrain the spiralling costs of advanced warplanes.

One thing likely to be common to all the next generation of Western fighters is an emphasis on high manoeuvrability and survivability. The Mach 2 "speed plateau" reached by the late 1950s designs such as the F-4 and Mirage III will still be accepted as a limitation of aircraft currently on the drawing board.

Key points of all the new fighter projects to be described below are maximum turn rate—both instantaneous and sustained (limited by lift and thrust respectively)—and specific excess power. For the moment, Mach 3 to 4 fighters and even more exotic "space planes" remain in the realm of advanced studies, and are likely to remain so unless the Soviet Union's Ramenskoye flight-test centre produces any surprises.

The advantages of recent techniques—such as variable-camber wings, lift-generating strakes and aeroelastic surfaces whose stiffness is tailored to suit the expected flight conditions—can be fully utilised only if fully active fly-by-wire (FBW) controls are used in order to augment stability and adjust the manoeuvrability to match wing incidence. This must involve eliminating the mechanical backup controls fitted to earlier fighters, but can allow the pilot to fly his mount right to the limits of its performance, ignoring the risk of spinning or over-stressing the aircraft. The pilot simply makes control demands, and relies on the flight-control system to "interpret" them in the optimum manner, moving the control surfaces so that the last few per cent of performance is provided to make the difference between success and failure in combat flying. No human pilot could perform this task unaided, or cope with the inherent instability of aircraft designs intended to offer the maximum manoeuvrability.

In addition to exotic aerodynamics and FBW control systems, most of the designs under consideration in the West have other common features, such as canard layouts. Until the arrival of FBW, only the Viggen had successfully used the canard layout, but a modern "smart" flight-control system makes such configurations as efficient as a conventional tailed design in subsonic cruise conditions. At high incidence the wing and foreplane work together to provide increased lift while at supersonic speeds the aft movement of the centre of lift of the wing and foreplane demand that the latter be used to create upload for trimming purposes, a more useful force than the download associated with conventional tails.

Coordinated movement of the foreplane, flaps and rudder could be used to offer direct-lift control, allowing the aircraft fuselage to be moved about the current line of flight without pitching, yawing or rolling movements. This type of unconventional flight is currently being explored by the canard-equipped experimental AFTI/F-16, but it is too early to predict the degree to which it will be exploited in the coming generation of fighters.

Another common feature of most designs is the large-scale use of composite materials as a means of keeping airframe weight down and minimising the radar cross-section of the aircraft. Carbon composite materials do not suffer from fatigue in the same way that metals do (promising maintenance bills), although they do suffer problems at high temperatures and in the presence of moisture.

THE STEALTH FIGHTER

Most mysterious of the new projects currently on US drawing boards is the Stealth Fighter currently being developed by Lockheed. This may be the project referred to as CSIRS (Covert Survivable In-Weather Reconnaissance Strike Aircraft). The US Defense Advanced Research Projects Agency (DARPA) is known to be involved in a project known as XST (Experimental Stealth Tactical), perhaps an alternative designation for the same aircraft.

Stealth involves not a single technology, but a blending of several established techniques. Careful shaping of an airframe can

Below: The AFTI/F-16 is not planned as an operational fighter, but is exploring new methods of combat flight. The USAF is confident that the hardware can outfly conventional designs, but sceptics wonder if the pilot will cope with the manoeuvres the canards will permit.

Above: The sleek and smoothly blended lines of the B-1 bomber are among factors which reduce its radar cross-section, early "stealth" technology which is being applied to new Western fighter designs. Other stealth features include masking of heat emission and low radar reflectivity of materials. This B-1A is on "B" tests.

greatly reduce the amount of radar energy it reflects, while the use of radar-absorbing material can cause still greater reduction in the radar "signature". Stealth designs avoid flat surfaces and sharp angles which can serve as radar reflectors, smooth shapes being used with the aim of deflecting rather than reflecting the incoming radar energy. Some evidence of this design technique may be seen in the shape of the Rockwell B-1 bomber. Specific airframe features which require careful shaping and the use of radar-absorbing material include air intakes and the leading edges of all aerodynamic surfaces.

The use of advanced materials such as carbon or even more exotic composites can also reduce radar cross-section. The degree to which such materials are used in US Stealth projects may be gauged by the tight-lipped response to any enquiries relating to the electrical properties of composites.

A typical jet fighter such as the F-4 has a radar cross-section of around 2sq m, but in the new Stealth designs this is reduced by a factor of 100 or more. Some reports even talk of radar cross sections of less than one millionth of a square metre.

The techniques described so far are purely passive, but Stealth aircraft will also rely on the use of deceptive electronic countermeasures. Given the fact that the aircraft returns only a minute radar echo, the ECM designer can proceed to mask this by means of false target returns intended to mislead radars as to the size, nature, position and course of the aircraft.

Stealth technology is highly classified by the US Government, and the companies involved with such work maintain a rigid level of security. Early "leaks" of information were ruthlessly suppressed on the orders of the US Government, and in some plants Stealth-related work is carried out in areas of the facility off-limits to most employees.

Several aircraft have been test flown, mostly from a classified site in Nevada. These are thought to be technology demonstrators rather than prototype fighters, and to be in the 20,000lb (10,000kg) class. Since flights started in 1979 several have crashed. Details of the aircraft are fragmentary, but one design is understood to resemble the lifting bodies tested by NASA in the late 1960s. Designations reported for "stealth fighter" projects in-

Below: The flat bottom and dorsal intake of this Grumman artist's stealth proposal are to reduce its radar cross-section from below, while engine exhausts in upper fuselage could screen the engine hot section from the attention of missiles launched from below.

clude F-19 and at least one YO-series number.

Possible features of an operational Stealth Fighter could include:
- large-scale wing-body blending;
- a wing of delta planform perhaps incorporating buried engines;
- rounded leading edges on all aerodynamic surfaces;
- absence of a conventional vertical fin in favour of winglets or a vee-tail;
- cranked inlet ducts which take the incoming air through a zig-zag route to the engine;
- jetpipes fitted with extensive infra-red suppression devices;
- a radar using spread-spectrum techniques to make interception of its emissions unlikely;
- millimetre-wave radio transceivers for short-range air-to-air communications;
- frequency-hopping radio transceivers for long-range communications;
- advanced electro-optical sensors for long-range target identification and tracking.

Every effort will be made to reduce the distinctive radio/radar "signature" of the aircraft. Conventional radio and radar transmissions effectively yell "Here I am!" to modern ESM sensors and data processing systems, so the Stealth Fighter will either use passive sensors which do not involve transmission, or rely on spread-spectrum techniques to "bury" the transmission among the normal background of radio/radar signals. The use of low-power millimetre-wave transmissions for communications between aircraft in a formation relies upon the fact that highly-directional but compact "smart" antennas may be used accurately to beam the radio energy in the direction of the intended recipient, while the high level of signal attenuation associated with such frequencies (due to absorption by atmospheric water vapour) will make it difficult for hostile eavesdroppers not directly on the line-of-sight of the transmission to detect and intercept the signal.

USAF's ADVANCED TACTICAL FIGHTER

The most important of the non-Stealth USAF fighter projects is the Advanced Tactical Fighter (ATF) programme. This is intended to develop a next-generation fighter able to handle the air-to-air and air-to-ground missions of the mid-1990s and beyond. The project is currently at the concept-definition stage. Emerging technologies in the areas of aerodynamics, propulsion, materials, manufacturing techniques, and avionics will be used to create an aircraft capable of operating in darkness and adverse weather, and of coping with the predicted threat systems which the Warsaw Pact will be able to develop and deploy.

Above: Artist's impression of an advanced STOL version of the F-15 Eagle. The inlet-mounted canards and thrust-vectoring engine nozzles of rectangular cross-section would be linked to an advanced flight-control system, resulting in increased lift, reduced drag and greater manoeuvrability.

Air Force programme PE 63230F contains parallel development projects for the new fighter and its advanced-technology engine. Concept definition study contracts were awarded to Boeing, General Dynamics, Grumman, Lockheed, McDonnell Douglas, Northrop and Rockwell in June 1983. Once these are completed in 1984, the USAF requirement will be reviewed, then one or more designs will be selected for further development. Most of the initial development funding will be allocated to the design of a new engine (perhaps featuring a vectored-thrust nozzle) with the aircraft itself and the demonstration of some of the required technology being assigned a lower priority.

There are no plans for a competitive fly-off; the USAF hopes to select a single contractor and aircraft design which should begin flight testing in 1987. Full-scale development of the aircraft (the task of converting the flight-demonstrator prototype into a Service aircraft) is scheduled for Fiscal Year 1987, while a production decision is required in FY 1990. If the planned 1995 operational date is not to slip, the programme must remain on the timescale indicated. By the end of this decade, the USAF will probably have spent almost $4,000 million on development of the new fighter and its engine.

Left: Dornier and Northrop have collaborated on this design for a lightweight agile ND-102 fighter for the Luftwaffe. The aircraft has a unique trapezoidal wing, no horizontal stabiliser, and non-afterburning engines featuring vectored thrust.

Above: The "canopy" on the Rockwell HiMAT (Highly Manoeuvrable Aircraft Technology) is a dummy. This structural and flight-control research aircraft is air- launched from under the wing of a B-52 then flown remotely by a ground-based pilot who "sees" the external view via a TV camera inside the "canopy".

One current project is already developing some of the technology which could be applied to the ATF. Scheduled to fly in the autumn of 1984, the Grumman X-29A Forward Swept Wing (FSW) Aircraft is being developed for the Flight Dynamics Laboratory of the USAF Wright Aeronautical Laboratories at Wright Patterson AFB, Ohio, and the NASA Dryden Flight Research Center at Edwards AFB, California. The project started in 1977 with the award of initial study contracts to General Dynamics, Grumman and Rockwell International.

Potential advantages inherent in FSW designs over conventional aft-swept wings include higher maximum lift, reduced drag, lower stalling speed, better low-speed manoeuvrability, and improved distribution of internal fuselage volume. A FSW tactical fighter could be up to 30 per cent lighter than a conventional design, resulting in improved payload/range performance and lower cost. Tests with models also suggest that such aircraft will have good short take-off and landing (STOL) capability without the need for conventional high-lift devices or vectored-thrust engines (like the Harrier's). Aircraft of this type could be operated from short airstrips, taxiways, straight lengths of road, or from small aircraft carriers.

Right: Although the long-term usefulness of forward swept wings seems promising, some experts question whether successful flight testing of the unique Grumman X-29A demonstrator will make forward-swept wing technology mature enough for use on the new fighters.

The design, fabrication and testing of large-scale aeroelastically-tailored test structures successfully solved the divergence problem inherent in FSW design without appreciable increase in weight, while a suitable fly-by-wire flight control system was designed and successfully tested.

In 1980 the individual companies submitted proposals for a manned flight-demonstrator aircraft. This led early in 1981 to the selection of the Grumman proposal. Two single-seat X-29A test aircraft are to be built and flown. To speed the programme and save money, components from existing aircraft are being pressed into service wherever possible. The nose section and cockpit are from the Northrop F-5E, the landing gear is from the General

Dynamics F-16A, while the single GE F404 turbofan engine is used on the McDonnell Douglas F-18, Northrop F-20 and Swedish JA-39 Gripen. These proven components are being mated with new centre and aft fuselage sections and a supercritical wing made from composites. The X-29A is 48ft (14.6m) long, 27ft (12.2m) in wingspan, and weighs 11,300lb (5,125kg) empty. Maximum fuel load is 3,000lb (1,350kg), and the maximum take-off weight will be around 14,800lb (6,700kg).

The first X-29A has already been assembled and is due to fly in the autumn of 1984 after a series of static tests. Construction of the second has already begun. Once initial flight testing by company pilots has been completed, the two aircraft will be

delivered to NASA's Dryden Flight Research Center. Following flight testing by NASA personnel supported by the USAF, the aircraft will probably undergo further trials tailored to future Service requirements. Grumman anticipates a top speed of Mach 1.6 for the X-29A, and expects it to sustain a 5.5g turn at Mach 0.9 and 30,000ft (9,000m) and 5.1g at Mach 1.2.

EUROPE'S FUTURE FIGHTERS

Much publicity has been given to Western European attempts to develop a lightweight fighter able to replace tactical fighters such as the Mirage III, Mirage F1, Jaguar, F-104S and F-4 Phantom currently deployed by the air arms of Britain, France, Italy and West Germany, but which will need to be replaced in the early 1990s. A common requirement exists for an all-weather multirole type able to fly air-superiority and ground-attack missions.

British Aerospace, MBB and Aeritalia are promoting a joint design based on the earlier BAe P.110 and MBB TKF-90 projects. Known as the Agile Combat Aircraft (ACA), this design was unveiled at the 1982 Farnborough Air Show as a replacement for the earlier European Combat Aircraft (ECA) tri-national programme. ACA is a twin-engine delta-wing aircraft powered by two developed Turbo Union RB.199 turbofans and weighing between 30,000 and 40,000lb (13,500 and 18,000kg). Only the British government was prepared to back the project, announcing at the 1983 Paris Air Show a $180 million programme covering the construction and flight test of a single experimental prototype. Funding would be split 50:50 between the British Ministry of Defence and aerospace industry. Designated the Experimental Aircraft Prototype (EAP), this is intended to serve as a technology demonstrator for the Agile Combat Aircraft, and will fly in 1986. The other Panavia partners are expected to participate in the programme, despite the absence of a firm commitment by their governments to the ACA.

Above: If the political will of the British, German and Italian governments matches the determination of their aerospace industries, the Agile Combat Aircraft could fly in the late 1990s. The project is currently funded by the UK MoD and with company money.

Right: The design of the Agile Combat Aircraft (now part of the UK's Experimental Aircraft Programme) is based on the earlier MBB TKF-90 and BAe P.110. BAe abandoned side intakes in favour of the MBB's ventral design, allowing a single design to be agreed.

France used the same air show to unveil its national project, a twin-engined ACX design under development by Dassault-Breguet. This is a technology demonstrator for an eventual ACT production aircraft. The prototype will be powered by two General Electric F404 turbofans, but any production design would receive the new SNECMA M88 currently under development in France, but this would not be available in time for use in the experimental ACX.

Much of the technology needed for the ACA is already being developed. MBB planners, working on the assumption that a future combat aircraft would have some 40 per cent of its structural weight and 70 per cent of its surface made from carbon-fibre composites, have designed a complete forward fuselage with 120sq ft (11.2sq m) composite side shells. At BAe, designers have built a number of experimental composite components including Jaguar engine-bay doors, a Tornado taileron, a complete Jaguar wing, and a bonded front fuselage section.

ACA's canard layout and artificially-maintained longitudinal stability results in 35 per cent more lift than could be obtained from a conventional wing/tail design of equivalent size. The all-moving foreplanes will work asymmetrically to control roll, and move symmetrically with the flaperons on the wing to control pitch. The twin fins and rudders will provide the surface area needed to ensure good directional stability and turn co-ordination up to the highest angles of incidence likely to be met in combat.

The FBW flight-controls will use a four-channel digital system, and experimental

Left: Seen from above, the air intakes of the Dassault-Breguet ACX are masked by the wings and canards. A prototype powered by GE F404 turbofans will fly in 1986; production aircraft would have a French engine now being developed.

hardware is being flight tested in a heavily-modified Jaguar testbed. Data transmission within the aircraft will probably be by means of optical fibres.

Although the systems of a production aircraft would be built internationally, the equipment used in the EAP prototype are likely to be the British units originally intended for the P.110. Wherever possible, these were to have been derived from existing equipment.

Maximum potential thrust of the basic RB.199 is around 17,000lb (7,710kg), some 1,000lb (450kg) more than that of the existing Service version. ACA would use the considerably developed RB.199-67 version. Higher operating temperatures, improved compressor and turbine stages, plus digital controls will probably be used to provide the extra thrust needed for ACA. Maximum thrust of the RB.199-67 will be around 21,000lb (9,525kg), giving a fully loaded aircraft a combat thrust-to-weight ratio (with 50 per cent fuel remaining) of better than 1:1. The location of the twin vertical stabilisers—directly above the engine nozzles—seems to rule out the use of vectored thrust to maximise manoeuvrability.

The UK is still putting some design effort into next-generation vertical take-off and short take-off designs. Configurations publicly revealed include the P.1214, a Mach 2 design incorporating a forward-

swept wing and Rolls-Royce vectored-thrust powerplant with plenum-chamber burning.

In many ways the French ACX flight demonstrator will be similar to the British-backed ACA. The most obvious external differences are the use of a single large vertical fin (Dassault refused to follow the current fashion for twin verticals), canards placed higher on the fuselage and further to the rear (improving the pilot's view), plus the novel intake position on the lower sides of the fuselage. The last feature is almost certainly intended to reduce the radar cross-section as seen from above by an enemy aircraft equipped with lookdown radar.

Dassault estimates the likely cost of the ACX programme at 1,800 million francs—the equivalent of around $125 million. The aircraft will fly in 1986, the same year as the ACA. If France opts to press ahead with the definitive ACT design, the national defence budget will have to cope with the strain of developing the aircraft, the M88 engine, the radar and other avionics.

SWEDEN'S NEW FIGHTER

Having developed the highly successful Viggen, Sweden was forced to spend much time during the late 1970s in devising a suitable replacement. The mainten-

ance of a national aerospace industry has always been important to the Swedes, but rising costs made it look increasingly likely that Viggen would be the end of the line.

In early 1980 the Swedish Parliament finally approved the development of a new aircraft to replace the Viggen, so an industry group, (Saab-Scania, Volvo Flygmotor, LM Ericsson, and SRA Communications) was formed to draw up proposals, which were submitted in June 1981.

Following an evaluation of the proposed Jakt Attack Spaning (Fighter, Attack, Reconnaissance) design, plus foreign types such as F-16, F-18, F-18L, F-20 (at that time still known as the F-5G) and Mirage 2000, the new aircraft was approved by the Swedish Armed Forces, then by Parliament. In June 1982, a contract for the development plus production of the first 30 aircraft was formally signed.

The JAS-39 Gripen is a lightweight multirole aircraft only about half the size of the Viggen, but with comparable "straightline" performance, greatly improved avionics, and agility in the class of the F-16. Wing span is approximately 26ft 3in (8.0m), while the maximum take-off weight is expected to be 17,600lb (8,000kg).

In order to reduce development costs and technical risk, Sweden decided to seek help from overseas. To power the new aircraft, the group selected an uprated version of the General Electric F404 turbofan. Rated at 18,000lb (8,165kg) in afterburner, this will be developed to meet Swedish requirements by a joint GE/Volvo Flygmotor effort. The Swedish company will build much of the engine, and handle final assembly.

Saab-Scania planned to make extensive use of composite materials in the wing of the JAS-39, and signed a short-lived agreement with Rockwell under which the US company could have produced the wings for the first six aircraft. They would have been of advanced design, but the Royal Swedish Air Force decided that the anticipated performance was not worth the likely cost. A new deal with British Aerospace will see these first prototype and ground-test wings designed and built in the UK, with production deliveries being the responsibility of Saab-Scania.

Five prototypes are to be built, with the first to fly in 1987. This trials fleet is being supplemented by two modified Viggens being used for system development. (The first is flight-testing the FBW flight-control system, while the second will be used for avionics testing.)

The radar for the new fighter will be developed by L.M. Ericsson, with assistance from Ferranti in areas such as the antenna and signal-processing. Smaller and lighter than the set carried by Viggen, it will have a similar performance and more operating modes. Hughes Aircraft is developing the HUD and will deliver the first unit for flight testing in mid-1984. Design of the flight-control system is being assisted by Lear Siegler.

Service deliveries of the new fighter are due to begin in 1992, with all 140 aircraft currently planned being handed over by the end of the decade. Follow-on orders could take the final production run to more than 300 aircraft. The only variant being considered is a two-seater for use as a trainer and special-mission aircraft. Any decision on the future of this is unlikely to be taken until 1985.

LIGHTWEIGHT FIGHTER FOR ISRAEL

In order to replace its current Kfir, F-4 Phantom and A-4 Skyhawk fighters, Israel has started the development of a new lightweight fighter. The Israel Aircraft Industries Lavi is being configured for the air-to-ground role, but will have secondary air-to-air capability.

Work on a new fighter started in the late 1970s under a short-lived project designated Arye. Work on this was halted, ostensibly when it became obvious that the US Government would veto any export sales of the type. Attempts in the late 1970s to get coproduction rights for either the General Dynamics F-16 or Northrop F-18L were unsuccessful, but the US Government approved the export of the GE F404 engine as the powerplant of a new Israeli fighter in April 1980.

Although Israel was in fact to reject the GE engine a year later in favour of the Pratt

Above: Artist's impression of the JAS-39 Gripen (Griffon) lightweight fighter intended to replace the Viggen in Swedish service. Development is being assisted by the UK and USA, and the first prototype is due to fly in 1987. A two-seat trainer is also being considered.

& Whitney PW1120, the fact that a US engine would have been available seems to have cleared the way for development of the aircraft now known as Lavi. The decision to proceed was taken early in 1982, the eventual goal of the project being to field some 300 aircraft starting in the early 1990s.

Currently still in the early design stage, Lavi is a lightweight single-engined fighter of delta-wing configuration. Advanced technology such as composite structures, a canard configuration, and sophisticated avionics including a fly-by-wire control system will be used.

A key feature of the project is substantial technical cooperation from the US aerospace industry, particularly in the fields of flight control and advanced composites. This help was not initially forthcoming, following a US Government veto on US industrial participation, imposed as a result of the Israeli invasion of Lebanon. The US aerospace industry had also expressed concern that the new fighter might capture export orders which might otherwise have gone to the USA.

On June 1 Grumman was chosen to develop and produce composite wings and vertical stabilisers for Lavi, the initial contract covering development, and the production of the first 20 shipsets of components. Subsequent transfer of the appropriate technology to IAI to permit local manufacture seems unlikely. The current US DoD position is that sensitive composite-material technology will not be transferred to Israel.

The design has already been frozen, and the first aircraft is due to fly in February 1986 with the first production aircraft to be delivered in June 1988. A go-ahead on series production is tentatively planned for April 1987. Operational testing and evaluation of pre-series aircraft should begin in 1990, but it is likely that a production decision will have been taken before then, probably in the first half of 1987.

Deliveries to front-line units could begin by 1992, and the IDFAF hopes to receive around 300 aircraft—240 single-seat fighters and 60 two-seat trainers. Unit cost of the aircraft is likely to be between $11 million and $13 million, with the total cost of development and production being between $6,000 million and $7,000 million. Much of this money will come from US Foreign Military Sales Credits. Late in 1983, the Reagan Administration announced its approval for Israeli plans to use such US funds for work to be carried out within Israel.

Few details of the Lavi design have been published. The design seems almost a hybrid of the European ACA and ACX, with a simple delta wing, single tail fin, and ventral air intake. It will be smaller than Kfir, only 41ft (12.5m) in length with a wing area of 350sq ft (32.5sq m). Maxi-

Below: Development of the Israel Aircraft Industries Lavi light fighter will pose a considerable strain on Israel's war-torn and inflation-wracked economy, so the type's future is far from secure. This drawing shows the canard configuration and a payload of Maverick and Python 3 missiles. The latter is an indigenously developed "dogfight" weapon.

Above: A significant setback to the joint Italian/Brazilian AMX STOL strike fighter programme occurred early in the flight-test programme when the first prototype was written off in an emergency landing during its fifth test flight. Construction of further prototypes continues.

mum take-off weight will be around 30,000lb (13,500kg), and typical combat weight for air-to-air combat around 18,700lb (8,500kg). Thrust:weight ratio will be greater than unity; maximum speed around Mach 1.85.

A high priority has been placed on instantaneous turn rate, recent Middle East combat experience having convinced the IDFAF that the ability to point the nose of a fighter directly at the target during a dogfight is essential.

The wing will have full-span trailing edge flaperons plus a movable outboard leading edge. These may be moved differentially for roll control. Lavi will be fully unstable, but "tamed" by a quadruplex fly-by-wire control system. The most critical items of avionics will be developed in Israel. Elta is working on a new multi-mode radar incorporating a programmable signal processor, also on the aircraft's wide-angle HUD and EW systems.

The IDFAF represents a "captive market" for Lavi, but exports beyond the 300 likely to be accepted by that air arm are unlikely. Attempts to offer Kfir on the international marketplace have been hampered by US Government vetoes of re-exports of the J79 powerplant; the same situation is likely to apply in the case of Lavi.

LIGHTWEIGHT STOL AT MINIMUM COST

Although in most respects a conventional design rather than what might be considered an advanced-technology fighter, the AMX light strike fighter currently being developed by Italy (Aeritalia and Aermacchi) and Brazil (Embraer) will form part of NATO's front-line air strength in the late 1980s when it replaces the Aeritalia G.91s currently in Italian Air Force service. It could also score significant export sales with nations needing light strike aircraft heavier than armed trainers such as Hawk or Alpha Jet.

The aircraft is intended to be a low-cost STOL ground-attack fighter able to operate from semi-prepared airstrips. In its basic form, AMX is a single-seater, although a two-seat version capable of anti-ship strike, all-weather attack and EW missions as well as operational training has been proposed.

The design is conventional, with a shoulder-mounted swept wing incorporating double-slotted Fowler flaps and full-span leading edge slats, plus a combination of ailerons and spoilers for roll control. The high-lift devices give the desired short-field capability, while the spoilers also act as lift dumpers and airbrakes. The powerplant is a single non-afterburning Rolls-Royce Spey 807 turbofan, developing 11,030lb (5,010kg) of thrust.

First flight of an Italian prototype was on May 2, 1984, but it was destroyed on a subsequent test flight.

PRECISION GUIDED MUNITIONS

Faced with the numerical superiority enjoyed by the Warsaw Pact, the West's air forces must rely on advanced missile technology in order to even the odds in aerial combat. As Soviet designers improve their own products, introducing new and sophisticated air-to-air missiles such as the AA-9, the West must introduce corresponding improvements at the same rate.

The West's latest microchip technology must be used to create the "smart" air-to-air and air-to-ground weapons required in the 1980s and 1990s. Guidance and control technology will be the key to combat success. Modern developments have already greatly improved established patterns of missile such as the AIM-9 Sidewinder and AIM-7 Sparrow. Latest models of these weapons may resemble their predecessors of a decade or more ago, but beneath the skin they are virtually all-new weapons of greatly improved performance—an ideal starting point for any survey of the high-accuracy guided weaponry which will form the "cutting edge" of Western air power until the end of this century.

SIDEWINDER AAM

AIM-9 Sidewinder originally entered development in 1949, and was first test-fired in September 1953. Eary-model Sidewinders required a fighter to fly stern-chase attacks in order to obtain lock-on, but the current AIM-9L and -9M can respond to the lower levels of infra-red energy seen during frontal aspect attack. The pilot is thus free to choose his own attack profile or to attempt shots against briefly-presented targets of opportunity. AIM-9L is a USAF/USN missile with a range of 10nm (18.5km). Production began in 1976 and it was superseded by AIM-9M in 1981.

The latter is an improved AIM-9L and is based on technology developed during an AIM-9L improvement programme. Features of the -9M include a reduced-smoke engine and a closed-cycle cooler for the detector element. Target tracking (particularly against adverse backgrounds) and ECM resistance are better than that of the -9J.

The AIM-9P series were developed specifically for export. AIM-9P-1 has an active optical target detector (proximity fuse) instead of the standard IR fuse. The AIM-9P-2 has a reduced-smoke rocket motor, while the -3 features the new motor, IR proximity fuze, plus an improved warhead whose explosive filling is less sensitive to high temperature and has a longer shelf life. Despite their high performance, these improved Sidewinders are inexpensive (at least by missile standards). Unit cost of an AIM-9M is approximately $60,000 to $80,000.

SPARROW AAM

Development of the Sparrow missile began in the late 1950s. Over 34,000 AIM-7C, D and E models have been produced, with the -7E seeing extensive combat use in Vietnam. The AIM-7F and the AIM-7M are the only programmes still active.

Introduced in 1977, the AIM-7F has solid-state guidance, a heavier warhead and a more powerful rocket motor. By switching to the use of solid-state electronics, the Raytheon designers were able to miniaturise the seeker and guidance electronics. The space saved was shared between a new and heavier warhead and a longer rocket motor. What the designers failed to do was to eliminate the mechanical scanning motion of the seeker antenna, thus leaving the weapon vulnerable to deceptive jamming. The AIM-7F therefore had procurement limited to 5,000 rounds.

Key feature of the current AIM-7M is an advanced monopulse seeker providing improved resistance to ECM plus better lookdown shoot-down capability. As its name suggests, a monopulse seeker can derive the position of the target with respect to the sightline of its non-rotating antenna by receiving a single return signal. The monopulse seeker stares directly at the target and uses a number of beams (normally four) to monitor instantaneously the region of the target and its surroundings, instead of sampling them during a rotating scan. By comparing the strength of the return signal in all antenna beams, the aiming error may be deduced directly. This technique is difficult to counter, requiring jamming systems of complex design.

AIM-7M has the same outside dimensions and general performance as the AIM-

	AIM-9B: 80,900 produced by Philco and GE and C15,000 by European consortium; 10,000+ updated by Ford.
	AIM-9C/D: 9C SARH model by Motorola (1,000+), 9D with better IR/speed/manoeuvre, 950+ by Ford for US Navy.
	AIM-9E: 9B rebuilt with new cooled wide-angle seeker, about 5,000 for USAF by Ford (Aeronutronic).
	AIM-9G/H: 9G improved 9D with off-boresight lock-on (2,120 Raytheon, USN); 9H solid-state (3,000 Ford AF).
	AIM-9L/M: 9L 3rd generation all-aspect (Ford and Raytheon, also Europe); 9M improved ECCM/motor (Raytheon).
	AIM-9J/N: J rebuilt B/E with new front end (Ford c14,000 for AF); N (formerly J1) further improved (c.7,000).
	AIM-9P improved B/E/ J or new production, new motor/fuze and better reliability, c13,000 by Ford for USAF.

Left: Years of development effort have matched the AIM-9 Sidewinder to the ever-evolving threat, making the weapon one of he most cost-effective missiles ever fielded. The original AIM-9B was similar in electronic complexity to a domestic radio of contemporary vintage (early 1950s), while the latest versions are intended for modern dogfight combat.

Below: Early-model Sidewinders had to be fired from almost due aft of their target, and the seeker had to be accurately aligned with the target if its limited search pattern was to result in lock-on. The latest versions carried by this USAF F-15 search a wide conical angle for targets, and will even lock-on to aircraft approaching directly from astern.

7F. The weapon entered production in FY81, and unit cost is $203,000.

Similar upgrading programmes are being applied to other air-to-air weapons produced by the West. Having taken orders for more than 6,000 rounds of its R.550 Magic IR-homing "dogfight" missile, Matra is now working on an improved Magic 2 intended to arm the Mirage 2000. Flight trials have already begun. The seeker of the current model carries out an autonomous search procedure before launch, but the seeker of the Magic 2 may be slaved to the parent aircraft's air-interception radar.

A new active proximity fuze will be fitted to cope with the triggering problems inherent in head-on interceptions. Attacks from the front hemisphere involve very high closing rates, so the warhead must be detonated without delay in order to ensure that the explosion takes place close to the target.

Technology from existing weapons is being applied to several designs which have just entered service and which may be considered "half-generation" improvements over established types such as the AIM-9L and Magic. First revealed at the 1981 Paris Air Show, and taken into combat over the Bekaa Valley, the Rafael Python 3 is a development of the earlier Shafrir 2. Intended for both close-in air-combat and long-range interception duties, this new weapon has highly-swept tail surfaces, and incorporates passive infra-red homing using a single element infra-red detector. Performance is claimed to be superior to that of the AIM-9L.

The Armscor Kukri is a heat-seeking weapon of South African design. Although based on Magic technology, it incorporates several advanced features. Slightly larger than Magic, it uses a novel control system with Magic-style control surfaces (a moving surface mounted directly behind a fixed canard) in one plane, and simple Sidewinder-style delta surfaces in the other.

A helmet-mounted sight is used for target designation. The pilot aligns a sighting reticle projected onto the helmet visor with his target, and the aircraft fire-control system then slews the missile seeker head into alignment. Should the target lie outside the missile's performance envelope, the reticle will disappear. An audible tone signals that the seeker has detected the target. After lock-on, the seeker will follow the target until a fire command is given. The pilot thus has time to assess the tactical situation before launching his missile.

MICROELECTRONIC ADVANCES

These improved versions of existing missiles all incorporate features which will be found in future weapons—solid-state electronics of high reliability, high-accuracy seeker systems able drastically to reduce the high values of miss distance associated with earlier weapons, and emphasis on high manoeuvrability and resist-

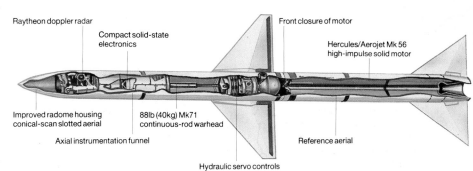

Raytheon doppler radar · Compact solid-state electronics · Front closure of motor · Hercules/Aerojet Mk 56 high-impulse solid motor · Improved radome housing conical-scan slotted aerial · 88lb (40kg) Mk71 continuous-rod warhead · Axial instrumentation funnel · Reference aerial · Hydraulic servo controls

Above: The definitive AIM-7F and -7M versions of Sparrow overcame many of the limitations of earlier models. The use of miniaturised guidance electronics allowed the size of the motor and warhead to be substantially increased without exceeding the dimensions of the existing airframe. It is likely that the small number of Syrian MiG-25 Foxbat Mach 3 reconnaissance aircraft downed by Israel fell victim to F-15-launched Sparrows.

Above: Matra's R.550 Magic has proved a resounding export success, and has even been retrofitted to Soviet-supplied MiG-21s. In its current form, it is a direct replacement for the AIM-9 Sidewinder, but the new Magic 2 Mirage 2000 may be slaved to the radar of the parent aircraft for fast lock-on to targets. **Below:** During the 1967 Six Day War, Israeli pilots relied on cannon during air-to-air combat. Six years later, the Rafael Shafrir 2 was responsible for most Israeli air-combat kills in the Yom Kippur War. Such comparison graphically sums up the limitations of early-model missiles and the lethality of later systems.

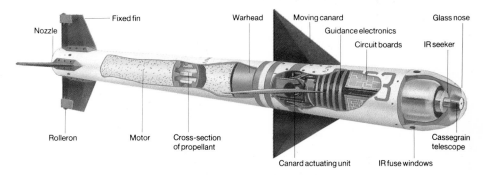

Nozzle · Fixed fin · Warhead · Moving canard · Glass nose · Guidance electronics · Circuit boards · IR seeker · Rolleron · Motor · Cross-section of propellant · Canard actuating unit · IR fuse windows · Cassegrain telescope

ance to ECM. All are a direct result of Western progress in microelectronics, a field reported to be a major target for Soviet intelligence-gathering operations.

The impact of such technology on existing weapons must not be underestimated. The Egyptian air force considers the retrofitting of AIM-9P Sidewinders to its MiG-21 fleet in place of the AA-2 Atoll to have virtually doubled the combat effectiveness of the Soviet fighter. When applied to new missiles, microelectronics promises even greater combat effectiveness, allowing pilots greater freedom to manoeuvre in combat and to carry out attacks from any direction and at any height. The two most important current programmes are the US

AMRAAM and the West European ASRAAM.

Under joint development by the US Air Force and Navy as a replacement for Sparrow, AMRAAM is an all-weather weapon able to attack targets from any approach angle and at both visual and beyond-visual ranges. It is intended to cope with threat systems likely to be fielded over the next two decades. Compared with the earlier Sparrow, AMRAAM offers a higher missile velocity, an extended performance envelope, plus the ability to take on several targets simultaneously following a multiple launch.

Work on AMRAAM started in the late 1970s, with Hughes winning a "shoot-off"

competition in December 1981. Extensive Development, Test and Evaluation/Initial Operational Test and Evaluation firings are now under way to prove the new missile.

Initial procurement is expected to begin in 1984, with a decision to proceed with full-scale production following early in 1985. The missile will enter operational service in FY86 aboard the F-16C/D. The two Services have a joint requirement for 24,000 missiles (13,000 for the USAF and 7,000 for the USN). Despite the high performance of AMRAAM, the unit cost is expected (somewhat optimistically) to be around $110,000, half that of Sparrow and not much more than that of the Sidewinder.

On August 14, 1980, the governments of West Germany, the UK, France and the USA signed a Memorandum of Understanding (MoU) covering the joint development and production of next-generation medium- and short-range missiles. The European partners agreed that the USA should continue to develop AMRAAM, which would become the standard medium-range weapon for all partners, while they would develop the complementary Advanced Short Range Air-to-Air Missile (ASRAAM), which would in turn be adopted by the US Services. Under co-production licencing arrangements, both weapons would be built on both sides of the Atlantic. (At present France is not a full signatory to the agreement, but retains the option of becoming a full partner at a later date.)

The AIM-120 is smaller and lighter than the AIM-7 it will replace. The airframe is only 140.7in (357cm) long, 7in (18cm) in diameter and 20.7in (53cm) in wingspan. Ready for launch it weighs 327lb (148kg). Boosted to supersonic speed by a solid-propellant rocket motor, it has a maximum range of between 30 and 40nm (55 and 75km).

Sparrow used fixed tail fins and movable wings, but on AMRAAM this arrangement is reversed. The wings are simple

Above: Development launch of a Hughes AIM-120 AMRAAM missile from a USAF F-16. The GD aircraft urgently requires an all-weather missile capability, so the new missile is being rushed into production even before final testing with high-speed, high-altitude targets and system software has been completed.

Below: After launch, AMRAAM cruises much of the distance to a long-range target under the control of an inertial guidance system. In the final stages of flight, an active radar seeker is used to locate and home on to the target. The process is automatic, so the aircraft can turn away to engage another target or leave the area once the round has been launched.

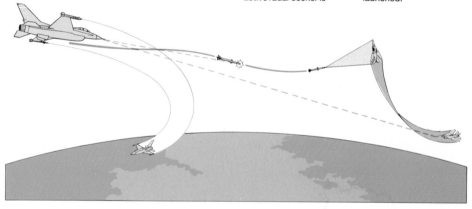

fixed surfaces, while the tail-mounted fins are moved by electrical actuators—the missile design eliminated the complex hydraulic systems fitted to earlier weapons.

Simultaneous launches of up to six AMRAAMs against multiple targets are made possible by the missile's two-stage guidance system. Before launch, the inertial navigation system is given details of target position. The launch aircraft is then free to fire several rounds against a number of targets. In the final stages of flight, the missile switches on its active-radar seeker, aquiring and homing in on to the target. Unlike the seekers fitted to semi-active radar guided weapons such as Sparrow and Skyflash, AMRAAM does not require the launch aircraft to keep its radar antenna aligned with the target in order to provide a source of illuminating energy. During long-range engagements, the launch aircraft will transmit updated target data to the missile, to ensure that it will be able to detect and lock-on to its victim. A "home-on-jam" operating mode is also available.

The 48lb (22kg) high-explosive warhead is of blast-fragmentation type and is triggered by a proximity fuse. This weight is well below that of Sparrow, a reflection of the high accuracy anticipated from the missile guidance system. During the first-ever guided flight, the missile scored a direct hit on a QF-102 drone.

EUROPE'S ASRAAM

Few programmes offer a greater contrast between the fast pace of a US project and the lumbering pace typical of Western European ones than the ASRAAM. Covered by the second part of the international MoU which established the AMRAAM as a NATO-standard weapon, ASRAAM is planned to be a lightweight "dogfighting" missile able to replace existing types such as the AIM-9L Sidewinder.

The project is currently being handled by British Aerospace Dynamics (UK) and Bodenseewerk Geratetechnik (West Germany), although France could in theory join the programme at a later date. British work on short-range missiles of this type

Above: ASRAAM will form part of the armament of the planned Agile Combat Aircraft (ACA). These mock-ups of ACA show wingtip and triple-round multiple launchers for the wingless ASRAAM design favoured by BAeD. Also visible is a mock-up of ALARM, the new lightweight and fully autonomous anti-radar missile under development by BAeD.

Below: French air force Mirage 2000 interceptors will be armed with the latest version of the Matra Super 530 radar-guided air-to-air missile. This is designed to carry out snap-up and snap-down attacks, allowing an individual fighter patrolling at fuel-economic medium altitudes to police a large volume of airspace above and below its own cruising height.

MICA (Missile Intermediat de Combat Aerien) will probably be the main air-to-air missile armament of French fighters in the 1990s. Rather than attempt to create equivalents to the AMRAAM and ASRAAM, the French Air Force has decided to concentrate efforts on a single intermediate-range type able to cope with most likely missions. Under development by Matra as a replacement for the R.550 Magic, MICA will probably be fielded in two versions—one for short- and medium-range interception missions, the other for close-in air combat. Like AMRAAM, MICA will have two-stage guidance. A strap-down inertial system will be used in the early stages of flight, handing over to either an infra-red (air-combat) or Doppler radar (interception) seeker.

MICA will be marginally larger and heavier than Magic, and is expected to weigh around 220lb (100kg). The weapon will be powered by a solid-propellant rocket motor, and will have a maximum range of 27 to 32nm (50–60km).

The airframe used in early flight tests uses long-chord wings of modest span, a configuration similar to that used by the current Matra Super 530. In this case the wings are of even shorter span, making the weapon visually similar to the US Standard SAM. This is probably intended to minimise airframe drag while still giving high manoeuvrability. To give the high post-launch agility needed for short-range air combat, the aerodynamic control surfaces will be supplemented by a thrust-vectoring system. Flight tests of this system, which uses small movable surfaces to deflect the exhaust of the rocket motor, started in 1982.

OTHER ADVANCED MISSILES

Looking beyond the weapons described above, several more advanced studies are known to be under way. MICA will probably be the main French air-to-air project into the 1990s, but the UK is known to be studying another air-to-air missile.

USAF plans to improve further its air-to-air missile firepower based on AMRAAM. Under a project designated PE 63313F Advanced Missile Subsystem Demonstration, USAF is already flight testing a new passive/active radar seeker and two new patterns of rocket motor for use on enhanced versions of AMRAAM.

The passive/active radar seeker will provide additional passive operating modes, allowing missiles to lock on and home on the radar or ECM emissions of their victim. The launch aircraft would no longer need to make such extensive use of its radar, thus reducing its own vulnerability to passive-homing missiles, while the enemy would be denied a warning that missiles were in the final homing stage of an attack.

The PE 63302F Advanced Missile Propulsion programme is developing a reduced-smoke two-pulse rocket motor for use on future AMRAAMs, plus a ducted rocket motor (basically a solid-propellant

dates back to the late 1960s. The design of the national Short-Range Air-to-Air Missile (SRAAM) was completed in 1970, but the British Government, true to its traditional timid defence procurement policy, decided not to adopt it for service, reducing the project to technology-demonstrator status in January 1974.

To date, very little "hard" information has been released on ASRAAM. The missile will be smaller and lighter than Sidewinder. The two partners initially followed different development paths, with BAeD favouring a SRAAM-like design, while Bodenseewerk favoured a Sidewinder-like configuration with conventional controls. The latter is reported to have been selected for further development. Some work has been carried out on exotic direction-control systems such as secondary rocket thrusters—small directional nozzles able to bleed off hot gas from the main exhaust.

No decision has been taken concerning the guidance system. Passive IR, active and semi-active radar homing and even laser guidance have all been considered, while at one time the possibility of creating several variants with different guidance systems was suggested. The active-radar scheme would use a Marconi Space & Defence Systems three-axis gimballed seeker able to operate at the same off-boresight angles as an IR seeker, but offering longer range and all-weather operation.

The prospect of national missile projects must be regarded as a serious threat to the future of ASRAAM. Given the pressure on the US Services to "buy US", and the virtual collapse of the US Roland programme (the only serious attempt in several decades by the US Services to deploy a European missile system), long-term US backing for ASRAAM could be lukewarm at best.

FRANCE'S MICA FOR 1990

France remains an observer in both the ASRAAM and AMRAAM programmes, and here too the prospects for long-term support of an international weapon seem doubtful, given the existence of the national MICA intermediate-range missile programme.

ramjet) which might increase the range of the weapon by up to 100 per cent. The latter powerplant would have a longer burn time, giving improved AMRAAMs higher speed, longer range and greater manoeuvrability.

To date, guided gun-launched projectiles have been restricted to calibres such as 155mm, but by the 1990s integrated-circuit technology should allow "smart" guidance to be fitted to small-calibre weapons such as aircraft cannon. The Armaments Division of the USAF has examined the feasibility of 40mm or even 20mm guided cannon shells.

The sensor will inevitably reduce the space and weight available for the round's high-explosive filling—a problem familiar to the designers of proximity-fuzed ammunition. Experience with the latter suggests that 30 to 35mm is likely to be the minimum calibre for a "smart" round.

AIR-TO-GROUND MISSILES

The most important air-to-ground missile carried by Western fighters is the AGM-65 Maverick. The USAF alone plans to deploy the missile on more than 3,000 aircraft. Maverick was developed by Hughes to meet a USAF requirement for a highly-accurate weapon which could be used for close air support or as a stand-off weapon able to attack high-value targets. More than 26,000 TV-guided AGM-65A

and AGM-65B Maverick rounds were built. During 1,221 firings the average hit rate was 86 per cent. Mean radial error from the centroid of a tank-sized target was only 3ft (1m) during trials with telemetry-equipped rounds.

The latest USAF version is the AGM-65D IIR (Imaging Infra-Red) version which entered low-rate production in April 1983. Simple IR seekers such as those fitted on Sidewinder and Magic are designed to detect and track "hot spots" such as engine jet pipes or warm airframes. IIR units are the thermal equivalent of TV, creating a video image which reflects the temperature level of the individual objects or items of terrain in the field of view. Like a TV image, the IR "view" may be used to guide a PGM, but in this case the weapon may operate by night or in conditions of poor visibility, and is not confused by smoke.

Since the image is thermal rather than optical, the AGM-65D will be a useful anti-radar weapon for the F-4G Wild Weasel anti-radar aircraft. Radars have in the past avoided attack by anti-radar missiles simply by switching off their transmitter. AGM-65D allows the "Weasel" to cope with such countermeasures by launching a round to home in on the residual heat emitted by radar sets.

Trials have shown that the IIR seeker is less likely to lose its lock on a target than the digital centroid tracker fitted to current

TV guided rounds. Loss of lock has proved a problem in the past, the centroid tracker having been substituted for an earlier gradient-edge tracker. The AGM-65D seeker will also be used on the GBU-15 and Walleye glide bombs, and may also be fitted to later models of the Harpoon.

Full-scale engineering development of the AGM-65C laser-guided version of Maverick began in 1975, with Rockwell being given the contract to develop a seeker able to acquire and track targets illuminated by a laser designator. This component was also intended for use in the US Army's Hellfire helicopter-launched anti-tank missile. Although the resulting Block II seeker successfully completed flight trials in April 1978, the USAF decided not to proceed with the AGM-65C. The programme was reorientated to meet the requirements of the USN and USMC, the revised AGM-65E featuring the low-cost seeker, an improved safety device for the rocket motor, and a new pattern of warhead. The latter is a 300lb (135kg) dual-role device fitted with a fuze which may be set to explode on impact or alternatively to allow a short time delay so that the warhead can penetrate the target structure.

The weapon is intended for close-support, and will be fired at targets close to friendly forces. If the missile seeker loses lock on the target, the warhead fuzing system will automatically be inerted as a

Right: Internal arrangement of the TV-guided AGM-65A and B versions of Maverick. The seeker optics are located in the nose and mounted beneath a transparent hemispherical transparency. The latter is protected by a cover until the missile is ready for launch. The heavy warhead relies on the shaped charge principles

to break through heavily protected targets. To allow the hot-gas jet from the warhead to reach its target, a narrow tunnel is provided through the electronics section of the weapon. The gas jet easily burns its way through the remaining lightweight components of the seeker and reach the target – with devastating results.

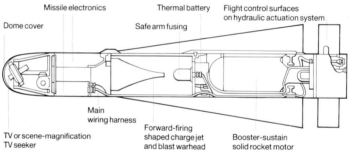

Missile electronics | Thermal battery | Flight control surfaces on hydraulic actuation system
Dome cover | Safe arm fusing
Main wiring harness
TV or scene-magnification TV seeker | Forward-firing shaped charge jet and blast warhead | Booster-sustain solid rocket motor

Below: Graphic proof of the accuracy of precision-guided munitions. This TV-guided maverick is heading straight for the door of a bunker during development testing. The weapon has demonstrated a combat success rate of greater than 90 per cent, with a miss distance of only a few feet (around a metre).

safety precaution to reduce the risk should the now unguided round impact near USMC positions.

To meet the needs of the USN, another specialised variant designated AGM-65F is under development. Intended for use against ships and coastal targets, this combines the IIR seeker of the AGM-65D with the heavy warhead and propulsion section of the AGM-65E. The USN is expected to buy about 7,000 rounds. Trials started in October 1981, an early series of captive tests showing that the crew of an aircraft could recognise ship targets at a longer range by using seeker imagery than by relying on the naked eye.

NEW LAUNCH METHODS

In parallel with development work on improved versions of missiles, the USAF is developing new launch methods. At present, missiles are individually aimed using a cockpit-mounted video display, then launched. In the future, the USAF hopes to use ripple firing techniques and eventually to introduce automatic targeting using the Martin-Marietta Low Altitude Navigation and Targeting Infrared System for Night (LANTIRN) pod.

A modified version of the standard Hughes three-rail LAU-88/A launcher has been used for experimental ripple firings. To accomplish this, the seekers of the two rounds are slaved together. Once the first round has been aimed and fired, the next is automatically activated. The circuitry in the modified launcher begins the pre-launch sequence for the second, jettisoning its seeker dome cover, and displaying the missile's video signal on the cockpit CRT. At the same time, the seeker of another missile is slaved to that of the round now being aimed.

Tests have confirmed that the rocket motor efflux of the first round does not obscure the field of view of the second,

Above: Major John P. Bland inspects an AGM-65E round mounted on his A-4M Skyhawk before setting off on a mission which would make him the first USMC pilot to launch the weapon. The laser-guided -65E was based on the earlier but abandoned -65C missile.

and that warhead detonation of the first missile does not cause the next round to break lock. During tests at Eglin AFB, an F-4 fired three Mavericks at three stationary truck targets within 12 seconds during a single low-altitude pass. All three targets were destroyed. This test used TV-guided rounds, but the USAF is interested in applying the same technique to the IIR version.

USAF aircraft normally carry Maverick on triple-rail launchers, but the new single-rail LAU-117A launcher provides greater flexibility in devising armament loads for the F-4G, F-16, A-7D and A-10A. It will also be used by the USN.

"SMART" ZUNI ROCKET

By mating a modified version of the AIM-9B Sidewinder seeker head with the body of the standard 127mm ZUNI unguided rocket, Bendix hopes to be able to offer a low-cost "smart" weapon. The basic rocket is a standard US Navy/USMC weapon, while large numbers of obsolescent AIM-9B seekers currently in storage could be reworked as 1.06 micron band. The AIM-9B seeker operates at a wavelength of 3–5 microns, but company studies suggest that the optical system could be used at the shorter wavelength without unacceptable losses.

A low-cost alternative to Maverick might be produced as a result of the USAF's Hypervelocity Missile (HVM) programme. This resulted from industry proposals to develop an anti-armour missile weighing less than 40lb (18kg) and costing less than $5,000—half the price of a TV-guided Maverick. A single aircraft could carry 40 HVMs in two 14 to 16in (35 to 40cm) diameter launch pods. The HVM is designed to reach speeds of around 5,000ft/sec (1,500m/sec), and to have a range of up to 3.3nm (6km). Instead of relying on a conventional high-explosive warhead, the HVM would destroy an AFV target by piercing the armour with a tungsten-carbide nose. (Tank guns often fire solid tungsten-alloy anti-armour projectiles, so this method of knocking out AFVs is well proven.)

Guidance would involve a laser scanner carried on the launch aircraft acquiring multiple moving targets anywhere within its 68deg field of view. This field would be scanned by a Multifunctional Infrared Coherent Optical Scanner (MICOS), a carbon dioxide laser able to penetrate smoke, haze, dust and some water vapour. The missile would incorporate a laser receiver able to detect the MICOS beam which would be switched rapidly from one target/missile combination to another so that each round received a course correction at regular intervals.

HVM is currently in advanced development. Vought and Lockheed were issued contracts in September 1981 for technology demonstrations of their respective designs, but the Lockheed proposal was dropped within months. During flight testing in 1982, the beam from the laser-based guidance unit proved it could penetrate the rocket motor efflux and pass steering

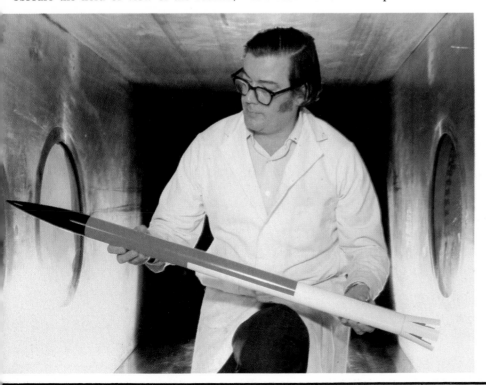

Left: A 2-inch (50mm) hypervelocity missile is prepared for testing in a wind tunnel. Operational hardware is unlikely to enter service until the end of the decade. It would rely on its high speed, rather than a conventional high-explosive warhead, to pierce enemy armour.

demands to the guidance system. Tests of the steering system's ability to respond to laser-generated commands started a year later.

Ground tests have shown that the planned laser-guidance system is technically feasible, but the crucial test will come when several missiles are guided simultaneously against independent targets. Flight tests are continuing into 1985, with improvements being made to the fire control system. If these trials are successful, the weapon could move into full-scale development, but production rounds are unlikely to be fielded until the late 1980s or eary 1990s.

The only non-US air-to-surface guided missile currently in production in Western Europe (except for specialised anti-radar weapons) is the Aérospatiale AS.30 Laser. The earlier AS.30 used command guidance, and almost 4,000 were built. Intended to arm the final 30 French Air Force Jaguars, AS.30L combines the proven airframe, propulsion system and warhead of the original missile with a Thomson-CSF Ariel laser seeker. The parent aircraft carries a Thomson-CSF/Martin Marietta Atlis 2 pod-mounted target tracking and laser-illumination system. The original Atlis 1 required the use of a two-seat aircraft, but Atlis 2 is suitable for use on single-seaters.

SMART BOMB DEVELOPMENTS

Following a combat debut during the Vietnam War, guided but unpowered weapons—usually referred to as "smart" bombs—still play a major role with the air arms of the USA and its NATO allies. Under a rebuild programme, 3,600 Hughes/Martin Marietta AGM-62 Walleye electro-optically-guided bombs are being converted to the Walleye II ER/DL (Extended-Range/Data Link) standard, receiving larger wings to extend the range, plus a data link which will allow the launch aircraft to carry out evasive manoeuvres while a second aircraft takes command of the weapon.

The need to field LGBs which can be released at low altitude resulted in the

Above: Outside of the USA and the Soviet Union, France is the only nation known to have developed "smart" bombs. This is the Matra laser-guided bomb mounted on a Mirage F1. (The existence of an Israeli TV-guided weapon named Luz has never been officially confirmed.)

Texas Instruments Paveway III LLLGB (Low-Level Laser-Guided Bomb). Similar in general configuration to the earlier Paveway models, this uses microprocessor technology, an improved nose seeker, and high-lift folding wings. Under a preplanned product-improvement programme, Paveway III will receive an IIR seeker plus a new signal processor. The latter will probably be the first application of technology developed by the Very High Speed Integrated Circuits (VHSIC) programme.

The Rockwell International GBU-15 long-range glide bomb entered service in 1982. Standard Mk84 2,000lb (900kg) or M118E1 3,000lb (1,360kg) bombs are converted into "smart" weapons using modification kits consisting of add-on television or infra-red guidance systems, rear-mounted control surfaces, and longitudinal strakes. Initial Service deliveries used the TV seeker; the IR variant uses the imaging infra-red seeker originally developed for the AGM-65D Maverick.

The only other Western nation to have developed LGBs is France. The Matra laser-guided bomb is similar in general configuration to Paveway, and carries a Thomson-CSF Elbis seeker and tail-mounted steering fins. The weapon is available in 880lb (400kg) and 2,200lb (1,000kg) forms, and can be launched at low level and at stand-off ranges of 1 to 4nm (2 to 8km), depending on launch conditions.

Several patterns of submunitions dispenser which either carry precision-guided munitions (PGMs) or incorporate built-in guidance are under development for service in the late 1980s or beyond. Northrop's NV-150 carrier vehicle for conventional payloads such as PGMs is a long-range weapon powered by a single Williams International turbofan engine. It uses "stealth" technology to minimise the chances of interception by hostile defences, and would rely on a ring laser gyro navigation system backed up by a Global Positioning Satellite receiver to help it find the target after a flight of 200nm (370km) or more.

The Low-Cost Powered Off-axis Dispenser (LOCPOD) is being promoted as a NATO-standard next-generation weapon, and could be combined with the current USAF Stand-off Attack Weapon project, becoming an international collaborative programme. Since a range of 8 to 16nm (16 to 32km) is contemplated, some form of guidance will be required, probably a low-cost inertial unit.

Alternative payloads include anti-tank and anti-runway munitions, such as the Avco Skeet. This terminally-guided submunition was successfully tested during the now-defunct Assault Breaker and ERAM (Extended-Range Anti-armour Munition) programmes.

After being dispensed from its carrier, the spin-stabilised Skeet locates targets by

Left: Following a combat debut during the Vietnam War, the Paveway laser-guided bomb has been widely exported to friends and allies of the USA. This is the Mk2 version; the latest Mk3 is designed for low-level release.

means of a fixed sensor. The round is designed to wobble while in flight so that the seeker—a two-colour IR unit—scans a circular area of terrain.

If no target is detected, the submunition reverts to a secondary fragmentation mode, exploding in an attempt to knock out nearby APCs, soft-skinned vehicles and personnel. If the seeker locates an AFV target, the warhead is detonated in its primary mode, generating a self-forging fragment warhead able to break through the relatively thin top armour of a tank.

Several national projects for submunition dispensers are being studied. The Matra/MBB Apache now being studied for service in the late 1980s is a 500lb (1,000kg) modular weapon able to engage targets up to 5nm (10km) from the point of weapon release. The payload may consist of anti-tank or anti-personnel mines. These sub-munitions could be guided by a millimetre-wave homing head currently being developed by Electronique Serge Dassault (ESD). This active-radar unit is based on large-scale integrated circuits and uses digital signal processing.

ANTI-RADAR MISSILES

Proliferating air-defence systems force attack aircraft to carry dedicated anti-radar missiles. Early weapons of this type, such as the AGM-45 Shrike, had a limited frequency coverage, but the new Texas Instruments AGM-88 HARM (High-Speed Anti-Radiation Missile) has a broadband seeker head of advanced design. Development of the weapon was authorised in 1972. At that time the project was backed by the USN, but the USAF joined the programme in 1975 in order to obtain a better weapon to arm Wild Weasel anti-radar aircraft.

HARM is an undoubted technological success, but its cost has forced a search for

possible alternatives such as the Sidearm (based on Sidewinder) and new versions of existing anti-radiation missiles. The likely unit cost of production rounds will be more than $390,000.

Around 50 per cent of the missile's massive price is due to the seeker, so an alternative has been keenly sought. The most obvious replacement was the seeker used on the Anti-Radiation Projectile (ARP). Although in its basic form the ARP seeker lacked the wide-band coverage of the HARM unit the significant growth potential of the former suggested that this problem might be overcome given further development. It is now planned to use a seeker based on the ARP design in a new version of HARM. Designated AGM-88B, this will probably replace the current missile on the production line in 1989. The new seeker has an estimated $118,200 price tag, and the AGM-88B is expected to be 20 per cent cheaper than the AGM-88A.

The British Aerospace Dynamics ALARM (Air-Launched Anti-Radiation Missile) is under development for installation on RAF Tornado IDS strike aircraft, and might also be fitted to Jaguar, Harrier and the AV-8B. Slightly larger than Sparrow, ALARM will supplement rather than

Above: The USAF has scaled down its planned procurement of the effective but expensive AGM-88 HARM anti-radar missile – seen here on an underwing hardpoint of an F-4G Wild Weasel – from more than 14,000 to only 9,000, but the USN still plans to buy 8,000.

replace existing stores, so does not greatly reduce an aircraft's normal weapons load. Being completely autonomous, it requires little modification to the launch aircraft.

After release at low level, ALARM is intended to climb to around 40,000ft (12,000m) then deploy a parachute. As it "loiters" at altitude, it can detect and analyse radar signals. Once a target is selected, the parachute will be released, allowing the round to dive on to its chosen victim. Should the latter cease transmitting, an on-board INS guidance unit would allow the missile to complete its attack.

The original AJ37 anti-radar version of Martel still serves with the French Air Force, but will be replaced by the Aérospatiale ARMAT (Anti-Radiation MArTel). This combines the proven airframe with a new Electronique Serge Dassault (EMD) homing head. Back-up INS guidance also seems likely. A second version specifically intended for export has also been reported.

Right: Sea Eagle has a longer range and "smarter" guidance than Martel, while the new ALARM anti-radar missile is much smaller than the anti-radar version of Martel. SRAAM was an experimental dogfight weapon.

INDEX

PICTURE CREDITS

The publishers wish to thank all the organisations and individuals who have provided photographs for this book; they are listed by page number below.

Front cover: Frank B. Mormillo (via World Photo Press). **Back cover:** Top, Grumman; bottom left, Northrop; bottom right, Dassault-Breguet. **Endpapers:** McDonnell Douglas. **Pages 1:** General Dynamics. **Pages 2-3:** McDonnel Douglas; **4-5:** Panavia; **6-7:** US Department of Defense (DoD); **8-9:** Dassault-Breguet; **10-11:** British Ministry of Defence (MoD); **19-20:** British Aerospace (BAe); **21:** MoD; **22-25:** BAe; **28-33:** Dassault-Breguet; **34:** Belgian Air Force; **36-37:** Dassault-Breguet; **38:** Top, Dassault-Breguet; bottom, Belgian Air Force; **39-44:** Dassault-Breguet; **45:** Matra; **46-62:** Dassault-Breguet; **65:** US DoD; **67:** Top, DoD; bottom, Fairchild; **68:** Fairchild; **69:** Top, Fairchild; bottom, US DoD; **70-71:** Fairchild. **72-78:** General Dynamics; **79-85:** US DoD; **86:** Grumman; **87:** US DoD; **90:** Grumman; **93:** US DoD; **94-100:** Grumman; **101:** Top, NATO; bottom, Grumman; **100-103:** Grumman; **104-109:** Israel Aircraft Industries; **110-120:** McDonnell Douglas; **122:** US DoD; **125:** Top, Pratt & Whitney; bottom, US DoD; **127:** Top, US DoD; bottom, McDonnell Douglas; **129:** Top, British MoD; bottom, US DoD; **130-133:** US DoD; **135-138:** McDonnell Douglas; **139:** US DoD; **140-147:** McDonnell Douglas; **148-150:** Northrop; **151:** Top, Northrop; bottom, US DoD; **152:** Top, General Dynamics; bottom, Salamander Books; **153-154:** Northrop; **156-162:** BAe; **165:** Turbo-Union; **166:** British MoD; **168-175:** Saab-Scania; **176:** Dassault-Breguet; **178:** BAe; **179:** Top, British MoD; bottom, Dassault-Breguet; **180:** Left, Matra; top and bottom, BAe; **181:** BAe; **182:** Dassault-Breguet; **183:** British MoD; **184:** US DoD; **187-189:** Vought; **190:** General Dynamics; **191:** Top, US DoD; bottom, Grumman; **192:** Top, McDonnell Douglas; bottom, Dornier; **193:** Top, Rockwell; bottom, Grumman; **194:** Top, BAe; bottom, Dassault-Breguet; **195:** Top BAe; **196:** Saab-Scania; **197:** Aeritalia; **198:** Raytheon; **199:** Matra; **200:** General Dynamics; **201:** Top, BAe; bottom, Dassault-Breguet; **203:** Top, Hughes; bottom, Bendix; **204:** Top, Matra; bottom, US DoD; **205:** Top, Texas Instruments; bottom, BAe.

PRINTED IN BELGIUM BY
proost
INTERNATIONAL BOOK PRODUCTION